Springer Biographies

The books published in the Springer Biographies tell of the life and work of scholars, innovators, and pioneers in all fields of learning and throughout the ages. Prominent scientists and philosophers will feature, but so too will lesser known personalities whose significant contributions deserve greater recognition and whose remarkable life stories will stir and motivate readers. Authored by historians and other academic writers, the volumes describe and analyse the main achievements of their subjects in manner accessible to nonspecialists, interweaving these with salient aspects of the protagonists' personal lives. Autobiographies and memoirs also fall into the scope of the series.

Stephen Hill

In Defence of Our Humanity

Real Life as a United Nations Ambassador in a Troubled World

Stephen Hill
Faculty of Arts, Social Sciences
and Humanities
School of Humanities and Social Inquiry
University of Wollongong
Wollongong, NSW, Australia

ISSN 2365-0613 ISSN 2365-0621 (electronic)
Springer Biographies
ISBN 978-981-97-2362-1 ISBN 978-981-97-2363-8 (eBook)
https://doi.org/10.1007/978-981-97-2363-8

© The Editor(s) (if applicable) and The Author(s), under exclusive license to Springer Nature Singapore Pte Ltd. 2024

This work is subject to copyright. All rights are solely and exclusively licensed by the Publisher, whether the whole or part of the material is concerned, specifically the rights of translation, reprinting, reuse of illustrations, recitation, broadcasting, reproduction on microfilms or in any other physical way, and transmission or information storage and retrieval, electronic adaptation, computer software, or by similar or dissimilar methodology now known or hereafter developed.
The use of general descriptive names, registered names, trademarks, service marks, etc. in this publication does not imply, even in the absence of a specific statement, that such names are exempt from the relevant protective laws and regulations and therefore free for general use.
The publisher, the authors and the editors are safe to assume that the advice and information in this book are believed to be true and accurate at the date of publication. Neither the publisher nor the authors or the editors give a warranty, expressed or implied, with respect to the material contained herein or for any errors or omissions that may have been made. The publisher remains neutral with regard to jurisdictional claims in published maps and institutional affiliations.

This Springer imprint is published by the registered company Springer Nature Singapore Pte Ltd.
The registered company address is: 152 Beach Road, #21-01/04 Gateway East, Singapore 189721, Singapore

If disposing of this product, please recycle the paper.

Contents

1	**Introduction: "Death and Life the United Nations Way"**	1
	Death—A Surprise	1
	Discovering the Meaning of Life in the United Nations	3
2	**"Walking in the Door"**	7
	First Days	7
	Headquarters Briefing	9
	Dealing with the Headquarters—Field Divide	10
	Breaking the Rules to Do the Job	10
	Moving Back into the Real World	15
3	**"Learning to Walk the Diplomatic Path"**	17
	Protocol and Diplomatic Life	17
	My Debut	18
	Diplomatic Opportunity Even with Small Things—The Slovakian Stamp of Approval	21
	Diplomatic Tennis	22
	The Unwrapping of Traditional Javanese Culture	23
	Opportunity in Being Creative—Ocean and Underwater Diplomacy	25
	The Power of the Gift Rather Than the Deal	28
	The Power of Diplomacy in Dealing with Corrupt Governance	31
	In the Shadows of Diplomatic Privilege	34

4	**"Settling into an Expatriate World"**	37
	Living with City 'Planning' and Local Conditions	38
	Spiritual and Spirit Presence	43
	The Wayang Society	46
	The Wild Life of Jakarta	48
5	**"Jungle Hostages—I: Capture"**	55
	Just Another Birth Announcement	55
	Being There—At a Distance!	57
	Origins of the Strategy to Capture 'White Noses'	59
	Historic Context of Exploitation and Repression	62
	Stimulus for the Plan to Take Foreign Hostages	66
	Life as a Hostage	68
	The Military—Walking a Tightrope: Negotiation Versus Attack	73
6	**"Jungle Hostages—II: Negotiating Peoples' Lives Across Cultures"**	77
	Negotiating	77
	The Problem of Remoteness	78
	Side-Plays	82
	Contact Again—Core Values of the Conflict and Its Resolution	85
	The End Game	92
7	**"Jungle Hostages—III: A Deeply Troubled Resolution"**	95
	The Agreed Hand-Over Ceremony—So Close!	95
	The Trauma of Release	102
	Back in Jakarta	107
8	**"'Flying Pigs'—The Start of a Voyage into the Future"**	109
	Pigs Did Fly	109
	Legacy of Flying Pigs—Shift in the Mode of Development Assistance	115
	The 'Voyage into the Future'	116
	Creating a Cargo Cult?	119
	Legacies of the Voyage into the Future	122
9	**"Lighting the Way—Building the Future for Indigenous People of West Papua"**	125
	Return Voyage to the Tribes	125
	Responding to the West Papuan Drought: How Jungle Aid Programs Can Suddenly Go Terribly Wrong	133
	Edge of the Future	135

10	**The Critical Importance of Local Engagement and Listening**	139
	Working with the Mentawai People of Siberut Island	139
	Response to the Tsunami in Aceh	140
	Transition to Democracy in Timor Leste	142
	Timor's Violent Context and Indonesian Source	143
	Significance of the Loss of Sergio De Mello	148
	The Disruptive Impact of an International Donor with More Money Than Sense in Timor Leste	149
11	**"Changing Things in the Real World—Learning from the Edge"**	151
	Moving On	151
	The Challenge of Building Community-Based Sustainable Development with a Very Remote Indigenous People	153
	Development Assistance for the People is a Multi-disciplinary Affair	161
	A Tough but Successful Life	163
12	**"Community Empowerment—Lessons from Peace Building and Urban Environment Initiatives in Poor Communities"**	169
	Case 1: Education and Peace Building in the Post-conflict Zones of the Philippines	169
	The Danger of Too Much Success	175
	Case 2: Banjarsari—Building a Green Urban Village in a Polluted Developing Countries City	176
	Essence of the 'Idea' of Community Empowerment	183
	At the Centre of All—The Whole Person	185
13	**"Revolution—Lead Up"**	189
	May 1998, Indonesia	189
	Where It All Started	190
	Presidential Power	190
	Subtlety of Prior Opposition	193
	Signs of Unrest Round the 1997 'Festival of Democracy'	201
	The Double Whammy of Unexpected Economic Collapse	203
	Early 1998—Signals of What Was to Come	208
	The United Nations During Civil Crisis: Being Prepared for Security Breakdown	209

14	**"Revolution—Now"**	215
	Suddenly, It's Here!	215
	Escape	221
	The Chinese Citizens Issue	225
	Increasing Pressure to Evacuate All Families and Staff	227
	Resolutions Emerge	233
15	**Revolution—Aftermath**	239
	The Shifting Face of Trouble	239
	What Next?	247
16	**Opportunity Out of Challenge—Opening up Media Freedom**	251
	Opportunity—A Time of Change	251
	First Steps—Development of a New Press Law	255
	Building Investigative Reporting Through the Country: Powering a Local Radio Network	258
	Community Radio—Good Idea, but …	262
	A Way to Go	265
17	**The Time Was Right—Basic Education Reform**	273
	Discovering Local Commitment to Education	273
	Charting the Way	276
	A Momentary Aside on Accessing Money and the UN System	278
	First Steps	283
	Moving on to a National Program	287
	Including the Islamic Factor	290
18	**Tsunami—"The Day the Ocean Moved"**	299
	The Monster from The Deep: The Earth Shook	299
	And the Ocean Moved	300
	The 'Black Water'	300
	Being There: First Impressions	301
	Confronting the Task in Front of Us	304
	Travelling On	310
	Physical Impact of the Tsunami	312
	Infrastructure	312
	The Environment	312

19	"The Human Story of the Tsunami"	315
	The Deadly Game of Collecting Stranded Fish	315
	The Scale of Human Tragedy	316
	The Shadow of the Wave	317
	The Spirit of Survivors	319
	Recovery	320
	The Problem of Rebuilding	321
	Response by the International Community	323
	The Historical, Religious and Cultural Strength of the Acehnese	326
	Acehnese Cultural Resilience: Staring Down the Face of Disaster	328
	Assisting Cultural Strength to Handle the Trauma of the Tsunami	329
20	"Preparing for Another Tsunami"	335
	Transnational Versus National Issues: Some Observations	338
	Some Lessons for the Future	341
21	Bridging the Two UN Cultures—Reform for the Future	347
	An International Agency Ain't All That Simple	347
	Signs of Change	351
	Finally, Serious Action on a Decentralized Reform Agenda	353
22	Final Wrap—The Force of Cultural Empowerment	361
	Bibliography	367

About the Author

Emeritus Professor Stephen Hill, AM, FRSN, FTSE, FWIF, Ph.D. is a polymath, qualified at research level and experienced in both natural and social sciences, and Professor of Sociology at age 30 at the University of Wollongong, Australia, now Emeritus Professor. Over his career, Stephen was also awarded and founded the Australian Research Council's National Center of Excellence in Research Policy (1990–1995), served part-time as Australia's Foundation Chairman in APEC, the Asia-Pacific Economic Cooperation Organization (1990–1995), and has consulted broadly through Asia for international agencies and countries since 1965. His central objective over his career has been to foster knowledge for the sake of peoples' empowerment and welfare. For the last 11 years before retirement in 2006, Stephen served full time as the United Nations Regional Director for Science for Asia and the Pacific while in parallel as Ambassador and Field Director of the UN organization, UNESCO, the UN Educational, Scientific and Cultural Organization, across South East Asia.

Stephen has published prolifically across a broad field from global economics to dynamics and values of humanity and social change, including over 20 individually or jointly authored books. His published books already deal with real-life adventures such as those depicted in the current book, e.g.: *Captives for Freedom* in 2017, his personal story of dealing with the abduction into the jungles of West Papua of two of Stephen's UN staff, plus aftermath. In addition, he published two subsequent books with Springer in collaboration with Japan's Center for the Creative Economy in Kyoto from 2015 as Invited Visiting Professor, *The Kyoto Manifesto for Global Economics—The Platform of Community, Humanity and Sprituality* (2018), and *The Kyoto Post-COVID Manifesto for Global Economics—Confronting Our Shattered Society* (2022). Stephen launched his latest shared book *Cultivating Compassion—Going Beyond Crises* on invitation at the 10th International Humanistic Buddhism Symposium in Taiwan on December 16, 2023.

1

Introduction: "Death and Life the United Nations Way"

Death—A Surprise

I was *dead* two years ago

Not just my own fantasy. The United Nations *declared* that I was DEAD! So, it was Official.

I initially came across a clue that there was something seriously wrong because I checked my Bank Account as I do on occasion, to find that suddenly my life-supporting United Nations Pension had stopped being paid. My reward, after serving for most of my career as University Professor and Consultant, for then working full time for the last 11 years before retirement, based in Indonesia, as a UN Regional Director and Ambassador across Asia and the Pacific responsible for the UN Agency, UNESCO, the United Nations Educational, Scientific and Cultural Organization.

I sure needed to find out why the United Nations had declared me dead!

Thus, through somewhat frantic telephone research, I discovered that I was without Pension as the UN has a practice of not paying a Pension to Dead People. And, the United Nations had indeed declared me DEAD. True! Being told I am dead was something of an amusing surprise. But, not having income any more was much more serious. I still felt reasonably alive by normal standards of perception. Changing this official declaration thus become something of a priority.

After some difficulty, I finally managed to get through by phone to a United Nations Payroll Official in New York who shuffled around for a while and, with a sense of interested discovery, told me the clues that sufficed for the Declaration.

The problem started as in July 2021, they mistakenly sent my 2021 "Certificate of Entitlement" to the apartment I previously rented just up the road from where I live now in Wollongong, Australia—even though I had already informed them twice that I had moved. This Certificate is the form I must sign every year, and return by post, to somehow 'prove' I am still alive.

The man who took over my previous apartment *after* me *had* died—in the apartment—so the helpful next tenant who received my Certificate, confusing him with me, sent the Certificate back to the UN in New York informing them authoritatively—with detail—that I had passed on from this mortal United Nations administered world.

They believed it. And did not check even with my own previous UN Agency, UNESCO.

So, they stopped paying me my Pension. To rub it in, I then received a letter to my actual *current address* (note: they had it) shortly later from the Deputy Chief of Payroll in New York:

> Addressed to *The Estate of Stephen Hill*, then in compassionate caring terms, to my family, the letter requested my remaining family to send my *Death Certificate* to the UN in New York in order to complete administrative arrangements. I will be framing this epistle.

It's not often that, whilst still breathing, one is declared officially DEAD. Adds a bit of authority to it when it comes from the United Nations and is in writing.

Assuring them I was alive took some time, but finally the UN accepted that I actually was *not* dead and sent me an email a couple of weeks later, saying, and I quote,

> "Dear Mr Hill, we now recognize that you are *alive* … and apologize for the inconvenience".

Tempted by the precedent of Australian 'Goons' comedian, Spike Milligan, who had projected forward to have "I told them I was sick" inscribed on his tombstone, I am seriously considering having the above epithet inscribed on mine … signed, "The United Nations".

I could not help myself but observe in response to the UN email that it was indeed distinctly inconvenient being *dead*. Payroll in New York must have felt a little embarrassed as they reinstated my Pension within two months … not bad given the timing of common UN Bureaucracy practice.

Discovering the Meaning of Life in the United Nations

The experience of being (bureaucratically) declared dead shows a glimpse of one side of life in the United Nations … but it is only the one side. The other is very courageous people making a real difference in very challenging circumstances in the 'field situation, often extremely remote from the comfort of Headquarters life—coffee machine down the corridor, protection of self via procedure, and a safe and enriching European Capital or New York culture outside the door. In my case, this was Paris, backed by UN Headquarters in the New York bright lights of the United States.

Think of *this* side of UN life for a moment though—the one that *bureaucratically* declared me dead, as having the character and culture (and interactive complexity) of a National Government Bureaucracy *times 193*, the number of UN Member States joined into collective decision at that time. A peak in bureaucratic self-protection. Having worked in one role or another *with* the United Nations since 1965—as consultant, advisor, commissioned policy author, chair of UN networks, and conference organizer, I was familiar with this bureaucratic world, and, on successful selection, walked right into it when I was appointed to join the United Nations full time—in February 1995.

Eleven years later, I retired from the United Nations at the start of 2006, though I was requested to represent UNESCO in a number of capacities through the next few years. All of this time—eleven years before retirement and three years afterwards, I was embedded in the organization culture, though, under Director-General Matsuura's command, I did have the job of changing it globally in the early 2000s, a story I will return to later.

To you, the reader, this may all seem but a distant past of limited relevance now.

But not so. For these 11 + 3 years I was *inside* and because of enormous pressure of my very broad ranging field responsibilities (including covering Asia and the Pacific in my Regional tasks), kept a Day Book with detail I can return to of what was happening on each specific day, plus continuous reports to my Headquarters, the UN Security Council—when dealing with the serious real-life dangers that were part of my responsibility to respond to, plus, of course, Annual and other Reports to the public. So, I can write about life *within* the UN as few others can—capturing experience as an evolving real-life, almost novelistic, personal story, rather than a post-event set of observations from someone who was not there, or literature based analysis. Having kept in contact since, my stories about the Inner Life of the

UN are as relevant today as they were back in the early 2000s. But … with some distance of time, I am not constrained by any post-retirement censoring restriction.

I need to add, you will find detailed data about what happened through the text of this book without external citations. This is entirely justified as it was *my* experience at the time, noted in (recorded and filed) reports I made at the time—sent on to my UN headquarters and more generally, including to the UN Security Council, rather than being an unconnected academic report from someone not directly involved.

Focus of this book quite consciously, is as a *Biography*, that is, on my own experience of life and times in relationship to the United Nations when I was there. So, whilst the book lays down an insider experience of considerable relevance to history, and I do seek to 'glimpse' consequences over the last two decades to now, I am not writing a further 'external' analysis *outside* my direct life experience. Also, the observations and analysis are based on detailed records I needed to keep given the complexity of the work across a number of countries, much of it embodied in reports I then wrote—for my Headquarters, the UN Security Council and the public. I have kept the current book's story line clear now rather than bury it in detailed citations.

More importantly, the experience reported in my Biography of United Nations life reached way beyond the inside organizational and political domain to the *outside* world it is the United Nations' business to deal with.

Here, I was confronted by very real life experience of seriously important challenging events, indeed the real side of death out in the field, way beyond the reach of Headquarters Culture, at times putting my staff and me at serious direct personal risk. And I can report these events as they happened from the vantage point of *being there* day by day in a field of often unexpected adventures—including a Revolution, Staff Kidnapped, Militia Violence after the vote for Independence in Timor Leste, the Aceh Tsunami, and even being targeted personally for assassination myself, plus lots else. Most importantly, whilst confronted by these adventures as a 'normal' within UN life, I, with my UN staff, was also able to make a positive difference, bringing social liberation across a number of spheres of peoples' lives where it was seriously needed.

So, whilst I introduce my UN Memoir with the *inside bureaucratic fantasy of death,* product of what at times could be a 'near-dead' bureaucracy, this was *a very real possibility* when we went about our business in the world outside. But meanwhile, what we did made a positive, even *revolutionary difference* for the people as well. Here, the external events I am unveiling from personal experience, are still very much within present attention. I was *there!* And can present the stories in a day-by-day account as each event unfolded onto the public stage. Few others can do this across this range.

So, my readers, this book, "In Defense of Our Humanity—Real Life as a United Nations Ambassador in a Troubled World" takes you into some exciting places. To deal with these situations, I needed to leave the (inside) bureaucratic rules behind at times because peoples' lives were at risk, or, in the situation of a developing country in crisis, you could not follow the bureaucratic rules anyway. Timor Leste was a good example and I will later come back to this case in more detail. Directly after the paid militia violence that swept across the territory following their positive vote for Independence on 30th August 1999, *everything* was trashed, including the Banks. So, the *only* way I could transfer money there for essential support from my Regional Office in Jakarta was in a sealed large brown paper bag in Indonesian Rupiah cash, mutually signed with a UN official up from Timor for the day to Jakarta. Needless to say, my Headquarters financial people threatened dire consequences for my departure from the rules. They could offer no alternative however, so I did it.

I will take you, my readers, into a world you probably have never seen before, this inner world of United Nations bureaucracy, but do realize that out in the field of action, the rules needed to be broken at times. Always with specific and necessary purpose, however.

In Chaps. 2, 3 and 4 you will come along with me to my first days … walking into this UN world and being very directly confronted by its bureaucratic ways as well as demands as an accredited international diplomat—whilst also moving into the unfamiliar cultural world of Indonesia—home of my own Regional Headquarters, and then later moving on to explore organization of the United Nations more deeply across the world. My basis for talking about UN organization is complemented by my commission from UNESCO Director General Koichiro Matsuura in early 2000 to Head his Task Force to Reform and Decentralize the entire UN Agency of UNESCO globally, and be the Director General's Personal Envoy to the World in order to travel to the regions and negotiate directly with the Member States. I was then called on to successfully convince the UNESCO Executive Board of our Reform Plan, then the World General Conference. Immediately afterwards, we put our Reform into Practice across Asia and the Pacific to show the rest of the world how to do it. Meanwhile, not to be let too far off the hook, I was continuing with all my other responsibilities as UN Regional Director and Ambassador back in Asia and the Pacific, a key basis for being offered the responsibility to lead decentralization and overall reform of UNESCO globally. I will fill you in within my penultimate Chap. 21, "Bridging the Two Cultures—Reform for the Future".

Having settled into both the UN system as my organizational home, the focus of Chap. 2, and, as required, the new diplomatic world presented in Chap. 3, then Indonesia as my new cultural home, the story of Chap. 4, it was not long before I was directly confronted by the dangerous reality of adventuring into the field to make a difference from UN action. Six months after I first settled into my Jakarta UNESCO Office Director's chair, two of my UN staff were taken hostage by freedom fighters into the highland jungles of Indonesia's Provinces of West Papua. Suddenly my previous relatively safe University Professor life was thrown over a precipice of mortal danger for the people for whom I was directly responsible.

Chapter 5 will carry you out of the 'safe' internal world of the UN into this wider reality, drawing open the curtain on the excitement of the rest of my *In Defense of Our Humanity* story. Along the way, I will take you into what is involved in handling serious UN change programs and more particularly, major crises, when they arrive, most often, quite unexpectedly.

The overall lesson that emerges so very strongly is the potential power of community to make change happen and to take care. Our United Nations support worked when we kept this human collective power as our focus.

I will start though from the beginning. Walking in the door of my UNESCO Office in Jakarta, Indonesia, in June 1995.

2

"Walking in the Door"

First Days

There were some distinctly unexpected experiences and adventures for me when I entered into the inner world of the United Nations—even though I had spent some 30 years previously while in my more academic role as consultant and advisor to the UN, other international agencies, and a number of countries as well as chair of some regional networks.

The UN Agency I entered full time was UNESCO, the United Nations Educational, Scientific and Cultural Organization, originally founded in 1945 at the time the United Nations as a whole was created in the aftermath of the horror and violence of World War II.

Our guiding Logo was inspiring:

"Since wars begin in the minds of men (sic), so too do the defenses of peace."

Our focus within the United Nations portfolio of responsibilities was leadership in addition to the areas identified in UNESCO's name, with World Heritage, Social Science, as well as Communication and Media Freedom—all within our 'defenses of peace' mandate. In confronting major human crisis, as we did in handling the aftermath of the Boxing Day 2004 Aceh Tsunami, the immediate need for overall United Nations intervention was rescue, medical support, provision of food and shelter and re-developing the agency of the government to cope. Within this frame, UNESCO's immediate priority was to rebuild media and communications so the people had information they could trust on what was going on, and because unsubstantiated rumor was immensely dangerous in a panicked population. Our longer term mission within the UN portfolio was then the rebuilding of the society, knowledge base and culture of the people so they could handle the aftermath of the present crisis, and move beyond it. I will tell this story in Chaps. 18, 19 and 20.

I remember the first day in the Office in June 1995. Arriving at work off the plane from Australia in my newly pressed suit and color-coordinated tie, seeking, despite severe inner misgivings, to convey an image of confidence and authority, I walked into the quite spacious Director's suite in the UN building on Jalan Thamrin, Central Jakarta. Having introduced myself to Ida, the long-standing Balinese secretarial guardian of the Office, I then disappeared around the corner to take 'command' behind the imposing glass-topped desk that I had inherited from my predecessor. On the desk to my left was an enormous pile of files and signature books, literally about 90 cm high. To my right, an empty out-tray. Somehow, I had to move each item on the left to the right and make a decision that crossed unknown bureaucratic territory in between.

Finding one's way was something you pretty much had to do by yourself. The Office had been run well, though with a certain Teutonic flair by its previous German Director: there was, for example, a strict dress code and meticulous precision about the timing of meetings. Under his tutelage, the Office had embarked for the first time on expansion from a narrow science project base to some early innovation in education and culture through non-regular budgetary staff, that is, young 'associate experts' appointed to UNESCO for international experience by their governments, or consultants employed on specific extra-budgetary funded projects.

Meanwhile however, the interim *acting* Director (or, in UN parlance, Director *a.i.*) of the previous few months had left me with his style of management and little else. His approach had been to manage by post-stickers and yelling a lot. He was not comfortable with people. My desk therefore confronted me with seven very neatly arrayed piles of colored post-stickers, to the left, the dramatic crimson '*do now*, do not question my instruction!' stickers; to the right, the quiet beige 'for information only' reminders. 'Robert', for want of another pseudonym, suffered no dissent. Staff had learnt that quiescence was the better alternative to the valor of venturing a question of direction, invariably met with a Director a.i. response in the 110 decibel sound range. 'Robert' informed me further that not only did his post-stickers regime provide definitive direction that brooked no further discussion, but that it had to be applied to *all* correspondence. Indeed, I should read absolutely *everything* that came in and went out of the

Office. 'You can't trust these guys' he remonstrated. As a responsible UN official you *must* know *everything* that this Office does and is responsible for!' I did a quick calculation for the 30 or so staff at that time in the Office and worked out, with e-mails as well as faxes, letters and reports, that this task would probably absorb at least 60 h per week, leaving me no time whatsoever to actually think about my job, develop a vision for the future and *do* anything.

The previous full Director had left nearly a year before I arrived however, so the Office was 'spinning its wheels' a bit whilst still emerging from 'old ways', that is, basically just implementing science projects designed and mandated in Headquarters, not particularly adapting to local conditions and interests, and only just starting to explore the other sectors of activity that makes UNESCO such an interesting organization, dealing as it does with education, science, social sciences, culture, and communication—the *human face* of development.

Procedures were highly bureaucratized, but 'management by objectives' and accountability for performance outside simply spending the budget, were still relatively alien concepts. UNESCO's Paris-based Headquarters did however provide introductory briefings for outsiders like me who arrived into the organization without previous employed UNESCO experience. I felt that it was important to have some sort of feel for what the Office actually did before I went along for this briefing, so instead of going to Paris on day 1 of my posting as was normal practice, I spent a month in-situ in Jakarta before heading off to Paris to learn what I was *supposed* to do.

Headquarters Briefing

The problem in those days, this was 1995, was that few in Headquarters actually *knew* how a field office needed to be managed. Indeed, I learnt quite quickly that UNESCO culture was highly centralized and forged within the fires of Francophiliac addiction to Paris-based control from the 'center', as well as the lifestyle imperative of Parisian café society. There was an inside joke that was actually half serious that 'decentralization' meant moving from the main UNESCO building in Place de Fontenoy overlooking L'Ecole Militaire and the Eiffel Tower, to the Bonvin-Miollis Building, a 5 min walk deeper into the 16th arrodisement or district; and further, that the greatest demotion sanction that could be levied in Headquarters while still staying in Paris was to be moved to 'Basement 3' several levels below a view of the Eiffel Tower, and at the furthest distance from the coffee machine. No one even wanted to contemplate the greater sanction, that was to be moved to a field office—from which there was a very real fear that you would never return, having been discarded onto the scrapheap of invisibility from the distance of Paris.

Dealing with the Headquarters—Field Divide

As I got to know UNESCO from the inside over the next year or two I came to realize that I had joined an organization with two quite different managerial faces. In the field, one had to *manage uncertainty*; in Headquarters, one had to *administer an illusion of certainty*. The reason for the distinction was pretty obvious. In the field, we were confronted by real developing country worlds of unexpected events and change. In my own experience, for example, this included staff taken hostage, economic collapse, a revolution, anarchy and evacuation of international staff, terrorist bombings, earthquakes and a tsunami. You simply could not go about normal business according to a plan adopted at an international General Conference two years before, but constantly had to adjust, confront new challenges whilst recognizing and capitalising on opportunities as they emerged. But, in Headquarters, life is directly accountable to the Member States through a Director-General who is likely to be highly aware of the complex politics of keeping somewhere near 200 of their ambassadors or representatives happy. Consequently, the main game in Headquarters is to *show* that plans have been put into place and budget spent according to decisions made within the formal process. Thus, the concern with maintaining appearances of certainty and responsible delivery of promises becomes paramount. However, this division in managerial priority sets a paradox into the organization that I found myself addressing on a daily basis for the decade I worked *inside the house*. The organization had still not fully transcended this contradiction by the time I retired.

Breaking the Rules to Do the Job

Indeed, no matter what our introductory instructions demanded, if you were looking after things in the back blocks of Cambodia or Timor Leste, you sometimes *had* to disregard the UNESCO Manual and Codes of Practice and *break the rules*—because they would otherwise *prevent* you doing what was needed in a developing country environment, in particular when dealing with a crisis.

A dramatic example:

Shortly after the plebiscite-related militia violence that tore apart Timor Leste in September 1999, Kofi Annan, Secretary-General of the United Nations visited the capital, Dili. We had already started on a program requested by the new Government to renovate a historic Portuguese fort on the waterfront, Uma Fukon into a national cultural exhibition site, its priority being to facilitate the development of consciousness of a national identity after more than 400 years of colonization. This was a particular interest of Xanana Gusmao, ex-leader of the Fretlin freedom fighters and subsequently President then Prime Minister. We had only just started on the renovation and both the officials in the UN Administration in Dili plus the Timorese themselves were keen that Kofi Annan visit the inaugural exhibition depicting 'who' Timorese were, even though the building renovation was nowhere near complete. We had to urgently get $(US)5,000 to Dili in Indonesian Rupiah to pay the local builders to fix the roof and construct one part of the space. We had less than two weeks. But ... Dili, the capital, had been totally trashed by the invading militia, including the banks, so there were still no banks operating in Timor Leste. Consequently, there was no way of transferring money or changing travelers cheques; and at this stage I had not had time to establish our UNESCO Office there. My only solution was to package the $(US)5,000 in Rupiah (roughly 80,000 Rupiah at that time) in Jakarta in a *large* brown paper bag and have it transported to Dili by the UN Official who at that stage was serving in the transitionary UN Administration as equivalent to Minister of Education and Culture. We took appropriate steps of sealing and signing the bag and signing *for* it, and we already had been working with this guy so knew him quite well .... but I was still moving United Nations money around by giving it to someone else in a paper bag in small denominations of cash. Viewed from the distance of formal financial accountability procedures and banking arrangements in Paris such an action would have been inconceivable, but for the arrangements to be in place for the UN Secretary-General's visit, I had no alternative. I did of course account for and regularize things later. Both the Timorese authorities and the Secretary General were pleased, so fortunately the good politics resulting from what *had* to be done helped me through the internal administrative censure that inevitably followed.

This event also required unexpected flexibility and breaking other rules. We needed to raise the profile of science in the country as Timor had been seriously disadvantaged in education and use of science while under Indonesia's 'colonialist' rule. Consequently we decided to fill the museum with an interactive science performance for the visiting notables to see and therefore for wider publicity. We brought in school children to participate. Unfortunately President Gusmao's security guards came to check out the safety of the venue in advance and immediately objected to children being present *for security reasons*. They evicted them, then left to pick up the President and other dignitaries.

Here lay their error. It was ridiculous to have the museum fully set up with equipment for a science show and no children to present it—before key world leaders. So, I sent local members of our team out onto the streets to bring back street children to fill in for the school students that the security guards had ejected. The street kids had an absolute ball as it was *so* different to their normal world, making the display that much more charming and connected than it would have been otherwise. The security guards came back with the President but could do nothing to change our presentation as it was too late. The dignitaries fully enjoyed the event … and were, of course, totally safe. Media brought the high level visit and show widely to the public. So, there was no way the guards could punish us for disobeying their (frankly stupid) instruction and action.

The paralysis of rules
Back to my briefing however. In 1995 only a trivial amount of organization budget was devoted to training, somewhere around 0.3 percent—an anathema in an organization of the international community responsible for taking the lead in *knowledge* application to development and peace building.

Priority of moving towards becoming a 'learning organization', I should immediately point out, shifted greatly under the incoming Director-General Matsuura's reforms initiated from the end of 1999. Now, $(US)6 million or 2 percent of budget was spent on training.

However, back in 1995 when I joined, absence of attention to serious training was obvious. Briefing was entirely conducted by staff who really were supposed to be doing other things, or retiree volunteers. I recollect that not one of our mentors had actually worked out in a field office. By the end of the first day, we had passed through the exhortations to learn the rules of UNESCO, including the seriously proffered advice of maintaining the (turgid, complex, legalistic) UNESCO Manual under our pillow so we could read a little more each night until we were totally familiar with its content. And, in other sessions we were being lectured by an intellectually desiccated retiree, whose instruction consisted entirely of reading directly from the United Nations codes of practices.

A few moments reflection with some of my fellow trainees over our first 'official welcome' Parisian aperitif that evening was all it required for me to decide to bypass much of the rest of the briefing sessions. Instead, I discovered the real Bible of the organization, the Internal Phone Book, checked out who was responsible for what I needed to know about programs and administration, and went to talk with them directly.

Perhaps like all organizations, but particularly in the United Nations, learning to 'work' the networks, and understand where influence (as opposed to authority) was located, was an essential tool of both learning and management as well as getting things done oneself.

In reflecting back on the Headquarters mentality of the time I am reminded of what has to be a criterion example of the bureaucratic paralysis that can so easily infect an organization where many of the people remain remote from being directly responsible for making things actually happen out in the real world. This was a meeting I had at the time when I travelled to Paris several months before joining the organization to be interviewed for the job. I wanted to enquire on the conditions of appointment, things like, how much support was provided for moving goods around the world, possible options and expectations in salary and seniority level given my previous academic post and experience, non-salary benefits, and so on. I went to what in those days was called the Personnel Office and spoke with a very helpful secretary.

> "You must see Mr Azizi!' she advised ("Azizi" is my pseudonym), the desk officer responsible for field staff. 'However, as it is just 12.30, he will have gone to lunch. Come back at 2.01pm. He *will* be there."

I should have recognized the danger sign of such attention to precision timing. I did indeed arrive at Mr Azizi's office one minute past the stroke of 2.00 pm, admitting myself after knocking and hearing a deep African voice on the inside saying 'Entré', to find Mr Azizi sitting with hands folded across an entirely empty desk, looking me over with a not-unfriendly but distinctly Gaelic attitude. He only spoke French, an immediate challenge for me, a neophyte with classic Australian non-linguistically pluralistic background. I acquainted him with my request, that is, to learn what the conditions of potential appointment were. He immediately asked if I had my file with me. This, I pointed out in limping French, was not yet possible as I had just come along to be interviewed and, if selected, needed to know the conditions in principle so as to decide whether to accept the job if it was offered to me. UNESCO did not yet have a staff file for me as I was not yet a staff member. 'Ah', he said (with East African French accent), 'then I cannot talk with you!' I felt it was a quite reasonable ask to question this assertion, as if this was the case, then *no one* who had not yet joined the organization could learn from the apparently responsible official what conditions to expect in their employment. 'But, I *cannot* talk with you without a file to refer to', he reiterated, with the implication that to do so could lead to him offering possibly inaccurate advice, a position he could not responsibly violate. I think I may have sought once more to express a voice of reason, but to no avail. I finally left his office defeated.

I should qualify this example by immediately emphasizing that I had the joy to work with UNESCO colleagues of the highest commitment, integrity and intelligence, and found the shared culture of such an intensely multicultural organization very rewarding indeed. However, all too often these highly valued colleagues maintained their capacity against the background of a constant fight against distinctly countervailing tendencies from within the structure and cultural expectations of Headquarters sanctions and rewards that emphasized doing things within the constraints of proper procedure even if it meant not delivering the results that we were screaming out to have delivered when confronting very real life problems.

As long as people followed 'proper procedure' and did not put their heads up they remained 'safe' and would proceed unproblematically up the hierarchy of promotions.

The time I got most upset was when we were in the middle of a *revolution* in Jakarta in May 1998, the time when President Soeharto fell from power. We were confronting major civil unrest, with anarchic mobs burning and looting through the streets, and murders being committed quite literally within sight of our United Nations offices. The police and military were entirely absent from controlling the riots in the streets—part of a power strategy being played out around the President's office. Although I elected to stay as 'essential' UN staff, along with our Administrative Officer, Moussa, who did not want to miss the action, I had to evacuate all other international staff and families of my UN Agency, but in advance, knowing what hardship they would otherwise suffer, arrange ongoing payment and leave for our locally employed staff. With some difficulty—as all phone lines out of the country were overwhelmed—we got through by telephone to the desk officer in Headquarters responsible for the payment arrangements. After a few minutes of listening to the requirements she said, 'Oh, I've just realized. It's 6 o'clock. It's time for me to go home. I'll fix this problem tomorrow.' And, then she hung up. Needless to say, I was not happy, and, under considerable duress, finally was able to find a colleague I knew personally in Headquarters who took it on himself to walk around the organization until he found senior people who had the authority to fix the problem.

After the 'briefing'—and my initial networking exercise, I returned to Jakarta, to be greeted at the airport by the warm evocative smell of the tropics and the city that over ten years became so significant a reminder that I had again returned to 'home' in a developing country just south of the equator.

Moving Back into the Real World

And, I moved on.

Somehow I had no problem recognizing that coloured post-stickers, yelling, and not trusting people was not going to work in managing my own office. So, counter to the advice I had received from the Director. a.i., and in an approach that was not a part of either our briefing or the UNESCO Manual, I adopted the fairly obvious management strategy I had learnt over the years of managing academic institutions. That is, to ensure that each person *could* do the job—in terms of training and ability; second, to provide clear parameters to what they did—which in my case said, once we, together, are clear about overall direction, *do* it, but check with me when things cross into policy, funding and public/government relations; and third, make sure they realize that they are accountable within pretty clear guidelines. *Encourage* innovative ideas, and build *sharing* between people and teams into the culture of the organization. Then back the people to the hilt—even when things start to go wrong. Hang in there. *Trust.* A basic lesson of management. As I subsequently learnt from what worked in the field, these were also the basic lessons of helping communities to empower themselves. Finding local champions and listening to what the people needed and wanted, self-empowerment of their communities, facilitating the development of appropriate capacities, and then building mutual *trust*—were the platforms for being effective in just about everything we did as a UN Agency in helping to foster development that the people themselves wanted.

3

"Learning to Walk the Diplomatic Path"

The other side—to administration and management—of moving into a United Nations organization with responsibility to cooperate with Member States is that one must learn to be a diplomat.

Protocol and Diplomatic Life

As a Field Director in the United Nations, and in the present case specifically UNESCO, one has formal diplomatic license to officially represent the organization *across cultures* and to speak *for* its Director-General as Representative or Ambassador of the organization. This protocol *is* treated very seriously both within the Secretariat and by Member States. The representative status confronts you on the one hand with a critical responsibility that one really must treat very carefully—particularly if speaking *as if* the Director-General. On the other hand, the status also equips you with a quite serious political *clout* that can be of enormous use in working with the most senior levels of government either on highly sensitive issues like freedom of expression or human rights or in convincing the government's representatives of activities they should support.

No NGO Head has this valuable tool of change management in their hand.

International diplomacy is ruled by an iron hand of protocol—with absolutely strict rules of precedent and seniority: as an ambassador stays longer in the country, standard protocol is for them to move further along the protocol hierarchy until they finally reach the top. The Dean of the Diplomatic Community in Indonesia therefore was the ambassador who had served there longest—a protocol that will be maintained even in the face of embarrassing ineptitude or recalcitrance to represent the *whole* community. In Indonesia, for example, in the early 2000s the longest serving Ambassador was a representative of Palestine who was there longest only because Indonesia had agreed with the Palestinian Authority to pay all costs and the guy refused to leave, fully recognizing he was onto a good thing. The Ambassador was a 'colorful' character who caused serious dismay locally when he chose to shoot a man in the foot rather than drive off when the man 'accosted' the Ambassador in his car at a traffic light. The European and American Ambassadors were frequently incensed as the Dean spoke supposedly on their behalf at official Foreign Affairs functions, but instead, called on the world to support the Palestinian Cause and berated Israel in distinctly undiplomatic language.

The protocol for UN Agencies left us further down the order of seating at official occasions. The UN 'Coordinator'—assigned from New York and most frequently from UNDP—had full Ambassador status and sat amongst the greats. As Acting UN Coordinator at times, I occasionally had this status that elevated my seat at official occasions down to the front. Otherwise, we were on the Ambassadorial seating list but really somewhere towards the back, amongst the more newly arrived Ambassadors of rather smaller countries and Deputy Ambassadors of the major powers. *But*, although a little closer to the end of the protocol line, we still had been formally approved as Representatives and therefore Official Ambassadors by the National Ministry of Foreign Affairs so had full envoy status along with diplomatic privilege and immunity. This mattered as far as doing things was concerned.

My Debut

When I first arrived in Jakarta during the week when I came in to see what the Office did before heading off to Headquarters to be 'briefed' on what I *should* do, I knew I was supposed to be a diplomatic 'representative', but really had little idea what this meant.

The first social signal came when I had been in place for a day, was staying at the Hotel Borobodur—not too far away from the Palace end of town but also within hitting distance from my office—and I had to attend a function hosted by the Philippines Ambassador. This was my first official diplomatic National Day Reception—of which, I should add, there turned out to be around 100 a year. My car arrived at the Hotel Entrance. My predecessor as a proud German had purchased a silver Mercedes for the UNESCO Representative, so the car seemed of appropriate diplomatic significance. Flying on the curb-side front fender was the United Nations flag. The car, suitably promoted through the lobby cue of vehicles, drew up to the Hotel Entrance to the immediately obsequious attention of the uniformed master of vehicle ceremonies: 'Your Excellency', he intoned to me, the guest to whom he had previously paid marginal inattention, 'I had not realized you were Ambassador, I'm so sorry to have not looked after you better, however, your car has arrived. Please let me assist.' Pushing the crowding assembly to the side he opened the car door, bowing significantly more deeply than for his previous patrons. 'Good Lord' I thought, smiling in passing to the assembled throng, 'Is that right?' … and sat in a warm glow of new-found pretense in the rear seat behind the waving flag of my diplomatic status. It took about three such occasions to level my pretense to the blasé normality of weekly ritual. I did realize quite quickly however that these ritual National Day functions were extremely useful in getting to know the heads of diplomatic missions and government ministers, and 'doing business'—opening the door for formal follow-up to gain government approvals, or for setting up subsequent private meetings to convince heads of diplomatic missions to fund UNESCO activities. I rarely missed a National Day Reception unless I was out of the country.

Apart from appearing for drinks and a few early greetings at this initial Philippines National Day Reception, my first really serious experience of what diplomatic life as a United Nations official could mean came two months later and was dramatic. The occasion was the 17th August 1995 Indonesian National Day celebration.

By this time I had settled into Indonesia—after the initial week-long orienting period in Jakarta during which I had attended the Philippines National Day Reception, and after the subsequent briefing in our Paris Headquarters. Jill, my wife at the time, and I had moved into our residence Not only was it National Day but also this was the 50th Anniversary of Indonesia's Independence. President Soeharto was at the zenith of his kingly power and chose to stage a massive military display plus entertainment for the people—played out in the open in Monas Square (where the National Monument to Independence is located), just down from the State Palace.

As was the custom at that time, all Ambassadors were sent the materials, decorations and hat, the Pecci, to dress similarly in traditional Javanese costume. All Jakarta, it seemed, was migrating to Monas Square. Fortunately, with diplomatic license plates inscribed with 'CD-1' indicating Ambassador status, and the right official passes displayed on the car, my wife, Jill, and I were swept past the crush right to the entrance of the park where the celebration was being staged. I had never seen a crowd so large, somewhere over an estimated two million people. The Palace Protocol people were however used to large numbers and greeted us as our car pulled up, allocated a young couple dressed in traditional Javanese costume to escort us to our seat just behind the President's—through the jostling mob who were held back by military escorts on horseback. The President arrived with due pomp and ceremony and the formal part of the parade started—with the President reviewing the passing troops, then finally engaging in a ceremony to hand over the carefully preserved original national flag, symbolizing the significance of the Fiftieth National Day celebration, to a youth brigade couple who, with military precision, raised the national flag to the thunder of a 21-canon salute. Then we settled back to watch the staging of the 'party' for the people, what promised to be a fabulous show—of Indonesia's best in performance, athletic exhibition and massed person displays.

But the President left! Just as the show was starting. Normal protocol, we then rapidly learnt for the first time is that when the President goes, so do you. *Never* before, but always shortly after as an appropriate sign of respect. I also noticed good reason to leave, that is, as the Presidential entourage moved towards the entrance his minders went too and the crowds started to close in behind them. If we left our departure for more than a few minutes we were destined to have to fight our way through a couple of million people unescorted and somehow find what had happened to our car and driver. By hanging close to a couple of experienced ambassadors we made it through and onto the street, where I looked in desolation at the thousands of cars that were crushed into the surrounding space. While searching the horizon, I felt someone in the crowd picking at my sleeve and brushed them off—only to find a moment later that it was my own driver, Lukman, one of the most senior diplomatic drivers in town, totally devoted to having the car in the right place at the right time, and who had managed to steadily progress my UNESCO Mercedes to the front of the queue and was signaling me to get in quickly.

So, we left. Outside the initial crush the streets were almost deserted. Everyone was at Monas. We arrived home in record time, having spent a full hour at what we expected to be an all-day occasion. We then saw the Monas celebration, but on television in our lounge room. As far as the show was concerned, we hadn't needed to even get out of bed. However, we did at least try and capture a bit of the ambience by watching TV dressed in the traditional Javanese costumes that we had taken so much time putting on early that morning.

Meanwhile, as I increasingly appreciated when in the Field, mastering Diplomatic Life was, on the one hand, an essential element of national and international relationships for senior UN officials, but equally could be both source of opportunity as well as entertainment.

It is quite easy to become distracted by the style and opportunity of diplomatic life. Just turn up for the parties, smile a lot, make a few friends, and participate in a very privileged lifestyle. For some Ambassadors, particularly from small diplomatic missions, this really was about all they did. And their countries missed out on enormous opportunities that could, with a little creativity, be conjured up even for the less powerful who 'played' the diplomatic circle.

As an example:

Diplomatic Opportunity Even with Small Things—The Slovakian Stamp of Approval

The Ambassador of Slovakia in 1998 and I did a deal that would, with larger diplomatic missions, probably never have been conceived—that was, to follow his personal interest in stamp collecting to release a *joint* UNESCO-Slovakian 'first-day cover' letter and stamp series that celebrated the two World Heritage sites —of Spis Castle in Slovakia, and Borobudur in Indonesia, "Seen through the eyes of UNESCO". To profile this bilateral relationship mediated via UNESCO's World Heritage nominations in both countries, the Ambassador and I arranged for the Minister of Tourism, Jupe Avé to launch the bilateral stamp series—published I should add in parallel in *both* Slovakia and Indonesia. There was a side-play, for the Minister decided to use the occasion to show to the world his interest in high tech video linkage. The stamp series was therefore launched in a rather large event at one of the local five-star hotels—with broad media coverage and good attendances, given that the Minister was officiating. However, following from Jupe Avé's commitment to highlight video connectedness as well, I was to remain in my office being filmed by a camera crew, with two-way communication of both the Minister and Ambassador's speeches at the hotel, and my speech delivered from my desk in my UN Office in front of the United Nations flag.

What I had not quite appreciated at the time was that at the other end of this communication link, an enormous screen had been installed in the hotel's ballroom, and my face was being beamed through the satellite link as a 10-m-high image on the wall. What I also did not appreciate was that as soon as they started filming in my office, my image was up there—spreading

UN goodwill across the event and the ballroom wall. Consequently, I was nervously sitting at my desk casting a last-minute eye over my speech notes, scratching my leg, blowing my nose, and sipping the last drops of my cooling coffee—totally unaware that all this was being watched by millions, the ballroom wall and event being broadcast live across national Indonesian TV … until the Minister's voice came over the line suggesting that perhaps I might like to start my officiating remarks. At the end of the filming, the TV producers replayed the footage, neglecting however to tell me this was what they were doing … so this time I thought that they had *again* jumped into my office privacy, so immediately struck my official speech pose …. until one of the camera crew pointed out that the event had finished five minutes before.

Meanwhile, in spite of these glitches, the Slovakian Ambassador had pulled off a major media presentation of his country, and its bilateral interest in Indonesia—when Slovakia was hardly known within Indonesia—for virtually nothing—courtesy of the mediating role of UNESCO, and a casual conversation that Peter and I had had at a National Day Reception some time before.

Although he became a good friend, I tended to stay at a distance from the Slovakian Ambassador at official Presidential events however. The Ambassadors were always close to the President on such occasions and therefore under very tight scrutiny from the President's armed security minders, who with communication devices in one ear, were very clearly militarily hardened men with menacing holstered bumps under their jackets, and whose lives quite literally depended on keeping the President alive and unharmed. This scene was very familiar to the Ambassador. His diplomatic status was acquired from his previous job as head of armed security for the Slovakian President. The Ambassador was an ex-military man too. And he delighted in testing the security system surrounding President Soeharto, occasionally sliding his hand inside his jacket as if about to draw a gun, or moving in an unpredictable way towards the President's chair, all the while watching how the minders responded ….. This seemed to me to make Peter unacceptably risky to stand next to when the President was around!

Diplomatic Tennis

I also found that diplomatic representation of the organization sometimes needed to take an 'unusual' path. One particular challenge I faced was that my UNESCO Director-General in the early 2000s, Koichiro Matsuura, loved playing tennis as exercise for his 70 year old physique. I therefore needed to arrange tennis matches for him in each of the countries under my watch when he visited on official missions. BUT, given the protocol that Matsuura had Head-of-State status I had to develop what I called "Diplomatic Tennis". Opponents needed to be of either Ministerial or Ambassador status but also play at a level *nearly* as good as the Director General … but not significantly better. I played tennis a fair bit at that time myself so had to take on a few advance challenges to test the alternative invitees. Plus, I played opposite to Matsuura who was pretty good though his agility across the court was a little restricted, and I needed to *just* lose. Not too difficult given my own standard. Calling the match "Diplomatic Tennis" provided my excuse to my friends who were watching as to why I could never beat this guy who was significantly older than me.

The Unwrapping of Traditional Javanese Culture

Playing out one's diplomatic role across Asia also meant handling relations across cultures and this could be challenging.

Without doubt the most memorable entrée for me to an inner cultural world because of my UN representative responsibility for culture occurred on 14th March 2002. Following is what I wrote in reports at that time:

"On 14th March 2002 I was invited, along with my wife, Jill, and the head of USAID and spouse as the only foreign guests, to attend the celebration of 1 Muharram or Moslem New Year at the Surakarta Palace, Solo, by the Sunan, or King of Surakarta, Sri Susuhanan Paku Buwono XII. Solo, or Surakarta, to give the town its traditional name, is the cultural heart of Javanese society and 1 Muharram is the most important event celebrated at the Palace.

Lunch set the scene. This was shared with the Sunan and his royal family. This was a rather large family as he did have 38 sons and daughters by a variety of six wives. The location was the main royal pavilion—an enormous glassed-in platform, with a table in the centre for the Sunan, three princes and us, a gamelan orchestra at the one far end, and the line of the Sunan's family at tables at the other end of the pavilion.

Lunch was served, Rijstaafel style—with 24 courses, each served by a different servant girl who arrived en-masse in a long line when the meal was to be delivered.

But it was the evening that was really special. At midnight, the evening 'procession of sacred weapons' was celebrated by the Sunan and 3,000 palace officials, family relatives and supporters, all dressed in traditional Javanese costume. The sacred weapons were brought out of their sanctuary, ritually cleansed, and then the velvet sheathed spears and kris knives were carried by the chosen through the streets of Solo, the procession lit by burning fire brands and following a sacred white Ox—which, we were assured, knew the way, and would wander around the city until he chose to return to the palace. As it turned out the sacred ox found his way back around 4.00am along with those officials and followers who had managed to last the distance.

As I have learnt from past experience of my participation in occasions like this, things never go smoothly. We too had to be dressed in traditional Javanese costume for which the palace sent out two assistants to our hotel to do the honors of helping. Getting dressed for me involved a lot of wrapping up by sarong, various belts and so on. All fine, though a bit constricting."

Jill, meanwhile, was also wrapped in sarong and various belts and 'made-up' with blackening of her hair, attachment of the 'mandatory' ibu's hair bun at the back, along with a stylized 'widow's peak' above her forehead, and a *severe* wrapping of her sarong. The problem was that Jill kept her legs together. For, after the final wrapping by her palace assistants was complete, Jill could hardly walk beyond short 10 cm shuffles. Confronting a staircase was a major problem as she had to shuffle fast enough for a final jump to the next step to succeed in getting up the long, long staircase to the palace entrance.

The crunch came however, as we hurried up the steps to the giant wooden door of the palace compound an hour or two before midnight—having pushed past a crowd of some 50,000 bystanders. At that moment all 4 meters or so of my outside belt decided to relieve itself of the obligation to remain around my waist and dropped uncurling like a relaxing snake to the ground, trapping my ankles in boa-constrictor coils whilst releasing at the same time my ceremonial kris sword to clatter noisily onto the palace stairs in front of me. I felt the eyes of all 50,000 people watching. An assistant fortunately was near at hand and reasonably quickly re-wrapped my dignity. With my hand ever-near the offending belt we then moved as quickly as one can with legs constrained by a tight sarong past the courtiers and the giant wooden entrance door and on to the most extraordinary of traditional cultural evenings."

After we had made it past the heavy wooden palace doors, we walked into a scene that could have been a thousand years old—3,000 traditionally clad relatives of the royal family, palace officials and notables—milling about or sitting across the main palace platform with burning torches providing the light. We were guided to the front, but then separated—with Jill sitting with the women and me sitting in the men's group—with the previous President Gus Dur sitting alone just to the front. At the end of the pavilion however was a small room with closed door. Every so often the Sunan would open the door and poke his head out—whilst the grey flickering light of the TV in his room provided background. The Sunan had to signal when the time was propitious for the sacred white Ox to leave, thus leading the procession—all antique kris swords and spears having now been released from their vault and blessed. But while the Sunan waited, he (alone) sat in a side-room watching a soap opera on TV .... Something of a contradiction, I thought, to the heavy weight of tradition that otherwise hung over the ceremony outside his door!

I did follow the Ox out of the Palace compound into the city—along with many others. After an hour of wandering however, he did not seem to be too committed to heading back home to the Palace, so, with the alternate prospect of wandering about behind a disinterested Ox until the sun came up, I quietly moved out of the procession and walked back to where I was staying."

Opportunity in Being Creative—Ocean and Underwater Diplomacy

In late 1998 I had a particular diplomatic task to complete where I needed to involve the Presidents of the two countries for which at that time I was Representative, Indonesia and the Philippines. The task was to get the respective Presidents to sign 'The Ocean Charter' a declaration under UNESCO's stewardship of good intent to promote ocean conservation at the highest level of government.

In the case of Indonesia, the government decided to put on a show up in the far eastern islands at Manado in North Sulawesi during an ocean sports festival. Bacharuddin Jusuf (or B.J.) Habibie, President at the time, therefore signed the Charter on board a naval ship with me standing next to him looking down approvingly, witnessed by his top military personnel, accompanied by fly-past of a dozen naval aircraft, and review of a flotilla of vessels including traditional tall square-masted sailing ships. President Habibie further had had a large container equipped as a surgical operating theatre and loaded onto the rear deck of the ship—where through side-windows the guests were able to witness Habibie's generosity to the people in the provinces—free operations to fix hair lips of children, demonstration of an ongoing program of care for coastal community people by the navy .... a somewhat curious element in the overall event!

Habibie was regarded generally as something of a fool, in particular by the military leaders. I had been sitting next to General Wiranto, Head of the Military, in a preliminary speech by the President on land before we boarded the ship. All the time while Habibie spoke, Wiranto kept trying to talk with me ... though I was doing my best to avoid responding so as to be polite at a Presidential occasion where I was sitting in the front row of seats. Wiranto's dismissive intent became very clear at the end of the final ceremony on board the ship however. Against every protocol rule in the book, General Wiranto turned his back as Habibie was climbing into his helicopter, and stared at the ocean.

I should add, Habibie had publicly embarrassed General Wiranto a month earlier at a Presidential Reception at the Palace. Both Habibie and Wiranto prided themselves on their singing prowess—Wiranto having even recently released a CD of himself—including his version of the song Johnny Mathis made famous—"Feelings" … a little unsettling when sung by a Military General implicated in civilian disappearances and human rights abuse. At the Reception, President Habibie was ready to entertain the crowd and had set up a band with microphones on the balcony half way down the steps to the garden from the back of the Palace Reception Room. He invited Wiranto to join him and sing together for the audience … an anathema to many in the audience who associated a President, namely previous 26 year President Soeharto, with serious protocol and reserved dignity. Wiranto joined him, almost certainly feeling he could easily outshine Habibie. However, Habibie had only *one* copy of the words, and kept hiding it from Wiranto who was seriously embarrassed by his own stumbling with the lyrics.

But it was the Philippines that posed me with the greatest challenge.

I knew that President Ramos was both committed to marine conservation as well as being a scuba diver. So, I made the proposal to the Palace—really only half seriously—that perhaps he might like to sign the Charter *underwater* to attract more media attention. Unfortunately for me, he agreed!

I was certified as a scuba diver but not very good at it, so my first priority was somehow to come up to speed before the event. The designated dive site in Batangas Bay was known for swift moving currents and the idea of diving with a President scared the wits out of me. I went back to dive school in Jakarta and descended into the shallows of a couple of relatively deep swimming pools; and then, fortunately, a casual remark by Jill, my wife, to Sofian, her neighbor at a formal diplomatic dinner party, elicited an invitation to practice diving off one of the three islands the guy owned out in Jakarta Bay. A wealthy businessman, he had bought the islands some years earlier by paying the locals, according to traditional practice, for the *number of palm trees* on the islands. So, we went visiting—taken out on Sofian's rather large launch to the outskirts of Pulau Seribu, Jakarta Bay's 'Thousand Islands', to his private resort. He called in a Master Diver, and I went diving along with Sofian's two sons. I must admit that this was the first time that I had had the luxury of someone carrying my air tanks, dressing me in the rubber gear—including putting on my fins while I comfortably reclined next to the water—and then carefully lowering me into the water before following at a cautious but close distance in a launch to make sure I was always OK. This stress-free scuba diving was in sharp contrast to my previous experience. I had learnt Open Ocean Diving at Bass Point near Shellharbour in Australia—where access *in* to the water required carrying the air tanks plus gear for a couple of hundred meters across rocks, and getting out required ascending with the same heavy gear up the appropriately named very steep 'Cardiac Hill'.

I also had the Ocean Charter made up on Dive Board material—which the marine staff in my office used for recording in underwater scientific surveys they conducted. However, a week prior to the event the President's staff informed us that they *also* wanted the Ocean Charter to be written on a very large board because this was increasingly becoming a major media event—with CNN, American ABC and other TV channels flying in to watch. I commissioned the Manila-based UNDP office to make this up for me. The plastic product looked very impressive. But unfortunately it came with a problem.

At the last minute, the President's minders decided that we would sign the Charter both on board the ship that was available for Presidential cruises as well as *in* the water, but the Charter would be signed *in* the water snorkeling rather than while diving, as the President's health was problematic. Then when *in* the water, we confronted the problem. No pen would register on the surface of the large plastic board UNDP had prepared for me. We tried everything. Finally, a female reporter from CNN came to the rescue, and the Charter was signed under the water in her lipstick. The Charter is now, I am reliably assured, appropriately laminated, and resting in 20 m of water in Batangas Bay, next to a Christian Cross previously installed by President Ramos—the only official international Charter signed underwater in lipstick by a President! …. President Ramos invited me to have lunch with him afterwards and I asked him why the Cross was down there. He told me that he loved diving, but the only day available in his Presidential schedule was Sunday and being Head of State for the deeply religious Philippines people, he needed to show his Christian commitment and go to church. But, he assured me, with the Cross 20 m underwater, he could now go diving on a Sunday with a clear conscience that he was diving in his own private underwater chapel. Meanwhile, as the Signing Ceremony was quite a media event, it was subject of a later feature film on CNN.

The Power of the Gift Rather Than the Deal

Stepping outside the normal could indeed be powerful. The general principle of international diplomatic negotiation and assumed success is most generally self-interest. Making sure by 'The Deal' that one's own national (and perhaps personal) interest is rewarded.

Across a range of interactions though we discovered the perhaps unexpected but strong power of "The Gift" in international diplomacy—right up to high levels of official authority—rather than the more general international diplomatic strategy of achieving a positive self-or-national focused advantage in "The Deal". The reason: *trust* is basic to success when one reaches up to high levels of official authority as well as far down at community level … not a *deal*. And, giving a gift without any immediate expectation of reward or response is, by my experience, enormously powerful in building trust.

> The *gift* however *must* be based on *listening*—understanding what is needed—from an external perspective but based on hearing how the target community sees things, and then locating action within the context of what the people themselves value. *So* many development assistance projects fail because the agency does not *listen* but acts in the way *they* have determined is best for the people.

With this 'listening' principle at the heart of UNESCO action, a 'gift-based' strategy worked wonderfully across a broad range of programs and levels, with return favor or desired action usually happening subsequently at the initiative of the recipient country or agency without the need for this to be required by contract. The most significant case concerned North Korea where, under responsibility as the UN's Regional Science Bureau, we were seeking to develop an initiative in the first instance to get North Korea to participate and cooperate in the broad range of UN Science programs and debates—across all disciplines. Building cooperation was important in achieving wider peace and security goals, but also served potentially to strengthen North Korea's own National Science Capacity. In keeping with *listening* to North Korea's own objectives and crafting action that was politically acceptable, though still guiding where needed, dramatic results were achieved … including *the introduction of Internet* into North Korea—as a vehicle for connecting North Korea more directly into the wider international community, in particular, of science cooperation and knowledge. Initially the very idea of us proposing internet for North Korea would have been strongly against the country's official self-protective rhetoric, so, whilst highly desirable on both political and knowledge grounds, we did not approach North

Korea and say, "I will make *internet* happen for you". Such an initiative would have been rejected out of hand—and it was not our plan in the first place. At first, we just wanted to help them to be more connected via science with the outside world. But the closer and more far-reaching relationship developed, mainly, as an evolution of increasing trust.

Very briefly here is the sequence of events—identified as elements of a 'gift' strategy:

> *Gift No. 1:* North Korea would not come to any of the conferences and programs we ran 'for the Asia Pacific Region (across all disciplines), or participate in agreements or support (across all areas of science). I assumed they were rejecting such participation.
> But the problem was different. We only had funding to offer *one 'ticket'* for each scientific conference or event per country across the region (for some meetings we had 44 to deal with). I then realized that North Korea wanted *two* tickets, so the second person could watch the first person watching the second person—so preventing one of them escaping. So, Gift No.1 was for us to unilaterally offer North Korea *two* tickets to everything (overriding a considerable amount of flak from my UNESCO Headquarters Bean Counters). The North Koreans came, and back home, their bosses were pleased.
> After a year of cautious participation, North Korea invited me to Pyongyang on an Official State Visit (1999). The officials showed me eight research institutes—every one with problems largely because they had had almost no international science interaction for 12 years, whilst *all* international research publications were chosen by the government "Central Information Agency"—the "CIA" of North Korea—a rather paradoxical acronym. North Korea's CIA bureaucrats chose 60 publications per year, translated them and sent them to the Research Centers and Scientists *they* chose.
> As a previous Research Chemist myself, whilst I could not solve the problems, I knew they *could* be solved. Our own UNESCO science specialist staff, together via correspondence with representatives of the eight North Korean Research Centers, then identified the one *most* important problem for each of them. So ...
> *Gift No. 2:* I offered North Korea that we would bring in a scientist for each of the eight North Korean Institutes to solve their key problem—from countries acceptable to North Korea. We put this team together and with me leading, brought in the mission 6 months later. They solved each Institute's key problems within two to three days.
> Again, North Korean authorities were very pleased and asked me to help them introduce *Intra*-net across the country. But, this time, I said "*NO*. Your problem is not *internal* but *external access.* You need *inter*-net." "Oh No. Too hard!"

So ...

Gift No. 3: Trust was critical. So, I arranged for *China* to agree to host a person from each of the eight Institutes to show them how to solve their next most important specific problem *just using internet*. China was acceptable for North Korea diplomatically so North Korea agreed. Again, in quick time the North Korean scientists visiting China solved their Institute's problem —using (the previously forbidden) Internet.

North Korea was impressed, and then asked me if I could arrange for the Deputy Head of Science for North Korea and colleague to have a look at internet internationally.

So ...

Gift No. 4: I arranged a Mission to Australia to show these guys what Internet could do. I am a Fellow of the Australian Academy of Technological Sciences and Engineering, and was able to arrange with them to *fund* a Mission for North Korea's Deputy Head of Science (+ colleague) to come to Australia to see what Internet had to offer, and also I arranged for CSIRO to support them in Australia and spend 3 months showing these two guys how important internet was in informing and supporting scientific research. CSIRO took them around the country to a number of scientific institutions on a well-orchestrated learning program.

Then ...

Gift No. 5: On their way back to North Korea, the Deputy Head of North Korean Science and colleague primarily responsible for Korean-English translation (Mr. Hong ... he had by now become my friend ... and this was important for internal trust and support by North Korea) stopped over in my UN Office in Jakarta to Debrief. They asked me to help them set up an official international Internet Address for North Korea.

My staff did this, and internet was introduced into North Korea.

So, *The Power of the Gift!* Through this series of gifts (asking for nothing in return) we became *trusted,* and North Korea opened up internationally via Internet for the first time. Limited and controlled indeed. But still there and showing the people more generally. For example, computer students at Pyongyang's University of Science and Technology NOW can access Internet ... albeit with restrictions, as I confirmed just a few weeks ago. But ... these are *students* ... who communicate more generally to their friends if no-one else. A small chink in the armor of totalitarianism ... but a potential step towards wider liberation .... *because of the Power of the Gift!* Meanwhile the country's research related to food supply and more general support for the people was strongly enhanced.

The Power of Diplomacy in Dealing with Corrupt Governance

Corruption can be very near the surface of relations with some countries, particularly in the developing world. Diplomatic sensitivity can be far more effective in dealing with this rather than direct conflict. What I found worked was not to confront but *surround*. Whilst this strategy was so useful in general in my UN diplomatic experience, I will present just one story here. It is about using the power of music in our work which, at one stage required dealing with major corruption. I need to prepare the way to show where corruption crept in by providing some brief background.

Originally, back in 1995 when I first arrived in my UN Post in Indonesia, a local altruistic entrepreneur, Rano Sianturi (who became a close friend) and I founded an NGO which we called "Sacred Bridge"—dedicated to using music and performance to heal or bring communities together. I was particularly attracted to this opportunity having been a part-time musician in a professional rock band while a Sociology Professor by day back in the late 1970s to mid-1980s—the band's name, "Sons of Beaches" and whilst being also a keyboard player, my main role in the band was as a Blues Harmonica player. We worked with children caught up in Christian-Moslem fighting in Sulawesi, the Street Gangs of Jakarta, and as I go on to describe more fully in Chap. 19, helping to heal the desperate trauma of children seriously traumatized by the Tsunami that was so enormously destructive of Aceh at the end of 2004.

While primarily targeting using music and performance to heal traumatized children, we also developed public performances with a message for youth. Starting back in mid-1997, we developed an international concert—to be held in Bali—to be called the "Sacred Rhythm" Concert, a follow-up of two other smaller International Festivals we helped organize and support in 1997 and 1998. It was our intention to target this Millennium-turning date also as it heralded the first moments of the United Nations International Year for the Culture of Peace—the core business of UNESCO. Our Millennium Concert became the official start of this UN Year. We organized for ten international and nine national groups to perform—including drummer Mickey Hart from the USA, Japanese percussion virtuoso Stomu Yamash'ta (a 'National Treasure' of Japan), and groups from Burkino Fazi, Senegal, India, the Republic of Korea, Switzerland, Italy, the USA and from across a number of provinces of Indonesia.

Now I come to the money needed to make this event happen … and where high level corruption crept in.

All was going well, including raising funding to bring in the international performers—from the Ford Foundation, UNESCO, and local business, and we had developed good support from the Government of Indonesia through the Ministry of Tourism, Art and Culture, the Ministry of Education and Culture as well as the Governor of Bali. But we still had a problem in paying all costs, including in particular, the cost of building the stage—a large-scale affair to be located in Jimbaran Quarry where the acoustics and landscape were perfect for a truly magic performance and the local village leaders accepted our initiative. I mentioned this problem to the Minister of Forestry—with whom I had been working for some time, including when he was previously the Minister for Culture. He came up with a suggestion—why not try the current Minister of Trade and Industry to stage a fund-raising event? I knew this Minister already quite well as when I had to move on to my full-time UNESCO post in 1995, he had been nominated by President Soeharto to take over Chairmanship of STEPAN, the UNESCO Science and Technology Policy Asian Network which I had founded and for which I then served as Foundation Chairman. The Minister agreed to host the fund-raising evening.

So the fund-raising evening went ahead—opening with a dramatic competition between two dueling Jegog Gamelan groups (a form of Gamelan from West Bali where the instrument consists of giant bamboo pipes played from a saddle on top). I was impressed by the Minister's property—which included six houses on 11 hectares of land that used to be a village in South Jakarta, one house for his wife and family, another for his art collection, another for the gamelans, another for the 60 automobiles, and so on—all funded, theoretically, from his $(US)150 per month salary. I was particularly impressed by how much money was committed by the businessmen who the trade minister had invited to the Fund-Raising event, and were no doubt seeking his favour, a total of near $(US)250,000—enough for what we needed. The Minister showed me the written commitments, a number of which I, fortunately, recorded.

Three weeks later however, and we had received none of the money and I was running seriously out of time with contracts already being written for international performers for a fixed date that *could not* be changed. I discretely enquired why. What I found caused me a problem. The Minister had allotted responsibility to organize the fund-raising evening to one of his Directors—a woman who also, it appeared, happened to be his mistress. She had decided to take $(US)150,000 for herself to support her own artistic pursuits. At this stage, not to be outdone by a mistress, the Minister's wife decided to avail herself of the remaining $(US)100,000. So, I was left with a very high level love triangle, source of a major diplomatic problem—as I had provided very public support for the event on behalf of the United Nations ….. but had no Ministerial fund-raising money in the kitty.

This situation did tax my diplomatic skills considerably.

Finally, I decided to employ what I came to understand as 'the Javanese way'– never confront … but surround'. So I sent the Minister an official letter—hand delivered personally to his desk rather than via his secretary by my Deputy, Qun Li, who had diplomatic privilege to do this. My letter congratulated the Minister on having organized such a highly successful event where I had personally sighted the extraordinarily generous financial commitments of the guests, a selection of which I included in my letter. I then informed him that because this was such a major achievement—both for the international image of Indonesia and for world humanity generally, that I would be on his Ministerial doorstep first thing the next Monday morning with the entire media of Jakarta to highlight his success and transfer the money. Well, the event happened, and the money started to move—not all of it, and not quickly, but we started to gain access to the funds that had been committed.

The delay however had been critical, and we did not have the total amount of money in time, so we were unable to build the Jimbaran Quarry stage. Instead, we organized the festival at midnight in locations linked to Bali's most sacred temple sites around Ubud—in some ways, as it turned out, more appropriate as venues anyway. It had been a serious test of my diplomatic mettle however from which was reinforced the successful diplomatic lesson to 'not confront but surround'.

Meanwhile, as sequel to the story, the Minister was caught in the post-Soeharto net of prosecutions for corruption in Indonesia and ended up in gaol—with a small suite of three cells, next door, I was told by others, to the more splendid suite of *five* cells (including a billiard room) that were occupied by President Soeharto's murder-convicted and corrupt son, Tommy—with open doors, and small warungs or food outlets down the corridor to the telephone repair shop at the end. Like Tommy, who was frequently seen around the golf courses of Jakarta—when sent down to Jakarta for 'medical' reasons, the by now *ex*-Minister also seemed to have good external leave conditions. As an aside, local residents near the gaol were starting to complain about the noise from frequent helicopter flights coming in and out of the gaol to transport these privileged 'prisoners'. At one point some time after the Sacred Rhythm event when his sentence had yet to expire, I was surprised by a well dressed, well tanned ex-Minister with fashionably long mullet style hair, bouncing down the staircase at Senayan Mall in Central Jakarta, a young attractive woman on his arm. An eternally friendly man, he recognized me and called out "Hello Steve", a greeting I returned. I found it a little difficult to work out what to say next however as I knew he was supposed to still be in prison.

In the Shadows of Diplomatic Privilege

Further in the national diplomatic scene, I should also add that sometimes quite senior Ambassadors did some supremely undiplomatic things in public—but usually got away with it. One of the more dramatic examples of this was at a private party I was invited to that was hosted by a South American Ambassador—a gentleman of Latin passion whose main claim to diplomatic fame—apart from running a thriving coffee import business (where, I should add, a good proportion of the 'coffee' was a *white* powder from unnamed Southern American sources)—was that his wife was the sister of the country's President.

Suddenly the guests were stunned to see the South American Ambassadorial host grappling on the floor with an Ambassador from Europe, a Baron, whose claim to high diplomatic status was bolstered by aristocratic lineage. They had come to blows in an argument over who had access rights to the same Indonesian mistress—also present and watching, apparently horrified but perhaps secretly pleased. The wife of the South American Ambassador was quickly retired to the kitchen where, held separate by the calming ministrations of other Ambassadors' wives, she continued a Spanish tirade of readily understood expletives against her husband and the mistress and their obvious moral failings. With a little encouragement from the less intimidated guests, the two rutting ambassadors ceased their conflict and stood glowering at each other across the room before the Baron, a heavy-set and serious looking man, strode off into the evening for a restitutive glass (or bottle) of scotch at a local bar before returning to his residence and cuckolded wife.

The next day both Ambassadors appeared at Parliament observing the traditional Presidential 'Accountability' speech, chatting calmly with groups of other Ambassadors, and though not meeting eye-to-eye, but with a polite "Good Afternoon Your Excellency" greeting, appearing as if there was no serious dissension between them. The prior evening's event did not hit the press, although it became the salacious source of behind-the-hand gossiping entertainment amongst the diplomatic glitterati for a month or two afterwards.

On the serious side however, the most important benefit of Representative Diplomatic Status as a United Nations Representative or Ambassador for me was that I was able to withstand pressure from government to capitulate on contentious issues to local power interests, and instead maintain a strong voice for maintenance of international standards. In the national political context where I was responsible, I particularly needed to withstand pressure in areas of my specific United Nations responsibility—for example, on environment sustainability standards, education reform, the rights of cultural minorities, freedom of expression, and media freedom, whilst constantly confronting the specter of hidden or quite blatant corruption and abuse of power.

4

"Settling into an Expatriate World"

Apart from learning to handle the organization culture of UNESCO and the essential (new) skills of international diplomacy, I also needed to establish my home base within a very unfamiliar cultural and social environment.

Returning to Jakarta after my introductory briefing in Paris then meant setting up house and learning to engage with a seemingly alien world as an expatriate.

We found our first house fairly quickly—taking it over from an Australian Embassy Official whose posting had ended. The house was located in the popular expatriate district of Kemang, a seemingly appropriate choice at the time for it meant a quite good concentration of houses of a style that people such as me from Australia would find comfortable, and a sprinkling of 'western' style restaurants, cafes and shops within walking distance.

Houses that were available varied enormously in style and taste, but most commonly they had a faux-western luxury stamp, usually including at least one chandelier and locally manufactured faux-antique furnishings. Size mattered, so many of the houses from which one could choose were simply enormous by our previous standards. All were characterized by building to the absolute limit of the block and high perimeter walls—to ward off the outside world and in particular, burglars. First impression was of pervading gloom—partly a product of the high walls, partly as dark meant cool, and partly as electric lights provided were often 20 to 40 watts to save on the rather expensive commodity of electricity. The kitchen was usually separate and the domain of servants rather than the householders. Often there were sinks for washing hands in the lounge room itself. That is, there was an initial sense of tainted and somewhat gloomy opulence. The tropical climate is not kind to the outside appearance either. Owners normally sought to minimize paying money for anything once they rented the house out until they *had* to repair or renovate to attract the next tenant. In 1995 the only way that foreigners could own a house was as a silent partner to a local; apartments were still quite rare: as they started to grow in numbers and popularity, apartments became available for purchase by foreigners, but not on the ground floor and with no ownership implied of the land underneath.

So, when we found a house that was reasonably light and not too unreasonably large with an owner who, according to the previous tenants, actually did repair things, we were delighted. The main problem was, however, that as an expat, you were required to pay the entire three year rent up front—at that time, around (US)$150,000 to (US)$200,000. Fortunately for me the UN was prepared to cover this cost on a monthly return basis. The owners meanwhile, would use that funding to purchase yet another house for profit from more expats.

And, we started to appreciate the exotic feeling of the country. Rapidly growing tropical flowers and palm trees, dramatic storms, the smell of the tropics hanging in the invariably warm air, sounds of a village life interwoven into the fabric of the city and its traffic …. a feeling of magic. The first day we felt we had actually settled in we sat by the swimming pool just absorbing the new and extraordinary atmosphere of the place. Jill, my wife, was writing a letter home. At that moment a ripe mango fell from the overhanging tree next door into the swimming pool at Jill's feet. Our sense of wellbeing was complete.

Living with City 'Planning' and Local Conditions

But, Kemang came with a downside. Getting through traffic bottlenecks was enormously time-wasting for the roads were really village tracks rapidly set in cement in a city where development under the 30 years or so of the Soeharto regime was ruled by the financial benefits to a very small elite close to the President—in particular, his own children. They simply had no interest in matching new high-rise buildings they owned or controlled with the supportive surrounding infrastructure that was required to service and transport the new concentrations of people moving into the area. Indeed, the President's son, Tommy Soeharto, made one of his many fortunes from selling … and then buying … the cement that was used in his own building program rather than from subsequent *use* of the building. High rise development was nourished by such financial benefits, often with little or no assessment of tenancy potential. Meanwhile, the development of a rapid public transport system across the city was paralysed by Soeharto family politics. Soeharto's son, Tommy, wanted to develop a Rapid Transit above-ground Light Rail system, whilst Soeharto's daughter, Siti Hardiyanti Rukmana or Tutut, already owner of the majority of the Motor Tollway System, planned to develop an Underground Rail System. No bureaucrat or advisory panel was brave enough to choose between the President's own children, so no decision was made, no action taken. And the volume of cars continued to grow and congeal in traffic jams across the city.

And, we learnt that having a river close by, though somewhat picturesque—except for the flotsam of discarded rubbish that stamped careless environmental policies and practices onto the character of the city—was a bad decision when the rain season came. The rain season, for anyone who is not familiar with tropical life, descends with thunderous force onto daily events. Dramatic to an extreme, the experience is as of a very large bathtub suddenly being upended over your head, and house, and car, whilst lightning forks ominously from soaring storm heads and the continuous rumble and periodic crash of thunder shakes the security of walls that previously felt so safe. Our street, along with quite large sections of Jakarta, was in a flood plain—an unzoned fact that had escaped our initial euphoric attention to discovering a reasonable house. We also were located on a street in a dip between two hills. Under *normal* seasonal flooding, the water rose just to the lip of our front door—right through the garage and into the servants' quarters and kitchen, but, just to the lip of the area where we had carpets and furniture. We could normally keep the water out with carefully positioned sandbags.

The problem was the traffic. Little 'tututs' as they were called, three-wheeler motor scooter taxis—imported second hand from India—cheap local transport, would rev up to full pace at the top of the rise and then charge, with passengers clinging on for dear life, into the flood waters, hoping to make it through to the opposite hill before their engine died. Local kids would sit on our front fence with their feet dangling in the rising waters and cheer. Our problem, apart from the screaming noise, was the waves the tututs generated …. breaching our sandbagged living room door sill.

We were however fortunate compared to many. For us, the water levels breached only just into the ground floor area, but did not rise too much further. For many locals, the rain season commonly meant flooding to the second-floor level of their house, loss of any of the local household possessions that could not be lifted out of the way in time, and an enormous filthy clean-up operation thereafter.

Within our UNESCO operations and led by our Italian hydrology expert, Guiseppe, we actually did try and assist this situation. We could not move the houses, so had to assist locals to *cope*. Under our hydrology program we were already cooperating with local scientists monitoring river levels and flows, so we assisted the establishment of up-river measurement of flows at critical points and linked this monitoring with an 'alarm' system that alerted communities downriver which were likely to be affected. But we went further than simply providing an alert, and sent forward estimates of how high the waters were likely to be. We then worked with the local communities to plan what to do next—'calibrating' village altitude above the river and housing heights in order to identify where possessions could be moved to remain out of the approaching flood waters; and we instituted training in handling the polluted water once it arrived, that is, 'capping' existing village wells to prevent their contamination, and working out how to store and provide drinking water until the crisis had passed. This project provided a good example of how combining contributions from both natural and social science platforms could make a difference. But, because of the woefully poor city planning, the people were still regularly flooded—in 2006 particularly badly.

The tropical drains were often blocked or inadequate for the high-rise developments that sprung up like cement mushrooms amongst former villages and agricultural fields. Because city planning was generally overridden by the interest of elites who sold land and developed local housing, there were many communities built on flood plains where houses should never have been located in the first place.

Even senior diplomats were not immune.

The Danish Ambassador, newly arriving to set up Denmark's diplomatic presence in Indonesia, chose a Residence just down the road from us in a quiet picturesque backstreet just off the main road through Kemang, and invested in a 25 year lease to secure the house for Denmark's diplomatic future. The main river through Kemang, under most circumstances a quiet ambling stream, albeit also serving as vehicle for local rubbish disposal, was directed by nature straight at the rear wall of the Ambassador's property where a cement corner had been fashioned to re-orient the river flow down the side boundary. The house was just one storey in height but rambled through many luxurious squares in size—centerpiece, adjacent to the dining room being a large very carefully imported grand piano. Then the rains came. Unfortunately, nature took its course—quite literally, and blew apart the artificial cement protecting wall, breaching the rear fence with a two meter high deluge of rushing flood waters. These swept the ambassador's entourage and household through the lounge room and out to the street—including the grand piano. Needless to say, Denmark had to break its 25-year lease and move on to higher ground.

City flooding was further exacerbated by a little corruption upriver in the mountain area of Bogor just out of Jakarta. It was not uncommon when their own water levels started to rise for Bogor locals to bribe the river-control official to open the local flood gates, thus providing relief to their own problems. The effect was to lower the water levels around Bogor, but to throw a sudden deluge down the rivers into Jakarta.

Even when it was not raining (and local lore said that the Rain Season lasted through every month with an 'r' in it ... that is, from September through to April ... and you could never trust the so-called 'Dry' Season anyway), we quickly learnt whilst commuting from the depths of Kemang that one had to re-learn the habits of driving to survive in the local environment.

Driving in the city was a fundamentally new cultural experience. Jakarta traffic is infinitely flexible. Road rage does not appear to exist. It is possible, and indeed, reasonably frequently practised, to break any road rule whilst other drivers will patiently wait until you are finished. Quite literally, it is regarded as not unreasonable to do a U-turn in six-lane traffic, and everyone else will wait without blowing a horn—as long as you make the turn slowly and patiently so that other cars can take action to avoid collision. But, to negotiate the road successfully means being prepared to be flexible oneself. Indonesian drivers seem to be able to judge distances between cars in millimeters, and casually drive at top speed accordingly whilst we Australians, having learnt to drive in a land where safety and rules to protect us from ourselves were paramount, became extremely uncomfortable at the distance of a meter from our driving opponents' extraordinarily *un*-rule bound behavior. The only basic rule of Jakarta traffic is that if the nose of your car is slightly in front of the opponent, then you have right-of-way.

At one stage I took Philippe, a young Belgian member of UNESCO staff, on mission to Canberra in Australia. He had already been driving in Jakarta for a year or so and had fully absorbed local practice.

Arriving at the airport in Canberra, we each rented a car for separate activities, but both on my credit card. We drove off. Five minutes later, a frantic phone call came through from Philippe. He had reached his first roundabout, of which there are many in Canberra, the city of total design. *One car was on the round-about. He hit it.* The woman who was driving simply followed Australian rules, that is, if you have right-of-way, you take it. It's almost a religious act in Australia. But, Philippe followed Jakarta rules, 'traffic is flexible, this other driver will adjust!' Bad mistake. My credit card suffered severely on that day.

Obtaining a license itself required a very direct acquaintance with local ways. To acquire a license was normally a full-day enterprise—with numerous forms to fill in, lines to wait in, and a driving 'test' before being photographed and having your image etched onto a hologram-equipped license card. Being Head of Diplomatic Mission helped me a bit—as my local staff did a lot of the form-filling and waiting on my behalf. But it was still *required* that I complete the local test—both of questions asked in Indonesian, and driving skill. As with all other aspiring licensees, payment at the appropriate time by one of my staff (from his own pocket, and without my realizing until later) of an expected 'facilitation fee', helped things along enormously—removing the formal requirement for answering questions in Indonesian and doing the test. The fee levied to avoid the test turned out to be almost exactly the same amount of money that you had to pay anyway to actually *do* the skill test, as the aspiring licensee had to *hire* both car and the testing official's time. One's own car had to wait outside in the Motor Registry carpark. The test itself was conducted amongst the odd witches-hat on a totally enclosed course set up in an internal quadrangle, that is, without another car in sight. Once the skills test was completed in this inner world—or, more accurately, once the examiner was satisfied with his own pecuniary advantage having been met, the successful driver was released onto the totally chaotic anarchic streets to fend for themselves. Even driver training prior to the test was equally as unconnected to the reality it was supposed to represent. Most commonly, because of cost, four or five young persons would hire the instructor and van between them. One would drive, the others would learn by watching from the backseat…. and then *they* would progress onwards to their license before being unleashed on the streets of Jakarta. It was no wonder that as a new driver in Jakarta one had to learn flexibility very quickly.

Accessing the system also revealed the way that society's organizations had absorbed the endemic corruption of the 32 years of Soeharto's New Order Government—right down to the very roots of daily action. People in positions of whatever power they could acquire, basically were paid to 'sit there in their job', not to actually *do* anything: to *move* the person into action normally required ex-gratia payment. Payment for services rendered to supplement pretty low incomes became a way of life, and stretched from the very top of the status heap, the President, his family and Government Ministers, all the way down the food chain to the local block official responsible for ensuring garbage was picked up in your street. Many of the local block officials were ex-low ranking military personnel, formally awarded the job as a retirement privilege, but in the position informally to cement military observation and control deeply into the everyday life fabric of the society.

Spiritual and Spirit Presence

As one quickly starts to appreciate, Indonesia is the world's most populous Moslem country.

Daily life starts and finishes with the exotic sounds of the Moslem call to prayer wafting from local mosques across the morning and evening tropical breezes. And there are *a lot* of mosques. At first, as a foreigner, this Islamic reminder of God's command is a magical complement to a tropical quite exotic environment.

There is however a downside. We had two mosques close by. One, I finally decided, was a 'practice' mosque. That is, the call to prayer was often carried by a young man newly introduced to the rigors of precise tonality, but who exercised great pleasure in maximum volume of output. Call of the two mosques would intersect—and this started, we quite rapidly discovered, well before dawn and was repeated through all five statutory prayer times of the day.

Furthermore, we discovered that the speaker systems used to call the faithful were sometimes utilized as a weapon—turned at full volume towards the living rooms of expatriates whose financial contribution to local religious opportunity was in need of supplementation. Fortunately for us, this approach to ecumenicalism did not target us. However, one of my UN colleagues who lived directly opposite a small mosque with a large speaker system was not so lucky. Visiting him for evening dinner became an exercise in shouting. Sleep, he blearily informed me through weary blood-shot eyes, was a luxury experienced when on international mission, not at home.

Religious festivals were lived in the local streets. In particular, the prophet Mohammad's Birthday was celebrated with the sacrifice at each local mosque of donated animals—particularly goats, but also cattle where somewhat richer benefactors lived nearby. There are local mosques around virtually every corner, so the morning suburban experience flows directly from the unsettling sounds of bloody sacrifice to the engaging smell of local BBQs as the sacrificial meat offerings are distributed to the people. The problem was that most sacrifice and butchering was done by amateurs who paid scant attention to hygienic practice. So, streets on the celebration day were filled with bouncy playing children enjoying kebab skewers of recently killed meat; but the evening would be full of many of these same children, clutching their stomachs and vomiting from acquired food poisoning.

At the same time superstition and engagement with a world of spirits, an inheritance of traditional village culture, was deeply ingrained into the whole society, even in very unexpected places.

My driver showed me local newspapers, for example, where good-luck 'spirits' were advertised for sale. Spirit merchants took their job seriously. They would first come to the home of the prospective buyer to check out *which* spirit was right for them specifically, advise accordingly, set the price, and then 'deliver' with appropriate rituals. And a spirit did not come cheap. 'Local' spirits were cheaper, although even these would sell for up to $(US)20,000; 'international' spirits were more expensive, presumably as they came with more power, up to $(US)50,000—and this was at late 1990s rates. I understand that most spirits are purchased within the business-wealthy Chinese ethnic community. I never discovered how the return policy worked for any clients who were not adequately satisfied.

What was ever-present however through all communities were the 'dukans' or spirit men. In particular, a specialist group of dukans, called 'rain-pushers' were available for hire to assist at important outdoor functions—'pushing' the rain away from the event. Hiring rain-pushers was common practice at the opening of shopping centers, wedding festivals, and even for Presidential occasions. Indeed, for the most important Presidential functions, not only 'rain-pushers' but also 'rain-pullers' were employed, the theory being that they would work in tandem to provide double strength in the insurance against rain disrupting the event. In perhaps the most curious case of modernity absorbing tradition, dukans were employed for important outdoor occasions by the Indonesian Institute of Sciences.

We remained skeptical about the effectiveness of these guys. But, then again, there were times when we were not so sure. Most dramatic of these was one evening when we had to attend a major Diplomatic Function and Concert in the grounds of the Bogor Palace an hour's drive up into the hills near Jakarta, and hosted by President Habibie. Full rain pushing and pulling expertise, we were reliably assured, had been targeted at the event. Bogor is known for raining much of the time, so I guess the Palace Protocol staff felt they really needed to be careful. Bogor is also around an hour's drive from Central Jakarta. The moment we left the city we drove into an enormous tropical storm. It stayed with us through the full hour's journey into Bogor and as we drove the circle around the outside of the Palace grounds towards the entrance gate. We nearly gave up as we were sure the event would have to be cancelled. But then at the gate … and at first we were totally incredulous … the car stopped while we checked in with Security, and whilst the rear window and boot remained under a torrent of rain, the front window and bonnet were dry. There was *no rain* in the Presidential Garden. I guess the magic wore off around two hours later. After the patrician power and presence of President Soeharto, President Habibie, a short and rather more clownish figure, was never regarded too seriously by either his own Palace staff or the people. He came to sit at a table to dine near the front of the gathered throng just as the rain arrived: most of the diplomats left—unusual as normal protocol was to depart immediately *after* the President, never before; but Mr Habibie remained seated, looking somewhat forlorn in the failed-Dukan rain-soaked grounds of the Palace…… Shortly afterwards he was deposed from power.

Rumors of the impending downfall of the next President Abdurrahman Wahid, or Gus Dur (Uncle Gus) as he was popularly known, were also accelerated by superstitious signs that I saw directly. Just as his impending impeachment was being considered, a diplomatic event was held at the Istana Negri, the main palace in Jakarta, where Gus Dur gave a welcoming speech. Just as he approached the microphone, a black cat raced across the stage out of the wings and urinated on the speaker system. The audience was stunned. Later that week, at a major outdoor event held in the main Senayan Stadium in Central Jakarta, just as President Wahid arrived, an enormous storm broke out, crashing with thunder and illuminating the grounds with vivid lightning. The audience gasped. Around twenty minutes later, Megawati Sukarnoputri, the daughter of the founder of Indonesia, President Sukarno, arrived. She was at that stage being tipped as the next President of the Republic—a status she did later acquire. The sun came out. The people applauded. Perhaps indeed sheer chance. But, spirit life *is* close to the surface of everyday affairs and perceptions in Indonesia.

In fact, appeal to the Spirit World was a powerful factor in the maintenance of the power of President Soeharto himself. Just before the May 1997 'Festival of Democracy' as the sham elections were euphemistically called, when signs of public disillusionment and student protest were starting to emerge with some force for the very first time in Soeharto's rule, wide-spread speculation started to emerge that the President had lost his *wahyu*, the magic powers thought to accompany a just rule and a concept believed by millions of Indonesians. Soeharto consulted regularly with his spiritual advisors in the city considered to be the spiritual heart of Java, Solo, or Surakarta, its ancient name. The President's Spirit Advisors informed him three months before the 1997 election that the nail that anchored the island of Java to earth had come unstuck, a sign of impending calamity. Soeharto put great stock in such portents, and in February 1997 sent a trusted confidant to Yogyakarta, a traditionally mystical site of Java, to perform a ritual designed to repair the damage. As the economy subsequently collapsed and fires spread across Indonesia, a historical prophesy re-emerged amongst the people of a Javanese king who fell from power amongst social chaos and fires. Just a few months later this is exactly what happened.

The Wayang Society

Jakarta therefore posed for us as newly arrived expatriates the enchantment of setting up everyday life in an exotic culture and land. It did not take too long before we 'settled in' and, with a few tentative words of Bahasa Indonesia to make us feel at home, became quite blasé in the face of unexpected difference, whilst meanwhile enjoying the fact that each day brought with it fresh and fascinating new colors of the country and people we had adopted as home for the next few years.

However, the wayang or shadow puppet theatre for which Indonesia is famous provides an excellent metaphor for the way the society functioned. Behind the relatively smooth and apparently unproblematic progress in everyday life, there was a deep shadow side—a repressive political regime that maintained the President's and the army's absolute rule, and which was bedded into a dramatically volatile physical environment.

At first the menace that lay in the shadows was well concealed—its corruption of human values and freedom a dim background to the surface reality of rule by an apparently benign dictator. Little criticism ever emerged into the public domain as freedom of expression was fully controlled—managed by 50,000 bureaucrats of the Ministry of Information scattered across the whole country, and whose job was simply *censorship*. All News that was available was formed and edited in Jakarta and syndicated out to the provinces 16 times a day.

As economic crisis started to impact on the country from 1997 onwards however, things started to change—first in the remote provinces, where the fingertips of centralized power penetrated, extracting profit from the peoples' own lands and handing it directly to the center of Javanese-based rule—on to the President and the rings of connected and sycophantic political, military and business figures that surrounded and supported him.

The President's power had been bolstered by impressive economic performance that, despite its plundering by the President's own family, did deliver financial welfare generally across the country. Meanwhile dissent was rigidly suppressed by militaristic control. Whilst the people could afford to live, with relatively little abject poverty through the country, affordable rice and kerosene, and whilst the people were afraid to shake the political scaffolding that sustained this daily order, the President's power was inviolate, even with democracy severely constrained. But, as the economic woes of the Asian Economic Crisis washed over Indonesia's economy from 1997, exposed as it was by corrupt movements and offshore stashing of vast amounts of the nation's wealth, the people became dissatisfied.

Some of the first signs we saw were in the provinces remote from Jakarta—Sumatra and West Papua (Irian Jaya at that time), where photographs for the first time started to appear in discrete corners of rooms and shops of President Sukarno, the founder of modern Indonesia, who had been deposed by President Soeharto in 1967 following the bloody violence of the previous two years that killed between a half million and a million people and was associated with the military crackdown after the so-called Communist Coup attempt of 1963. Meanwhile, the first glimmerings of a pro-democracy student movement emerged out of Yogyakarta's Gadja Madah University from 1992 onwards. Heavily suppressed for 'undermining the state ideology', a voice of serious protest did start to be heard for the first time.

Consequently, in spite of the enchantment of living in an exotic culture with unexpected new colors of experience entering into household life every day, we had by this time, 1997, started to experience directly the other side of the Indonesian order.

However, even a few months after we arrived, we realized by the alien noises and power losses when communicating, that our phones were being tapped and we were being watched. As we got to know and be trusted by new friends associated in particular with the arts and universities, we also started to learn a lot more about disappearances, sudden incarcerations without trial, and intimidation by hired thugs and police. What was exotic for expatriates experiencing the richness of life in Indonesia for the first time papered a surface reality over the underlying wall of inequity, power, and suppression onto which the wayang society was projected.

It did not take long before the underground rumblings of the social volcano that was hidden in the shadows of wayang society exploded across the fully lit face of the city. And even our home, our 'domestic retreat' from city life, was not safe anymore. I talk about this in Chap. 14 when I take you with me into the center of a revolution.

The Wild Life of Jakarta

Meanwhile, as we were initially settling into a somewhat more informed understanding of expatriate urban life, we were confronted by the unexpected consequences of city and tropical country life being so closely interwoven—and the richness of animal life that is so easily brushed aside by urban sprawl and careless or exploitative environmental practices so common in many developing countries.

For, then there was the dragon! …….. actually a monitor lizard which had been washed down the river from the mountains around Bogor, and then swum up the street canals to our house. This was not a small monitor lizard. Rather, it was around 1.5 m long, and with the classic Jurassic dinosauric ugliness and threatening drool of Komodo dragons. Our jaga, the young man who looked after our security and the garden, was clipping the front hedge, not paying really special attention to the reptilian appendages hidden amongst the leaves. He clipped the dragon who was not pleased, and immediately attacked in retribution. Wawan, the jaga, retreated backwards into the garage, and then through the house to alert me. The monitor lizard had grabbed his leg, fortunately only catching his trousers, and had then hung on as a terrified Wawan dragged himself with attached dragon back into the apparent safety of our garage.

I was quietly typing on my computer in the back garden ….. but not for long.

We had hired this guy only a couple of weeks earlier. He was a young man who gave off an aura of gentle youth—except for the knife scar slash down the left side of his face and the spiked club contrived from a timber offcut and nails that he maintained in the shadowed corner of the garage. As part of his job was to guard the house, I had confidently told Jill, that, in spite of his youthful slight build…. and perhaps in the light of the scar on his face, he was really a wiry tough young village lad who would look after us.

This however was *not* my impression when Wawan rocketed through the kitchen door as white as a ghost calling 'Pa', 'Pa' for my urgent attention and support.

With no idea whatsoever about what had scared the living daylights out of my jaga, I accompanied him to the house's access door to the garage. Though with some trepidation as I did not know what to expect, robber, military official, a plague of rats or …… whatever, I was about to go through when Wawan totally blocked my path, signaling that I should first look through the crack at the bottom of the door at what evil lay on the other side.

And there HE was. The Dragon! One point five meters of Jurassic anger crashing his more than ample leathery tail repeatedly into the wheel of my new diplomat-plated Mercedes … and glaring at the eyes under the door with venomous intent. Now with good reason for trepidation, I unlatched the door into the garage, and with the help of a convenient piece of lumber, initiated what I hoped were appropriate noises to scare the dragon outside again. Scare the dragon? He did not regard me as anything much more than an inconvenient bite between him and the source of his discontent, Wawan. But, with enough noise, and by trying to look as tall an alpha-male as I could, we did finally drive the lizard through the garage doors into the garden and then ….. he disappeared.

Relief! I should tell Jill, I thought. While all this was going on, Jill had been sitting over the other side of the wall separating the swimming pool from the front entrance garden where the dragon had appeared. Jill was in the study that fronted onto the pool, with the door open to the warm tropical breeze, languidly typing her latest poem, contemplating an environment where the greatest danger so far had been from errant perfectly ripe mangoes dropping from the neighbor's tree into our swimming pool. Safe, I thought. At least, the other side of a two-metre wall, she was totally protected from the 'monster'.

So, with all the casualness I could muster to avoid conveying a feeling of disquiet I meandered around to the study and calmly reported an 'interesting' event in the entrance garden.

Then, I came back. And looked at the wall. There, to my horror were the claw marks of the monitor lizard which had climbed up apparently to the top. On immediate and closer inspection I recognized that he had actually climbed to *just under* the two meter height, and not making it over the rim, had slid back down into the surrounding foliage. Had HE flopped over into the pool at Jill's feet, I seriously doubt that my posting in Indonesia would have survived another day.

A colleague down the river, Henri Fournier, Head of the International Committee of the Red Cross (ICRC) in Indonesia, told me that he too had had a very large Bogor sourced monitor lizard seeking new residency in his garden. However, in his case, being somewhat closer to a local village community, the dragon was a rather attractive source of nutrition, and had been the subject of a local village shock troop which dispensed with it using local weaponry thereby facilitating an opportunistic village barbecue.

The experience at my own residence made me realize something I had not yet fully appreciated about Jakarta. That was the close interweaving of modern city and the traditional rural environment that presaged the urban complex.

The city had expanded very fast over the last decade. Before this there was one serious 'international' hotel, the Hotel Indonesia, a building in the center of town on the traffic circle opposite the British Embassy and donated to Indonesia as war reparation by Japan. This hotel was the centerpiece location of the Australian movie depicting the violence of the 1963 'communist' suppression and subsequent overthrow of President Sukarno, 'The Year of Living Dangerously'.

Even by 1995, the year we moved to Jakarta, whilst there was a mushrooming population of high-rise office buildings, there were *very few* apartments, so expat living required finding a house. That was not easy because of oil money. What had happened with the burgeoning wealth of Pertamina, the national oil monopoly, was that the local elite who directly benefited from the profits, invested in building modern houses—targeting the associated influx of foreign managers. As I reported earlier, as an expat you could not rent a house without paying three years or more of rent in advance.

The whole system was fed initially by foreign oil companies and executives who had very little limit on their accommodation expense, so set the pattern for everyone else. The effect was a mushrooming of large, westernized houses—usually VERY large—across whole new areas of the city. Pondok Indah was the criterion example—on the south side of the city, location of the International School and many richer locals plus expatriates. And it was in these areas that the interweaving of modern city and rural worlds collided. For much of the development displaced traditional villages within the general Jakarta environment, or nestled into the surrounding agricultural fields, leaving the village houses intact, but overshadowed by new high-rise offices or very large boundary-to-boundary modern style houses. In highly developed areas you would therefore find a village behind the six-meter walls of the modern world, or a still productive agricultural field just off the traffic roundabout. The animals of the country remained in the city, and the city was a patchwork of global and traditional life.

It was because of this close interweaving of city and rural environment that Jill therefore had her own experience of Jakarta's animal world too.

In her case, it was the unseen presence of 'something' that was not finally revealed to us until quite literally the last night we spent in our second house in Jakarta, in the suburb of Permata Hijou, closer in to the city, a choice of residence that, apart from anything else, relieved the tedium of dreadful traffic jams en-route to Kemang. But, as with the patchwork character of the city, across the other side of the 6 m back wall was an agricultural forest and village.

4 "Settling into an Expatriate World"

Our second house was quite lovely. Built by an architect for herself, this two-story residence in a middle-class generally ethnically Chinese area, it was well endowed with stained glass windows, a spacious light living area fronting the swimming pool at the back through 3.5 m high glass folding doors.

The curious thing was that we kept finding berries, some of which were crushed, and half eaten, on an internal balcony overlooking the pool. We assumed that they were probably the result of a bird harvesting dinner from the surrounding village gardens, but never were able to surprise the animal or bird to actually see what it was.

And then came the problem. By virtue of the nature of my job—covering a rather large group of countries on behalf of my UN agency, I travelled a lot, heading overseas every few weeks. Jill often needed to suffer the rigors of Jakarta living by herself. We had heard odd noises on the roof, but never found anything when we checked. And we were a bit concerned as the local youth had an incredible ability to climb just about anything—frequently clambering up what looked like smooth three-story walls to retrieve a kite that had become entangled. In Permata Hijou we had several servants living in the house, two satpans or security guards ostensibly to guard the place at night, but still, there was an ever-present risk of high climbing robbers.

Then one night when I was away and the servants were on their Sunday holiday, Jill heard a powerful man-sized thump as something landed on the roof directly above the bedroom and then proceeded to walk to the central courtyard, step by readily audible step. Sensibly, given the circumstances, Jill fled. Calling a taxi, she arrived on the doorstep of a couple of our friends in her pajamas—thus ensuring that the robbers, if that was what they were, could access the household valuables if that was what they were after, but at least ensuring she was safe. The next day Jill ventured back. Nothing was missing or out of place. …. but the berries were back on the balcony.

Two years later we found the culprit. On the last night in our house before moving on to other accommodation following the riots and pillaging of the 1998 revolution that swept right through our Permata Hijou suburb, we sat up late, admittedly with the odd glass of champagne as we reminisced on the joys and sorrows of living for three years in Permata Hijou. It was near 3.30am. Suddenly we noticed the shadow of an animal carefully picking its way across the razor wire on top of our rear 6 m wall. Incredible agility. Cat-like but with spots and large—around the proportions of a medium sized dog. Moving, careful step by careful step towards the balcony where it had been quietly feasting on local berries for the last three years of our tenure. It was a civet cat, and came from the local forest just over our wall.

A momentary aside for those who are aficionados of coffee. There is a brand of coffee sourced from North Sumatra in Indonesia called Kopi Luwak. It is arguably the most expensive coffee in the world, is prized for its unique quality—even currently sold at a dedicated coffee house in New York—at, what I have been informed, is a premium $US)869 per kilo (for wild-collected beans). The house specialty. The unique character of this coffee is the role of the civet cat in the coffee's production. The civet cat loves coffee beans, but only the best quality coffee beans. On the dedicated plantations that produce Kopi Luwak there is a good-sized population of indulged civet cats. The coffee is harvested *after* the civet cat has had its way —by collecting the feces which contain semi-digested and therefore semi-processed coffee beans. I have been assured they are washed before packaging. And the taste, so they say, is very special! Interestingly, the poorer locals initiated this practice as they could not afford to buy the local coffee, so started picking up and using the remnants of civet cat coffee bean feasts. Somehow the global market discovered this practice and took its newly acclaimed exquisite value to New York. A marketing triumph—selling cat pooh to the elite at a luxury price!

And a second aside that moves on to the wildlife heritage that UNESCO protects—I actually did have the chance to enter the world of the real Komodo Dragons later—in November 2003. We had decided to sign a formal agreement with the American-based conservation group, The Nature Conservancy (TNC) with which we were already cooperating in conservation of Komodo Island in East Indonesia and other marine sites across Southeast Asia. The President of TNC, Steve McCormick, and I agreed to sign the agreement while taking a joint mission to Komodo to inspect the ongoing work, the pristine reefs and dragons—all of which made Komodo into a very special World Heritage site.

Komodo is the land of the dragon. Komodo Dragons are very large monitor lizards that have been around since the time of the dinosaurs, inhabiting just this one island, Komodo, and its neighbour across a narrow strait, Rinca—plus there are maybe a few dragons that strayed as far as Flores. When I say 'large', I mean really, really large—up to four metres or more in length, not known for their cuteness and very definitely to be avoided because of their breath. The Komodo Dragon's reputation is impressive. The monitor's normal way of killing its prey is just to bite them and leave. The prey dies over a day or two from the most obnoxious collection of bacteria one can imagine, all of which thrive in the Dragon's mouth.

When one comes across a Komodo Dragon one's first impression also is that they are rather slow lumbering creatures that must catch their meals by the prey accidentally falling on them. Bad mistake! One must immediately be reminded that the most common prey of the Dragon are flighty and rather fast deer and local goats. Komodo Dragons can accelerate from a sleepy prone start to the speed of a horse. Maybe not for all that far. But, if you are foolish enough to be seeking a 'shot-of-the-month' close-up for the kiddies, the Dragon does not *have* to move very far.

Indeed, the last person eaten by a Dragon was a Swiss tourist some years ago. All that was left was his indigestible camera. It is rumored that the last photo on the film-roll was a very close close-up of an approaching monster.

The last person *bitten* by a Dragon at the time I was there was the Harbor Master of Komodo. With maybe three yachts a week to monitor, his job was relaxed to say the least. On this, his day of misfortune, the Harbor Master, as had become his regular practice, therefore retired from the midday heat to his hut next to where a number of the Dragons hang about, and took a quiet nap. That is, he took a quiet and very relaxed nap until he was suddenly awakened by a Dragon that had crept up the steps, taken a preparatory nibble at his foot and was now glaring at him from the end of his bed sizing up the next course. The Harbor Master survived, but only just. He was evacuated to hospital in nearby Flores Island as rapidly as possible, but fought off the rampant infection for some time, leaving him with a rather nasty scar, a limp, and a new-found respect for Dragons and locked doors.

So, on my mission we went to view the Dragons—accompanied by several local staff and a park ranger carrying a long but thin forked stick. He claimed it was an effective protection, but my personal view was that the real purpose of the stick was to trip the person next to him as you both ran from the rampaging Dragon—leaving behind a tasty alternative.

We came across a half dozen of the monsters drooling quietly in the shade of the house where the Harbor Master was bitten. I was just lining up a quite excellent photo of monitor's beady eye when I noticed the young ranger's assistant walking behind me and re-tuned my awareness. She was carrying a full medical kit with syringes of antibiotics already loaded. The Dragon quite suddenly moved a foot or two. I jumped two meters in one bound.

To return to why I was there, Komodo's real claim to World Heritage status is not its landscape—dry, rocky and quite barren as it was during the dry season when we visited. Instead, Komodo's beauty lies in the waters that surround it. Pristine coral reefs that boast some of the richest biodiversity in the world, one of the very best dive sites there is—but, as with all such bounties in the developing world, at risk in particular from local overfishing but also men from other islands who engaged in illegal cyanide fishing for stunned aquarium species, and indiscriminate bombing for just about everything that moves and can be sold at the local fish markets. Needless to say, the impact of these practices on the reefs themselves is disastrous.

Quite central therefore to the conservation of Komodo was the development of alternative and sustainable employment opportunities for the people, and serious policing to prevent outsiders poaching fish stocks late at night. This was what we really came to inspect. However, as a monitoring mission, we *did* have to leave the schooner on which we were housed for a couple of days, to check out the quality of the reefs. My *job* as UNESCO Director therefore *required* that I snorkel through warm tropical waters across the most beautifully colored and diverse seascape imaginable, and drift in the currents along with the local manta rays. Although I had been informed that the Dragons do not tend to take to the water, I suffered a moment of disquieting reflection when at my furthest point from the dive boat whilst I was marveling at the passing parade of enormous drifting manta rays the question occurred to me ... how, exactly *did* the Dragons cross the strait to the other island just over there? From then on, I saw dark ominous shadows everywhere.

These shadows were more imagination than reality and I could readily escape them by climbing back into the dive boat. I had already experienced much deeper real shadows in our field experience of the United Nations however—the first signs of which dropped unexpectedly out of the jungles of West Papua eight years earlier. Two of my UN staff were captured and held for political ransom while on an official ecology mission in the highland jungles of West Papua. Martha, the Dutch female, was pregnant!

5

"Jungle Hostages—I: Capture"

Just Another Birth Announcement

"15 July 1996.

> Dear Stephen, Ish and all others.
> We proudly present … *Mick Lorentz*. Mick is strong and healthy (3820g) and joined us on the 13th July at 00.17 hours. Pleased and proud as hell, what more is there to say? Regards to all of you down there. Mark and Martha"

Just another Birth Announcement. Nothing unusual about that.
But there was!
Martha and Mark had escaped from the jungles of Indonesia's Irian Jaya (now since 2000, "Papua" or "West Papua") only seven weeks earlier after spending 128 days as hostages of the Organisasi Papua Merdeka or OPM, the rebel group of Freedom Fighters seeking Independence of Indonesia's Papuan people. Martha and Mark's original capture had occurred only six months after I took over my UN job in Jakarta and was still adjusting into a new tropical and cultural life. Having so recently arrived from a quiet academic post running a small research institute in Australia where 'danger' consisted

---

I have written a related and more detailed version of much of the Papuan Hostage Story of Chaps. 5, 6, 7 and 8 before, in my earlier book, "Captives for Freedom: Hostages, Negotiations and the Future of West Papua", University of Papua New Guinea Press, 2017, itself based on my earlier account in "Merdeka", Perceptric Press, 2014. Detail of sources used in the current book are available there—including of the many daily reports I wrote to my UNESCO Headquarters. Focus here is on integrity and readability of the story.

of dropping your coffee cup on the fax machine, suddenly I confronted *very* different responsibilities indeed.

'Lorentz' the baby's name, was the jungle home of the hostages during their ordeal, the National Park that Martha and Mark had been responsible for monitoring as part of UNESCO's World Heritage program and World Wildlife Fund for Nature, WWF's, conservation support. This was a name that became indelibly inscribed on the lives of Mark, Martha and the other hostages who had finally escaped. Mick, had he been born *in* the jungle and continued to be held by the OPM, would have been called 'Merdeka' or 'Freedom' by the rebel leader, Kelly Kwalik, and served as mascot at the head of the battle lines of Papuans and protect them from bullets as they continued to fight the Indonesian military. Mick had been conceived just prior to the ill-fated jungle trek of Mark and Martha that had ended in their abduction, but a trek that had been intended, in personal benefit beyond its official UNESCO monitoring objective, as a two-week mind-clearing 'let's work out our future' relationship-building experience.

After eight days of walking, Martha and Mark, along with another WWF consultant, Frank Momberg, walked into Mapnduma village, perched in perpetual mist 1,000 m up the highland range, surrounded by mountains as high as nearby 4,000 m Mount Trikora, and around 30 km east of the Baliem Valley town of Yiggi. They sat down in the home of the local Protestant missionary, Adrianne van der Bijl, regarded as 'father' of the village by the people of Mapnduma. It was there that they met up with the ill-fated 'Lorentz'95 Group' whose future had already been decided by the OPM and was played out within two days, when, led by Daniel Yudas Kogoya, 200 OPM warriors attacked and took them hostage, sweeping up a total of 26 people on the way, the majority locals. Martha and Mark had been caught up in events not planned for them, but as the OPM reported to an Indonesian Human Rights Commissioner involved in early negotiations, even though the OPM were targeting the Lorentz'95 Group, they *had* to kidnap the others as this was a 'gift from Jesus Christ'. The rebels did actually apologize to Martha and Mark at the time for they valued the conservation support that both UNESCO and WWF were 'giving' to the Papuan people.

Needless to say, Martha's pregnancy with Mick was then a pretty grim time, characterised by fear, starvation, and strenuous walks across very difficult jungle terrain as the rebels moved ahead of the military, violence and malaria.

Being There—At a Distance!

My own engagement with what happened to Martha was at a distance. As Representative of the United Nations, it was impossible to be engaged directly in negotiations with the OPM separatists because this was proscribed by the Government of Indonesia, as it is for any State conscious of its own integrity, as external and diplomatically unacceptable interference in the State's internal affairs. The same condition applied to diplomatic representatives of the national governments from whose countries the international hostages had been taken, that is, the Netherlands, Germany, and the UK—in these negotiations represented by their Deputy Ambassadors. So, although the Embassies had the resources to bring in military support personnel to liaise with the Indonesian military closer to the action, all of us had to work through intermediaries—eventually settling on the International Committee of the Red Cross, the ICRC. Representing the UN, I was part of the negotiating team however, involved in deciding strategy and bringing in key people and interventions that we hoped would influence the negotiations in a positive way. But we could not talk directly with rebel leaders in the jungle.

Meanwhile, the OPM were doing the best they could to *hide* in the jungle and keep ahead of the Indonesian military who were doing their level best to track and find them. At the same time, we had to exert maximum pressure from every diplomatic source we could muster at all levels of government to call off the rather more belligerent elements of the military from following their more normal practice at that time for dealing with jungle people …. repressing through gun-wielding 'diplomacy' and *attacking*. We were extremely worried about the risks that would inevitably follow of our people being killed.

As it turned out, for long periods of time the military *could not find* the rebels. The tribal Papuans were masters of the jungle and could move very fast leaving behind hardly a trace of their passage.

So, we often did not actually know what was going on in the jungle and had to guess. Our only information was scheduled radio contact—which suddenly and inexplicably stopped—though we did have village reports of people passing through, rumors, and occasional traces of previous camps. My daily reports to UNESCO Headquarters and the UN Security Council therefore read rather like a Jean Le Carré spy novel—exciting traces of a future trail of negotiation, imminent threat, and intrigue which I would project in one report would simply dissolve or be derailed by unexpected circumstances or as-yet-unknown events that were occurring but totally hidden from us until later. So, next report, I had to adjust and project new interpretations and possibilities, though perhaps the ongoing epic was being increasingly etched a little more clearly in our developing understanding of what the rebels were trying to do. Often however, as we subsequently found out, the OPM were not sure of where they were going either.

Given the nature of what I was recording I did adopt a literary style in my reports that deviated considerably from normal rather dry UN reports in favor of engagement with the events and their color. I later discovered an unexpected consequence. The Reports I sent to my Headquarters were transmitted directly and confidentially to the designated senior official in our External Relations Sector—the Director of our Personnel Operations Unit in our 'Foreign Affairs' office. There was good reason for caution on confidentiality as release to the media of my internal reports at times could have seriously derailed the negotiations and therefore the safety of the hostages. Therefore, only staff members at Headquarters who could justify legitimate reason to read the reports had access. But knowledge of my daily updates of the extraordinary epic that was evolving in the jungles of West Papua started to spread. More and more people were able to legitimize some remote reason to read them. And the result, I was later told, was that every morning when my reports from the hostage crisis arrived at the senior official's office fax machine there was a line-up outside for the latest instalment of the ongoing serial.

Back at my end of things in Indonesia, this was a time when I needed to devote many long hours and occasional overnight sessions in support of the negotiation process—partly as I needed to talk with people in Europe and because of the time difference: my Head Office only really woke up after dark as far as we were concerned. And I was grounded in Indonesia by personal decree of the UNESCO Director General until the hostages were released, unable to take any overseas missions to look after the rather large number of other countries included under my mandate—specifically so I could keep as close an eye on things as I could, and to be seen as doing so. At a personal level, my first grandson was born in Australia on the day the hostages were captured but I was unable to go and welcome him into the world for over six months until Martha and Mark were finally released.

What I particularly found during the time of engaging with the rebels was that we could expect to make fundamental errors unless we started paying very close attention to the way that cultural difference was being played out, sometimes in very subtle ways that had dramatic and political consequences. And we could not understand the situation and dynamics of the rebel movement unless we developed a good grasp of the historic and political context in which both the rebels and we were operating. For what happened at the front end of negotiations was a play which the key actors influenced as they went, but which was cast within circles of historic, cultural, and political determination. To act as a responsible UN official in this very difficult circumstance one had to do the hard yards of analysis.

This chapter therefore takes you into this account and the way our understanding evolved from hard practical experience as the hostage drama unfolded. As with all the faces of what worked in UN interventions presented in this book, *'In Defense of Our Humanity',* we did have to base our interventions in field practice of the UN on an informed understanding of the people we were seeking to help or influence and the dynamics of their lives and society. The alternative is funded irrelevance. So, if I am seeking, as I am in this book, to convey what UN life is like and the role of the organization in our current globalized world, I need to take you, the reader, along with me into the West Papuan jungles to *see*.

In West Papua in 1996 we were dealing with life and death. In the back of our minds all the time was the specter of the fear, deprivation, and danger that our friends and colleagues were confronting every moment of their days in their jungle prison.

I have told this hostage story in detail in my 2017 book, "Captives for Freedom"—using, in particular, my daily reports to Headquarters and UN Security to communicate what we knew day by day. My intent now is to show more briefly in this real-life drama, the complexity of interactions across cultural and institutional boundaries that may be involved, but also the power that follows from 'deep listening' across cultural difference. I do not follow up the longer-term consequences to the present of the hostage drama here as this can be found in *Captives for Freedom.*

Origins of the Strategy to Capture 'White Noses'

The immediate catalyst for the OPM taking hostages was a jungle excursion by four young students from Cambridge University who formed the 'Lorentz'95 Group' accompanied by 17 Indonesians, including local bearers and members of Jakarta's Biological Sciences Club and Irianese (Papuan) Officials. Martha and Mark were accidently caught up in an abduction targeting the Cambridge group; Frank Momberg, a German consultant working with WWF in cooperation with UNESCO, had also walked into the village where the abductions occurred along with Martha and Mark.

There were two basic problems with the Cambridge team itself—both of which were contributing factors to the abduction.

The first was that the young Cambridge students, with no experience of the Papuan culture or jungles, broke many of the cultural 'rules' of engaging with the local communities. In particular, the Lorentz'95 Group came to *collect* biological and geological specimens, not to contribute to or exchange with the people. As the OPM stated to negotiators, the group was taking away 'the leaves from our forest and the dirt from our ground, and that is exactly what happened before when the miners and the foresters came and took our sacred mountain and our trees.' Additionally, the team travelled with a barrage of supportive but alien high tech equipment that set them well apart from the bare simple lifestyle of the highland people. Indeed it took *two* plane loads to get them and their equipment up into Mapnduma.

The second problem was that being Javanese or connected with the Indonesian Government was associated in the eyes of the OPM with the Jakarta-led military and political repression of West Papua. Two young men were killed by OPM rebels in the last days, Javanese students Navy Panekenan from Jakarta and Theis (Yosias Matheis Lasamahu) from Bandung, both associated with the Jakarta Biological Sciences Club. Papuan academic, Markus Warip, who narrowly escaped from being murdered after Navy was killed, was regarded by the OPM as a traitor for he worked for the Indonesian Government.

The young Cambridge students were warned.

Whilst in Jakarta preparing for their Papua mission, the Lorentz '95 Group had come to speak with WWF and our UNESCO ecology team—including Martha—who was responsible for UNESCO action in West Papua on conservation of the Lorentz National Park—currently being considered then by UNESCO for World Heritage status. However, the Cambridge students had disregarded most of UNESCO and WWF advice on practical cautions—in particular to value local 'ownership' of the very plants they were collecting and land they walked across, and *not* take Javanese assistants with them as they would be in danger. Ben Bohane, an Australian photojournalist, met the Cambridge team after they had arrived in Mapnduma and also warned them that given the level of antagonism to non-Papuan Indonesians, the mere presence of Javanese within the Cambridge Group was creating tension so they were all risking their own lives being there[1] However, the Cambridge students remained in the highlands for several more weeks, hiring Ben Bohane's guide, Daniel Yudas Kogoya as an assistant, a fatal move as it turned out. Daniel Kogoya (or Yudas as Daniel Start, leader of the Lorentz 95 Group called him)

---

[1] Reported by Jim Elmslie in his PhD thesis, based on an interview with Bohane: Jim Elmslie, *Irian Jaya Under the Gun: Indonesian Economic Development versus West Papuan Nationalism*, PhD Thesis, Department of Government, University of Sydney, 2001, p195.

was an OPM leader who used this time to monitor the group before leading the attack to capture them in Mapnduma.

Once the Cambridge mission started, the tensions then built up quickly. Indeed, a recovered diary note left behind by one of the Cambridge students as the OPM fled the military with them as hostages, and dated the day *before* the kidnapping, expressed deep concern for their safety because of conflicts developing between the Cambridge Group and the local villagers. The WWF/UNESCO team reinforced these concerns when they arrived at Mapnduma. Meanwhile, even before the WWF/UNESCO team arrived, the Indonesian counterparts to the Cambridge team who came from Jakarta had been worried enough to start making plans to get out as soon as an aeroplane could be arranged to pick them up. They, like the WWF/UNESCO group, were unable to make the arrangements quickly enough.

Although eight Javanese students had been captured and killed by the OPM in 1986, the idea of capturing *foreigners* was a new strategy of the OPM in the struggle for an independent Papua. The OPM independence movement had come to life after the Dutch gave up their colony in 1963 and Indonesia annexed Papua as the most southwestern piece in Indonesia's national archipelagic jigsaw, then legitimised their take-over with the United Nations General Assembly through a contrived plebiscite. In this plebiscite 1,025 people voted out of a population of one million. A representative of the OPM interviewed in the UK talked of how his father was included in this process:

> They selected those people based on who they wanted, and they trained them in some Indonesian sentences, like "I agree with Indonesia", or "I don't want the Dutch"—at least 5 or 6 sentences. My father didn't know the meaning of these sentences. After some weeks, they tested who was doing good in those sentences and my father passed the test, and he was asked to say one of those whole sentences in a meeting.
> Interviewer: "So the process was basically a complete joke, would you say?"
> Yes. My father is now feeling very, very sorry. He is saying, 'Don't repeat my mistake anymore.' At the time they thought Indonesia was coming to help, supporting independence.
> Interviewer: "Right, so they didn't realize that they would actually be taken over as part of Indonesia?"
> Actually they realised later. And all of the 1,025 are now against Indonesia. When I am here, they are now protesting. They are standing and they say 'I signed these and now I want to pay it back.'

Historian, John Saltford claims that such 'educational' techniques were supplemented by naked threats to the voting delegates of being shot if they voted the wrong way.[2]

Moses Weror, an acknowledged leader of the OPM Council and exiled resident in Papua New Guinea, speaking during the kidnapping in early March 1996 to *Forum Keadilan* claimed that the OPM was now in the seventh stage of its struggle, a stage set between 1994 and 1999 to attract world attention through hostage taking.

The hostage-taking act was therefore planned, although the specific hostage group targeted was probably more the result of local opportunity and idea rather than OPM wide decision.

Behind this action by Kelly Kwalik, Daniel Yudas Kogoya and their fellow OPM guerillas was the history of Indonesia's exploitation of both the land and people of West Papua.

Historic Context of Exploitation and Repression

At the core of their concern, as Kelly Kwalik told the ICRC negotiators in 1996, the OPM claimed that 43,000 of their fellow Papuans had been killed since the early 1960s.[1] Indeed, TAPOL, the Indonesia Human Rights Campaign claim that,

> ... it is widely agreed that about 100,000 Papuans have lost their lives as a result of military operations or occupation-related disorders since the beginning of Indonesian rule in 1963.[2]

No official statistics were kept. As the people lived in arguably one of the most remote parts of the world, not much of what happened in the jungles was reported to the outside world. But we can be sure many people died.

As a momentary aside on the *lack* of clear information of what happens in the West Papuan jungles outside world scrutiny, we (i.e. my own people and myself in UNESCO) mistakenly believed a couple of years later, in early 1998 during a drought relief program, that we had uncovered evidence of genocide

---

[2] Some diplomats reported open threats were made against delegates "a Council Member asked what would happen to him if he opted for Independence; the reply was that he would be shot." On May 24, the Tjenderawasih newspaper reported that Major Soewondo addressing 200 village chiefs stated that "I am drawing the line frankly and clearly. I say I will protect and guarantee the safety of everyone who is for Indonesia, I will shoot dead anyone who is against us and all his followers." See John Saltford "The United Nations and the Indonesian Takeover of West Papua, 1962–1989: The Anatomy of Betrayal" (London, Routledge, 2003), p. 147.

in the highlands. In cooperation with the UN Food and Agricultural Organisation, FAO, we were sending an agricultural scientist by helicopter into the primary drought-affected areas to assess what could be done to rapidly build up or exchange food stocks. He met with the people in one area where official government statistics declared there to be around 2,000 Papuan people. They met in the local village, and as with the other such consultations, given the people were desperate for food, all would normally trek down to the village to participate. Only 200 or so people turned up, and we became worried about what had happened to the other 1,800 people. We later discovered however, that what we were observing was not a product of militaristic genocide at all, but of bureaucratic corruption. The local official had been massively overestimating population numbers in remote areas where no one else could check his census polls, as this significantly increased his budget and personal income. The people were never there in the first place.

The one thing that was clear to us in our own contacts with remote West Papuan communities however was that the people were *very* afraid of the military, whilst up to the time of the 1996 hostage crisis, maintenance of the integrity of national unity in the remote provinces of Indonesia was almost invariably accompanied by unflinching military control and harsh retribution for any deviance such as protest or raising an Independent Papua OPM flag.[3]

The military had a lot to lose with movement towards autonomous control of West Papua as well. At that stage, the Indonesian military received only 25% of their income from Parliamentary vote, and had to raise the rest of their budget themselves through assorted 'business' interests. As Peter King observed:

> Through its *yayasan* (trusts or foundations established to oversee military business) the military became a largely self-financing 'industry' in its own right—its impunity on this front strengthened by the absence of any serious accountability to the civilian authorities of the state. Around 75% of military outlays continue to be 'off-line' supplements to the minuscule official defense budget, which on its own barely kept or keeps the soldiers fed, clothed and housed.[3]

As Ed Mc Williams, Political Counsellor at the US Embassy in Jakarta from 1996 to 1999 reported in November 2005,

---

[3] See also Ajay Singh and Keith Loveard, 'Now a Threat in Irian Jaya—Once Counted Out, a Rebel Group Seizes Hostages', *ASIAWEEK*, January 26, 1996, p30.

TNI profits tremendously from its presence there (West Papua), extorting money from Indonesian and foreign firms and operating illegal logging, prostitution and other "businesses." The U.S. mining giant Freeport McMoran paid the TNI more than ten million dollars over a recent two-year period. Military service in West Papua also is rewarded with extra pay and faster promotion, as had been the case in other conflict areas like pre-1999 East Timor.[4]

The military were therefore deeply embedded in economic gain from the remote provinces, crossing the edge fairly smoothly into illegal activity such as support for pirate logging to complement legitimate economic enterprise. There was clear evidence that came to us during the hostage crisis (1996) of arms sales by some 'renegade' military interests across the border into Papua New Guinea. The weapons simply 'disappeared' from secure army warehouses in Wamena, where the local military officials claimed they had been stolen by 'unknown robbers'.[5] At least some of the weapons ended up back in West Papua in the hands of the OPM rebels shooting at the military, making this a distinctly Faustian economic bargain. It was pretty sure that somewhere along the way, Indonesian military men were gaining a tidy profit, and had every reason to suppress any slight movement towards local independence or accountability, and indeed to mobilize direct retribution against local Papuans in an attempt to move the blame onto the OPM and away from the military itself.

In parallel, the New Order Government of President Soeharto had instituted a policy of 'transmigration', or resettling Javanese from the crowded islands of Java and Madura (in particular) where 60% of Indonesians live, into the remote provinces of West Papua, Kalimantan, Sulawesi and the other eastern islands—providing land expropriated from the locals, along with housing and foundational financial assistance, thus moving Javanese influence and culture into the heart of the relatively unpopulated and culturally alien reaches of Indonesia's empire. Transmigration therefore fundamentally transformed the demographics of West Papua. As *Human Rights Watch* report,

> The Government appropriated, usually without compensation, large tracts of land from traditional owners to support the new arrivals. For example, "Operation Clean Sweep" in June 1981 was reportedly used to force Papuans off

---

[4] Ed McWilliams, 'Response to Efforts to Deny Crimes Against Humanity in West Papua, East Timor ETAN/US internet site, www.etan.org/news/2005/11mcfet.htm, November 2005.

[5] Carmel Budjiardo, 'West Papua: Land of Peace or Killing Field', Paper presented to the 5th International Solidarity Meeting for West Papua, Manila, Phillppines, 30 April 2005, Tapol: The Indonesia Human Rights Campaign (Surrey, UK), internet site, http:/www.tapol.gn.apc.org/reports/r050430.htm

their lands in the border regions to vacate land for incoming transmigrants. This resulted in entire Papuan communities being displaced and increased feelings of marginalization by the indigenous population, especially in the mining towns where non-Papuans sometimes vastly outnumbered Papuans. Non-Papuans also dominated government bureaucracies and had better access to higher education and employment.[6]

As a consequence, non-Papuan born residents rose from 4% of the West Papua population in 1971 to 35% in 2000 when the transmigration program was terminated.

Transmigration, as many of the neo-colonialist policies of Indonesia, was culturally insensitive to local norms and practices. The only prism of value was the Indonesian way. Papuans were often viewed by bureaucrats as primitives to be dragged into the Indonesian culture-set of the modern world. At one stage, the central government in Jakarta decided, as a token to the local Papuan people around Timika, to build houses for the locals to match the ones being built for the Javanese immigrants, designed as a cheap suburban house for a family of two parents and two kids. The problem in Papua was that the locals did not know what to do with them. Papuans in this area near Timika traditionally live in shared accommodation set into a rectangle—with a women's house down one side, the men's house at the end (with space underneath for honored mummies of their key ancestors), and the house for pigs on the other side. Four-person family homes simply did not fit local cultural design, and ended up not as residences, but as a place to keep the pigs.

Economic and human rights policy in the provinces were neo-colonial, commanded from the center in Jakarta, and in particular by President Soeharto's family financial and other interests and military support. The massive gold and copper mine of the American multinational, Freeport, near Timika in the south of West Papua was therefore developed with no local consultation or recompense—and the scale is massive, grinding down the total 4,500 m Grasberg Mountain to its foundations, operating from sea level to the snow-capped peak of a tropical mountain glacier and meanwhile producing massive run-off from post-production tailings down the river systems. In return, tribal inhabitants of the Freeport-targeted mountains and lowlands were simply displaced, and there was not even the recompense of a single pig-giving ceremony, an action that locals told us would have been an appropriate first step in compensation. Jakarta's return was 10% of the

---

[6] Human Rights Watch, *Out of Sight: Endemic Abuse and Impunity in Papua's Central Highlands: III. Background,* Internet site: http://hrm.org/reports 2007/papua 0707/4.htm#

profits of the largest gold mine in the world to the Soeharto family directly plus royalties and taxes to the Indonesian government.

Meanwhile as far as one of the main displaced tribes, the Amungme, were concerned, a major sacred site had been totally desecrated. The Amungme called this mountain 'Nemang Kawi'—the mountains were their mother, the highlands her head full of thoughts and ideas, the middle zone containing all the productive assets for survival—gardens, wild game and so on, whilst the lower region below the waist, was unclean and unhealthy. As Jim Elmslie observes,

> Thus the Amungme stuck to the hills until they were forced to the lowlands by the government, where malaria and other diseases have taken a savage toll, since the mountain people have no natural resistance to them. While the Amungme suffered in the lowlands, their traditional sacred site of Nemang Kawi was slowly and inescapably consumed by Freeport. The mountain has been levelled.[7]

Stimulus for the Plan to Take Foreign Hostages

Various incidents sparked the fire of the resolve of the OPM to take hostages as a strategy for fighting the repression they were experiencing—including the killing of Papuans by the military at the abortive 1989 Independent Papua flag raising ceremony and attempt to seize power in Jayapura, West Papua's capital that had led to the jailing of Tom Wainggai, an event that had further consequences later. Tom Wainggai died in Indonesian custody, an event which, amongst other things, led to the release of his brother, Bram Wainggai, who had been taken as one of the hostages, and to violence on the streets of Jayapura when Tom Wainggai's body was returned from Jakarta.

Probably most important though was the betrayal of Kwalik himself when he had sought to develop compensatory negotiations with Freeport during the year before the kidnapping. He sent a letter to the company proposing the donation of pigs as a sign of compensation at a planned feast in his family village. Instead of Freeport management dealing with the issue directly, the letter was passed through the hands of Freeport security and on to the Indonesian military.

---

[7] Jim Elmslie, op cit., p 169.

The military did not arrive with pigs. They came at the time of the feast with guns and shot up the village, killing, amongst others, Kelly Kwalik's three brothers.

Kwalik in his earlier life had been a Catholic seminarian under the tutelage of Bishop Meninghoff of the Jayapura diocese—subsequently a key figure in early hostage negotiations. The incident where his three brothers were killed however is thought to have converted Kwalik's previous religious basis for care of his fellow Papuans to a strident political base—into which the legitimacy of killing for political purposes was admitted—and at the same time, as subsequent events appear to show, it 'turned' Kwalik at a much deeper psychological level towards a need to maintain power for himself even against the commitments and interests of his own people.

Kelly Kwalik's political agenda therefore was forged into a trenchant critique of the effects of neo-colonialism on his own land and people. He observed during the course of negotiations, 'God gave us a nice country, but we cannot keep it for ourselves' ….. 'outsiders usually come to West Papua only to take away things that belong to the people of West Papua, and never to bring things which will help the people in return.'

However, although Kwalik sought an independent Free Papua by whatever means, this could be achieved. The OPM had little power to fight a battle of independence against the Indonesian military. Formed as a jungle-based resistance force in the late 1960s following the Indonesian army's brutal suppression of dissidence that followed the 1963 take-over of West Papua by Indonesia, the OPM had remained a loose jungle-based movement, equipped with a handful of bolt-action rifles and many traditional weapons—bows, arrows, spears, and axes. Warriors would move in and out of OPM operations, not to hide so much as to simply return for periods of time to village life before taking to arms again. Indeed, the OPM describe themselves "as a state of mind" with actual numbers of fighters varying according to the ebb and flow of relations between Indonesians and the Irianese. Jim Elmslie further observes,

> The term OPM represents much more than a military force; it is the expression and symbol of the desire for independence that is shared by the overwhelming majority of the West Papuan people. One expression of this desire is violent confrontation.[8]

With various claimed overall leaders in West Papua and in exile, including Moses Weror, the exiled leader in Madang, Papua New Guinea, and a small

---

[8] Jim Elmslie, op cit., p 30.

number of spokespeople in Australia and Europe—not always speaking with one voice, communications and strategy were primitive, and the OPM's campaigns were overwhelmed in general by government military repression. Although OPM sympathy was wide-spread in West Papuan towns, OPM support there was strongly suppressed, thus weakening linkages between what was happening in the jungle and those supporting the OPM internationally. Consequently, communication between the exiled and those fighting in the jungles was extremely poor, so lines of command were highly ambiguous.

Even with few modern weapons, the main strength the OPM had was its jungle warriors, and it was ultimately the jungle commanders who really made the decisions in 1996 (although there has been a rise in the authority of civilian leadership since 1998). With excellent bushcraft, they could move extremely rapidly through seemingly impenetrable terrain leaving behind almost no trace of their passing. To counter them the military often hit their food supplies, occupying or destroying the gardens of villages through which the OPM was passing, bombing or napalming villages and valleys sometimes in retribution for OPM actions, causing enormous distress to the local tribes who may have had nothing to do with the rebels in the first place.

What happened in the capture of the Lorentz'95 Group in Mapnduma was a case in point. The OPM overwhelmed the village food stocks of the Mapnduma N'duga tribe with 200 mainly Amungme warriors. Within days the OPM had killed *all* the pigs of Mapnduma and then moved on, taking the hostages with them. When the military came, they occupied or destroyed the village gardens whilst the people fled into the jungle, barely surviving the sudden depletion of the food stocks now available to them. The N'duga were not pleased with the Amungme for creating this mess and considered the hostages to be theirs as well, given that they were captured on N'duga land—a problem that derailed our own hostage negotiations sometime later while the tribes worked out this ownership question. And meanwhile, the hostages, although well cared for, were often very hungry. Frank Meyer, the ICRC doctor involved in hostage negotiations, reported in early March 1996 after examining the hostages, that several of them had lost 15 kg to 18 kg in weight.

Life as a Hostage

The threat of potential violence followed the hostages all the time.

When I spoke with Martha the day after she was released, she described the capture of hostages at Mapnduma as terrifying. Many men dressed in war feathers, paint and pig fat, brandishing bows and arrows and spears, much yelling, trashing of the missionary's house—creating an environment of total intimidation. In retrospect, Martha observed, the arrows were not fired. At the time, it was singularly threatening.

The British hostages, interviewed by Kirsten Garrett on Australian ABC's *Background Briefing*, on Sunday 18th May 1997 reported the capture this way:

Daniel Start: We'd been in Mapnduma about eight weeks of the ten weeks that we planned to be there, and it was 8th January when about 200 tribespeople, warriors, came down from the ridge, and I was initially surprised by the fact that I didn't recognize them.

Anna McIvor: We hadn't seen that number of people running before in the pose that they were running; they all had their arrows out, bows strung, they were wearing a lot of face paint, feathers in their hair, very ceremonial, warlike dress.

Daniel Start: Suddenly there was a gunshot which went straight past my head, and of course we were in a wooden house, and someone had fired up into the room. I mean at that point we really knew then that it was the OPM, because I knew the OPM, the Free Papua Movement, had guns.

Bill Oates: Everyone ran upstairs, except myself, and I ran into the room that I'd been sleeping in on the ground floor and hid under the bed, courageously. In my bedroom I had a tape recorder that I'd been recording the stories and the exploits of us in Irian Jaya, and I grabbed this, and I was recording my farewell words to my family and my girlfriend. I thought that was it, they were going to kill us.

Anna McIvor: The house had this kind of funny little porch that wasn't really a porch, it was just enough space for us all to crouch down in there basically. And Yudus was pushing us out, and they were trying to pull us out onto this thing, and we didn't know what they wanted to do to us, and to be honest, I think we almost thought our time was up.

Bill Oates: Pretty soon they worked out where I was, it wasn't a very big house; and so I was given the choice to either come out or have the door broken down and be dragged out, so I came out.

Daniel Start: And then the warriors came with machetes and they started slamming those into the wood of the porch, and close to our faces. It was almost as if the crowd could erupt at any moment, and commit some uncontrollable or unknown deed.

Anna McIvor: And finally, we couldn't hold back any more, they dragged us each out, one by one, and we saw that they were just tying us up, they didn't do anything worse.

Daniel Start: And then I saw a line of people stand on the low garden wall, and they all had their bows and arrows drawn, aimed towards us. And it seemed almost as if we were being prepared for execution. And then suddenly it began to rain, and clouds came down over the mountains to the north of the village, and that did seem to kind of quell some of the excitement.[9]

When the rebels were fleeing Mapnduma taking the hostages with them after initial but abortive negotiation attempts of church representatives, they moved the greatest distances of the whole period of capture. This was mainly because they were being followed by trackers from the Nduga tribe, employed by the army, naked except for shorts, carrying machine guns, and *very* fast through the jungle. It was a very tense time for both rebels and hostages. Whilst the hostages were therefore under very considerable physical duress, Silas, one of the kidnappers, spent the first couple of weeks constantly sharpening a knife to a razor's edge and brandishing it around the faces of the hostages.

But, with the West Papuans, violence is part of primitive tribal life and is contained by tribal ritual and practices. Silas fortunately was held in check this way.

Back in Mapnduma at the time of the abduction, many of the N'duga villagers objected to the kidnapping, saying this is not *our* way of waging war. One particularly brave man, Philippus, a preacher, stood up alone and directly to Daniel Kogoya and declared personal war on him and his 200 rebels, telling them to go back to their own villages and cause trouble there— he was, at that stage, singularly unsuccessful. Subsequently, Naftali the radio operator, hearing of the intimidation being experienced from Silas by the hostages, brought the fresh heart of a pig to the hut where the hostages were being held. He cut the heart into two pieces, giving one piece to Silas. Holding up the other he said to the hostages, "all of you must eat this! No-one can kill another who has eaten from the same plate." Even the English girl who was, up to this moment in life at least, totally vegetarian, found the stomach to take a nibble. Silas caused no trouble thereafter, and indeed later sought to be the hostages' protector.

As a further example of the interaction between violence and everyday life, Martha reported that one night a villager came to offer them a large pumpkin to eat. The man, previously known as a lovely and gentle person, simply said, when explaining how he could afford to offer it, because "… it grew in the garden where I killed a man. I cannot eat it because of the spirits."

Life for the hostages was absolutely simple. The people have nothing. Nothing in their huts, nothing. They travel with a woven fiber blanket to sleep on and which is used to keep the rain off, and a small carrying bag or

---

[9]. Reported on internet site, 'www.converge.org.nz/wpapua/friends.html'.

noken for food. In absence of a convenient pocket, the naked tribesmen carry their tobacco in the tip of the kodakai, or penis sheath—a fact worth knowing for any future trekker in West Papua who borrows a cigarette from a local. Penis sheaths by the way are universal male fashion amongst Papuans, formed from a collected root crop gourd that can come in an enormous variety of long but erratic shapes and sizes, is worn to protect (or perhaps to emphasize) one's private parts, and is usually held in erectile place by a thin strand of fiber or thread attached around the man's waist.

As soon as they became engaged in negotiations the International Committee of the Red Cross, ICRC, sent in food parcels for the hostages, supplemented in order to provide some food for locals' consumption as well. Given the absolute poverty of their supporters, the hostages were therefore, at times, embarrassed about taking these dedicated food supplies. However, the local people understood. Indeed, they said—and insisted—that foreigners die if they do not eat at 7.00am, midday and 7.00 pm. So, they did. Whether the hostages liked it or not, they ate to schedule—that is, when food was around.

Some of the hostages did however become very sick, one with an untreatable liver problem, another with a kidney stone and several with malaria. Martha and Mark had not expected to be at risk of malaria, so had taken no prophylactic drugs early in the trip: they expected to be traveling only in the highlands above malaria infested areas. But, the rebels took them down into malaria zones as they escaped the military. A month after the hostages were captured, we received a letter carried out from Martha and Mark—and letters transmitted by the hostages, it turned out, could be quite open. The abductors could not read English or Dutch and did not seek to censor the correspondence, although the hostages took the precaution of never naming their captors, only referring to them via nicknames. I'll quote their letter:

6 February 1996
At last, we are in a position again to write you a short message. This note is written from yet another shelter. We are still alive but both physically and mentally at the end of our reserves. Especially the last week was very hard. Due to military activities close by, the OPM felt itself forced to change our location frequently. Extreme walks, unhealthy living circumstances and a lack of food have seriously weakened us all. Three of us, including undersigned have suffered from severe malaria attacks. Martha's condition in particular gives us many reasons for concern. Beside a general lack of food (no protein, no calcium) she suffered from several fever attacks during 3 days (40 °C). The fever has been treated with Paracetamol, 3 x 200 mg chloroquine, 3 tbl Fansidor. Martha is now over 18 weeks pregnant and any medical advice which can help her is more than welcome.

Martha was in a terrible position given that she was pregnant. On the one hand, anti-malarial drugs are contra-indicated for the health of the fetus, but on the other, a 40 °C body temperature could kill the developing baby. Martha's own doctor was of course helpful with advice that we passed on—mainly that as Martha had just passed her first trimester, it was probably more important to control body temperature rather than worry about the anti-malarial drugs crossing the placenta wall. As the Birth Announcement at the front of this Chapter shows, her baby, Mick Lorentz, came through unscathed.

Although, in their weakened condition, continuously moving was extremely taxing for the hostages, they never carried anything when they were trekking. The Papuan villagers did. Normally naked, they carried all the possessions of the hostages, sleeping bags, clothes, food, and so on. It took 20 men to accompany the group, just as bearers. The Papuans walk in such a way that they do not create tracks, just momentary clearance. So, finding their trail is very difficult. They walk extremely fast. They are very, very fit. They make log bridges across rivers very rapidly—with the logs often just below the current, and confidently stride across, whilst foreigners, particularly Martha—who increasingly was developing a pregnancy-inspired 'waddle', were quite terrified of being swept away by the current. The Papuans can quickly make fiber rope suspension bridges, then simply cut them down after they cross, making pursuit again very difficult for people without the same skill. Being in the bush with the rebels was therefore both an extraordinary lesson in bushcraft, and a very basic simple life as well. Furthermore, respect for the Papuans increased as the people *cared*—particularly for the foreigners … 'white noses' who they mainly associated with the few missionaries or men of peace with whom they had come into contact. The Papuans really did treat the hostages as guests who needed to be looked after in a world for which these guests were ill-prepared.

But the people had absolutely no concept of the outside world. As Martha described it, they would sit around all day and simply wait. They were in the jungle, simply *waiting* for independence—whatever that is—to arrive. Martha observed that communication with the rebels was extremely difficult as they spoke little Indonesian and had no reference point to relate to the outside world. At the time of the abduction the abiding impression for the tribal men involved of the outside *Indonesian* world was of the military. Meanwhile, the military—and particularly their attitude to and use of violence outside the tribal rituals that contain it—did not fit into any concept of the Papuan's own world. The people are very simple. The people were very confused.

Indeed, after all of this was over, we were asked by tribal chiefs of the Baliem Valley to take them into this outside world. For them, even the main town of Wamena had no road access and could only be reached by air or by walking down jungle trails. "We have been requesting the local Bupati (or senior government official) for years", they said. "But he won't help us. All we see is people stepping off an aeroplane. We have no idea of the world from which they come, so do not know how to deal with them. We want to see." As I show in the next Chapter, I therefore mounted several UNESCO "study tours", the first in April 1997 bringing the tribal leaders of 20 villages to Jakarta, an epic journey into the future that had extraordinary consequences. This is another story and I will come to it in the next chapter after we get out of this hostage mess.

The Military—Walking a Tightrope: Negotiation Versus Attack

We were quite worried about the way the military was going to handle the abduction.

Traditionally, they took a hard line stance in the provinces, and we were concerned that they may attack the rebel camp putting the hostages at very serious risk of being killed. Indeed, this was the position of the local Regional Commander in the first week of the crisis who insisted on a "search and rescue" operation.

Within a week, command was firmly taken over however by Commander of Special Forces, Brigadier General Probowo Subianto, a western-trained fast-rising star in a military career that was considerably assisted by being married to President Soeharto's second oldest daughter, Siti Hedijati Hariyadi. Probowo took a much more "peaceful persuasion" line and generated considerably more confidence amongst the diplomatic community and negotiators, although we were still wary as Probowo had previously been a hard-line exponent and implementer of military control against the rebel Fretelin Movement in East Timor.

Probowo turned out in the present case however to be genuine, and took the new negotiating line even against the position of his bosses in Jakarta. Armed Forces Commander General Feisal Tanjung, having just consulted with President Soeharto, announced to reporters from Jakarta shortly after Probowo had taken over dealing with the hostage crisis, "Who said we will bow to terror? We will not. There are no negotiations. We will handle this in a good way. We want the captives released without being harmed."

Probowo did however exercise appropriate Javanese caution in his public front. He maintained publicly an official though 'softer' position supporting General Tanjung, emphasizing that the soldiers needed to be close to the hostages in case any harm were to come to them in which case they would need to arrest the OPM rebels as criminals; but if the hostages were not harmed and were released, then the military would allow the OPM to leave the area unmonitored. More privately Probowo was strongly supporting negotiation. In late February, when the hostage crisis was already 6 weeks old, he was instrumental in supporting our advice to bring in the International Red Cross, ICRC, to take over negotiations, even though this was not fully endorsed by his more senior commanders, and there were initial disagreements between ICRC and the more senior military about the groundrules for ICRC involvement: ICRC insisted on taking a high profile position where they were able to make clear security guarantees as part of the negotiating strategy, but military interest was highly antagonistic for they wanted to claim all the credit for hostage release for themselves, and even took steps to try and discredit the head of ICRC, Henri Fournier. Meanwhile, Probowo had firmly maintained considerable caution to avoid military engagement with the rebels, keeping the troops outside well established perimeters. It is thought that he was able to maintain this softer military line because he had at least the tacit support of the President, Soeharto.

However, Probowo trod a fine line. With his acceptance of working towards a negotiated settlement, he was out of step with the long-standing doctrinal military position on controlling restive provinces, so he was likely to face censure from above in the hierarchy and opposition at the same time from restive troops below.

Indeed, there were numerous instances of other elements in the military 'white-anting' Probowo's ability to operate. Several times, mischievous press reports were released from military sources. For example, even after only four days into the crisis, an unnamed military officer declared that 11 hostages had been freed by military force, a claim that was totally untrue and very destructive to negotiations. In mid-February, Daniel Kogoya sent a message out to the military for them to drop a radio near a village, Ndzouma, as Kelly Kwalik wanted to talk directly with Probowo. But the message did not get through to Probowo for several days, held up, we thought, by the 'forceful solution advocates' who were itching to attack the area rather than talk. Probowo was furious.

The longer negotiations went on without resolution, the more Probowo was seen to have overplayed his hand. He was therefore desperate for signals of negotiation progress. Initial engagement of the ICRC was successful, as they obtained their first objective of establishing dialogue with the rebels within a fortnight where it had been totally absent for several weeks before, and then they met their second objective, to meet the hostages to assess their health and welfare—in 3 days. When the ICRC negotiators subsequently returned to the main Baliem Valley town of Wamena on 29th February, they were met by General Johny Lumintang, Probowo's second-in-command, who was absolutely delighted—also expressing Probowo's view—and bought cartons of beer for the troops and the ICRC negotiators, and then spent the evening celebrating at the hotel where they were staying.

We, the international community, were very concerned however that Probowo would lose power and his role in maintaining negotiations. The diplomatic community therefore sought to put as much pressure as possible on both the local military in Jayapura, and in Jakarta to maintain a 'soft' negotiating stance. I was personally involved in arranging for a stream of diplomatic initiatives towards this end from senior United Nations Heads—the Secretary-General of the UN, Boutros Boutros Gali and Federico Mayor, Director-General of UNESCO—through Indonesia's Minister of Foreign Affairs, Ali Alatas.

6

"Jungle Hostages—II: Negotiating Peoples' Lives Across Cultures"

Negotiating

Negotiations for the release of the hostages commenced almost immediately after their capture—initially by radio and scheduled interactions, called 'scheds' between the rebel group and the negotiators. Consular officials from the British and Dutch Embassies flew almost immediately to Wamena to assess the situation and to communicate with the military. Shortly afterwards, the British, Dutch and German Governments brought in military attachés to work with the Indonesian military from Wamena, the main town of the Baliem Valley, and the British Government shortly afterwards brought in hostage negotiation experts from Scotland Yard to advise. WWF initiated carefully crafted communications to align their own captured people with conservation in the interests of the people of Papua and therefore, the OPM. But the United Nations was unable to be involved directly: as far as Indonesia was concerned this was an internal political issue; if the UN became involved directly, it served to legitimate the case of the rebels against the national government. We therefore had to remain in the background, building up trust with the government, embassy, and military officials so that they would share intelligence reports with us on a daily basis. We were directly involved however in framing negotiation positions—in particular with ICRC a little further down the track, and bringing in international pressure from high ranking UN and church officials on the rebels on the one hand to recognize the negative attitude to kidnapping in the world outside the Papuan jungles, and on the other hand, on senior government officials, in particular through the Minister of Foreign Affairs, to hold back hardline military action.

I was reporting to both my Headquarters and to the UN Security Council on progress and potential action on a daily basis. Meanwhile, the Minister of Foreign Affairs, Ali Alatas, assured the world community that Indonesia would adhere to a persuasive negotiation strategy; but the frequently bellicose attitude of the military still left us continuously concerned.

The Problem of Remoteness

What we discovered very quickly was the enormous complication of dealing with a hostage crisis that was being played out in remote jungles where access is extremely limited and communication almost impossible. As a result, there was a continuous flow of rumours and *partial* information—indicators of steps forwards vs sudden dangers that came to us in an atmosphere of complete uncertainty.

My Reports to my Headquarters and the UN Security Council therefore read, as I observed earlier, rather like a Le Carré spy novel—glimmerings of what was really happening and might happen next that were likely to be revised within one or two subsequent reports. On many occasions, we really thought that negotiations were about to be successful, only to find a day later that some new constraint had sprung up and our hopes were dashed. At times the distance from the jungle arena where the hostages were being kept quite directly impacted on our understanding of the rebel's position and demands.

rumors abounded, some turning out to be true, many completely baseless. In early March 1996 for example, a rumor was current for two weeks that the person everyone was referring to as 'Kwalik' was not Kwalik at all. The only outsider who had actually met Kwalik was the priest Bishop Meninghoff who had known Kwalik 23 years earlier when Kwalik was a seminarian, and described him as inarticulate—yet the person negotiators were dealing with was intelligent and highly articulate; a photo emerged reputedly taken 23 years before of Kwalik with Meninghoff and people who saw the photo said it was not the Kwalik they now knew. The rumor evaporated when Meninghoff actually met Kwalik.

Meanwhile, two-way radio frequencies and contact were totally controlled by the military, so Kwalik could not interact with other OPM leaders unless the military allowed it. But, as short-wave radio reception *was* possible, the media *did* have an influence on Kwalik and on the whole hostage situation, sometimes extremely negatively. In February, the second month of the crisis, Kwalik had completed his 'strategy', made his point, and was, as far as we understood, prepared to release the hostages. Then he heard a Radio Australia interview with Moses Weror, self-proclaimed Chairman of the Revolutionary Council of the OPM and living in exile in Papua New Guinea. Weror called on Kwalik to *not* release the hostages but negotiate. Kwalik immediately reversed his decision to release the hostages—but he had no ability to talk the issue through with Weror or any other outsider, and became very confused. Moses Weror subsequently changed his advice—perhaps influenced by the reminder proffered by the Papua New Guinean Government and the international community that as he had called for revolution in another State he was subject to incarceration in Papua New Guinea. We were eventually able to get the new view of Weror through to Kwalik, but by this time he appeared to be confused, not able to talk with his senior commanders and not trusting in external 'advice'.

Hardline military interest played the media in such a way as to directly interfere with negotiation as well, the intent seemingly to derail the possibility of peaceful settlement, thus opening the way for the military to attack, forcefully release the hostages and gain the credit. On 14th January shortly after the abduction, an unnamed military source reported that the military had forcefully released 11 hostages—a straight lie. On 15th January, Indonesia's official news clearing service, ANTARA, announced that the OPM was demanding a plane as its price of releasing the hostages, that the hostages were sick and hungry and being held tied up, and that the army was in direct contact and negotiating with the OPM—all untrue: the army only knew what was going on by monitoring the early radio contacts between the OPM and the church. Meanwhile, Indonesian Press interests generally were unable to release the actual demands of the rebels, whereas these demands were known and widely distributed internationally through Reuters. But on 25th February, at a critical time in Kwalik's consideration of hostage release a military source in Jayapura announced to the Indonesian Press—also broadcast worldwide - that the hostages were going to be released "today"—totally wrong, a potentially dangerous lie if heard by Kwalik, and the subject subsequently of strong diplomatic interventions with the Indonesian government to seek to control such mischievous reporting in the future. Then the international press got it wrong as well. CNN's reports were very frequently shallow or out of date. A press report in the European media appeared in late February that a battalion of South Sulawesi troops had moved into position near the rebels. The report was based on a mistranslation. The Indonesian source report had said that the troops were 'ready when required to be sent'. The troops had not moved out of South Sulawesi. And an Indonesian media report that Australian journalist Ben Bohane had suggested to Kwalik in the first place that he should capture 'white noses' rather than 'brown noses' in order to attract world attention was sourced to the military and most likely was an attempt to discredit Bohane who had been meeting illegally with the OPM in the town where the hostages were captured, Mapnduma. I should add however that the international media picked up this report uncritically, as they did with most others: there were no other journalists able to be on the ground.

Several times we 'interpreted' the meaning of what was going on in the negotiations in ways that seemed eminently sensible at the time but turned out to be quite wrong.

Ten days after the hostages were abducted, for example, we really thought that the radio 'scheds' were working well towards final resolution and a direct negotiation meeting had been established. The OPM had agreed to a negotiating group—consisting of the Dutch Bishop Meninghoff—who had been former mentor of the rebel leader, Kelly Kwalik when he was a seminarian years before; the Dutch missionary, Adrianne van der Biel, whose house had been the meeting site of the Lorentz'95 group at the time when they were captured; and a West Papuan priest trusted by the rebels. Both sides accepted that access to negotiations would be provided by a local US Christian church whose mission included airflight support of the villagers. Safety of the hostages was guaranteed by the OPM, and the military faithfully pulled back. After some delays due to weather and access difficulties, a meeting was held with Daniel Kogoya, leader of the kidnapping group. Negotiations were looking positive, though Daniel said that any agreement he made had to be endorsed by the OPM leader, Kelly Kwalik. Kwalik arrived at the rebel camp and things started to go sour, as he took a harder line, sending out a series of letters with the visiting priests to the involved national governments and the UN demanding recognition of the OPM and its cause, conditions they or we could not agree to under any circumstance. We were worried, but partially assured by the British hostage negotiation experts who pointed out that this was the first time that Kwalik had had the opportunity to get his message to the international community, and commonly that first contacts involve aggressive assertion of cause.

But then *all radio contact ceased*. We assumed that Kwalik was playing hard-ball and refusing to communicate.

My Report five days later to UNESCO Headquarters and the UN Security Council read,

> There has been no information since Thursday 25th January. The arrival of the OPM leader, Kwalik, has changed the situation entirely. It is clear that he is playing a new hardline position, has cut off all radio contact, and refuses at this stage to negotiate.

6 "Jungle Hostages—II: Negotiating Peoples' Lives ... 81

… it is also possible that lack of radio contact results from the rebels not having access to a radio' …. Information is very limited and speculation is rife'

Through clergyman van der Biel, four runners were sent in to search for the rebels and hostages and report back. No word. It appeared they just kept running.

Then, almost straight after my Report, a radio broadcast came in from the person who was acting as radio operator for the rebels, Naftali Wanimbo. It turned out that at the end of the abortive discussions of the negotiating team with the OPM, van der Biel had told Naftali, one of his previous assistants in the mission, that he would be wise to get out of Mapnduma as the military might attack given the failure of the talks. So, Naftali, thought *not* to be a rebel group member, just a guy from Mapnduma, took off into the jungle in the opposite direction to the rebels, scared out of his wits. Naftali finally re-established radio contact on 30th January, but meanwhile Kwalik had taken the OPM group and the hostages off to the west towards his homeland, not being prepared to travel east where the tribes were totally antagonistic to the idea of kidnapping and potentially would have waged war on Kwalik. Daniel Kogoya was left behind in Mapnduma along with five of the OPM group. We did not know at that stage whether this meant that there had been a breakdown in Daniel and Kwalik's relationship or not.

After this, even though military scouting patrols and the runners came back with some information on movement of the rebel group based on recently evacuated camp sites discovered and local tribes reporting, no-one had any idea of where the rebels actually were for some five weeks. The rebels meanwhile *did not have* a radio. They were not playing hard-ball, just unable to communicate.

Invariably the weather was a major factor in the ability to negotiate and communicate. The only way to get a team of negotiators directly to the rebels was by an eight-day walk or more realistically, by helicopter or small airplane. But this required a 45 min flight from Wamena through 4,000 m mountains, landing on an airstrip carved out of the side of the mountain and perched on a 600 m ravine. *Generally* the area around Mapnduma was shrouded in thick mist, so that usually the only time when flights could fly in was very early in the morning, with negotiators getting out around mid-morning to avoid having to stay overnight, when their safety would have been much more significantly at risk. Numerous times negotiations were delayed because the plane simply could not get in.

I would add that these flights were not for the faint hearted. The landing strip was on the *side* of the mountain, that is on a slope, and not very long. Arriving by airplane required the pilot to fly *through* the nearby mountains, corkscrew down, and then land uphill and apply the airplane's brakes immediately its forward momentum ceased in order not to slide back down the mountain. And taking off? Well, there was one chance, and only one. The pilot had no alternative but to race his plane down the hill at top speed, drop off the edge of the runway into the valley below and …. eventually … pick up enough air current to fly.

Side-Plays

Meanwhile, there was a range of side-plays going on.

Whilst the rebels were running and hiding and heading west in late January into February, other concerns started to emerge back amongst the military and foreign participants in this saga. The military had lost faith in Adrianne van der Biel, as he seemed now to have been playing a side agenda. The military were *very* angry with him as he (and his wife) had falsely taken the credit for the distribution of food supplies flown in by the military for the people of Mapnduma when they returned to the village out of the jungle where they had fled for fear of military attack. Van der Biel was reporting military activity that was strenuously denied by senior generals; and it was thought that he may have encouraged Naftali to take the radio into the jungle to *prevent* the rebels having it, with the intention of forcing the rebels to come back to Mapnduma where he could assist and establish credit in negotiation success. Probowo and the military attachés of the three involved countries agreed that van der Biel was now compromised with his interest in being seen as a benefactor of the tribal people, so was playing a political game and could not be trusted. Again, the dynamics underlying negotiation were obscured at a distance.

At this stage, the military accepted that the International Red Cross, ICRC, could be brought in, although as I noted earlier, given the military's own interest in claiming success in resolving the hostage crisis, this entry by the ICRC was not without conflict and difficulty.

Then later in mid-March Moses Weror, claiming to be Commander of the Revolutionary Council of the OPM, exiled in Papua New Guinea, finally reversed his earlier instruction to Kelly Kwalik and strongly proposed release of the hostages, claiming that the OPM would be in serious trouble if any of the hostages were harmed and the longer they were held, the greater was the danger that they would be harmed. This message was sent by fax, followed by original letter and an audio tape of Weror reading the letter. It was then followed by a further plea through UNESCO …. all of which was communicated on to Kwalik by the ICRC. Kwalik's response was to declare that he had to consult with the other members of the OPM group as there had previously been serious internal disagreement over whether to release or keep the hostages. We were waiting however with baited breath as the sign was pretty good.

Totally out of side-field we then received a fax out of Papua New Guinea from a man calling himself Simon Along who claimed that he, not Moses Weror, was the Supreme Commander of the OPM, and that there could not be any hostage release until he and his four top commanders, Bonny Angemea, Jacob Prai, John Otto Ondawame and William Tonganael, agreed that 'their' OPM demands had been met. He further stated that if those demands were not met quickly then he would order all of the hostages to be killed. Along's core demand was immediate freedom for the West Papuans, totally unacceptable to Indonesia. Otto, one of the named commanders was in Sydney and was contacted by the ICRC: he claimed he had never heard of Simon Along so the letter was a lie and a hoax. Subsequently, even though the core group of negotiators for the release of the hostages attributed little credibility to the Along fax, every effort was made to ensure that Kwalik did not hear of it.

Kwalik himself was bedeviled by the impact of his remoteness on communication. While on the run and without a radio he could not contact the outside world, or other units of the OPM. Meanwhile, in particular after the Weror instruction in mid-March, he was in deep conflict with two strong-willed members of his own group, Spears and Titus who were strongly opposed to release—to the point where this disagreement nearly erupted into a fight. Meanwhile, other tribes such as the Hattam tribes around Arfak who formerly supported the OPM, were very upset that Kwalik had kidnapped conservationists who they regarded as their friends. Kwalik was effectively alone then, unable to consult, himself, with leaders or wider OPM units, reported to be committed to forming consensus, but unable to do so …. he was, as Henri Fournier, Head of the ICRC in Indonesia, commented at the time, "like a cornered cat".

Outside the immediate situation, other events were also impacting on the OPM's decision and strategy just as these mid-March negotiations were looking quite hopeful.

In February the OPM—led by a man not involved in the Mapnduma incident, John Magai Yogi, captured another two hostages in Paniai regency towards the Papua New Guinea border—a Frenchman, Frederic Penti and an Indonesia, Gabriel Go, both employed by PT Nabire Bhakti Mining. In this case the regional military commander, Lt Col. Armentony, mounted an operation to capture the rebels 'dead or alive'. Penti and Go managed to escape after just one day as a military helicopter came in over the rebels' hiding place. They ran down the hill 500 m and were picked up by the military helicopter. The military commander Armentory claimed the rebels fired on both the helicopter and the hostages, but it is more likely that the rebels were intimidated by the helicopter and fled, leaving the hostages behind. For us however this incident was disquieting as it demonstrated the military *taking* a hard-line attack position just when negotiations with the captors of our own people were at a quite critical stage.

Meanwhile, other events were also intruding on the negotiations from the outside.

On Sunday 10th March, following a Freeport Mining truck hitting and injuring a local, an apparently staged riot hit Tembagapura where the injured Papuan was in hospital. The attack by three groups was coordinated, including by two-way radios, and appeared planned—some suggesting, by the Indonesian military. Two days later the same groups attacked the larger town of Timika below the mine and basically trashed it. Probowo's troops were called in, and to their credit were able to quell the riot peacefully with minimum force. The local Amungme tribes were reported subsequently to be embarrassed by the incident, but what was worrying for us as this stage in negotiations was the possibility that it had been stimulated by outside provocateurs.

Shortly afterwards Tom Wainggai, the activist gaoled the previous year by Indonesia for raising the rebel OPM flag, died in prison—apparently of natural causes. But, when his body was brought back to Jayapura from Jakarta on 18th March, and was being carried out to the family village, the convoy was suddenly attacked, allegedly, by university students, who kidnapped the body, until confronted further down the road where they had to give it back. The students then rioted and burnt the main market in the university town of Abepura—an act that seriously destabilized the main West Papuan town of Jayapura.

Kwalik requested ICRC to provide independent assessments of both the way the military handled the Timika riots and the death of Tom Wainggai. In both cases ICRC reported that from their own investigations Indonesian authorities could not be held responsible but had acted quite appropriately. ICRC were confident in their conclusion as they had one of their own doctors present at Wainggai's autopsy. This was an essential assurance for Kwalik at the time—even though an unconfirmed suspicion lingered that Tom Wainggai had in fact been poisoned.

The hostage negotiation scene was therefore one of continuingly swirling mists of events, conflicts of political interest being played out within the church and within the military, economic interest of both multinationals and Indonesia that was continuing to ride rough-shod across the Papuan people and their land, cross-currents of tribal politics and in the OPM authority structure, and jungle-remoteness that severely impacted on clarity of communication and resolution. It was little wonder that Kelly Kwalik was feeling rather like a 'cornered cat'.

Contact Again—Core Values of the Conflict and Its Resolution

Penetrating through these swirling mists however was the cornerstone of both the crisis itself and the development of a successful negotiating strategy. This was the fundamental conflict that became increasingly clear between the cultural values and interests of the Papuan people and the values of the globalized world that waited outside the Papuan jungles unseen and unknown by the indigenous villagers except through the excesses of mining exploitation by Freeport and other multinationals, contact with a repressive Indonesian military and occasional local officials, and, of course, church missionaries. Local understanding of what the world outside was really like was extremely distorted; their understanding even of what they were seeking to achieve, 'freedom', immensely simplistic. As I observed before, Martha reported that quite often the local OPM-supporting tribespeople would simply just sit and wait .... believing that something called 'merdeka' or 'freedom' would somehow descend on them. Also, at an early stage in the negotiations where focal issues for negotiation were at the lofty height of freedom for the Papuan people, UN recognition and so on, a new negotiation demand was made—to fly in a plastic bucket to the people when the negotiators next returned.

Meanwhile, the outside world did not fully understand the Papuans either. The ICRC were however very constructively engaged.

After the military accepted that the ICRC could take the lead role in negotiations—this was during the time when the OPM group was heading west but the precise whereabouts of Kwalik and the hostages was not known, the ICRC took a range of actions to re-establish contact, including messages left with tribes in areas where Kwalik might go, presence of ICRC personnel in the jungle in places where they could be contacted, and so on. Eventually contact was established. And then the first helicopter flight of the ICRC went in—led by Belgian doctor Frank Meyer. The detail of what happened is highly revealing.

Frank Meyer was taken 400 m from the helicopter, sat on the edge of a 100 m deep ravine, surrounded by a large number of naked tribesmen in pig-fat, feathers, with spears and the occasional gun, and confronted by the OPM junior leader, Titus, who Meyer described as very tough. Titus simply stared at Meyer for a good two minutes and then said,

> What do you prefer me to wear? T-shirt or Koteka (penis sheath)?

Meyer, momentarily taken aback, then replied,

> That is your choice, whether you choose to wear traditional or modern clothes, not mine.

And after a short pause,

> But I have three T-shirts to give you if you are cold.

Perhaps sitting on the edge of a 100 m ravine surrounded by a naked rebel army dressed in penis sheaths but carrying spears and rifles sharpened Meyer's perceptiveness, but this was the correct answer to the test and allowed further communication to be pursued. Meyer had said two things that resonated with the OPM cause, 'you are the people who have the right to choose', and I come to bring you a 'gift' not to take something. The Lorentz'95 group had broken these rules and thereby invited their own capture by the OPM.

These two issues, gifts and offer of choice, became the core of the subsequent series of tests that Meyer confronted. Each time, passing the test led to a further stage in the negotiation, or a higher level of OPM leader who he could subsequently consult.

At the later meeting where Meyer was scheduled to meet Daniel, Meyer asked on arrival.

> Is Daniel (Kagoya) here?
> No!
> Then", said Meyer, "I will come back tomorrow.
> Am I not worth talking to?" questioned the OPM representative, to which Meyer responded,
> Of course, if you have something to say.

Meyer then ordered the helicopter away for 30 min. (The helicopter could not stay on the ground at that stage as it contained Indonesians to whom the OPM could have been hostile).

Meyer did not know Daniel by sight. *One minute later* Daniel appeared, saying to Meyer,

You are here. *I* decide when you will leave, not you.

Meyer had passed the second test—by being prepared to communicate with the people rather than being directed only to the hostage negotiations.

Daniel's first question then was,

What are you coming here to take away, the hostages?

Meyer's response passed the third test as he replied,

I do not come to take away anything. I come to give you these (packages of food and supplies). You will *give me* the hostages when you decide.

Meyer subsequently noticed that Daniel had a wound in his foot, and medically treated it. He gave Daniel several T-shirts. Daniel brought back pig meat, saying to Meyer,

If you eat this with me we will be friends for life.

Meyer took out his Swiss penknife, cut the meat for both of them, and gave the knife to Daniel. Daniel gave the remainder of the pig flesh to Meyer.

At their next meeting Daniel asked Meyer who he had eaten the pig meat with. Meyer responded, 'My boss', which, honoring the gift, pleased Daniel.

Meyer was concerned however that Daniel was carrying his automatic rifle and asked Daniel why. Daniel's response was, "I carry this gun to protect *you*!".

After Meyer medically examined the hostages, he then also examined the villagers and the OPM, including Daniel. Daniel, he noticed, was now carrying Meyer's gift of the Swiss penknife on a cord around his neck.

Following the medicals, Meyer recommended lifting out the village chief by helicopter, who he described as *very* sick, indeed in appearance like a Papuan 'mummy' in colour and appearance, but breathing. Meyer was concerned that the chief might die anyway.

ICRC flights into Ngselma continued after this—with little direct progress on negotiation. In the context of concern that the chief could die—in a place remote from his tribe with some possible responsibility attributed to the ICRC the main purpose of these flights was—specifically to bring 'gifts' of highly valued information from the hospital about the chief's health.

Relations continued to get better. Meyer had already passed the tests to move up the OPM hierarchy in his negotiations from Titus to Daniel, and eventually got to Kwalik.

On 29th February, Meyer met with Kwalik.

By this stage Kwalik had received Moses Weror's new liberation message, he recognized that the world had woken up, that maintaining an OPM presence around Ngselma was difficult and a continuous drain on the economies of the local villages. But, on the other hand, he knew that other OPM members, including in his own group, did not want the hostages released. In absence of a high-power radio transmitter—that the military had expressly prevented being taken in, Kwalik could not talk to outsiders or more senior OPM people. He really did not know what to do.

Kwalik therefore asked Meyer what the outside world thought of the current hostage situation, and what Meyer's view was about what he should do. Meyer's response was,

> I will not tell you. Think it over.

Again, Meyer was strictly adhering to the value of choice being in the hands of the Papuans, not of outsiders …the Papuan way.

The values of choice, of exchange rather than domination, and of the right of the Papuans to their own land were central to all negotiations. But, at times we did not appreciate adequately what this implied.

In the very earliest days of the crisis, I sat down with the Resident Representative of UNDP for virtually one whole night accompanied by a fax machine, several cups of coffee and a telephone. By morning we had organized letters to the OPM from the Secretary General of the United Nations, Boutros-Bouros Gali, and the Director-General of UNESCO, Federico Mayor, both calling on the OPM to release the hostages. We also set up action that later was played out with letters from the Head of the European Union, the Archbishop of Canterbury …….. and the Pope. Both letters from the UN heads emphasized the role of the kidnapped hostages as conservationists seeking to assist West Papua and called on behalf of the international community on the OPM to release them. Mayor wrote, for example,

> The taking of hostages is condemned throughout the world, whatever the circumstances and whatever the purpose.

It wasn't until later, when Kwalik received the letter from the Pope—actually, a draft read to him by Bishop Meninghoff at his negotiation meeting on 25th January, that we realized that the international interventions had *not* shown adequate cognizance of the Papuans' values and cause. Kwalik, a former seminarian, would, we thought, be particularly likely to pay attention to an entreaty from the Pope. At the time of the Bishop's meeting the actual letter had not reached him as he had travelled from Jayapura, his base, to Wamena, and then up to Mapnduma—just as the original letter arrived in Jayapura. Meninghoff therefore read to Kwalik the letter as reported to him over the phone.

Kwalik listened attentively to the Bishop's report. He then observed that the Pope expressed concern about the plight of the hostages, but said nothing about the troubles faced by the West Papuan people. This brought to an end discussion of the Pope's correspondence. It would appear that Kwalik interpreted the Pope's intervention as a *misdirected moral directive* rather than a positive sign of international attention.

It was also reported to us that the letter from the Archbishop of Canterbury had been dealt with in a curiously Papuan way. The OPM leader who received it, Daniel, looked at the letter, held it in one hand as if weighing it, and said,

> "On this side I have this letter, and on the other, the hostages. This (the letter) weighs almost nothing". He then threw the letter away.

Within the negotiation discussions Kwalik had with the ICRC he continuously moved into monologues about the sins of the colonizers and the United Nations and all 'white faces' who have come to 'take' from West Papua. These monologues represented a catharsis of his past for Kwalik. The reason he gave for bringing in the Netherlands and British officials to a meeting was because he wanted to 'vomit' on them. As the ICRC negotiators observed, the dynamic of negotiation required people who can listen, accept, and acknowledge Kwalik's and the West Papua peoples' history, not argue. Hence, there had to be time in the negotiations for Kwalik's bile to be exhausted. More importantly however, the very basis of being able to negotiate at all required an understanding by the outside world that what was fundamentally at the heart of dialogue was the Papuan values of exchange of gifts and of choice in redressing the exploitation of the land and its people in the past.

Similarly, we misjudged the valence of Papuan values in early negotiations to have Martha and another woman—who was sick—released as a signal of good faith and because of their at-risk medical condition.

Already we had taken heart from the fact that the OPM had released hostages. Jacobus, a West Papuan, his sick wife and child, were released to go back to their village, Mapnduma, in the first few days, and initially for Jacobus to make a clear statement of the rebels' demands to the outside world. Indeed, by this time 14 of the local Papuans taken in the original abduction in Mapnduma had been allowed to go back to their families. The OPM leaders then allowed Frank Momberg, the German hostage, fluent in Indonesian as well as English and a WWF member, to fly out of Mapnduma with the negotiating clergy—after swearing on the Bible that he would return—to convey the message of the OPM clearly to the outside world. This was on 15th January.

Through the negotiators we persistently were sending message for the rebels to allow Martha to be released.

What we did not realize was the prize she represented.

First she was a woman. In Papuan society, women are prized by men as valued exchange objects—with a status that arguably was contested by pigs, that is, of very high value. More importantly, Martha was a symbol of the United Nations—no matter how many times we kept insisting that really she had been on holidays and did not represent an official UN person or view. She was still the UN for the OPM, the international body that had recognized the legitimacy of Indonesia's right over their land in the first place, and therefore with the power to reverse this earlier decision. Martha was therefore very *unlikely* to be released until the very end. Indeed, Kwalik had, as I noted earlier, already made plans for her baby when born in captivity, to be named 'Merdeka', to be kept as symbol of the OPM's struggle, and to be swept on-high into battle at the front of the warriors as they engaged their enemies.

The people, at heart however, dealt with the world in terms of straightforward values honed from millennia of isolated tribal life, and with honor. For example, a major problem of 'honor' arose when, as a sign of respect at the death in a Jakarta prison of Papuan activist Tom Wainggai, the OPM released his brother, Bram Wainggai, who had been held as one of the hostages. The problem arose because Bram was allowed to fly out from the rebel camp by helicopter direct to the main Baliem Valley town of Wamena, and not through Mapnduma, the place where he was captured. Already there was tribal rivalry over who 'owned' the captives. The N'duga claimed the hostages as they were kidnapped in their territory. But Kwalik's own tribe, the Amungme, claimed them as Kwalik had run with the hostages from the military into his own tribal lands and this was where they were now being held. The kidnappers were a mixed group containing both tribes. The N'duga were incensed when Bram Wainggai was released as they believed he should have been released through Mapnduma so that the N'duga could formally 'apologize' to him for allowing him to be kidnapped on their territory. This tension came to a head in the week of 22nd March during an ICRC visit when fighting nearly broke out between the groups, and Kwalik then demanded the negotiators bring him firearms so that his people could 'hold off' the N'duga. As a sign of honor, also remember the individual Mapnuduma villager who I mentioned earlier and who declared personal war on Daniel Kogoya and all his 200 warriors at the time when the hostages were taken because he disagreed so strongly with the kidnapping. Indeed, as the hostages could see, the people of the Lorentz where the four-month drama took place, mainly wanted to just live their lives with dignity and to share in the fruits of development, such as health services and education. The villagers shared their food and made sacrifices on the hostages' behalf, and towards the end were telling the hostages that they were anxious for the captured group to be allowed to return to their families and their normal lives. But, as Mark Van der Wall observed, the villagers' quite simple interests did not seem to be of any concern to Kelly Kwalik, the rebel leader. His goal was political. As Mark is reported in Jakarta Post on 28th May 1996,

> Kelly Kwalik proved he had no interest in the will of the people or in their welfare when he broke his promise to release us peacefully on May 8th.

And, in keeping with traditional culture, the tribal Papuans entered negotiating interactions in ways that made sense within their own tribal life. Titus, when impersonating Kelly Kwalik in interview with Ben Bohane observed—in Ben Bohane's words,

> They (Kwalik's followers) looked at the OPM rebellion from a tribal law perspective because it was the only way, the only prism, through which they could make sense of what was going on around them, and it gave them a solid pretext for armed struggle. If someone comes into your village and steals your pigs, and does not tell you, and does not offer compensation, you have a right to kill them. That is tribal law. They saw Freeport and Indonesia as coming in and taking their assets and offering no compensation; therefore they had the right to kill them. That was the essence of their legitimate struggle.[1]

In the midst of the hostage negotiations, parallel negotiations started with Freeport on 14th March at the Sheraton Hotel in Timika– stimulated by the serious riots that had just occurred. The meeting of around 70 people was attended by General Probowo and several other military and administrative personnel. Chief Executive of Freeport, James R Moffett—a larger-than-life

---

[1] Reported to me in a personal meeting with Ben Bohane, September, 2014.

no-nonsense Texan known otherwise as Jimbob who, to appropriately sycophantic and applauding audiences did serious Elvis Presley impersonations at Freeport functions (which I had the privilege of seeing, by the way)—was confronted by the highly respected Amungme woman, Mama Yosepha. She spoke simply and colourfully in Amungme language.

> My son Moffett, in the past I put you inside my noken (the native woven bag used by Amungme women to carry babies and piglets). I took you with me wherever I went, but I did not realize that you actually suck my blood until its all drained, and I remain only in bones and without flesh. Now, I pick you out of my noken and will throw you far away

At this stage, to the shocked response of the audience, Mama Yoken threw the noken to the floor. As Moffett later responded, offering to consider the tribal demands seriously, he asked Mama Yosepha,

> "Mama, can I be put inside your noken again?" Mama Yosepha answered, When I have thrown something, I will not pick it up again. But, if you promise to fulfill our demand, written on paper, then I will put you inside my noken again.

After this, Mama Yosepha and the other Amungme put forward their demands.

The End Game

The saga of the hostage crisis continued—with reversals, delays, false hopes, derailing cross-currents—but finally, the ICRC's continuous presence as mediator worked, and Kwalik agreed to handing over the hostages in a formal ceremony to be held on Wednesday 8th May 1996—symbolically chosen because it was International Red Cross Day.

Demands of the rebels had moved through several stages, as had the negotiation strategy from our side.

Initially, until Kelly Kwalik entered the discussions directly, the basic demands were those carried out to communicate with the outside world by the German hostage, Frank Momberg, just a week after the hostages were captured, that is, respect for and recognition of their land (the essence of a 'Free Papua'), compensation for land lost to mining development and for lives lost, involvement in decision making, return of tribal people to their land from coastal areas to which they have been displaced, and an end to devastation caused by Freeport and other commercial interests, particularly, logging. From the Western negotiators' point of view, the objective of negotiations until 24th January was to obtain the quick release of the hostages from the kidnappers headed by Daniel Kagoya, leader of the original attack. We were seeking to convince the kidnappers that their objective of calling the world's attention to their plight and objectives had been achieved. Kelly Kwalik then showed up with harder line demands for freedom and recognition and communication broke down—for around six weeks when we simply did not know where the rebels were and they kept moving, unable to communicate anyway without a radio.

The second phase of negotiations proceeded during this time, with the ICRC taking over, establishing listening posts through the jungle and leaving messages until contact was finally re-established on 18th February.

The third phase, lasting until the last week of March, initiated in Frank Meyer's clifftop interaction described earlier, sought to address all the issues related to releasing the hostages. These included any OPM demands, assurance of the safety and welfare of the hostages—and dealing with or waiting for resolution of internal tribal conflicts and issues. By the end of this phase, it seemed to us that all possible answers had been given and it was now up to the rebels to release the hostages or take full responsibility for the military and other consequences if they did not.

The fourth phase was a time of waiting. The ICRC 'tightened the screws' on the OPM, ceasing to play the role that ICRC Chief, Henri Fournier, described as 'Santa Claus'—delivering food and medicines or whatever the rebels or hostages asked for. At this stage, full responsibility was placed on Kelly Kwalik to come to a decision. It was critical on our side to dissuade external interests expressing impatience, for the military were looking for an excuse to move in—given the length of time the 'soft' approach had been taking.

At last Kwalik agreed to the release and a hand-over ceremony. Final arrangements were put into place in a series of meetings during the first week of May. The signs of assurance that the liberation would go ahead lay in the commitments of the OPM to the liberation ceremony itself. The supply of pigs and food for such an important event is symbolic. These supplies therefore had to be gathered from specific representative villages - and brought by ICRC helicopter into Geselema where the ceremony was to be conducted. Ten key leaders of the tribes also had to be present, including Kwalik's father. Meanwhile the ICRC had obtained approval from Geneva for a long-term commitment to the West Papua people—including medical clinics with doctors and a full-time presence monitoring human rights—together with a promise of no military retribution—as long as Kwalik released the hostages.

On our side, representation was tricky. The UN could not be formally involved, nor could anyone as a diplomatic representative of any of the countries of which the foreign hostages were citizens. The solution, agreed by the Government of Indonesia and the rebels was to bring in representatives of the National Red Cross Associations of the countries from which the hostages originated—that is, a diplomatic sleight of hand appearing to symbolize national representation but not having any formal diplomatic status as such. The ICRC assured me that Kwalik accepted that there was appropriate international representation.

Kwalik specifically committed to Henri Fournier, Head of the ICRC mission, that given the enormous financial and political commitment that the ICRC was making to the event he *would* go ahead with the ceremony and hand-over of hostages. And two of the rebel leaders, Silas and Titus, commenced goodbye celebrations with the hostages four days before the scheduled event. Things were looking good. We believed that for Kwalik to change his mind, given the degree of preparation, ritual, and tribal commitments, would have meant enormous loss of face in terms of traditional values. It seemed highly unlikely that Kwalik was setting up the whole show to mock his own people.

At the same time, we also discovered that the OPM had built a shelter for the media representatives. Kwalik asked for a radio so he could hear the international news reports, and insisted on having a video camera brought in to record the event—not just any video camera, but a *very large* video camera, as in his mind, the larger the camera, the more it represented the internationalism of the news recording of the event. It was my job as Head of the UN Office whose brief was to handle media issues and freedom in the country, to find and supply the camera. This was not easy, as camera hire stores these days are increasingly moving towards smaller and micro-size equipment; large cameras are a thing of the past. After a lot of footwork around Jakarta, my staff finally found a *giant*—and quite old—camera, crated it up, and sent it off to the ceremony. (Getting the camera *back* out of the jungle to the video hire store, was, I might add, a whole other saga).

7

"Jungle Hostages—III: A Deeply Troubled Resolution"

The Agreed Hand-Over Ceremony—So Close!

On Wednesday 8th May the arranged celebration proceeded to schedule, starting early in the morning after several helicopters flew in to Geselema shortly after 5.00 am with the ICRC, the foreign Red Cross representatives and supplies. Four to five hundred people were present. Seventeen pigs were sacrificed. Speeches were given about the end of the drama, some of the original abducting group started saying goodbye to the hostages, certificates were brought in for signature.

Then Kelly Kwalik entered the scene, having not participated until now. Dressed in a brown possum-skin balaclava, he played to the camera—indicating his belief that the speech would be broadcast worldwide. To the surprise of the crowd, he spoke in Indonesian—a language little understood by most of his fellow tribespeople, so at the end of the speech the people applauded but did not know what Kwalik had said—he was speaking to a world stage, not to them. Kwalik had however stridently claimed that *the hostages would not be released until Papua was free*.

Suddenly, the ceremony collapsed.

The hostages had been happily sitting, watching the ceremony's progress in the belief that at last it was all over. Initially they did not comprehend that Kwalik had reversed everything.

Simple interests and values did not seem to be of any concern to Kelly Kwalik. His goal appeared to be entirely political. As Australian journalist Mark Davis was reported saying in the Jakarta Post on 28th May 1996:

Kelly Kwalik proved he had no interest in the will of the people or in their welfare when he broke his promise to release us peacefully on May 8th.

Kwalik later claimed on the Australian ABC *Four Corners* TV program, *Blood on the Cross,* in an interview with Mark Davis, that the ICRC had betrayed him by not passing on his messages to the international media and by not being 'serious' during the negotiations to set up the Liberation Ceremony. Given what Henri Fournier, Ferenc Meyer and their ICRC colleagues had done, and the ICRC level of commitment of people and resources to support the agreed hand-over ceremony, this claim is not credible. Kwalik claimed to ABC Four Corners journalist Mark Davis that the whole point of the kidnapping had been to publicize the struggle of the West Papuans, and that the ICRC had betrayed him by not releasing the press reports he gave them. He complained that official government representatives from overseas were not present which was a key part of the deal. From the ICRC's point of view their use of international ICRC participants had been fully transparent and agreed by Kwalik. It seemed to us at the time, that Kwalik had simply reneged because he wanted more publicity for the cause or for himself personally.

Significantly and disturbingly, within 24 h of the aborted ceremony a related but more radical group in London, TAPOL, issued a press statement describing the happenings of the Wednesday event in detail, applauding the non-release of the hostages, and claiming the key reason was that the ICRC had sold out by allowing the military to come in close to the event.

This was totally untrue. From the information available to us, the military stayed outside the agreed 12 km perimeter, and on that day, they were actually 60 km away. The ICRC continuously overflew the surrounding areas by helicopter prior to and during the ceremony to ensure the military stayed out.

What was disturbing about the press release was that it contained information that could not have been known by an outsider or by someone who had not been briefed about what Kwalik was intending to do.

It was generally agreed that TAPOL had advance contact with Kwalik and that his strategy had been communicated some time prior to the 8th May ceremony. Kwalik, perhaps alone amongst his tribal partners, had planned all along that the ceremony would provide him with a massive 'big man' platform to speak to the world about the OPM cause.

Meanwhile, although Daniel Kogoya may have been aware of what was taking place, the rest of the OPM's hard-core leadership was taken completely by surprise.

What followed was utter chaos. Fortunately, there was no violence.

Devastated by the turn-around, the hostages were taken away by the OPM freedom fighters into the jungle, under the command of Silas, leaving everyone else in total disarray.

But Silas disagreed with Kwalik. He asked the ICRC team to return the next day. Kwalik stated that he wanted to talk with his troops anyway. Fournier agreed, although he was very angry at being 'duded' at the last minute.

At 7.00am on the morning of 9th May Sylvianne Bonadei and Ferenc Meyer came back to the village of Geselema—Ferenc to check on the health of the hostages, and Sylvianne to talk with the OPM leaders. Henri Fournier flew to Prabowo's military base, Keneyam and waited for General Prabowo. Sylvianne and Ferenc spoke with Daniel and Silas.

After three hours in Geselema, Sylvianne and Ferenc flew out to Keneyam and reported to Henri Fournier. Sylvianne asserts that she brought 'good news' to Fournier. There was still hope. They just had to wait three days. Daniel had said that he was confident if given three days to contact Kwalik that Kwalik would agree to hand over the hostages. Sylvianne would have reported to Henri Fournier somewhere between 10.00am and 11.00am in the morning of 9th May.

The precise time lines matters. From here on accounts of what actually happened vary.

At 11.30am Fournier, from his direct information to us, told Prabowo that negotiations had failed because Kwalik had had a 'change of heart' and reneged. There was no longer any chance of further negotiation so the ICRC was pulling out.

Fournier—and his boss, Michel Monod—later claimed that Sylvianne had been sent to Geselema to take a final offer to the OPM, 'release the hostages now or the ICRC will withdraw immediately'. This is also what we in the negotiating team were told. Sylvianne says this is not the case.

Subsequently the OPM said that they did not know that negotiations had ended with the ICRC pulling out. According to Sylvianne, neither did she.

Then again, it is possible that Sylvianne did not effectively communicate to the OPM that Fournier's position was an ultimatum: "Release the hostages now, or the ICRC will pull out". Not, "maybe he could accept yet another promise". Whatever the case, it appears that after Sylvianne's three hours talking with Daniel and Silas, the OPM believed that the ICRC would fly back three days later.

After meeting with Sylvianne and Ferenc, Henri Fournier immediately issued a Press Release stating that negotiations had failed and the ICRC would not be involved any further. It took until 3.00 pm before the statement was actually made public through Geneva Headquarters. The declaration could not have reached the people in Geselema as communications of international media communiqués into the West Papuan jungle only happened some time later by radio. From what Sylvianne reports, the OPM and the people who were gathered in Geselema believed they had three days to put a hostage transfer into place.

Fournier and Ferenc Meyer started organizing their trip back to Jakarta, but left Sylvianne in West Papua, sending her down to Timika to maintain an ICRC presence, monitoring and assisting the hostages if possible, and in particular with medical support. Martha was of specific concern. Fournier and Meyer flew out of the Keneyam military base for Jakarta at 3.00 pm.

What we knew at the time was that Henri Fournier and Ferenc Meyer returned to Jakarta that evening. Along with Russell Betts of WWF, I met with them. Fournier was furious and depressed. He told us that Kwalik had not only refused to release the hostages but had evicted the ICRC team from Geselema village. No more negotiation was possible.

Fournier told us that he had had enough. So many times, we had come close to the release of the hostages just for Kwalik to renege. Fournier had made an enormous commitment to support the 8th May Liberation Ceremony—bringing ICRC representatives from Europe, as well as people and pigs from many of the local villages, all the while ensuring the overflying of surrounding areas to monitor possible military movements.

Kwalik had thrown it all back in his face on 8th May. It is not surprising that Fournier was both furious and did not believe the (alleged) new assurance that in three days perhaps there might be a resolution—although he did not report this. The only curious thing is that Fournier claimed to us that the ICRC had been thrown out of Geselema by the OPM, whilst Sylvianne's later report stated that Daniel had offered a possible resolution if they waited another three days. We knew nothing of the conflicting accounts—just the explanation that Henri brought back to us on the evening of 9th May.

The reality was that in West Papua, Geselema was no longer a protected village. But it appears the people did not know this.

It was not until over a week later that we discovered what happened next.

No information at all emerged about what was going on in the depths of the West Papuan jungle at the time. Even a week later what had actually happened in Geselema was shrouded in military secrecy. More recently released information tells us more.

It was highly dramatic, almost the stuff of a Hollywood movie, but unfortunately, also a serious denial of the human rights of the West Papuans.

7 "Jungle Hostages—III: A Deeply Troubled Resolution"

Allegedly, Prabowo personally led an attack on Geselema at 2.30 pm on Thursday 9th May.

His troops had clearly left their Military Base at Keneyam whilst Henri Fournier and Ferenc Meyer were still there. It is unlikely however that the ICRC personnel knew anything of Prabowo's intention. Fournier claimed on the ABC 'Blood on the Cross' program that he did not know of the 'white helicopter' attack until two months after the incident. The attack was also 30 min prior to the release of the ICRC press statement announcing the failure of negotiations.

The villagers in Geselema reported seeing a white helicopter with the logo of the Red Cross fly in.

The villagers believed it was the same Red Cross helicopter that had previously transported the negotiators and medical support in to talk with the rebel leaders and to bring medical and food relief. They came out into the clearing to welcome the passengers. They had grown to trust the International Red Cross.

Instead, soldiers jumped out and began shooting. At least eight villagers were killed and many injured.

Daniel Kagoya was there along with a small number of his OPM freedom fighters. So too were a number of civilians from other villages who had come in for the previous day's ceremony and stayed overnight.

The Papuans had become used to the sound of helicopters and could distinguish between the ICRC helicopter and those used by the military. As a result they were not afraid of the 'white' helicopter as it approached.

Then, immediately after the white helicopter landed, five military helicopters arrived carrying soldiers. The people would have run into the jungle if they had known the helicopters arriving were from the military.

It was also reported by locals that the first people out of the 'white' helicopter were white. According to their reports, four white people jumped out and began firing on the villagers. Kagoya asserted in his ABC *'Blood on the Cross'* interview in 1999 that a female 'soldier' was first out and pointed, identifying him as the leader, then fell to the ground before the shooting started. Sylvianne was implicated but very strongly denies she was involved. Given everything else about Sylvianne's involvement caring for the Papuans and even, that morning, supporting the OPM promise of further negotiation, her involvement in the 'white helicopter' attack is not credible.

There is no question now that the incident happened. Nevertheless, there are conflicting reports about who the 'white' armed soldiers were and what the circumstances were surrounding the event.

What we do know is that Prabowo had a narrow window of opportunity for decisive action. The ICRC's departure from negotiations would very likely be reported by radio—and therefore be known by the OPM in the village within the next day. Prabowo had a green light to attack now rather than wait. His most personally beneficial option was to capitalise on the ICRC's distinctive helicopter colour and marking and the OPM and the villagers' trust that the ICRC was still engaged. And as Sylvianne reported, she had told the OPM that the ICRC officials were going to come back.

We know that the ICRC helicopter had returned to Prabowo's West Papua base at Keneyam and the Red Cross insignia was still emblazoned on it. It had been hired by the ICRC from Freeport, the mining giant, the target of much of the protests by the OPM, but via an intermediary contracting company, Airfast. Prabowo had the opportunity to pick up the helicopter set down at his military base and pay the contractor for its use. Although the 'white' helicopter took off from Keneyam at 2.30 pm, 30 min before the ICRC team left for Jakarta, there is no reason that the ICRC team would know that the helicopter might have a new mission.

The Papuans went out welcoming the ICRC into Geselema. But they were met with unexpected violence. Prabowo was the leader of the mission. White soldiers were at the vanguard. The result was that at least eight local villagers were killed in the shooting.

The military subsequently claimed that in the course of their campaign to release the hostages they had killed eight OPM 'rebels'. Martha and the other hostages were very clear that no OPM freedom fighters were killed by the military. Instead, the military sought to hide their murder of Geselema villagers by pretending they were all OPM rebels. It is highly likely that the body count of eight murdered Geselema villagers was conveniently disguised in the official military report of the hostage release operation under the claim that they were the eight 'rebels' shot in the line of duty.

The later (1999) Australian ABC Four Corners television documentary, *Blood on the Cross* by Mark Davis sought to implicate the ICRC Head, Henri Fournier. Neither his, nor Sylvianne's, direct knowledge or involvement in the 'white helicopter' incident is credible. Fournier was however, very angry at Kwalik's about-face and possibly may not have assumed that the villagers of Geselema and the OPM knew they were no longer protected. There can be no implication of involvement beyond even this possible allegation.

The ICRC formally answered these allegations. To quote a 1999 report from the ICRC Resource Centre after an internal review:

> Allegations have gone so far as to accuse the ICRC of actually taking part in the military operations, and an ICRC delegate of even opening fire on the village's

inhabitants. This accusation is as farcical as it is grotesque. It can nevertheless not be ruled out that Westerners posing as ICRC delegates took part in the operation.[1]

The incident however could do nothing but harm the reputation of 'white noses', the ICRC, and their ability to operate for peace in the area. Previously, the village people had extremely little contact with the outside world, and their prior experience of white people was primarily of missionaries who came in peace. It took some years before the ICRC was again trusted enough to re-engage in operations in West Papua. The Indonesian Government forced the ICRC to close its Office in Jayapura, the capital of West Papua.

Then, in 2013 Edmund McWilliams, US Foreign Affairs Counsellor in the US Embassy in Jakarta at the time (1996–1999), brought to light an extraordinary alternate scenario for the whole end-game of the hostage crisis.

Prabowo's alleged role in the 'white helicopter' incident remains the same. But explanation of the events that led up to it, in particular, the aborted Liberation Ceremony, is very different indeed. McWilliams claims that Prabowo had recognized that he would enhance his reputation domestically and internationally by arranging release of the hostages by negotiation where he was in control and the ICRC were mediators. Kwalik had finally agreed to hand over the hostages on 8th May in exchange for a military undertaking of no reprisals and an ICRC pledge to establish a network of health clinics in the Mapnduma area.

But, counter to all other information we received, McWilliams claims from 'separate interviews with the two most senior ICRC officials', that on the eve of the transfer (scheduled for 8th May), the 'senior ICRC official involved in the negotiations' (presumably Fournier) was summoned by Prabowo to his West Papua military headquarters at Keneyam.

> There, an enraged Prabowo told the ICRC official that Suharto's elder daughter, "Tutut", was planning to fly to West Papua the following day to officiate at the hostage transfer in her capacity as Indonesian Red Cross Chairperson. This, Prabowo told the ICRC official, would rob him of the credit for the hostage rescue.

Prabowo pressed the ICRC official to phone Jakarta to seek to get Tutut or, Siti Hardiyanti Rukmana—her formal name, to abort her mission. The 'official' made the call but learnt that Tutut was already *en route*. Prabowo

---

[1] ICRC Resource Center (1999) ICRC Role during the Irian Jaya Hostage Crisis (January-May 1996), Posted 27th August, Reference: www.icrc.org/eng/resources/documents/misc/57jpz.html.

then moved to scuttle the transfer of the hostages at the next day's Liberation Ceremony'.

> This was done by conveying to Kwalik through a source Kwalik trusted that the Indonesian military had been acting in bad faith all along and would immediately target Kwalik and his personnel once the transfer had taken place. This, the ICRC officials claimed, was the reason for Kwalik's last minute 'change of heart'.[2]

McWilliams' report is credible. The real truth remains hidden in the West Papuan jungles and in unreleased information in Indonesian military intelligence files.

All that is certain is that Kwalik aborted the Liberation Ceremony at the last minute, and that under Prabowo's command, the military attacked Geselema the next day disguised under the insignia of the International Red Cross.

We do know what happened next to the hostages.

The Trauma of Release

The military started searching for the OPM and their captured hostages from 9th May onwards.

It was a prepared strategic statement, not a spontaneous outburst. And suddenly, the ceremony collapsed and the hostages, devastated by the turn-around, were taken away by the rebels into the jungle under the command of Silas, leaving everyone else in total disarray. Kwalik stated he wanted to speak to his troops before he did anything now, and asked the ICRC team to return the next day.

On the morning of 9th May the ICRC team came back, but Kwalik not only refused to release the hostages but evicted the ICRC team out of the location. Henri Fournier and the ICRC team gave up and went back to Jakarta, totally depressed. No more negotiation seemed possible.

It appeared that Kwalik had been planning this about-face all along—even though it was at enormous cost to his credibility amongst his own people, perhaps to humiliate the military and Indonesian Government, but perhaps more because he had now tasted the power that came by being attached to a 'world' event, and could not put it down: once the hostages were gone, so too

---

[2] McWilliams, E (2005) Response to Efforts to Deny Crimes Against Humanity in West Papua, East Timor ETAN/US, Internet site, www.etan.org/news/2005/11mcfet.htm, November.

was Kelly Kwalik's presence as a 'big man' able to walk the world stage. Kwalik later claimed on the Australian ABC *Four Corners* TV program, *Blood on the Cross* interview with Mark Davis that the ICRC had betrayed him by not passing on his messages to the international media and by not being 'serious' during negotiations which set up the Liberation Ceremony.

Meanwhile, although Daniel Kogoya *may* have been aware of what was happening, the rest of the OPM's hardcore leadership was taken completely by surprise. There was however no violence.

Significantly and disturbingly, within 24 h of the aborted ceremony a radical group in London, TAPOL, issued a press statement describing the happenings of the Wednesday meeting in detail, applauding the non-release of the hostages, and claiming a key reason was that the ICRC had sold out by assisting the military to come in close—although this last statement was untrue, the military having been kept outside a 12 km perimeter, and on that day, being some 60 km away, with the ICRC constantly overflying the surrounding area by helicopter to ensure the military stayed put. What was disturbing about the press release was that it contained information that *could not* have been known by an outsider or by someone who had not been briefed about what Kwalik was *intending* to do. It was generally agreed that TAPOL had advance contact with Kwalik and his strategy had been communicated some time prior to the 8th May ceremony. In other words, Kwalik—perhaps alone amongst his tribal partners—had planned all along that the ceremony provided nothing but a massive 'big man' platform for him to speak to the world about his cause. Kwalik subsequently *claimed* to the ABC Four Corners journalist Mark Davis that the whole point of the kidnapping had been to publicise the struggle of the West Papuans, that the ICRC had betrayed him by not releasing the press reports he gave them, and that official government representatives from overseas were not present: From the ICRC's point of view their use of international ICRC participants *had* been fully transparent. Kwalik, it seemed to us, had simply reneged either because he wanted *more* publicity for the cause or because he feared dropping off the world 'big-man' stage.

What followed was chaos. The ICRC pulled out. The military engaged—at last being released to follow their most desired plan to prove themselves heroes by engaging the rebels and forcibly liberating the hostages by the means they knew best, military action.

It was not until over a week later that we discovered what happened next as at the time we could obtain no information at all about what was going on in the depths of the Papuan jungle.

In fact, the military moved in immediately after the failure of the 8th May celebration and subsequent last-ditch ICRC meeting. The hostages had already been taken into the jungle by the OPM. For the next week the OPM and hostages remained within a short distance of Geselema, primarily circling, but every day, walking continuously, and stopping only when it became dark. The military could not find them on the ground. Indeed, Mark and Martha reported to me that at least twice, once on Thursday 09th May, the first day after the failed celebration, the military were within 200 m of the hostages. The hostages could hear the winches winding down the soldiers from the helicopters, but the military could not find them. The military took over all the gardens. As a consequence the OPM and hostages had to remain in the jungle for five days without food. They started to become very weak. Meanwhile, the OPM had continued fairly loose guarding of the hostages, often with different people each day, constantly moving.

The military brought in tracker dogs. But most importantly they used a drone aircraft with infrared sensors operating at night, and through this they were able to identify that the hostages had been split up into two groups and their precise location. Although the Indonesian military denied any foreign military assistance, the *Far Eastern Economic Review* (which had a very well connected and knowledgeable reporter based in Indonesia) reported on 24th May 1996 that several Israeli-made Mazlat Scout pilotless drones were shipped from Singapore by a Singaporean Air Force C-130 cargo plane in late April, and subsequently flew pre-programmed routes over rebel-held jungle to detect body heat through thermal imaging, thus helping the Indonesian Special Forces to pinpoint the rebels. On 15th May the hostages actually *saw* one of these 'tiny' planes, described by one of the Indonesian hostages who escaped, Jualita Tanasale, as 'like a toy'.

The military then moved in to surround the two groups.

However, it was not the military that found the hostages, but rather a group of eight of the hostages which found the military—on Wednesday 15th May, after being separated from their guards who had hung back with other purposes in mind. Jualita Tanasale, one of the Indonesian hostages who escaped, reported in a prepared statement issued after the hostage release by the Jakarta Biological Science Club what happened as, to the overbearing roar of a helicopter overhead, the hostages reached a very deep ravine:

> We had to descend to reach the stream at the bottom. Most of the rebels were in front, the British hostages followed, then the Indonesians, then some more rebels, and our fellow Dutch hostages were the last.
> Before they reached the bottom, the squad's commander ordered everyone to climb the hill again. The line changed: the Britons were in the front and

followed by the Indonesians. The Dutch couple (Martha and Mark) refused to climb again.

And then something really tragic happened. We never expected it. One of the rebels swung an axe at our colleague Navy (Panekenan), who did not put up a fight at all. This incident was witnessed by all the other hostages.

We panicked. The Indonesian hostages felt that the rebels were eyeing us as if they wanted to kill us all. So we all scrambled to save our lives. Markus (Warip) became the next target of the rebels and he simply jumped into the deep ravine. (It was reported to me separately that Markus had been warned in advance by a 3-year old local child to run away, so was prepared). Then the rebels started heading towards Theis (Yosias Matheis Lasamahu). Unfortunately for him, they caught him. The others ran towards the stream below with all the remaining strength they had.

It turned out that the ABRI troops had been in pursuit all this time and were not far from our location. They were just across the stream ...

The official report of the Biological Science Club, perhaps being appropriately diplomatic in the prevailing Indonesian context, then speaks positively about the military gathering the hostages together to protect them, and, because it was dark, going to search for the missing people the next morning.

What actually happened in the end-game was very different, and not the story of ABRI heroism that the military later constructed about the event.

The hostages told me immediately after they were brought back to Jakarta that in fact the military patrol was further along the creek but the *hostages* worked out where the soldiers were and walked in the open towards them. The troops were an inexperienced unit from Bandung, not the crack Kopassus Special Forces elite of General Probowo. The Bandung troops, hiding behind rocks, terrified of being hit by arrows, fired shots into the air to discourage rebel attack, but refused to come out, even to assist or offer protection when called on by the hostages to help from 100 m away. Adinda Saraswati, fiancé of Navy who had just been murdered, badly injured her ankle and was having enormous difficulty getting across the rocks in the stream. Another hostage, British Anna McIvor, had become separated and was still in the jungle. When the hostages reached the troops, the troops refused to heed their call to go looking for Anna. She finally staggered out of the jungle from where she had been hiding after Thies was killed.

The radio of the troops did not operate as it had run out of battery, so it was not possible to call in a helicopter. Indeed, had they been able to do so, the hostages could have been transported out that night. Instead, as they had to remain on site during the night, the Bandung troops had to make camp for the hostages. Martha described the result as the most amateur campsite they had stayed in for their whole time in the jungle: they were poorly sheltered, got wet, and cold. The next morning the Special Forces troops of General Probowo arrived, having been searching for the hostages in the second of the two areas the military had targeted. And finally, the hostages moved into the care of highly professional competent soldiers who went back into the jungle and brought out the bodies of the two Indonesians who had been killed, Navy and Theis.

The rebels had planned for at least 30 min to carry out the killings. The two unfortunates who could not escape were killed because the OPM rebels simply hated the Indonesians, and Irianese working for them. The idea of killing the Indonesian hostages had been a constant threat through the ordeal. From intelligence we acquired, they were almost certainly killed by people who came into the group from outside at the time of the ceremony, rather than the people who had shared the jungle passage with the hostages to that time. Indeed, I saw film of a man brought in from Papua New Guinea who led the prayers at the failed Geselema ceremony who was identified by some who were there as the man who struck the initial blow to Navy. The murders were *not* committed by Daniel Kogoya or Kelly Kwalik: Kwalik, it appeared, was nowhere near the hostages, having already started to travel as far away from the military as he could get.

The military told a different and more heroic story, that is that the hostages were fleeing up hill away from the rebels, with the two men who were murdered at the front. *Time* magazine ran the official line on 27th May 1996:

> 100 Special Forces Red Beret commandos snaked down ropes from helicopters hovering above the jungle, hauling with them sniffer dogs and remote sensing equipment. On Wednesday they stumbled upon British hostage Anna McIvor, who was hiding in the jungle, and she pointed them in the direction of the rebels and hostages. Shortly afterward the soldiers encountered a group of men armed with M-16 assault rifles. They were no match for the Red Berets. After an 8½ hour gun battle, eight rebels lay dead and nine of their captives were free. Less than two days later, the hostages stepped off a military transport plane at Jakarta's Halim military airport, apparently healthy though dressed in hospital gowns.

In fact, no rebels were killed as far as we could ascertain; the murders were *not* committed as the military attacked, for indeed the soldiers from Bandung who were there were actually hiding behind rocks, too scared to stick out their heads although they did apparently fire their weapons into the air in an attempt to scare the Papuans. General Probowo's Red Beret troops, once they arrived *the next day*, did however move into the jungle to find and bring out the bodies of the two hostages who had been killed. Both had been killed by wounds received from an axe and machete. But the release was not the result of a direct military confrontation. Indeed, Jualita, in the official Biological Science Club statement observes that,

> a wound on Navy's forehead, which was apparent when he was buried, was from crashing into a tree trunk when he fell, and did not come from a stray military bullet. He was never shot at.

Subsequently, under the excuse that operations were to sweep up the rebel leaders, the military turned the whole area between Mapnduma and Geselema into a militarised zone, establishing military posts, burning houses and gardens. According to a report released in May 1996 by the three churches of the Geselema-Mapenduma area, at least 11 people had been shot dead by Indonesian soldiers as they returned to their gardens searching for food, 137 people had died mainly from hunger and sickness, 13 churches, 166 homes, 2 health clinics and 29 men's houses had been burnt. A later report on 21st June 1997 by LEMASA, the Foundation for the Customary Council of the Amungme Tribe and both the Catholic and Christian churches of Timika, claimed that 1,000 civilian parishioners fled into the forests, mountains and adjacent tribal areas after the military attacked. The people felt very directly and realistically threatened by this outside world that had suddenly descended on their heads from outside their jungle home.

Back in Jakarta

Martha and Mark were precipitated out of this jungle world suddenly. And so too were the other surviving hostages, the Indonesian members of the Jakarta Biological Science Club, Jualita Tanasale, Adinda Saraswati and Markus Warip, the four British Cambridge students, their leader Daniel Start, Annete van der Kolk, Anna McIvor and William P. Oats.

From Thursday 16th May onwards life re-entered another phase of surrealism. Flown by Hercules aircraft from Timika in West Papua to the Jakarta military base at Halim Airport, they arrived to be greeted by the highest ranking military, including General Probowo, the three country ambassadors plus ourselves and an avalanche of press—even though the main group of press was kept at a distance. As *Time* reported of Martha,

> Among them was Martha Klein, a 33-year old United Nations administrator from the Netherlands, who is seven months pregnant. Met by her boss, Stephen

Hill, director of UNESCO in Jakarta, she embraced him and broke down in tears.

The advance press conference was attended by around 200 journalists. Martha and Mark, plus the other surviving hostages were driven in a motorcade to the Indonesian Naval Hospital (where Ibu Tien Soeharto, the President's wife, had died a couple of weeks earlier). There was not just a motorcycle escort. The streets were actually *cleared* of all traffic, as was otherwise the case only with movements of the President or visiting Heads of State. The released hostages stayed overnight for observation and were reported as 'normal' at a press conference held at 11.00am on Friday morning 17th May before appearing at a hand-over ceremony when responsibility for the previous captives was passed on from military to civilian authorities—in fact to the Ministry of Forestry which had provided the original approvals for the Lorentz'95 Group to trek into the West Papua highlands, again all covered by the press which outside the hospital doors was almost in riot.

As Martha observed, the military handover celebration followed precisely the same format as the liberation ceremony they had been part of deep in the jungle the week before. The OPM, haters of the Indonesian army, had copied their protocol to the letter. The afternoon of the surviving hostages was spent at the funeral of one of the Indonesian students who had died—spoiled as an occasion of grief by imposed military protocol and a rampaging uncontrolled media.

On the first evening after their release from hospital following their kidnapping ordeal, Friday 17th May 1996, Mark and Martha were finally able to relax. They had a small dinner at the Dutch Ambassador's Residence where they were staying—with Mark Argello, a friend brought from the Netherlands to accompany them home, Russell Betts, my counterpart in dealing with the hostage crisis from WWF, the Jayapura WWF person responsible for Mark's mission, Ron Lilley, and myself. Indonesian-Dutch food. Waited on by the Ambassador's servant.

The final surrealism for Martha lay in her stomach. In just over seven weeks she became a mother when Mick Lorentz, the baby that had travelled with her through the whole hostage crisis, was born.

8

"'Flying Pigs'—The Start of a Voyage into the Future"

Pigs Did Fly

It was six months after the hostages were released. The surviving escapees had moved on in their daily lives back to the 'normal' world from which they had so suddenly been barred, Mick Lorentz was 4 months old, and life in the Papuan highlands settled back into the normal cycles of tribal life and ritual. But a deep wound remained festering in the fabric of tribal culture. For all the pigs of the Mapnduma area had been killed.

The pigs had been killed during the early stages of the hostage crisis—as a direct result of the kidnapping and conflict that followed. The OPM, as they invaded the village to capture the hostages, then stayed—and *ate,* killing pigs to feed the two hundred or so extra 'guests' of the village community. As the military subsequently moved by, tailing the rebels after they fled, they destroyed the gardens of many people and, as did the rebels, needing food, so killed any pigs they could find to feed the (non-Moslem) soldiers. And the village people themselves, unwittingly caught up in this drama, were terrified of what the military might do, so escaped for some time into the jungles, killing their own pigs to ensure they had some food while in hiding, but on their return to the village around 11th February, 1996, confronted a future without their most prized possessions, pigs.

Having no pigs was a disaster for the local community. For pigs are not only a source of food in Papuan society, but also a significant social commodity. Pigs are the 'cultural capital' of the people, used in gift exchanges, as dowries for weddings, as reparation after tribal wars, and as essential symbols of wealth and prestige. It should be remembered that the traditional tribal village is set out in the form of a rectangle, with the men's' house at the end, and the women's' house and pigs' house on the two parallel sides—effectively of equal status. Therefore, the people of Mapnduma not only lost their breeding stock for food as a result of the abduction, but they also lost the central component of those social and cultural exchanges and events that bind their communities together.

To replace the pigs was an entirely appropriate act for UNESCO as the UN agency responsible for culture support within the world community. It was particularly appropriate within the Papuan context as an 'exchange gift' to the community. The local people had resisted the OPM, and they had assisted the hostages as much as they could with food and protection. The women had travelled with the hostages, looking after the girls and in particular, Martha, physically caring for and carrying her in difficult terrain. Indeed, the local villagers carried everything during the long jungle treks; the hostages never carried a thing. We *owed* the community a gift of enormous gratitude, and as a development assistance action, replacing the pig livestock was a critical element of the restoration of 'normalcy' within the local area where the drama had been played out.

After putting all the final pieces of really rather difficult logistical arrangements into place, we then waited for several days in early November 1996 until the mists cleared, allowing the first of a series of morning helicopter flights into Mapnduma in the Jayawijaya local district on 19th November—delivering 84 pigs on that day, and another 32 pigs a couple of days later—again, with bad weather preventing flights on the day in between. Originally, we entitled the program in Indonesian, *Operasi Angkat Babi*, the 'Pig Lift Operation', but it was too tempting for me not to change this name subsequently to *Operasi Terpang Babi*, the United Nations (official) *'Flying Pigs Operation'*. It was under this title that the post-operation report went on UNESCO's books and was reported to the 187 nation General Conference of the organization in 1997.... the *Flying Pigs Operation*. What I found a little curious, though perhaps a statement more than anything else about how carefully delegates read the detailed reports, was that *no-one* from this General Conference asked me what on earth UNESCO was doing being associated with *Flying Pigs*—even though, I had absolutely no qualms about the project being more than fully justified.

Russell Betts, international head of WWF in Indonesia—my colleague in dealing with the hostage crisis, and I, had actually planned this operation a long time before, indeed within a month after the hostages had been captured. We recognized at that time the problem that had been already created with the loss of local pigs. Immediately we put most of the approvals into place and (after gaining UNESCO approval to bankroll the entire operation if necessary so we could establish this development assistance principle quickly) I had managed to raise the funding we needed from embassies whose nationals were hostages, leaving only a couple of thousand dollars needing to be committed from UNESCO. But we decided to wait. It was really not possible for me to give a gift of this magnitude under the auspices of the UN while the hostages were still kidnapped, as it could have seriously interfered with negotiations and political sensitivities of the national government. Nevertheless, in early February when we first developed the idea of flying pigs, we quickly obtained enthusiastic support from the Netherlands Embassy, then the British and German Embassies, local church authorities, and even the military: General Probowo communicated support for the initiative to me on 9th February on behalf of the Indonesian military, stating that he was personally 'delighted' with the idea. By 19th February I had all the agreements in place, had written to General Probowo to obtain his *formal* approval, but we had decided that we needed to *wait* until *after* the hostages were released before mounting the operation. At that stage, we still maintained what turned out to be a completely misplaced faith in the negotiation process, expecting that the hostages might be released any day now. I wanted to move quickly after their release to symbolically put a new peace-oriented model of development into place, and to show the local people in particular that this could be done without serious bureaucratic delay. Sadly, my faith in early timing evaporated as the hostage crisis wore on and on, finally ending another three months later, with repercussions given the violent way things turned out with a complex local environment that did require several months to pass before the pigs could hit the air - particularly given the heavy duty military intervention that the West Papuan highlands had been subjected to as follow-up and retribution for the act of OPM defiance that the hostage crisis had represented as far as the military were concerned.

It was then that I realized that the initial action of gaining financial and in-principle support from key authorities and funders was the easy part.

To put it mildly, getting 108 pigs to the people of Mapnduma nine months after we conceived the *Flying Pigs Operation* was not an easy task! In the context of a restive and largely tribal province of Indonesia, even though we had obtained general support at senior government and military levels, many specific agreements at grass roots levels had to be put in place before we could actually start purchasing and moving pigs around. These included the local Indonesian Government Bupati and Government Offices; KODAM, the regional military command; the Office of Livestock Breeding in Jayapura which was responsible for inoculating the pigs against swine fever; the church-based Mission Aviation Fellowship (MAF) which employ dedicated pilots and handle most of the flights into the remote tribal areas of West Papua, and were working with the people of Mapnduma; the local Catholic Church volunteers—who carried information to the Catholic influenced tribal areas; the Farmers Group YAKARA in the village of Walesi who helped to accommodate the pigs for 18 days prior to the flights while we waited for the weather to break; and finally, the village representatives themselves, for if the pig distribution was handled wrongly in terms of local tradition, values and status, we could well have initiated a tribal war rather than taken a step towards peace and local security. This constraint was uppermost in our minds when we introduced the *Flying Pigs Operation*, not as supply of a gift (although, in fact, it was our intention to present the pigs as a cultural 'exchange' for the support and care the villagers had given to the hostages), but as *replacement* of pig livestock lost. By following this definition of the situation and by being very precise to construct and use accurate lists of previous pig owners we were able to foster precise principles of distribution and avoid rivalry either within or between villages.

Purchasing and collecting the pigs added a further complication. They had to be Wamena black pigs. The tribal people would accept no others. Furthermore, to meet normal village pig-raising criteria, we had to end up with a 1:4 male–female ratio in those we collected. Wamena and environs had however recently been struck with an epidemic that killed large numbers of pigs. We therefore met some considerable hesitation amongst the locals to sell their own pigs, particularly, the females. Adding to the difficulty, the locations of many of the villages which had to be contacted were remote and difficult to reach by car.

But we finally got there—with 108 squealing pigs ranging in weight from 7 to 13 kg, of which 25 were male and 83 female. In boxes provided by the farmers' group, YAKARA, we flew the pigs to Mapnduma and distributed them to family heads selected by the local government or Camat representative in cooperation with churches and community elders, and according to a list prepared (by the villagers for the OPM originally, but now transmitted on) by the Parish Chief of the Kingmi Church, Mapnduma and the local Camat official.

And we did not have a tribal war!

Indeed, the local senior officials conveyed messages of gratitude emphasizing that this *Flying Pigs Operation* was a 'concrete example of the participation of the international world in solving the difficulties faced by the Mapnduma people'.

8 "'Flying Pigs'—The Start of a Voyage into the Future"

Total cost of the flying pigs: just over $(US)10,000. It is amazing the impact you can make with small amounts of money if a development assistance project is precisely targeted to what the people themselves decide is important. For a UN Agency like UNESCO that, as a 'technical' agency (rather than donor), relies on mere dribbles of international funding (and, I might add, where I found myself needing to raise around four times the dedicated 'Regular Budget' provided by the Agency from other multinational and bilateral donors, business, and so on), discovering the power of community targeting with minor funding was a godsend.

What was particularly important about the *Flying Pigs Operation* however was that it opened the door to subsequent donor support to the highlands people *in the peoples' own terms,* whilst carrying through and demonstrating the principles that set a model for local development cooperation—with particular emphasis on local engagement in decision, and allocation of appropriate roles for all interested players.

> The pigs were purchased by the most active development oriented local NGO in Wamena with assistance and supervision from WWF, and monitoring by UNESCO of overall arrangements and finances.
>
> The military were fully consulted at both national and local levels and gave their blessing to a transport arrangement whereby local church mission pilots commanded the helicopters flying into the previous conflict zone.
>
> The church mission within the villages took monitoring responsibility for the long-term, with a clear expectation that they would also exercise moral persuasion if the intention of the assistance was broken, for example through local rivalries.
>
> Decision on the precise number of pigs to be purchased and the precise distribution across villages was left to local officials and the military. Mapnduma was the most significantly affected village, but a small number of pigs was also lost in three other surrounding villages. The point was that there was a *list*. It was compiled in early February, that is, at the time, from the villagers who sent the information to the OPM for inclusion in a letter of grievance. The list was accepted by the authorities—passed on by the local church minister and government official as it was compiled *by* the local villagers and was not introduced as a demand by the OPM. But use of the list for arbitration symbolically brought the OPM into the arrangement—reinforcing a positive role they could play looking after the interests and grievances of their people. No negotiation with the OPM was carried out or implied as far as the authorities were concerned, just use of the list of property lost that was compiled by the village people. However, the OPM symbolically were indicated as fulfilling their function in a new peace process, that is, establishing and maintaining balance of equity.

The three Embassies, Netherlands, Britain, and Germany, supported the initiative. However, whilst they provided minor funding support, we decided collectively that the most appropriate role for national governments was in the longer-term development assistance that followed the *Flying Pigs* initiative. The embassies therefore 'blessed' the initiative in any public comment they made, but primarily observed that the model of cooperation being demonstrated was a potential basis for their own subsequent provision of serious development assistance to the West Papuan village communities, for example, in the form of water systems, schools and so on. In this particular case, via UNESCO, I was able to move faster than other donors and establish the commitment very quickly (through bankrolling it and looking for funding later) when timing was of the essence. We were therefore able to open the door for development and substantial development assistance in the subsequent attempts to promote a West Papuan peace process.

And finally, the arrangement allowed all the local interests to claim a role and credit. It was particularly important that the military did claim credit for their role as it symbolized a very different and social development oriented role as compared with their previous reputation for singularly militarist suppression. I kept UNESCO in the background, knowing that 'bush telegraph' and quiet background knowledge would give our UN agency a strong reputation for providing care and cultural support without political grandstanding. Meanwhile, as perhaps its most useful outcome, this tiny initiative costing less than a third of a small international workshop, set a pattern for peace in West Papua, and a practical test of a community 'listening' model of development. The people noticed, and as I talk about shortly when describing the subsequent *Voyage into the Future* of highland village leaders into the outside world that UNESCO initiated, so too did the President of the Republic!

I should point out though that whilst the military *were* cooperating and applauding this initiative on the one hand, they were hiding an ongoing military pogrom against the Highlands people in their other hand—action which they considered justified given that the hostages had been released through military intervention not peaceful negotiation, proof, as far as ABRI was concerned, that tough action was ultimately what worked to bring 'primitive' people into line. At that stage we did not fully appreciate just how serious this military violence was, although we did know that ABRI *was* moving aggressively through the areas around Mapnduma seeking to track down the OPM leaders who had escaped. As I observed in the last Chapter, the military had a strong interest in *not* changing their previous repressive ways. So, our *Flying Pigs* initiative was a small step in a path that Indonesia was *starting* to embark upon—with almost as many steps backwards as forwards. *But* (in the context of the Government's increasing realization that hard-line repression

8 "'Flying Pigs'—The Start of a Voyage into the Future"

was simply not working) the *Flying Pigs Operation* signaled the *possibility* of sensitive development assistance and *dialogue* could be thrown into the West Papua equation—and as is shown in the *Voyage into the Future*, perceptions back in central Government were now moving onto a different track.

Legacy of Flying Pigs—Shift in the Mode of Development Assistance

Back to the *Flying Pigs* however, the criterion case for the present Chapter's discussion.

We had been taught a valuable lesson about development assistance and its impact: *listen* to the heart of what the people most need *in their terms and according to their values* and *respond flexibly*.

Prior to the Hostage Crisis, we had already been working in West Papua from 1995 onwards with the University of Indonesia and local tribal groups on identifying, assessing and safeguarding the invaluable rock art cultural heritage of West Papua. In the course of these early contacts in Papua we started to collaborate with a local NGO, Yayasan Lembah Baliem, whose goal was to help build local income and empowerment for Baliem Valley tribal communities.

Following our *Flying Pigs Operation,* the NGO approached UNESCO requesting support for indigenous people to establish a local carpenter and wood carving center in Wamena, Highland capital of Irian Jaya. The purpose of the crafts center was to capture and revitalize traditional arts and crafts (where, for example, the number of traditional experts who could craft stone axes in the Highlands had dwindled to the point where the craft was in serious danger of disappearing), and at the same time to generate additional income for the community based on an increasing influx of tourism.

As was often the case, UNESCO's own finances for the initiative were heavily constrained by a very low activities budget and strict restrictions imposed on how it had to be used according to pre-arranged plans by what we all knew and 'loved' so well according to its document title, "the C/5" Program and Budget approved by UNESCO's 1996 General Conference, and fixed in administrative cement. We therefore convinced the Government of Belgium to provide an operating fund of $(US)8,000 with additional funds being committed from the Indonesian Ministry of Education and Culture, and then we helped the local people to build the Carpenter and Wood Carving Centre in Wamena, and extended the plan to also assisting the development of a Bark Painting Workshop in the Lake Sentani district. But we not only found the money and helped build the facility. We also were directly able to promote the concept—choosing and supporting, according to the indigenous people's votes, the very best carvers to act as teachers. Additionally, we then *certified* the items produced, mainly wooden sculptures, as quality items using UNESCO's logo on the sales ticket, and helped to build up the tourist connections to the centers. However, apart from some statues which we displayed on behalf of the indigenous communities through our own UNESCO Office in Jakarta, and a few that sold through selected Jakarta shops, the market for the West Papuan craft was limited to those relatively few tourists who flew up into the Highlands to Wamena. Nevertheless, what money was generated in Jakarta was sent back to the local community for redistribution within the community, and for savings and reinvestment. The elders and chiefs could see the possibilities for the future.

The 'Voyage into the Future'

It was at that stage that the chiefs came to us again, proposing that they should travel to Jakarta in order to meet government officials and to see projects in Jakarta that would be used as models to promote development and income in the very poor Baliem Valley. They had *never* been outside the jungle and remote smalltown environment before, and said to us,

> We keep seeing these people stepping off airplanes at Wamena, but have no idea what the world is like from where they come; we want to go and find out so we know how to deal with this outside world.

Even though they had proposed a similar journey to the local senior government official, the Bupati, for many years, the Indonesian Government had refused to permit or support the trip, preferring to keep the indigenous peoples quietly back in the province rather than 'connected' into the country's mainstream. But, as I found was one of the UN's great strengths, *we could make it happen* through our role as a credible and accepted 'fair witness'. The *Flying Pigs Operation* had been a raging success as far as the Government was concerned and showed the way to a new appreciation of the Government's presence by the indigenous people against the backdrop of either previous neglect or internal colonial administration and military rule, factors that had surely contributed to the established OPM conflict and emerging calls from within the province for autonomy. So, we had pretty good 'street credibility' and were listened to. By intervening on behalf of

8 "'Flying Pigs'—The Start of a Voyage into the Future" 117

the indigenous people, setting up collaboration with the Indonesian Government's counterpart agency for UNESCO relations, the Indonesian National Commission for UNESCO, and then organizing the trip, we were therefore able to bring the tribal leaders *for the first time* to the outside modern world they so much wanted to explore. The village leaders themselves helped to fund the trip with money they had generated from the sale of pigs, vegetables and other commodities. They really wanted to come.

What a trip it was. Our Culture Specialist, Philippe, flew down to Papua so he could accompany the people to Jakarta—twenty-seven village chiefs and tribal leaders including three women (itself no mean feat given the traditional subservient role of women in Papuan village communities). They came by ship, sleeping on deck amongst their few possessions and animals being transported, stopping off at a number of ports along the way, each time, gaining a further taste of what modern city life might be when they finally reached their goal, the capital. As they sailed slowly towards Jakarta, the media discovered what we had called "The Voyage into the Future", and became increasingly fascinated by what it meant—as 'first contacts' by jungle peoples. By the time the ship reached Jakarta, the Voyage was a major public event.

So, we decided we would have a Press Conference. The tribal leaders had no problem with this, reflecting on the occasion as being much the same as a village oration session where people presented and discussed plans, ideas, and village issues. They were used to public speaking! I organized the Press Conference in the United Nations Building in central Jakarta—just down the road from the President's classically designed formal palace, Istana Negri, and across the street from MacDonalds, and a shopping mall. The tribal leaders arrived. As we met they requested to dress 'formally' for the occasion. I, of course, agreed, and donned my suit and tie. To my considerable initial surprise, *they then took off their clothes*, and apart from a shell chest decoration, painted markings, and penis sheaths, emerged to greet the media representatives of the nation and the world in the main meeting room of the UN, quite independently of this occasion, entitled, the Irian Jaya Room. I declined to follow suit, and according to my own 'cultural convictions' (or cowardice) remained with collar and tie. As we were about to begin—in Bahasa Indonesia, the Dani tribal language and English, I realized just how different this Press Conference was to those I confronted rather frequently in my United Nations role when I noticed I could see *through* the nose of the delegation leader sitting next to me. He had neglected to bring the bone with him in his luggage. What was then very interesting was just how well the tribal leaders handled the situation—demonstrating an extraordinary if simple wisdom about their entry into what still for them must have been a world as alien as the moon.

Our Voyage into the Future was then adopted by the President. Soeharto nominated his Secretary, General Hendropryono, previous head of military intelligence, and later head of BIN, the Government's intelligence agency, to liaise with and look after us. This was the Hendropryono, a very helpful but distinctly shadowy figure, who remained allegedly implicated in the poisoning death on a Garuda Flight to the Netherlands of Munir Said Thalib, the civil rights activist—who, by that stage, that is, years after Soeharto's downfall, constituted no threat to government order. Munir was remembered however at least by one of the Deputy Heads of BIN at the time of Munir's death, Muchdi Purwopranjono, for his rights assertiveness when Soeharto was in power and subsequently. Previously a chief of the Army Special Forces (Kopassus). Muchdi was brought to trial for involvement in Munir's assassination by the Indonesian Government in August 2008, prosecutors arguing that Muchdi's motivation was revenge for his dismissal after only 52 days from the Kopassus post to which he had just been appointed because of Munir's exposure of Muchdi's responsibility for the disappearance of several activists in the late 1990s.

Back to 1997 however, and Hendropryono, with the President's full blessing, could afford to be extremely helpful to us. He organized for the President to travel out to where the tribal leaders were accommodated—at Taman Mini, a cultural theme park that Soeharto's wife, Tuti, had played a central role in founding—to represent in many separate cultural pavilions the cultural diversity of each province of Indonesia. And Soeharto met each of the leaders, all of whom were then able to take home a photo of personally shaking hands with the President. I still have one photo from this event that is particularly significant, for the President is shaking hands with Molokma, one of the tribal chiefs who was reputed at that stage to be an active supporter of the OPM; in the background behind the President is General Feisal Tanjung, the hardline Commander of Indonesia's armed forces; in the background behind Molokma is myself as UN representative. For the tribal leaders, their photo with the President was an extraordinarily empowering device. For they could display it prominently at home, scaring the wits out of any overbearing official who happened by, trying to intimidate or exploit the people in the way to which too many in the provincial administration had grown accustomed.

General Hendropryono also decided to entertain the tribal leaders and invited them to a restaurant he owned on one of the main streets of Jakarta, Jalan Rasuna Said, amongst rather a large range of other investments that came the way of all who counted themselves close to the President's family.

For the tribal leaders this was their very *first* experience of a city, let alone going out to a restaurant. And this was not just any restaurant. It was a Japanese Restaurant, moreover a Tepanyaki BBQ style restaurant, where the normal practice of the chefs, standing behind BBQ plates in a square of surrounding patrons, is showmanship. The chefs throw their instruments into the air, catching them behind their backs, toss eggs casually around to each other, and generally put on quite a performance. The indigenous leaders were spellbound at this display of what city life was like. At this point, Hendropryono, wishing to reinforce his generosity, came around to each of the delegates and presented them with a wristwatch, explaining carefully what it was, how to use it and how to read the time. The group was stunned by this display of what they took to be the culture of the city. I have this abiding (but really, not serious) feeling that perhaps this occasion on our Voyage into the Future may have created a whole new set of food practices in West Papua, where the traditional roasting of pigs for ceremonial occasions is now accompanied by the throwing and catching of stone axes, knives and bones! Perhaps not!

Creating a Cargo Cult?

There was another occasion earlier however, in the midst of the hostage crisis in early February 1996, when I really did think half seriously that we *may* have inadvertently created a 'cargo cult'.

Cargo cults sprang into life originally amongst the Papuan people when the Leahy brothers, explorers, walked into the highland of New Guinea in the 1930s and found large numbers of people and gold. Whilst one brother walked down to the coast to organise a plane to bring in supplies, the others stayed and built an airstrip using a local indigenous workforce who had no idea of what they were doing having never seen an airplane. With no concept that there was an outside world beyond their own jungle, they were totally amazed by the arrival of a plane with supplies, interpreting the event in terms of their own cultural understanding as a gift from the white men's ancestors. Needless to say, they thought they were now onto a good thing and built their own airstrips fully anticipating that their own ancestors would now send them 'cargo' as well. On the coast, the tribes picked up the idea and built wharves in the expectation that shiploads of goods would arrive for them too. During World War II the whole process was generalized as the locals observed the US and their allies successfully achieving the same results from construction activity. The indigenous tribes watched as the military-built jungle air strips and the subsequent cargo planes arrived with everything from weapons to refrigerators and food. But the locals had no external reference point so had to interpret the meaning of this largess dropping from the air in their own cultural terms. They built *symbolic* airstrips, displayed western-style symbols such as the Christian cross, and, as if a jungle snare for cassowaries, then waited for the 'cargo' to arrive. They were of course disappointed. But the belief persisted that entirely in keeping with local cultural understandings, if some particular ritual or symbolic acts were followed, great wealth or 'cargo' would flow to the people.

What happened in our own 'cargo drop' occurred a month into the crisis when we decided to send in 'Care Packages' to the hostages.

Our intention was to provide for quite real needs, replacement clothes as the jungle climate had already taken a serious toll on the clothes they had worn as they walked into the highlands, additional food rather than local yams, plus toiletries, vitamins, medicine, chocolate, and also letters, books, comics and games to keep the hostages occupied and to lift their spirits. When we mentioned the idea to them, the British Embassy told us that they would look after the group of four Cambridge University students, so Russell Betts from WWF and I went ahead to set up the care packages for the other nine people captured, with the expectations that the British contribution would arrive before we transported the packages down to West Papua. With support from WWF, my own UNESCO staff and offices were then dedicated for nearly two days while the staff put together the packages—large green garbage bags with 'Courtesy of the United Nations/UNESCO/WWF' in stenciled letters on the outside along with the name of the individual hostage for whom the package was intended. Each bag was then packed with just about anything we could find that we figured the hostages would enjoy and which we could fit in.

ICRC had the job of delivering them. They told us that they knew exactly where the rebels were and that they would deliver the packages by helicopter to the rebel camp. As it turned out however, the ICRC knew *approximately* where the rebel camp was and so dropped the large UN-inscribed green garbage bags on the nearest village. We did not see the scene on the ground when suddenly out of the sky, 15 large 'packages' fell to the ground amongst the people. We can only surmise that the people were suddenly surprised and delighted that 'cargo' had dropped onto their heads as manna from heaven courtesy of the UN. One can assume that the local village people fed well for a few days, enjoyed some new clothes, and that the hostages could entertain themselves as well, as whilst all packages arrived at the village, only one reached the hostages—containing books, games, and letters. I shall not speculate about the hypothetical possibility of a new species of 'cargo cult' arising from the hostage situation and the dropping of named green garbage bags from the sky, and whether the villagers set up subsequent cargo-cult like rituals to encourage the UN gods to drop further manna… !

I should emphasize the point for my present Chapter of these dalliances into cargo cult and first-contact stories. It is that we see in these stories in clear relief the way that people must understand and relate to an alien cultural world by bringing it back into the fold of their own cultural framework and assumptions. There is no other platform of meaning to jump from in diving into an outside world and finding means of communicating within it.

Sardono, a famous traditional Indonesian dancer from the heart of Javanese culture in Solo, told me a few years later about a voyage he organized for tribal peoples into the globalised world. In his case, he had decided to take a group of indigenous people from Kalimantan in Indonesia's east to New York. They had heard of this place as a city without trees.

> "We want to go there" they told him, "… and we want to dance and to see their dance". "For we cannot understand how anyone can live in a world without trees, and must see their dance to understand".

Sardono then took the tribal group onto their airplane to New York. Initial response of their leaders pointed out that they understood planes as they had seen something of them before though they had never been inside. But, they had two problems—not being able to fit their spears in the luggage rack, and finding a way of fastening the seat belt across their penis sheaths!

Whilst the local reference point for crossing cultural boundaries is shown with some clarity in these examples that cross broad cultural territory from remote jungles to modern cities, the same message also applies to intercultural dialogue that for most of the readers of this book would be in more familiar territory, daily life in a modern world.

In the last chapter I noted the way that quite unintentionally the letter sent from the Archbishop of Canterbury to Kwalik, rebel leader of the OPM, failed as a device for reconciliation or persuasion as it simply missed the point for the people sitting in the jungle remote from a globalized world's morality that did not include them. Frank Meyer's negotiations worked *because* he stretched into tribal values. But, even as far removed as in communications within my own Agency, UNESCO, we found people seeking… and failing… to communicate with each other across unseen cultural boundaries—drawn in this case between an administratively oriented Paris based Headquarters and the remote but operational field situation. In any dialogue one must look for varying platforms of cultural experience if one wants to communicate. I come back to this shortly.

Legacies of the Voyage into the Future

We did not stop with the one Voyage of tribal people into the modern world.

Three months after the 'Voyage into the Future', from 8 to 19th August 1997, we brought forty tribal and village leaders to Jakarta from the border area of West Papua between the Republic of Indonesia and Papua New Guinea, that is, an area stretching across broad terrain from mountains to the sea but collectively characterized by tribal movements and interactions that crossed geographically determined national boundaries. This program which I called 'The Cultural Borders Journey' built on what we had learnt from the first tribal Study Tour and followed a similar format—with a combination of meetings with government officials and tours of development projects in Jakarta. Our focus was on promoting the development of small-scale industries that were likely to be most relevant to local village resources and opportunities—for example, rattan furniture, cattle breeding, metal work, processing agate, processing salted fish, brown sugar production and vegetable packaging. We worked with the same local and government agencies, this time with the President's Office providing us with access to a Hercules aircraft for picking up the leaders and transporting them from and to a number of border villages. We sought to assist the leaders to cross the cultural bridges they needed to negotiate and to pick up the knowledge they required to become effective change agents in their own local communities—linked with economic opportunities provided by the world outside. But *they* were the ones who decided how these further outside contacts would be developed.

Meanwhile, as I noted earlier about the *Flying Pigs Operation*, without us appreciating it until later, whilst the President and central government were welcoming a new phase on dialogue with tribal Papuans, his military in Papua were bashing the hell out of the people, not so much in the border areas we were now targeting, but up in the hidden tracts of the highlands from Mapnduma to Geselema. The military had a strong interest in remaining there no matter what the President may have been doing—to protect their economic interests and, particularly after they were forced to exit Timor Leste, to justify the need for continued strength and support of the military to control 'restive' provinces. As I noted in the last Chapter, it took until 2000 before serious change to the Papuan's political situation occurred—but the new dialogue *had* started. It is still to be completed.

Consequently, as far as we could see in 1997, the program was developing well for us, and was rated as very successful at both ends of the cultural chain—the village people themselves and senior officials of the Indonesian Government in Jakarta—even though there were still reports of continuing military suppression seeping out of the jungles. So, we planned the next tribal study tour. This time we were able to arrange for the Indonesian Navy to provide us with a ship to pick up leaders from coastal communities, bring them to Jakarta and take them back. Target date for implementation, 18th May 1998.

Then, on Thursday 14th May 1998, the Revolution that led to the downfall of President Soeharto got under way - precipitated a couple of days earlier with the shooting of students by military-based provocateurs. I write about the experience of the Revolution in Chaps. 13, 14, and 15. The situation on the streets became really serious—with major riots starting to spread across the face of the whole city of Jakarta. Somehow, to bring eighty tribal leaders out of the secluded jungles of West Papua into the middle of the streets of Jakarta during a Revolution seemed a tad irresponsible. So, I pulled the plug on the program.

Events moved on. For some time, Jakarta life and the stable flow of politics and governance in Indonesia were seriously disrupted. The tribal study tour program had served its purpose, and faced with other crises in Papua, in particular a major drought and forest fires which accompanied the 1997 El Niño weather phenomenon, we were now paying more attention to on-ground needs of the Papuan people.

9

"Lighting the Way—Building the Future for Indigenous People of West Papua"

Return Voyage to the Tribes

Following the initial 'Voyage into the Future' I spoke about in my previous Chap. 8, I wanted to see what impact the experience of visiting the modern world for the first time by some of the tribal participants had had back home. Their land also was very special—incorporating a continuous intact transect from snow cap to tropical marine environment, including extensive lowland wetlands—at severe risk however from external mining and exploitative deforestation interests. Developing protection for this land was of global importance. Legitimacy of international monitoring also added support for the local indigenous people whose land it had been for millennia before exploitative national and international interests invaded. National Park status was awarded to this area, Lorentz, in 1997, and UNESCO was assisting—towards the longer term goal of World Heritage status.

In pursuing these two goals—follow up of the tribal leaders "Voyage into the Future" and development of protection status for their land, I travelled down to West Papua along with Philippe, Culture Specialist in our Indonesia UNESCO Office, to meet with a number of the tribal leaders who had participated in the Voyage along with representatives of the people of Mapnduma to whom we had flown the pigs. In parallel we were progressing the wider goal of protection. This was in the first week of August 1997.

Our first port of call was in the south-east of the province to visit, on invitation, the massive Freeport copper and gold mine site at Tembagapura near Timika. Our purpose of being there was to further develop the relations with industry that we had initiated at Central Jakarta level to determine borders and the continuing support that was needed for Indonesia to propose and for us, that is UNESCO, to define the area and declare the Lorentz National Park in West Papua as a World Heritage Site. You will remember that at least the official rationale for Martha Klein's walk into the hands of the OPM (reported in Chap. 5) was to monitor one section of the Lorentz National Park and assess its World Heritage potential.

Lorentz, as I noted earlier, is an outstanding geographic area—stretching from one of the three snow-covered tropical glacier mountain sites in the world (the others being in Africa and South America) through every conceivable kind of tropical jungle and lowland terrain to the ocean. Freeport's mine sits directly adjacent to the tropical glacier. Other mining companies had territory exploration claims on areas of the park, all of which had to be clarified and resolved; and the whole area is of course populated with tribal Papuan people whose land it has been for thousands of years anyway. So, moving Lorentz towards World Heritage status to ensure its long-term protection, along with the rights of its tribal people, was a complicated and sensitive process. Visiting the Freeport mine and seeing its operations at field level was quite critical.

The scale of the Freeport mine is mind-bending. Freeport was basically chewing up a 4,500 m mountain, Grasberg, to its foundations and sluicing its ore residues down the mountain into the river systems and land below, extracting its copper and gold residues along the way.

This World Heritage quest took time. Subsequently, in 1999, after long and sometimes difficult negotiations, agreement was reached—with full support from Freeport and the other main mining companies which potentially impacted on the Lorentz World Heritage site. In parallel, we successfully negotiated the support of all relevant Government Ministers—Environment, Forestry, Mining, Education and Foreign Affairs, along with their local representatives in West Papua.

We then were able to arrange to sign off Lorentz in a formal ceremony in Jakarta as a World Heritage nomination with the President of the Republic, at that time, President Habibie. Lorentz's World Heritage status was approved shortly afterwards by the UNESCO World Heritage Committee meeting in Marrakesh, Morocco, in early December 1999. Whilst there remained significant difficulties with adequate monitoring of the site by Indonesia—largely as funding was very limited and the site is enormous and complex—World Heritage nomination and attention did provide a powerful support for local Papuans, for it limits and exposes any attempts by the more unscrupulous mining and forestry exploitation interests to sneak into the jungles, dig it up and take it away. World Heritage status means the host country has agreed that the nominated cultural or environmental resource is a 'possession of the world' rather than just the country, so their own caretaking will be scrutinized legitimately by the international community. Thus, World Heritage attention also means that what happens in the jungles through military interventions is also more likely to be discovered and brought to the notice of the international public. An *ideal*, it must be recognized, as the concerned government may well bar foreign or international reviewers to have access, and this did happen for West Papua. *But*, the protocol expectation is in place and visibly agreed at international level *with the Member State,* so whatever the Member State does from there on, it is being monitored with entire international legitimacy by the world.

Anyway, back to our visit to Freeport. Having driven up the mountain to the lower base of the mine site we were whisked by helicopter to the top excavation site at the oxygen-deprived 4,500 m level directly under the towering peak of the tropical glaciers that are the unique feature of the Lorentz National Park. Dramatic. Breathless. Disoriented. Intimidated—by the four meter tall diggers and trucks that are required to demolish and collect the top of the mountain, transport it into the 'flotation' process that separates out profitable yield and sluices the residue down the mountain into its lowland dumping ground and into the sea.

Directly afterwards we flew on to Jayapura, the capital of West Papua on the north of the island, and from this staging point on to Wamena, the main town of the highlands Baliem Valley. There we confronted more *digging*. This time it was the women of the tribes digging out the sweet potato and pig flesh that had been roasting in underground ovens in preparation for the feast by which the local tribal chiefs provided my official welcome.

There was a problem.

Local Indonesian airlines are not renowned for their reliability—or for that matter, for their safety. As one example, when I flew Bourak Air to Kalimantan a little later, the nose wheel collapsed on this ex-East European antique plane as we landed at our half-way stop-over on the island of Flores, causing us considerable disquiet as we hit the tarmac at a very inconvenient angle. "Stay on board" the pilot insisted. A half-hour later the airline produced a teenager with a large hammer who arrived from across the runway on his bicycle and smashed the nosewheel back into place. We immediately took off again—sustained all the way to Nusantara, Capital of Kalimantan, more by prayers than airplane maintenance.

Indeed, flying by local airlines in Indonesia could be an inherently risky business generally. On my 1999 trip to Freeport, our subsequent charter plane from Timika to a very remote coastal Asmat tribal village area in the south of West Papua, made it to the grass landing strip a few kilometres from the village, but, whilst going back to base during the time we visited the villages by dugout canoe, crashed into a mountain on its return journey to Timika - without passengers, in particular, me and my three companions, but killing the pilot, a tragedy that is not too uncommon with air flights into the Papuan mountains. This trip, which then took me down a river to the Asmat village of Agats, included an auction of local tribal artefacts—another very colorful story. I'll be back with this.

Meanwhile, I return to my story within a story that takes us back to our 1997 meeting with the tribal leaders of the Baliem Valley highlands mentioned in Chap. 8.

The *problem* was that because of what I found to be a quite normal lack of concern about provincial timetable delays by Merpati, the operative airline from Jayapura to Wamena, we were five hours late landing in the remote jungle town for the feast the locals had prepared in my honor. The people were very patient. Perhaps this situation was not unusual for them as they were well acquainted with airline delays—with Merpati their only contact with the outside world. The roast pigs were *not* patient however. To prevent them being radically overcooked, the women had exhumed the bodies three hours earlier. By the time we arrived and with the tropical heat, the proffered carcasses were flyblown, and with the deeper internal reaches of the pigs remaining somewhat untouched by underground oven heat, the meal looked distinctly unappetizing to anyone with Western restaurant tastes such as myself.

I was the honored guest! What this means is that I had to have first try at the carcass—and they, the people, would all wait for their meal until I had sunk my teeth into it. As the honored guest I had first pick, but that meant taking the best bits by *their* rules, the heart, the tongue, and the jaw. I must admit to being seriously intimidated by the prospect. I could see reflected in the rancid pig fat in front of me the avalanche of Cambantaran anti-worming tablets that would irrevocably be my immediate destiny. Either that or the near-death experience of very serious developing countries diarrhea. However, as any United Nations field officer knows, *always carry a Swiss pen knife*. I produced my knife and cut a portion of heart and tongue from the proffered body parts. But, not a large and culinarily satisfying portion. Rather, the thinnest sliver that my knife could dissect. With ostentatious demonstration of pleasure and satisfaction with the quality of the carnivoran gift, I ate … and rapidly passed on the remainder of the beast in the tradition of sharing to those around me.

And then came the Tribute Ceremony, one side-product of which was the offer which I really do highly value, to become an Honorary Chief of the Dani Tribe. Eight of the leaders from Mapnduma had hiked for eight days to come to this ceremony and present me with tokens of their esteem. I was surrounded by 'whooping' tribal leaders, again with more tokens. And bedecked with the welcoming floral wreath I presented the expected oration, translated into local language of course, reminding the assembled throng of the past events, the debt of gratitude the United Nations and the hostages owed to the people who cared for them, congratulating the leaders who had ventured to Jakarta on my 'Voyage into the Future' that I had previously provided for their wisdom in confronting and dealing with the outside world, promising immediate attention to the range of requests the people had made for further assistance, and basically saying thank you for such an enormous honour as they had bestowed on me with this ceremony and feast.

Starting to sit down I was reflecting on the occasion so far with the observation to myself that 'that went well' and I could now relax. But I was immediately called to my feet to receive the tokens the people had collected and wished to offer. Starting with the 1.2 m statue carved by the chief carver of the Culture Centre we had founded, originally called the Carpenter and Woodcarving Centre, I was then presented with what can only be described as a *mass* of bows and arrows, spears, stone axes, and stone ceremonial objects, nokens (woven baskets) and other tribal and ceremonial objects—in particular a collection of eight penis sheaths for different occasions. Molokma, the leading chief, observed in his responding oration that the chiefs had never been out of the valley before, and whilst confronting the modern world as it came to them in the valley, did not know its roots. "Now we can see" he applauded.

The problem for me, and for Philippe, was that now we had to *carry*.... a veritable arsenal of stone-age weaponry back on the small Merpati plane that connected Wamena in the highlands back to Jayapura, then juggle our way forward to the airline check-in desk through the congested assemblies of locals seeking to join the Merpati flight back to Jakarta and the modern world. This took a very uncomfortable two hours, inching slowly forwards with our collected weaponry in our arms. The airline officials checked our luggage cautiously for plastic explosives but waved us past the security X-rays with our bows, arrows, spears, other armaments and penis sheaths onto the plane because, as they said, our weaponry was too difficult to put onto the x-ray screening conveyer belt anyway—enough weapons it seemed to me to take over the airport had we so desired. Perhaps my Diplomatic Passport may have helped assure him. The main subsequent problem I had was working out how to fit a bunch of spears into the luggage locker. I found this beguiling when compared with some of my international flight encounters with Security. Flying out of Paris from a Headquarters assignment on one occasion I had a potato peeler confiscated by particularly zealous airport Security Officials—I spent much of the flight back to Jakarta speculating on exactly how one might threaten a pilot with paring away his epidermis with an object dedicated to removing the outside layer of vegetable skin.

Also, between the Tribute Ceremony and the flight, five of the Tribal Chiefs from nearby villages requested I travel with them back to their villages to see and meet the people. 'No problem' I thought, and immediately agreed. The problem was that I was a prime target for kidnapping by the OPM, the Freedom Fighters—and the only transport available was a long wheel-base Land Rover provided by the government. ALL the Chiefs therefore *insisted* they travel very directly *with* me in order to protect me personally from capture in each of their own controlled village domains. We *all* packed into the Land Rover. I found myself in a very limited space with a driver and five tribal chiefs crushed around me in care, semi-naked apart from the pig-fat, penis-sheathes and unwashed odor—driving down poorly developed very bumpy jungle trails (that meant even closer direct contact) for some considerable time … eventually almost wishing to be taken hostage in order to escape. But it was a brilliant privilege nevertheless to be so warmly welcomed by the people.

I mentioned the Asmat Auction which I attended when again in West Papua in 1999.

We arrived on the subsequently ill-fated charter flight after a two-hour journey from Timika, landing on the grass airstrip near the coastal villages of the Asmat. I wandered off the plane while we waited to see what was going to happen next and walked across 10 m or so from the front of the plane to take a photograph of our vehicle. Looking up towards the mountain at the end of the landing strip I suddenly was alarmed to realize that an assembled mob of maybe 200 or more semi-naked tribal warriors in full jungle fighting regalia of feathers, bones, spears, bows, and arrows were gathered and rattling their spears … a very bad sign. Immediately, they charged down the hill towards me. Protected with no more than a camera, I felt distinctly exposed. The whooping mass, brandishing their weapons with entirely credible menace, kept coming …. but at the last minute turned to the left around the nose of the aircraft, surrounding the small group of other passengers that had alighted from the plane and were standing in awe under the wing. No danger, just a welcoming party!

We then had to get to the village of Agats where the Asmat Auction of local tribal artefacts was to be held. We loaded onto a small flotilla of motorized dug-out canoes and set off down the river through the mud flats and mangroves. An hour later we turned the final corner of the river to be greeted with a series of dugout canoes stretched across the entire river's breadth, each containing six standing warriors. Again, a welcoming party to the village. Built on mudflats and over water, the village houses were connected by ancient boardwalks. We found our way to the main village community house and sat, waiting for the show to begin.

In the meantime, I had the chance to chat for a while with the local Catholic priest, an Irish Jesuit who, 47 years before, in 1952, had initially ventured by dugout canoe into what at that stage from the vantage point of Europe was the end of the earth, the tropical jungle mudflat Papuan villages of the Asmat, pursuing the zealous missionary target of bringing the 'primitive Asmat heathens' to God. Forty seven years before the present encounter the Asmat were head-hunting cannibals, so his lone adventure into the unknown must have taken enormous courage … or faith in The Almighty's protective hand. Needless to say, my curiosity drove me to ask the priest how he survived as a lone outsider entering the previously untouched world of the Asmat. He was totally pragmatic about God's will, and told me that what mattered was that he had been blessed by the traditions of the Asmat themselves. Their spirit world, populated by those ancestors who had moved on from life into death, was a direct 'negative' to the sentient world's positive presence: in life the people are black; in death they are white. The priest, of an Irish Celtic complexion untouched by solar blemish, was revered on his arrival as a spirit descending from the afterlife *because he was white*, and as far as the locals were concerned, *very* strange. What more perfect introduction could there be for a Catholic Priest appearing from another world down the river through the Asmat morning mist to convert the flock to new practices that enhanced their apparent security of access into the afterlife!

The Asmat were not head-hunters anymore, having been touched by Catholicism. But this past tradition remained an influence on current village life. The guy who ran the auction, radio microphone in hand, a showman to his core, was the village chief, a status he acquired, so I was informed, at least in part because through his immediate ancestors, that is, dad and grandad, he had acquired the spiritual power of possessing the *largest* number of shrunken heads—somewhere near 100. All won in inter-tribal battles and source of continuing community power. A little intimidating as wall decoration in his Chief's hut, however.

The Auction, by the way, had developed over the previous few years with particular interest and support from the incoming head of Freeport mining company's community relations, Paul Murphy, a person who had carriage of developing an entirely new community-oriented reputation for the company. Whilst most of his work required being in West Papua, Paul Murphy also was dealing with the Indonesian Government, and, as we increasingly needed to connect over Lorentz and ensuring Freeport acceptance of our UN boundary and care rules, we eventually ended up fellow tennis contestants within the Jakarta Diplomatic Community.

But, by word of mouth and a little wider promotion, the Asmat Auction down in a very remote West Papuan village was starting to become famous as an exotic tribal experience which you could not only have permission to access, but also where you could purchase Asmat Art at source, thus saving vast amounts compared with the prices Asmat artefacts would fetch in the dedicated Art Galleries of New York and London. Groups on a number of private yachts had ventured down to this remote southern coast of West Papua to then travel up-river to participate in the event, as, apart from coming down by privately chartered plane this was the only way one could get there. Still, whilst the event was developing a certain *de rigueur* fashion-ableness for the aficionados who could afford to adventure so far, not too many outsiders were able to make it.

The Auction began.

Fierce bidding—for artefacts ranging in size from four meter ceremonial poles to intimately sculpted wooden depictions of the ancestor. At the front of the hall were the 20 or so outsiders who had learnt of the Auction and taken on a serious adventure to find it. At the back of the room, just a meter behind the money-spending foreign contingent, were the locals—observing these strangers with both curiosity and a certain sense of expectation. The 'locals' I might add were dressed in full jungle regalia—that is, the men were basically naked except for the mandatory penis sheath, bristling with primitive weapons, odorously endowed by pig fat and life in an unbathroomed jungle habitat. They were *watching* very closely. And, each time the auction response to a proffered artefact stretched beyond *satu juta rupiah*, one million rupiahs, the warriors would, as one, rise to their feet and whoop and cheer uproariously. At first this practice was pretty intimidating. After a while we relaxed and engaged with the up-beat mood.

Several hours later after the post-auction feast we traversed the board walks over the mangroves on which the village was built, back to our waiting boats. On the way we noticed a number of quite old looking statues discarded into the mangrove mud. Whilst of antique potential to the imported western collectors, 'old' was not good for the locals. For the artefacts had lost the spiritual power that is endowed in the objects when they are made for a specific ritual purpose in the first place. As we found so many times in our contacts across the modern-tribal culture divide, the value we attached to what on the surface were the same things, was very different indeed. The Asmat valued spirit in an eternal present. As modernist outsiders we valued competitive possession of objects in which the past was embedded in a reminder of progressive time. Reflections of two contradictory cultural and economic worlds which UNESCO was seeking to bridge when we flew the 108 pigs to the people of Mapnduma.

Responding to the West Papuan Drought: How Jungle Aid Programs Can Suddenly Go Terribly Wrong

In our continuing contact with West Papua tribes and districts through the 1990s and 2000s, we had access to direct information on the change in local conditions and living difficulties that a severe drought was causing. Needless to say, access to clean water was critical. In some districts the water was there, but given the mountainous folded geography of the place, the people could not use it—as the water was often located deep in ravines they could not reach with a bucket on a rope. In other cases, there were no means of clean water storage available. I therefore mounted a cross-sectoral program to address the problem, bringing in our culture, science and technology and hydrology units into a single team, giving birth to the UNESCO 'Clean Water Program' for West Papua, the objective of which was to enable the most at-risk local communities to access, protect and use the limited water resources that were available to them for both drinking and agricultural needs.

We set up the official agreements and financial supports that have to be in place for this kind of tribal development project—inside the UN, with UNDAC, UNDP and UNICEF, and with the Indonesian Relief Assistance Coordinating Body, BAKORNAS, along with agreements for assistance from the Danish and German Embassies. Again, the funding base was relatively small, around $(US)20,000 plus of course our own staff time and expertise, a lot of in-kind help and a separate contract for diesel pump supply managed by the Danish Embassy. But the project worked, allowing us to purchase water pumps for 13 villages in the Baliem Valley area, varying according to the local situation, from manual pump systems to small diesel-engine powered water pumps where the vertical lift required was too high for manual labor to bridge. The Danish Embassy's contribution was to contract the Danish pump company, Grundfos, to manufacture and deliver the three diesel-powered systems we needed. Meanwhile, we also established a training program for local communities in the Baliem Valley at the Handicrafts Workshop we had established in Wamena. With the support of specialized carpenters from Jakarta we trained the locals to produce wooden barrels to be used for water storage and therefore protection from the drought. UNESCO was in charge of the overall program as our organization was particularly well suited to manage this operation because uniquely as an international agency we had the combination of expertise *in-house* to measure hydrology requirements, understand appropriate cultural practices and supervise science and engineering application in a highly complex and sensitive cultural context such as one is confronted with in West Papuan tribal society.

So far so good. However, as we so often discovered when implementing development assistance projects in remote and exotic places, things can go wrong in unexpected ways. The base problem was the diesel engine pumps and clear communications. We were fully aware that the pumps had to be *carried* by tribal bearers up the jungle paths from the town of Wamena to the villages where they were to be installed—carried on a mountainous trek through the jungle for up to eight days. Consequently, the pumps had to be supplied in units that a man could carry, but which could be easily re-assembled once delivered to the village. We conveyed this requirement to the Danish Embassy, but unfortunately by the time the contract was signed with Grundfos in Copenhagen this 'detail' had slipped into the forgotten side notes. When the pumps arrived in Jakarta in-transit towards West Papua, we discovered the consequent problem: Grundfos had welded each of the entire pumps together making them transportable by forklift truck perhaps but certainly not by unaided humans walking up a narrow jungle path. The problem could be fixed, and it was—but with a delay of around two weeks from the promised schedule.

Meanwhile, the manager of the NGO in the Baliem Valley who we had brought in to handle the human transport of the equipment into the jungle had gone ahead without checking with us to hire the 100 or so bearers that were going to be needed to carry not only the pumps but also the pipes, cement, and other building materials into the highland jungles. The men were sitting relatively patiently in the grounds of the Handicrafts Workshop we had built in Wamena waiting for the pumps to arrive. After several days the manager grew impatient with the delay. Each day was costing him a proportion of his profits as he had to supply food for the bearers to eat while they sat and waited. Unilaterally he decided to act and sent the bearers off on their journey without waiting for the pumps. Several days later the pipes, cement and building materials arrived at their destinations, but no pumps. The manager had neglected to mention his intention to us before sending the bearers off into the jungle. We therefore were confronted with cement moldering away in the sweaty jungle climate into being unusable, and no bearers left to carry the essential equipment. We finally solved the problems, a feat that required multiple missions of my UNESCO staff down to West Papua and into the jungles to re-organize and put the pieces of a complex hydrology jigsaw into place once the by-now separated components of the diesel pumps had all arrived. When it comes to working with remote local communities, always expect the unexpected!

We had not forgotten culture however as a centerpiece rather than constraint in development assistance. Our experience in the post-hostage development of cultural connectedness and tribal voyages into modern life had allowed us to realize that demonstration of the rich social wealth of cultural difference was a very important tool to use in healing the conflicts that erupted along with the Revolution between Christian and Moslem communities. So, late in 1998 we brought a number of Papuans back to Jakarta, this time as people to assist us with conflict resolution in urban areas. The cultural dependency relationship had come full circle. This time we were relying on indigenous cultural practices to help young people caught up in inter-group conflict to become aware of how much they shared across the barriers of conflict even though there *appeared* to be irreconcilable cultural or religious difference between them. More on this shortly.

Edge of the Future

The kidnapping had shaken the West Papuan Highlands out of the Stone Age and onto the World Stage. The subsequent events demonstrated to the world that a significant number of West Papuans wanted independence. Indeed, Meanwhile, the Papuan people were confronting contradiction—with the Indonesian army stepping up its repression in the hidden jungle highlands, whilst at the same time, President Soeharto directly welcomed a new approach in establishing dialogue with the tribal leaders that had been initiated by UNESCO.

It was *after* the fall of President Soeharto however that serious political change did start to penetrate into Papuan affairs and the Government started to pay serious attention to the peoples' demands. When President

Wahid came to power after Jusuf Habibie's interim Presidency, the Indonesian Government terminated the policy of transmigration—though, by now, it left behind a legacy of 35 percent of the residents in West Papua being non-indigenous. The government changed the name of West Papua to Papua and in February 2000 organized a landmark Papuan political assembly, *MUBES - Musyawarah Besar*, or Grand Consultation. The Consultation elected a Papuan Council Presidium which included several high ranking OPM leaders—and the OPM started to disappear as a separatist force as they became incorporated into the Presidium's decision-making process, and the wider community of Papuan people, recognizing they would never defeat the Indonesian military, at the same time disavowed the violence that had previously been associated with OPM resistance.

Some further OPM kidnappings did occur, for example of a Korean forestry team at the turn of the century, but from the 2000s onwards, the incidents declined—with one notable exception, the capture of two Belgians on 25th May 2001, Johan Elias dem Dynde and Phillip R.D. Simon. Interestingly, the leader of the group which captured the two Belgians was *Titus Marup*—one of the leaders of the 1996 kidnapping, and impersonator prior to that to Ben Bohane of Kelly Kwalik. Again, five years on, he claimed to be Kwalik to the outside world. Kwalik was not pleased and shortly afterwards released a statement to the media denying any involvement in the kidnapping whatsoever. Both Belgians were released without ransom.

And in late July 2006, the media reported that OPM leaders, meeting in Papua New Guinea, had decided to end their armed struggle and to continue their demands for independence using peaceful means, though they did, however, maintain their right to defend themselves if attacked. In response, TNI Commander-in-Chief Marshal Djoko Suyanto assured that the military, though remaining 'vigilant' would no longer conduct offensive operations against OPM rebels. This action has not happened. An International Presence of the Free Papua Movement has been formed in the UK and Europe—though is not always seen as representative in West Papua. The OPM, as the armed wing of the overall Free Papua Movement has now become the West Papua National Liberation Army or TPNPB (Tentara Pembebasan Nasional Papua Barat)—blended in with the local indigenous communities.

Sporadic attacks continue from both sides, but it remains to be seen whether a new commitment has truly started to influence the maintenance of peace and restraint in West Papua—particularly as the Indonesian military would appear to have changed little. Ostensibly seeking to repress TPNPB warriors who are fighting a guerrilla battle, the organised military too often attack village communities as if *they* are the rebels. Meanwhile, current President Joko Widodo has visited West Papua six times since his election in 2014, and additional government presence is expanding within the sub-Provinces of West Papua officially to provide enhanced infrastructure service but unofficially further dividing an overall voice for the Papuan people and strengthening overall military rule. From the Papuan side, the 'Morning Star' flag, symbolizing independence, though illegal, is raised widely on December 1st each year—and the people of West Papua clearly want self-determination. In September 2017 the Free Papua Movement circulated a Petition through West Papua to test popular approval of the UN appointing a special representative to report human rights abuses and to hold an internationally supervised vote for self-determination. Declared illegal, banned by the Indonesian Government, and blocked on-line, the petition sheets had to be smuggled secretly from one end of West Papua to the other, right down to remote jungle village level. Even so, 1.8 million people signed, voting for Independence—often with their blood and thumbprint, *70% of West Papua's population.* Exiled West Papuan independence campaigner, Benny Wenda, presented the bound Petition to the UN Decolonization Committee. When considered by the UN General Assembly, a number of countries offered support whilst Indonesia predictably classed the vote a publicity stunt with no credibility, directing the delegates back to the completely orchestrated referendum then General Assembly Resolution 2504 (XXIV) 1969. The United Nations is yet to take action.

On the guerrilla fighter side, in early February 2023 New Zealand pilot, Phillip Mehrtens was taken hostage by the TPNPB when he landed his small commercial plane in the Nduga region - the same Highland territory as the 1996 capture of Martha and other hostages.

The impact of the 1996 kidnapping incident therefore introduced a new *uncertainty* for the Papuan people, one which has not yet gone away. For on the one hand, through focusing world attention on Indonesia's hardline militaristic policy for West Papua, the incident started to sweep away the Indonesian Government's freedom to justify the continuing exercise of naked and violent neo-colonial control, but on the other hand, the aftermath of the 1996 incident opened up for the indigenous people a new global world of opportunity but culturally alien values to deal with.

What was revealed in the events that unfolded over those ill fated 128 days was the prism the incident represented—of global-tribal values in conflict that stood at the heart of the kidnapping and negotiations.

As I concluded in my final Security Report No 63 on Saturday 18th May 1996,

West Papua therefore teeters on the edge of history. Events of the hostage crisis provided both prism and stimulus of this history. Martha is free. West Papua awaits its verdict.

10

The Critical Importance of Local Engagement and Listening

We confronted the lessons we learnt from *Flying Pigs* again and again, in particular when dealing with tribal and remote communities – the absolute necessity of placing emphasis on listening, local empowerment and engagement, and the impact that quite small but well targeted financial contributions could make. Lessons from working with communities across other areas of Indonesia follow. Far too often development agencies, though with the best will in the world, did not *listen* to the people and culture they were dealing with, and decided inappropriately from the outside what the people really needed and wanted.

Working with the Mentawai People of Siberut Island

Indeed, projects with high levels of funding can have a negative impact simply *because* there is too much money sloshing around without adequate attention to what is really needed.

We worked with the Mentawai people on the island of Siberut, west of Sumatra for a long time, starting as one of our early new initiatives when I came to work with the UN in Jakarta in 1995. I talk more about this initiative in Chapter 10. In parallel, one of the large development banks had brought water to the people of a nearby other Siberut village. It was a well-endowed hydrology system built in the coastal village of Maileppet by outside contractors at some considerable expense. But once the developers left, the locals did not know what to do. Access to the water for local use, for example, was difficult as the taps were in the wrong place; the system broke down and no one could fix it, so within a couple of years it descended into disrepair and disuse.

Our own UNESCO team recognized that water supply remained a priority so we came, on invitation, to help. But we did not bring in consultants and large volumes of cash – which we did not have anyway. Instead, we worked *with* the local community, and helped *them* to design and build their own very basic system. It cost $(US)10,000, could be repaired locally as we used pipes made from local bamboo rather imported steel, placed access where the villagers told us they needed the taps. In a short space of time the locals were actually selling excess water to the local government officials who themselves did not have access to clean water. What mattered was *connecting* with the local communities and helping to facilitate them to do things for themselves. I would add that this same major bank development project for the island—costing somewhere over $(US)1 million, of which the water supply was one element, was designed by international consultants together with central government officials, and clearly with very little local involvement. Siberut really is quite hard to get to, and one has to assume that these guys did not bother, or stayed for very short periods if they could handle the adventure. The aid designers *assumed* that the locals, like 80 percent of Indonesians across the whole archipelago, were Moslems, and in recognition, built a mosque into the development package. Unfortunately for the project's success, 90% of the Mentawai are *not* Moslem, so the only real benefit extracted by the locals from the mosque component in the project was use of the acoustic loudspeaker system intended to call the faithful to prayer. This ended up in the local karaoke bar.

Response to the Tsunami in Aceh

I talk about the interaction between donors and the Tsunami crisis in Aceh province of Indonesia in Chaps. 18 and 19 so will only mention it briefly here, just to indicate another negative dimension of money-led aid. In Aceh after the December 2004 Tsunami, vast amounts of funding flowed in from international sources, including from tiny NGOs and even individual towns and community groups in Europe, Australia and elsewhere. The immediately obvious problem was often the desire to *give* was more important than understanding and responding to what the communities really needed. As a result, boats were donated that were too powerful for local conditions and stimulated overfishing, houses were built in areas directly at risk from future tsunamis or in designs that were quite inappropriate for local Acehnese, clothes were donated that were more suited to European winter than Aceh's tropics, and so on. More insidious was the unintended consequence of large numbers of doctors from elsewhere flowing into health care for they displaced the jobs for local practitioners, and large quantities of funding into the free provision of pharmaceuticals as local chemist shops were robbed of any business in the critical rebuilding phase.

Moreover, when competing agencies are juggling for position—and credit—with large cheques in hand, the opportunity for corruption opens wide. 'Facilitation' fees assist quick official acceptances of projects, whilst projects are approved that are often poorly thought through in terms of critical relevance, but the side-flows of money are attractive. In the case of Aceh, it should be pointed out, that whilst endemic corruption and irrelevance could not be totally suppressed given the flood of money and international interest to 'help', strong action *was* taken to take control. Under new President Susilo Bambang Yudhyono, the Government established a supreme coordinating Agency for Rehabilitation and Reconstruction, BRR, which, led by an effective ex-businessman, *did* limit the opportunities for corruption and irrelevance in the use of funding dedicated to Aceh very considerably. More broadly in Indonesia, particularly when Soeharto was President prior to 1998, corrupt side-flows of aid funding down the pipeline from Minister to senior official to lowly official was a feature of doing business. When the World Bank was criticized in the late 1990s for losing between 20 and 30 percent of development assistance funding due to such side-flows, one of the mechanisms came to light in Indonesia. The highly career-oriented Director of the time, later to be retracted to Headquarters and re-assigned to a very remote Central Asian posting, was implicated—though not for direct financial corruption, but for a wider 'interest' in successful loan negotiation. His career aspiration to Vice-Presidential status in the organization depended on demonstrating that he could develop the largest loan portfolio for the Bank. These are no-interest loans, with repayments over extended periods of time, so are attractive to governments of the day which have little real concern about picking up the financial debt of today's decision 10 years later when they are no longer in the job. The Bank would conduct very detailed feasibility studies and calculations after which they would establish the level of loan required, for arguments sake for an expressway system, at $(US)90 million. But the senior government officials under Ministerial guidance would do their own costing to demonstrate that the project could not be done for less than $(US)115 million. The Bank's Director was under pressure for if he refused this level of funding the loan would not go ahead and along with this, credit to his career status would be diminished. He would therefore accept loans at levels well above the Bank's own initial costing, endorsing arguments from government officials that there were unforeseen local conditions or whatever that required raising the level of the loan. The residual $(US)25 million would then flow down the pipeline of local authority from the Minister eventually reaching those that actually did the work, with decreasing levels of facilitation fees or additional costs being extracted along the way.

Transition to Democracy in Timor Leste

Corruption is invariably a black shadow that stands behind development assistance simply because the context is often one where poverty rules, government officials enjoy considerable broad ranging power, and the recipient country's mechanisms of accountability are still at an infantile stage. However, even where there is no overtly corrupt behavior, the most insidious source of failure for development assistance lies in the power of the money overwhelming the need for project-shaping engagement at local community level. This is particularly the case for those international donors which can write the largest cheques, for often in my experience, a culture of self-absorbed arrogance can quietly creep in, distorting projects and even cooperation with more technically specialized but less generously funded agencies.

One reason for this is that particularly when the agency is responding to a major crisis, and where they are dispersing extensive 'new' money raised through public or national government appeals, they have no choice but to bring in a large number of contract staff at field level. Though these are often highly committed individuals, these (usually young) people have a direct interest in proving themselves both for maintenance of their contract and the possibility of moving into permanent employment in the agency. *Their* plan usually prevails; cooperation with less funded though technically mandated agencies, like UNESCO, is a distraction; and local engagement with the community must be done by newly arrived outsiders in a hurry. And the consequent project can simply miss the point!

In East Timor, or Timor Leste, the Portuguese language official name of the country since its May 2002 Independence, (and additionally, Timor Timor, the Indonesian name of what was previously an Indonesian province until 1999, and Timor Lorisae, the local Tetum language name during its UN-managed transition period, 1999 to 2002) we confronted a fine example of this 'funding-over-engagement' problem caused by a well-endowed donor, where the result was not only total failure of the intervention, but serious disruption of earlier successful low-scale initiatives. The key problem I am highlighting in a complex situation was the development of post-violence community radio, absolutely necessary communication during the early recovery process.

To demonstrate the very negative consequence of total lack of attention to the local situation, I need to spend some time setting the wider context—purposive Indonesian military-led militia destruction—with an Indonesian President, Jusuf Habibie, creating the situation because of his own ignorance.

Timor's Violent Context and Indonesian Source

Timor Leste was in a very sorry state after the militia-led violence that accompanied the Plebiscite for Independence from Indonesia in September 1999 that President Habibie initiated. The level of destruction was quite extraordinary. Dili, the capital, for example, was totally trashed to the point where, as United Nations officials the *only* accommodation we could find was in a storage container each on a ship brought into port by the United Nations, and all banks were destroyed.

The violence was planned in advance by the Indonesian military which supported hired external militia seeking to intimidate, then after the peoples' vote, to derail the conclusions from the plebiscite that had been offered to the Timorese people in January 1999. Even against a backdrop of a quarter of a century of direct intimidation, disappearances and killings, the post-plebiscite violence traumatized the population, many of whom fled into the jungles and hills to escape the spread of murder through the whole province.

Within my own UN responsibilities for Indonesia, I was there immediately after the initial violence when some level of order had been established—my first Mission along with Heads of other UN Agencies and Indonesian Government to assess what needed to be done.

For me a highly evocative symbol of the aftermath of the trauma that demonstrated the depth of the fear that had been instilled in the population was when I was walking (with some considerable caution) in the early morning down a street in the capital, Dili, shortly after Australian Major General Cosgrove's military unit had re-established protection from the marauding Indonesia-inspired militia and civil disorder. In front of me, a tiny girl, perhaps six years old, sidled up shyly to a tall, fully armed, and fearsome looking Australian soldier who was patrolling the streets after coming into Timor Leste on behalf of the international community to bring the orchestrated anarchy under control. She grasped the soldier's hand, smiled up at him, and walked down the road accompanying him on patrol—symbolizing the slow return of trust that some form of security had provided for a people who were terrified. The vision brought me to tears.

Within security information the UN had access to we had clear evidence that the Indonesian military was directly involved in forming and funding the militia which had led the unrest that so traumatized this little girl.

Accidental catalyst was Habibie, the President of Indonesia who had offered a plebiscite on independence versus remaining with Indonesia to the people of the province. Habibie was not evil in intent, simply naïve, seeking to pursue a good idea, but not thinking through how to do it. The stage was set by a letter to him from Australia's Prime Minister John Howard raising the prospect of self-determination of Timor Leste along the lines of an arrangement worked out by France for the French colony of New Caledonia. Habibie was offended as Howard's letter implied Indonesia was running Timor Leste like a colony. Australia's intervention proposed a long-term preparatory period of 10 years to prepare the way prior to a plebiscite. Habibie was fed up with being continuously criticized over Timor Leste and concluded that maintaining control over the territory wasn't worth the effort. Habibie scribbled a note across Howard's letter, "Why not independence? If East Timor becomes a burden for Indonesia, then it could be harmonically separated."

Dewi Fortuna Anwar, Habibie's political advisor from the Institute of Sciences or LIPI, told me that she had previously proposed to Habibie in January 1999 that if he wanted to appear a statesman as a result of his action during his tenure as interim President after Soeharto was deposed, Habibie should offer options for greater *autonomy* to at least one of the restive provinces of Indonesia, Aceh, West Papua (then, Irian Jaya) or Timor Leste. 'Autonomy' meant greater freedom *within* Indonesia's overall rule.

Anwar's advice was a very sensible idea, and one that was later emulated in a major shift in national policy towards Aceh, one of the two other provinces straining against the yoke of central administrative control, Irian Jaya (West Papua) and Aceh.

Australian Prime Minister Howard's letter therefore stimulated Habibie to make Timor Leste a formative case for dealing with the problem of restive provinces of Indonesia generally. He was immediately attracted to the idea as it allowed him to get the international community off his back, but, in a distinctly Habibie style, he wanted to do it *now* rather than wait, so announced to the media shortly after he had received Ibu Dewi's advice that he was going to offer the people of Timor Leste an immediate plebiscite on their future relationship with Indonesia, i.e.: staying within the State of Indonesia as is—serviced by current support, or being 'independent'. No preparatory period required.

There was a problem. Habibie had made a mistake and confused "Independence"—meaning total separation, with what Ibu Dewi Fortuna Anwar had proposed, "Autonomy"—meaning a level of freedom *within* the State of Indonesia. Habibie apparently consulted a few members of his own inner circle, but did not consider it necessary to consult with his well-experienced Minister for Foreign Affairs, Ali Alatas, who may well have suggested caution and a protracted preparation period. I knew both Ibu Dewi Anwar and Minister Ali Alatas personally, and Ali Alatas told me that the first he knew of Habibie's intention to offer a Plebiscite for possible Independence to Timor Leste was when President Habibie walked past his door on the way to the Press Conference where he was about to announce his intention to the media. Ali Alatas went out into the corridor to enquire if he could assist the President and what he planned to announce, and learnt for the first time that the President was about to offer Independence or Remaining with Indonesia with extra support … *now!* Too late for Ali to intervene.

Habibi's second major error was to not consult with the Military about his offering of *independence* to Timor Leste in advance of his Press Conference announcement.

ABRI, the Indonesian army, was then caught by surprise and had every reason to be upset, for the army had a significant stake in Timor Leste. In keeping with the stimulus of being required to raise a significant proportion of their military budget from their own economic activities, ABRI officers who had considerable authority in a province where they were battling a jungle-based rebel movement, controlled the mainstay of the Timor Leste economy, in particular, coffee production and distribution—which, with the possibility of Independence, was under severe threat of no longer providing continuing finance for their military and personal (corrupt) income. Moreover, in the long battle with the freedom fighters of Fretilin, a significant number of soldiers had been killed. Even though the number paled into insignificance against the number of Timorese reported to be killed or missing over this protracted internal fighting period, estimated to be around one hundred thousand people from a population of just under one million. The military retained an agenda. *Their* boys had been killed by the rebels; it was time for pay-back not reward!

Consequently, the senior military officials decided on the spot that they would do all in their power to derail the Independence Plebiscite. General Wiranto, head of the military, as required of his position, half-heartedly sided with the President, his Commander-in-Chief, *in public*, but in private, he joined the military - implacably opposed to Habibie on the Timor Leste issue … determined to not let Timor Leste loose from Indonesia, and *never* to forgive Habibie for what he had done. The planning that ended up in coordinated militia action immediately moved into place under a rubric I was told was "Let them eat stones".

The people voted in the plebiscite of 21st August 1999 (98.6% of eligible voters), but of the 451,792 registered voters, 78.4 percent rejected the offer of remaining with Indonesia, opting instead for full Independence. 'Autonomy' as a choice of *how* to relate to Indonesia was not defined. Kofi Annan, Secretary-General of the United Nations, concluded therefore when the results were announced, that the people of Timor Leste had thus rejected remaining under Indonesian governance, and expressed their wish to begin a process of transition towards Independence. *Habibie had not built a transition time period into the Plebiscite, so Independence for Timor Leste did not need to wait or be prepared.*

The Indonesian military, and thus the militia operating under their commission, had a different strategic view. The Timorese would be punished for arriving at the wrong answer to the question.

Amongst so many other acts of violence, Dili, the capital, was comprehensively trashed. There was literally hardly a single building left standing and unburnt—a relatively small town, but totally in ruin. Bacau, the second town of Timor Leste, was similarly devastated, except for the Catholic Church: the priest had done a deal with the military, money had changed hands and the church was left intact.

Appropriately perhaps, accepting 'burnt buildings' emerged as a symbol of the spirit of the Timorese. After the militia violence but prior to Independence, one of the earliest local businesses to re-establish was Dili's first post-violence restaurant, primarily, it must be admitted, targeting internationals who, like me, were on mission to Timor Leste and enjoyed enough income to go to a restaurant. It was called "The Burnt House", and it was. Lit by candles, one sat in various rooms of a roofless former house whilst the cook made do with very basic facilities including a portable BBQ rather than stove. Following Independence Xanana Gusmao *chose* to set up his Presidential Office in the burnt-out shell of a building in the middle of Dili. Above the remnants of the remaining ceiling over the entrance foyer, the second floor appeared as little more than a gaping and blackened hole. Xanana's office was more or less intact, but a tiny space in an otherwise blackened shell where makeshift offices had been established. It was here that I first met and appreciated Xanana Gusmao.

Not only the buildings were affected, however. The violence had totally taken out the infrastructures of communications, broadcasting and transportation systems—relatively undeveloped to start with, and now, simply not there. In Bacau for example, after some initial repairs, the only place where one could experience mobile phone reception was within the near vicinity of the one transmitter tower that had been re-commissioned. The only problem was that whoever was talking with you also had to be within the close proximity of the same tower—you could just as easily send directly sighted semaphore signals. We, in the UN, had to rely on satellite based radios. This was not an option for the Timorese.

Needless to say, the loss of communications infrastructure had an enormous impact on the ability of international agencies like my own to help in the recovery process as well as the transition of a country into democratic rule. As was also the case in responding to the Tsunami in Aceh, a story I will come to in Chaps. 18 and 19, for us as the responsible technical agency, initiating the rebuilding of the media and communications capacity of an area hit by disaster was a critical early priority rather than something that could be left until later. The people need information they can rely on, with an essential purpose to dispel the rumors that invariably spill out of situations characterized by fear and uncertainty, but also to indicate where help can be reached, what has happened to relatives, and so on. We also had found that in the post-conflict zones of southern Mindanao in the Philippines, local community-based radio was an immensely valuable tool of local empowerment, literacy development and conflict resolution, essential elements in peace building. I will talk about this specific initiative in Chap. 16. A local voice and trusted information source is therefore critical for recovery from crisis, and in the expression and information that must penetrate into a society for it to handle conflict resolution, new-found freedom and democracy. All of these conditions prevailed in Timor Leste.

Consequently, and we now come to the main point of the Timorese story for this chapter. One of the earliest UNESCO interventions in Timor Leste that we introduced following the April–May 1999 militia violence that had torn through the country, was to assist a number of local communities to build a community radio capacity. In a project implemented by Tarja, at that time from our Western Samoan Apia Office, UNESCO managed to get community radio systems into place in the two most remote provinces of Timor Leste, at Los Palos in the east and Maliana in the west. The design of the project included very careful mapping of radio transmission and reception in difficult mountainous terrain, and provision of basic equipment for both broadcasting and receiving along with local training. Getting the radio stations on-air at this early stage was particularly important for the grass roots civic education that was needed to bring the society for the first time out of a subjugated and violent past and towards democratic elections. The head of the UN system in Timor Leste at the time, Sergio Viera de Mello came to see one of the UNESCO stations, Radio Comunidade Lospalos, and endorsed it as a 'model project' for the UN at that time.

Significance of the Loss of Sergio De Mello

Sergio Viera de Mello himself deserves a momentary aside at this point for his story indicates both the unique role of the United Nations in countries-in-crisis, and the shift in openness that was forced onto the UN by the rise of terrorism at the dawn of the 21st Century.

De Mello, as 'Special Representative of the Secretary General of the United Nations' in Timor Leste was accorded enormous power, or to use diplomatic language, 'Plenipotent' power over what happened in Timor Leste, for he was effectively Head of State during this UN-managed transition period. Sergio de Mello, at a personal level also conveyed a commanding presence, and was enormously valued by the Timorese as their initial nation builder. He moved on after his Timor posting to a similar level of post in Iraq during Iraq's transition period towards a post-Saddam Hussein Government following the US invasion of the country. De Mello was widely touted, quite appropriately, as the next Secretary-General of the United Nations.

But then the UN Building in Baghdad was attacked by a terrorist bombing. This was June 2003. De Mello was killed, an event that sent shock-waves through the whole UN system, including back to Timor Leste, not only because of who was killed, but because of the change it reflected in UN relations to the countries we served. One of the reasons that the bombers could so easily get to the UN Building was that no-one in the UN seriously believed it would happen. Experience to that point through many complex emergencies and countries even close to the status of being Failed-States was that the United Nations was seen by all parties as the 'arbiter' not the enemy, a fair-witness forum within which opponents had a voice and the country itself had membership and a voice in a way that could not be the case in any bilateral relationship. There was a general view, even in dangerous places, that the United Nations and its Agencies needed to be accessible rather than removed from the people behind barriers of fear.

Consequently, as in Baghdad, whilst *basic* security practices were in place, the death of de Mello, suddenly signaled to the whole UN system that the world had moved on and the United Nations itself was now a clear political target.

We had confronted some really quite serious problems with security in Indonesia as well prior to this event, but these mainly were associated with demonstrations that stopped off at the UN building for international profile or with being caught up serendipitously in civil unrest. I talk about this in Chap. 13, 14 and 15. The Baghdad bombing was different. As compared with our Indonesia situation where the UN Building was a location for public attention to street marches and protest, the United Nations was now a direct political *target* and the stress through the whole system on raised security measures was immediate, along with which the UN became a little more distant from the people it served. Increasingly, the situation was continuing to get worse. A direct result was serious danger to our UN Offices in Jakarta, Indonesia. Enough for me to move our entire UNESCO Office to an alternative and very comfortable location in a securely monitored diplomatic quarter of Jakarta as I speak about in Chaps. 14, 15 and 16 shortly when dealing with the May 1998 Revolution—just, as it turned out, a few weeks before a terrorist bomb was exploded at our Jakarta UN Headquarters and *all* other UN Agencies were forced to move out immediately to alternative accommodation in a nearby dark and dingy office block.

Then, as 2007 drew to a close, the newly built United Nations Building in Algeria was bombed by terrorists apparently linked with al-Qaeda, this time killing 10 United Nations employees. The sole purpose of the bomb blast that was engineered by a local terrorist cell linked with global terrorist initiatives, was to kill UN people so as to heighten the world's attention to religious-based opposition to the Government of Algeria. The United Nations' status as the accessible international fair-witness to international peace and empowerment was forever recast into required (and expensive) self-protection against the encroaching world shadow of sectarian violence. Peace and justice are the larger victims.

The Disruptive Impact of an International Donor with More Money Than Sense in Timor Leste

Focusing back for now on the way that an international donor with more money than sense can distort things within the traumatic aftermath of militia violence that literally *trashed* the country, we come to the community radio projects in Timor Leste. After our initial UNESCO interventions and the development of an additional group of independent radio stations, the World

Bank arrived on the scene in 2003, a year after Independence was declared. Local field staff of the Bank picked up on UNESCO's 'model project' that Sergio de Mello had endorsed, and then poured money in to establish 11 community radio stations. Without experienced community radio experts on staff, just a lot of money, they copied the UNESCO model, used UNESCO's research on transmission and reception maps and options, but neglected to consult UNESCO's expertise or bring in UNESCO as partners, or for that matter, acknowledge the source of the design that the Bank was now using. As a result, they copied the model superficially, but missed its essence, that is, to make the radio stations sustainable without continuing donor funds. The Bank made several fundamental mistakes. They did not provide the training and other support that is necessary to get what is effectively an amateur operation off the ground and functioning as a new and effective broadcaster, and they 'used' the stations as 'propaganda tools' for the promotion of World Bank projects in Timor Leste, immediately causing conflict with the five ARKTL stations which prided themselves on independence, a conflict that remained unresolved for four years. Most importantly, the Bank, with its access to substantial funding, *paid* the staff of the radio stations salaries that were exceptionally good given the level of income available from most other jobs in Timor Leste. Needless to say, the staff got used to being well off, and had little incentive to build up alternative sources of local support for the stations as a whole or find a way of operating on minimal income levels, a key dimension of success I talk about in Chapter 16. Timor Leste is one of the world's poorest countries, so there was no way the local communities could support the broadcasters at the financial levels the Bank had introduced. As soon as the World Bank project finished after three years, the money flow stopped. And left behind was a group of highly dissatisfied radio people who refused to work anymore. The community radio system then simply disappeared without trace.

11

"Changing Things in the Real World—Learning from the Edge"

Moving On

I have, dear Reader, now taken you with me through the door as I entered full time into United Nations life, only to be suddenly thrown into the drama of dealing with the life-threatening abduction of my staff into the jungles of West Papua by freedom fighters. Relationships between our modern international society and some of the most remote tribal peoples in the world confronted me in high relief.

Serious work followed, as I have presented in the chapters so far, to then help bring light to a people deeply enshrouded in repressive darkness by the exploitative interests of the modern world—in particular in the Indonesian Province of West Papua. We learnt many very important lessons along the way, in particular, listening across cultural difference.

In parallel however, much more was going on in my own United Nations life. After all, a major commitment of my responsibilities covered other East Asian and the Pacific countries as Field Director of our National UNESCO Programs, and Ambassador, as well as Regional Director for the UN's Science, Technology and Development initiatives and cooperation. A long way, it would appear, from the remote tropical jungles where the lives of my own captured staff were on the line.

I will now take you into this wider domain—moving across the spectrum from other remote traditional societies under threat to contemporary urban communities. Danger remained—as with handling the May 1998 Revolution and aftermath in Indonesia I write about in Chaps. 13, 14 and 15 and Islamic fundamentalist-excused terrorist threats for loss of their coercive power which accompanied our work to rebuild general education, village literacy and community connectedness across the previous Islamic Conflict Zones of the Mindanao Province of the Philippines after the signing of the Peace Accord under the Presidency of Philippines President Ramos in January 1997. I present this story in Chap. 12. Through United Nations action we could make a real difference—to the empowerment of the people and their own abilities to take control of their lives and future.

What mattered was not just giving relief—although at times this *had* to be our starting point, as with handling the totally traumatic aftermath of the 2004 Aceh Tsunami which I talk about in Chaps. 18 and 19. Instead, what mattered was helping the people to do it themselves and to help strengthen their shared community connectedness that nourished positive collective action. There is no other effective *long* term empowerment strategy.

I will start here from the edge of global intrusion, where millennia-old cultural values persisted, the island of Siberut in the Mentawai Island chain across the tumultuous Sunda Trench from the northern Indonesian Island of Sumatra. Then in my next Chap. 12, I will take you, my readers, increasingly into the modern world. Although cultural difference may vary enormously, the lessons about listening and cultural empowerment are universal.

Rather a long way travelled from handling a hostage crisis in the jungles of West Papua only three to four years earlier. But that and my subsequent West Papua *local* experience had taught me a great deal about where international assistance most effectively connected. Still, in the late 1990s "development assistance"—even within bilateral relations, did not adequately recognize the critical importance of the local peoples' 'agency' within the development assistance paradigm. Perhaps, even more important, the *local* and its cultural *meaning* context, was largely viewed through *international modernist* eyes, not as the basic frame for design of intervention. I very nearly fell into this trap myself when, as I go on to show you now when we started to work with the very remote communities of the Indonesian Mentawai Island of Siberut who appeared to have a 'green' (modernist) view of forest conservation, but, instead, this was embedded in the meanings of a very different tribal culture. Had we not listened—in the peoples' terms, we could have destroyed the culture of the people, and thus their resilience.

The Challenge of Building Community-Based Sustainable Development with a Very Remote Indigenous People

Siberut Island is remote! Like *really* remote. Communication with the external world is highly problematic as can be transport in to the island. Local cultural mores can seriously get in the way but *have* to be honored.

Koen Meyers, our dedicated and courageous project team leader there in Siberut, tells a story of just how difficult such conditions can be for what on the surface may appear a very straightforward enterprise, in this case assisting an international film crew to tell something of the Siberut story. I will quote Koen directly from the report he presented in our 'Glimpses of a Field Office' Section of the Jakarta Office's 2002 Annual Report. Koen tells the story well.

> "One afternoon in the Siberut Biosphere Reserve Office, we received a phone call from the UNESCO Jakarta Office. As is so often the case here, the phone line was not very clear and in our insular, isolated island life, the only words we were able to catch were ' … please send … story on … television … *UN-TV* … *CNN* … chance … promote … Siberut Biosphere Reserve'. And then … nothing!
> A week later, we received another call, and all became clear. A team from UN-TV was going to visit the island to make a short documentary on UNESCO's Siberut Intersectoral Program for *CNN World Report* and *UN In Action*.
> On one hand, a documentary on *CNN* may seem like a golden opportunity to promote UNESCO's Siberut Program (and we had been proposing this idea for a number of months!). But, on the other hand, the logistics of preparing such a field visit can also be a nightmare. For example, for the indigenous people of Siberut, the use of cameras continues to be a sensitive issue, with many people reluctant to be filmed, even reacting aggressively if pictures are taken without the prior consent of the community. In order to avoid such conflict, we decided to send Richard, the education program manager, Yohan, the local program coordinator, and three community representatives working under the Collaborative Management Team, to three upriver villages and one small settlement. Their task was to socialize the goals of the documentary and secure permission from the clan council and local communities to film on location. A day after the team had gone upriver the telephone rings (again!) … The *UN-TV* crew was unable to come. Unfortunately for us, at the last minute, a UN Development Program project in Ambon was given priority over Siberut. So, we faced a new dilemma: five of our staff members are upriver, using UNESCO's only dugout canoe, on a task that doesn't have to happen anymore, and due to the isolation of the region, we are unable to contact them. Fortunately, a few hours later we found another dugout canoe to make

the trip upriver and we sent two other staff members to inform the first team that they do not have to seek out the permission from the communities about the planned arrival of the TV crew. However,

A day later, we got another phone call: the TV crew *is* coming and the whole filming program is back on again! At that stage, we had two dugouts and seven staff members upriver. After a series of late-night consultations with the remaining team members at the Siberut Biosphere Reserve Office, we decided to send in another team upriver to inform the other two teams about the latest developments and ask them to proceed with the planned preparation for the TV crews' arrival.

After three days of anxiously waiting to see what was happening upriver, one of the teams finally arrived back at the Siberut Biosphere Reserve Office, with the news that we had been granted permission to film at all of the sites. This left us only one more day to pick up the film crew at the Padang airport. The trouble was that the public ferry had just left for Padang, and with the next ferry leaving in another four days, we were forced to charter a dugout to Padang. We found one, a little worse for wear and tear, with two 40 HP outboard motors that was able to transport us safely to Padang, though it was still a harrowing trip of 150 km across what is considered one of the most dangerous stretches of ocean in Indonesia. After all of these obstacles, we were still able to comply with the deadline and welcome the TV crew with an exhausted smile at the Padang Airport. All of this before they had even started filming.

Crossing dangerous, shark-infested seas, asking communities to climb coconut trees five times just to get the perfect shot; buying pigs and giving them to communities as a traditional fine for unintentionally filming objects in community homes considered taboo; carrying large amounts of heavy filming equipment and generators over muddy paths that pass through long sections of dense tropical rainforest: all of this is part of working for UNESCO! And all of this, for four minutes of prime time!"

Koen told me another story that even more poignantly demonstrates the gap between global world knowledge and the lives and understandings of these Mentawai tribespeople. This story concerns our UNESCO response to developing community preparedness for a possible tsunami after the earthquakes that had spawned the devastating tsunami on 2th December 2004 that hit Sumatra across the waters from Siberut and had subsequently seriously damaged, and tilted by a meter, the island to the north, Nias.

In this case Siberut was hit by three serious earthquakes in a row on 5th April 2005—of magnitude 6.4 to 6.7.

I was on the phone to Koen by satellite from my car in Jakarta when the first one hit. Koen was in UNESCO's Siberut Biosphere Reserve Office and narrowly escaped as it collapsed, a story I return to in Chap. 18. The people of Siberut knew about the Tsunami that had hit Aceh and were scared stiff that the earthquakes may presage a similar wall of water hitting their own villages. They ran up the hills. But this was difficult as the only access was through narrow jungle trails.

Koen immediately pulled in the Mentawains who had been working with us and did a deal with an NGO working on the island, SurfAid from Australia, to supply tents and emergency accommodation equipment. One of Koen's early tasks then was to build escape routes in case any future earthquakes might produce a Tsunami. Basically, what his team did was to clear a wide starting point in the uphill paths that funneled over some distance into the narrower traditional path, allowing a crowd to run together over the initial distance up the hill whilst being progressively channeled onto the track.

However, the main initial priority was to settle the people into their uphill campsites. What happened then can be described in no other words than as a French farce. The people settled, pitched their tents, dug latrines, brought out their cooking pots and started to prepare dinner. However, one of the elders suddenly exclaimed, "we are not high enough, the Tsunami rose to 50 m when it hit Aceh". Panic set in. People immediately uprooted their tents, left their dinners, and climbed another 50 m up the mountain before again settling, pitching their tents, digging another set of latrines and returning to re-preparing the evening meal. Life was not meant to be easy, however. Another senior member of the community then remembered a poster he had seen. Produced by the Indonesian Institute of Sciences, LIPI, it promoted their geological research work on the Sumatran Mentawai islands under the banner headline, 'The Islands Are Sinking'. "We're not high enough" he declared, precipitating another rush to decommission the tents, gather the cooking utensils and flee up the mountain once again, this time to near the top. Again, tents were pitched, latrines were dug though this time rather superficially, and the final version of what was left of the meal was returned to. ………….. One of the community then looked *down*: "We are on the edge of a VOLCANO", he screamed……. One more move, this time down the mountain. Most didn't bother about dinner this time.

It was pretty clear to Koen and the Siberut team that their next task on Siberut was education about earthquakes, tsunamis, volcanoes, about 'appropriate' preparedness and safe heights. He immediately set this program in motion.

Siberut is a very special place. The northernmost and largest of the Mentawai Island chain, Siberut lies 150 km off the western coast of Sumatra within the West Sumatra Province. The Mentawai Islands are believed to have been separated from mainland Sumatra by the 1,500 m deep Mentawai basin for at least 500,000 years, with the result that its flora and fauna have followed divergent evolutionary paths from that of the Sunda Shelf to the east. Of the 33 species of terrestrial mammals, 28 occur on Siberut, of which approximately 65 percent are uniquely endemic, including two species of bats, five squirrels, four rats, a tree-shrew, two species of civets and four primates—the Kloss Gibbon/Dwarf Siamang, the Mentawi Macaque, the Mentawaian Leaf Monkey and the Pig-tail Snub-nosed Monkey. The number of unique primates on Siberut is exceptional; no other site in the world has a higher density of endemic primate species per unit area. With a hot and humid equatorial climate, 4,000 mm average annual rainfall and no extended dry season, the island supports several terrestrial ecosystems including thriving virgin rain forest. Forty-seven percent of the island, the western part of the island, was declared by the Government of Indonesia as a National Park.

The Mentawai people, now numbering between 30,000 and 35,000, were one of the earliest human populations to colonize Indonesia and, having arrived there several thousand years ago, are of Austronesian descent and referred to as 'pro-Malays', their prevailing social organization being a relic of the Neolithic socio-political structure. Mentawains are organized into autonomous political units called 'uma', a landowning patrilineal family group. They have lived on Siberut for millennia in *balance* with their forest environment, with communities living within the National Park still primarily dependent on the traditional use of forest resources. The traditional Mentawai economy is based on simple but effective agriculture, extended on the eastern coast of the island over many generations of human habitation into a transformation of the native vegetation into a mosaic of mixed fruit and timber tree agro-forests. This simple agriculture is supplemented by hunting and collecting forest products, and has evolved in harmony with the environment, being controlled by a complex system of taboos and rituals which incorporate ethical and religious codes. It was firmly believed that breaking or disregarding taboos will attract physical distress - illness, accidents, misfortune and even death. As an example, medicinal plants can only be gathered if a sick person needs them. To gather them without any purpose would result in heavy karmic consequences for not only the person who picks them but also their family. Respect for plants and animals and careful use of natural resources is *inbuilt* into Mentawain culture and customs. So, conscious attention to preservation of nature is itself an alien concept, and not a guide: tradition does the same job. So, outsiders promoting conservation on Siberut have to be highly aware of, and work with, local cultural ways, rather than try and impose an external regime of ecologically sustainable practice according to *our* alien cultural standards. I, myself nearly fell into this trap, as I initially interpreted traditional Siberut care for their forests through 'modern' eyes, ie:

awareness of nature's fragility and the need to care. Had we followed this way of seeing we could have destroyed the culture and thus the peoples' shared capacity to respond to the outside threats to their way of life. The people were cautious about taking too much of the forest's medicinal plants as they knew 'their grandfather's wife's cousin's son's dog might die!" We needed to work and help change to happen for the peoples' benefit from *within* their culture.

It is because of these qualities—that is, Siberut's status as one of the world's major remaining reservoirs of plant genetic resources, high levels of endemism, and the persistence of the traditional culture of the indigenous population—that the Government of Indonesia in cooperation with UNESCO declared Siberut one of Indonesia's six 'Biosphere Reserves' back in 1981. Biosphere Reserves are conservation areas declared and monitored under UNESCO's 'Man and the Biosphere' (MAB) program, where careful use of zoning is used to separate dedicated conservation sites from areas where open development can occur by use of 'buffer zones' within which any development must involve conservation-sensitive economic activity that minimally impacts on the pristine site.

The *problem* we confronted was that Siberut was now under serious threat. Over the last couple of decades, outside economic interests had started to exploit Siberut with forest logging and development of plantations. Active and pending concessions threatened to destroy 70 percent of the habitat outside the Siberut National Park with potentially devastating consequences for the persistence of the whole island's unique flora and fauna. These developments spread illegally into the Park itself. But, the island is so remote that government officials, particularly of West Sumatra who *should* be responsible, would rather stay back in the city of Padang than cross the dangerous waters of the Mentawai basin in a marginally sea-worthy ferry. The exploitative interests had therefore come in and had co-opted some Mentawai clan members into forest clearing and plantation development. Consequently, unsustainable, or unplanned development had already led to rapid degradation of the natural resources and ecosystems of Siberut through commercial logging, reef bombing and cyanide fishing, introduction of air guns for hunting, monoculture, road construction and habitat fragmentation. The writing on the wall for Siberut was already inscribed in bold capitals on the two southernmost Mentawai Islands, Pagai and Sipora, where three decades of commercial logging and changes in resource management had destroyed virtually all forest and indigenous based lifestyle.

As the forests disappear, so too do the traditional ecological management ways of the Mentawains, and along with this, their unique culture. Needless to say, conflicts were also emerging between clan members who were benefiting from the illegal exploitation and those who were still seeking to maintain their traditional life and land use: all adult members of the Uma or extended family group have the same rights and authority, no formal chiefs exist, so all members of the extended community are equally responsible for managing their lands and resources. Where clan members break out of traditional practice, the whole extended family is threatened.

The risk to Siberut had been recognized by Government and Development Assistance agencies for some time. Strong support for change came from many sides. But, up until the late 1980s, what had been tried was guided by outsiders' economic development models, lack of culturally appropriate cooperation at grass-roots levels, and lack of long-term commitment to the Mentawai communities. 'Development' support therefore was *imposed* on the people rather than being a product of community concern and commitment, and was often simply off-track as I observed back in Chap. 10 when a multi-million dollar project of one multilateral agency, guided by consultants who may have never been on the island, took central government advice to build a mosque for the people in one of the main towns. Problem—the Mentawains who represent 90 percent of the people who live on Siberut are not Moslems, and the only use of the Mosque development was to use the public speaking system in the local Disco.

Led by Koen, a social scientist by training, we in UNESCO came in to work with the Mentawain people at grass-roots level in 1998. Koen knew Siberut and had spent substantial time there already—mainly as a photographer of remote ecological areas. We saw our UNESCO role as low-key, and hopefully in line with what we already knew of local culture as well as UNESCO's 'Seville Strategy' the globally determined strategy for dealing with community-based Biosphere Reserve conservation, we were intent on *building on the traditional roles and knowledge* of the Siberut people in the management of their own natural resources and environment, rather than seek to bring in outside-style ecological management practices. Our job was to assist the Mentawai people to empower themselves through community development and sustainable income-generating activities. We did *not* see our job as 'protecting' the Mentawai from outside influences, as this would have been impossible anyway, but as assisting them to strengthen their own ability to judge for themselves how to build the bridges they need *on their terms* with the globalized world that was steadily advancing on them through the jungles—in particular, for us, *using* the power of local community and the wisdom of traditional ecology management practices.

Nevertheless, we also recognized that we had to confront the problem of illegal logging and traders, and ensure the voice of the people was being heard by local and central government authorities—again, our 'fair witness' mediating role. To this point, outsiders had tended to treat the Mentawaians in the same way as exotic plant and animal species—*subjects* for program action decided elsewhere.

Our initial activity was to find out more—to conduct a *participatory* rural appraisal (PRA) on current resource management in five of the Mentawai villages with particular attention to how the dimension of gender made a difference, to start talking with the people and hearing what they said, and to *see* what was happening with the illegal logging and illicit traders.

The first exploitative traders to confront UNESCO were then in for a surprise, and it was here that our own entry point for community development started with response to what was the immediate problem for the Mentawain people rather than what we would have necessarily *planned* had we come in as an outside agency concerned with promoting sustainable development.

Picture the experience. The traders had travelled to the city of Padang, perched on the far western side of Sumatra, then travelled by a marginally seaworthy ferry overnight across one of the most dangerous oceans of Indonesia to the island, been taken by dugout canoe for several hours upriver and then walked several more hours on narrow tracks through the deep tropical Siberut jungle. Breaching the village clearing, the intrepid profiteers suddenly found themselves being greeted by two young United Nations interns equipped with large UN logos on their jackets—representing the ethical propriety of the outside world, absolutely the last fear the traders had placed on their agenda of risks to overcome in profiting from the Mentawai.

One of our earliest tasks then was to help the Mentawai with numeracy skills so that they would be less subject to flagrant extortion by these same unscrupulous traders. Our team then helped with the trading, suggesting that the locals could be a lot more effective if they had a 'house' where the stocks could be stored, and trading could occur in the open for all to see. Together, our team and the local community built the common house and developed with the community, a small micro-credit concept, that is, they put aside a small proportion of the common profits to fund new small-scale developments in the village.

We then started to work with the indigenous people more generally—based on what *they* wanted to do—training on coconut processing techniques and the cultivation of cinnamon and coffee to provide supplementary economic income.

The Mentawai were still relatively invisible from the far-distant vantage point of central Indonesian Government. It was therefore important for us to establish a bridge between the indigenous communities and the various arms of the Indonesian Government whose decisions affected Mentawai life and prospects—to ensure the Mentawai peoples' voice was being heard and that interventions in the Mentawai communities from outside honored this voice and were coherent. Our starting point had to be to bring the various players together for the first time. It took around a year from our first entry to set this up. In December 1999, in cooperation with the Indonesian Directorate General of Protection and Nature Conservation (PKA) we organized a national workshop in Padang—across the water from the island. This meeting, entitled "Conservation and Sustainable Development in the Siberut Biosphere Reserve", brought together more than 100 participants—from central, provincial and local governments as well as representatives of Siberut tribes and local, national and international NGOs which were working on the island.

Given the conflicts already emerging between different clan interests plus the 'fixed' views of outsiders about what was going to be good for the Mentawains, the interventions and debates were distinctly feisty to the point where we genuinely feared that the whole enterprise may break down in irreconcilable conflict. But it finally worked. Within the context of our own concern that development needed to be sustainable yet still honor the forest management ways of the people, the Mentawaian participants collectively developed their own suggestions and recommendations for the Government and international organizations about the future of Siberut. These recommendations formed the basic platform for what we in UNESCO then did. But we also had a clear line for our own continuing dialogue with government in representing the Mentawaian interests back in Jakarta on what government's role needed to be out on this tiny remote island.

We kept this level of consultation going. Nine months later, we followed up in collaboration with three Siberut-based NGOs and Walhi, the national 'Indonesian Forum for Environment' NGO, with two workshops on 'sustainable natural resource management for the welfare of the communities', this time on Siberut itself—with 70 people in Sikabaluan, the northern district capital, and 120 people in Muara Siberut, the southern district capital. Now our aim was to bring together for the first time, representatives from *all* the local communities in the island's two sub-districts in order to facilitate exchange of information and discussion about current sustainable development concerns and to start to build effective networks *across* the communities.

Development Assistance for the People is a Multi-disciplinary Affair

Three main lines of action had emerged for our own immediate attention.

> The first was education. Siberut was very remote, its society ruled by quite specific indigenous practices. This made formal schools that followed what at that stage was still pretty much centrally determined practice very difficult to access from the communities and long-houses. We therefore introduced an approach that UNESCO (under our Asia-Pacific Program of Education for All or "APPEAL" program) had tried with good results elsewhere, to establish a "Community Learning Centre" or "CLC". We already had a building—the hut we had helped the people to establish for trading. In keeping with the more general CLC model, our aims were to increase opportunities for education in general and community empowerment, as well as to provide feedback on how to develop community-sensitive education in this particular indigenous community, that is, to provide a base for *participatory* research on alternative education models and approaches in cooperation with local NGOs and institutions. It was critical as far as we were concerned *not* to impose an external model on the locals, but to develop an approach that could work *here*, according to *their* rules and expectations. What was eventually taught therefore combined traditional and new approaches in working out how best to transfer knowledge into the community. And what was perhaps most important, our CLC model was designed as a *mobile* model, in which local teachers *visited* the community and long-houses regularly to provide the teaching. We confronted a particular problem with the development of education for young women because according to local cultural ways, girls over the age of eight years or so were supposed to pay attention to cooking which was women's work, and not to education or pursuits outside the household. We dealt with this by having the young females who were doing the teaching spend time in the village kitchens, teaching reading and writing as it related to kitchen objects and practices. At first the men who decided things in this patriarchal society did not notice, but soon accepted that literacy empowered the women and this was not necessarily a problem.

The second action we took, as I noted in Chap. 10, was to assist the people of the coastal village of Maileppet to improve their own system of clean water supply using local materials. Here we were developing a program under our UNESCO Water Program—funded by the Netherlands.

Already, you can see the multi-sector, multi-disciplinary inputs that we found were needed to work with whole communities—as we were already calling on UNESCO's technical capacity and mandate in ecological science (for the Biosphere Reserve intervention strategies), social science and culture (to conduct participatory rural appraisals and surveys of needs and interests), education (to develop the mobile schooling) and now we were adding water science to the mix.

In the third action, we brought in another string in UNESCO's bow, this time expertise from our Coastal and Marine Science team. Particularly on the east coast of Siberut facing Sumatra, the island consists of islets, bays, coral reefs and spits of land covered with mangrove forest up to 2 km inland. A large part of these mangrove forest areas is not included in the conservation area of the Biosphere Reserve, so the unrestricted coral reef fishing was becoming too heavy and destructive, with long-term consequences for Siberut's overall sustainable ecology. We therefore helped the villagers to develop alternative forms of income generation, including training people, particularly women, in seaweed culture.

Again, back to social science. In traditional Mentawai patriarchal society women did not have any rights of inheritance of land if their husband died. As a result, they were often left derelict without a source of serious income or food. As our team steadily built up trust within the community, they talked with the (male) elders about the problem. Finally, the elders accepted the idea of allowing the women to be trained to develop seaweed farming—which the men accepted as legitimate women's work, and most importantly, the elders decided to allocate sections of village land as a *common*—'women's land' to be used by unsupported women for generating their own income and food.

Eventually the elders realized that they needed to use social science for themselves. They recognized that they could make much more sensible decisions about the community if they knew more about what was going on across the more remote villages and small settlements. So, under Koen's guidance, they became involved in conducting more structured surveys of what the people needed, and responding to recognized needs.

A Tough but Successful Life

Koen and Richard meanwhile were building up a group of twenty—and later, up to fifty, local Mentawain people—as the Collaborative Management Team (the people mentioned earlier who helped Koen handle the consultations upriver when the UN-TV crew were coming, then not coming, then coming), thus broadening the ability to take initiatives *into* the community, creating a broad *change-agent* capability.

And Koen and Richard lived a pretty tough life. Both came down with multiple bouts of malaria and dengue fever. Richard at one stage had to confront the ministrations of traditional medicine when he contracted cerebral malaria and day-by-day was becoming sicker and sicker. The local 'Kerei' or traditional healer, figured he could handle the case, so spent much time in chants, waving specially collected herbs over Richard's body, and engaging the forest gods in Richard's protection from bad spirits. Richard's body unfortunately was not as convinced in the efficacy of these medical practices. After three days he realized that his consciousness was slipping increasingly into a pretty dangerous place. Thanking the witchdoctor for his interventions with the local spirits, Richard then got out to the world of westernized medicine, available at least in some measure in Padang across the Sunda Trench in Sumatra. By this time, he was lapsing in and out of consciousness. The locals had carried him for 11 h through the jungles and down the river, and were really very worried about his welfare until we were able to get a message back to them that Richard was finally recovering. Koen, meanwhile, was confronted in his third bout of dengue fever with the rare but life-threatening complication of steadily progressing paralysis from the feet up. He managed to get to Padang but the paralysis was creeping up his body and he had probably six to eight hours before it reached his lungs and heart. My Administrative Assistant and I worked through the night to pillage every dollar we could find out of *any* account (to be regularized later) and raised the $(US)20,000 needed to charter an emergency plane to Singapore for adequate medical treatment. He got there just in time … and after recovering went right back to Siberut to continue working with the people.

It was a tough life, but a fabulous adventure as well, particularly for young (healthy) interns or staff members from our Office that I sent up there on mission. One, a young Australian law graduate who I sent to Siberut to learn about traditional Mentawai law relating to forest conservation and to relate this to Indonesian (Dutch-based) law, came back a couple of months later saying that the experience taught him more about the social basis of law than five years of university training. He was then selected for study at Oxford on a highly competitive Rhodes Scholarship, and moved on into a blossoming law career—fundamentally enriched by the experience of living in and working alongside the indigenous Mentawai communities.

Meanwhile, we were encouraged by the fact that after only a year or so of operation amongst the Mentawai, Indonesia's national planning agency, BAPPENAS, took on our Siberut project as a reference model for sound development planning in remote areas and small islands of the country. Our basic principles: scientifically sound, environment friendly, people-centred, economically workable, culturally appropriate, long-term committed ... development with and for the people of Siberut.

We remained committed to building Siberut Island's own human capacity to manage the island's sustainable long-term future.

We initiated the Second Phase of the project during 2001, continuing our efforts to develop co-operative management, poverty anticipation (and new small-scale enterprise development), non-formal education for forest dwelling communities, and advocacy—supported by Belgium, Conservation International and our own limited UNESCO resources. Our particular focus now was on building and empowering customary environmental management of the Siberut Biosphere Reserve, and handing it *over* to local authorities and NGOs to ensure long-term sustainability.

In close cooperation with the Siberut National Park and local NGO, Yayasan Citra Mandiri, and through many meetings and consultations, we developed a 'Co-management Team' consisting of indigenous community representatives, National Park and local NGO staff. The team increasingly took over all levels of UNESCO's Siberut program, including planning, implementation, monitoring, and evaluation. The team targeted enhanced National Park programming to fully include both scientific and indigenous knowledge inputs, a more open and transparent Park management, and an information Bulletin edited by National Park staff and local communities that was distributed to *every* village on Siberut every three months. The impact these initiatives had on Siberut was demonstrated by a survey the Co-management Team conducted in Southern Siberut Island where the UNESCO team had primarily been working. Now, 60 to 70 percent of the local population supported conservation and understood the sustainable management practices needed, compared with barely 5 percent just two years earlier.

The Co-management Team had a major impact on broadening our reach into the communities of Siberut. A program that had started in just two villages with three field staff, now had expanded to a team of 50, representing not just UNESCO but a broad variety of stakeholders—indigenous communities, the Siberut National Park, NGOs and government institutions, now covering activities across much of the island. The strength of a local community-based program was enhanced significantly by the progressive changes that were now being made in Indonesia's post-May 1998 democratization and national decentralization policy. In particular, Act 22 that passed through Parliament in 1999 gave greater decision-making power to village authorities and allowed the establishment of village regulations.

By 2003, as the world community drew to the end of the United Nations International Decade of the World's Indigenous People (1995–2004), and with broad-ranging public acceptance across Siberut of the need for conservation, the time was well placed to develop new local regulations for Siberut on sustainable forest management based on *both* customary regulations and scientific knowledge. Along with our partners—now also including the Indonesia Legal Aid and Human Rights Association, we embarked on an intensive and interactive process to facilitate local communities and village governments to design village *regulations*—through mechanisms such as village meetings, awareness campaigns, training activities and workshops. The basic regulations were agreed by the village communities and established by the end of the year.

Also, years of strong advocacy paid off. In 2004 the Minister of Forestry (under the previous Soeharto regime until 1998 this had been a Ministry that advocated the virtually uncontrolled exploitation of the forests) established an independent team—of which UNESCO was a member—to investigate all logging activities on Siberut to determine whether they were in line with Siberut's status as a Biosphere Reserve.

Through 2004 we established a second Community Learning Centre through local NGOs and district education offices, and expanded the reach of local government in listening to the voice of the indigenous people—amongst other means of consultation, organizing a workshop between the newly elected district parliament, government agencies, NGOs and over 100 representatives of indigenous communities to discuss local government challenges in relation to the aspirations of indigenous people concerning development.

We also returned to the problem of clean water. Whilst the people lived a fully traditional life, clean water was not too much of a problem as each extended family lived in a longhouse located near a small river which provided continuous access to clean water; meanwhile traditional practices ensured sustainable water management in use of the rivers. But development had been at a price. Under the previous Soeharto New Order Government many of the Mentawains had been resettled out of their longhouses and into villages. The altered socio-economic context and relations of village life intrinsically changed pre-existing cultural attitudes to water. Water-related taboos were no longer respected. But the villagers were not equipped with technical know-how and financial capacity to introduce new systems and approaches to water management that would work in the village environment. The problem was particularly bad in the village of Rokdok. Backed by our own ecological, social science and hydrology experts, the Co-management Team went to work. In keeping with the approach which by now we were calling 'the Siberut model', all primary responsibilities regarding project management, including planning, implementation, and evaluation, were assumed by the local community through the establishment of a water management committee. Again, in line with our model, this process helped the integration between scientific knowledge and customary practices in the successful development of the community-based water management systems of the Siberut indigenous village.

As we approached the end of 2005 we started to move on from Siberut. Our job was done and UNESCO's role in UN-based development is more to stimulate action and build its sustainability, rather than to provide longer term support—more the job of UNDP and other UN agencies more responsible for funding. After 7 years of enormous commitment by the field team allocated to Siberut we were able to leave behind a sustainable long-term transformation of a society and environment that was previously under immediate risk. The community management commitments and mechanisms were now firmly in place, the people were aware, more capable of dealing with the encroachment of the outside world, and their traditional knowledge and aspirations valued and included in planning for the sustainable future of their island home of the last few thousand years, Siberut.

For us, after the Tsunami tragedy at the end of 2004, we had more urgent concerns for our UNESCO Biosphere Reserve team in Aceh, particularly, developing protection for the World Heritage rainforests straddling the border between Aceh and North Sumatra in Gunung Leuser National Park (home of all four big Asian mammals—tigers, rhinos, elephants and orangutans). The Park was already under enormous threat from agricultural encroachment and illegal logging before the Tsunami.

The Tsunami had two key related impacts here. The first was to weaken the government's conservation enforcement capacity through the killing of key forest protection personnel and the destruction of critical management infrastructure. The second related impact was to increase the opportunity for illegal logging. The disaster and need for a massive rebuilding program provided cover for the illegal loggers—who, claiming they were logging to assist the rebuilding program were in fact extracting highly valued exotic forest species that were irrelevant to Aceh's reconstruction and instead, destined for overseas illegal markets.

One of the last things we were able to do before I left my post in Jakarta at the end of 2005 was to secure substantial funding from Spain (as well as our own World Heritage Centre) to launch the project "Post-Tsunami Assistance for Gunung Leuser National Park, the Tropical Rainforest Heritage of Sumatra, and the Nature Conservation Agency in Aceh Province". Koen, our Siberut leader, was then appointed to lead this project.

On doing so I leave a debt of enormous gratitude for the committed, imaginative and courageous support provided by the UNESCO-based field team in Siberut, in particular, Koen Myers. Apart from anything else, he learnt to speak all the local languages and could communicate at grass-roots level with people across the whole island community. He became a welcomed and influential leader *within* the communities, an excellent model of what field people within the United Nations *can* contribute. It was *they* who led our Siberut Program.

12

"Community Empowerment—Lessons from Peace Building and Urban Environment Initiatives in Poor Communities"

Case 1: Education and Peace Building in the Post-conflict Zones of the Philippines

In February 2003 Babo Pampay Usman, resident of the remote barangay or community of Muslim-dominated Lower Katuli, Mindanao, the Philippines, who had never been outside her local area before, addressed the United Nations General Assembly in New York

The occasion was the Formal Launching of the United Nations Literacy Decade. The other two speakers were Kofi Annan, Secretary-General of the United Nations and Koichiro Matsuura, Director-General of UNESCO. Pampay was plucked out of her local community as a woman who at the age of 60 had just become literate and whose story needed to be told to the world.

Like many in poor communities Pampay had never had the chance to go to school. Although she could not read or write she managed a small market stall. Because she could not write down the name of her customers or the goods they purchased she had to remember their faces and every item they bought—and she was frequently cheated. She was embarrassed to accompany her children then grandchildren to school, unable sometimes to find her way as she could not read the street signs, and generally felt powerless.

However, in 1995 Pampay had taken the functional literacy course offered by the Notre Dame Foundation for Charitable Activities—Women in Enterprise Development (NDFCAI-WED) project (supported by UNESCO) and had then gone on to the Advanced Adult Education course, winning three merit awards. She admits that after acquiring basic literacy skills, including very basic abilities such as writing her name and address and reading the prices on groceries, Pampay felt different and proud, able to talk with her grandchildren about school, more confident about talking with people in general, able to find her way. Now at her small store she was also able to keep records of neighbors who bought on credit, and she was no longer cheated when she bought grocery items in the stores of Cotabato City. Pampay became an active community leader, instrumental in encouraging other illiterate Muslim women and men in her barangay to join the literacy classes. She came alive because of literacy, and with the help of a small loan from the Notre Dame Foundation, she established a small store, and her business grew.

On request of the UN in New York, and on behalf of my Office of UNESCO to represent the newly literate of the world, Pampay spoke in 2003 to the United Nations General Assembly with confidence:

> 'I was not afraid to speak about the impact of literacy on my life' she said, 'because I was speaking about my own life and from my heart: 'Literacy is Freedom'.

We found out about the Notre Foundation for Charitable Activities Women and Enterprise Development program and their inspiring leader, Myrna Lim, shortly after Fidel Ramos—President of the Philippines, overviewed the signing of the Mindanao Peace Agreement on 2nd September 1996 with the Governor of the Autonomous Region of Muslim Mindanao (ARMM). This Agreement ended more than two decades of armed conflict in the Southern Philippines, and led to a serious commitment by both Government and local leaders to post-conflict reconstruction for peace and development in Mindanao, especially in the Special Zone for Peace and Development (SZOPAD) where poverty and illiteracy were highest. Six of the poorest provinces in the Philippines were in Mindanao with real per-capita income across all provinces in SZOPAD being about one-third of that of the National Capital Region: poverty in Muslim-dominated Sulu was estimated to embrace 63 percent of the population compared to the national average of 28.4 percent.

It was therefore well understood that the difference in cultural and religious beliefs and the unequal distribution of resources were key stumbling blocks for the continued development of peace in the region. Education had also been a particular casualty of the war. While the Philippines could boast one of the highest literacy rates in the developing world (over 92 percent), only 65.5 percent of people in ARMM could read and write. Functional literacy was even lower with over half of people between 40 and 60 years of age being unable to read, write or count. We knew that high levels of illiteracy were directly associated with poorly performing economic activity and poverty. We *found out* that lack of literacy and job skills was directly associated with recruitment into the more extreme continuing Islamic movements, such as the criminal group that came to prominence kidnapping foreigners, Abu Sayyaf. In fact, kidnapping for profit was widespread through the province, with gangs even exchanging captives with other gangs at increasingly higher market prices as means of accumulating illicit income. Mindanao was not a safe place to work for us.

Nevertheless, from UNESCO's side it was clear that we needed to be there: lack of peace and illiteracy were our core business. We firmly believed that the power to change things lies firmly in the local communities and their potential ability to transform conflict and threats into challenges which can be met through cooperation and growth in a spirit of general solidarity rather than division. We knew also that women were particularly disadvantaged, but likely to be key change agents within family groups, so needed to build gender sensitivity and targeting of women into what we did.

The Notre Dame Foundation was working directly in this area and already had a good track record on functional literacy training. So, in cooperation with the Notre Dame Foundation Women and Enterprise Development program, we established what we called our 'GENPEACE' (Gender and Culture of Peace) program for Mindanao, initiating our first activities at three sites, Jolo in Sulu, Sultan Sa in Barongis and Ipil Zamboanga Sibugay, chosen *because* they were main conflict areas and havens for criminal elements. This was to be a community-based education project implemented through local NGOs under the leadership of the Notre Dame Foundation and targeting men, women, and children among ex-combatants of the Moro National Liberation Front (MNLF), the Moro Islamic Liberation Front (MILF) as well as Christian communities and the indigenous Lumad People.

But we did something different. We needed to extend the reach of the literacy program to remote communities as well as to the urban complexes. So, in cooperation with the Notre Dame Foundation, we designed a two-part strategy in line with which we built non-formal education programs that combined peace education with literacy training, whilst at the same time we founded *community radio stations* as a tool for both extending the reach of the education program through distance education, and promoting the development of a cohesive community voice for peace. UNESCO had already assisted the development of a successful community radio station at Tambuli in the northern Luzon Province, so we brought in their experience and expertise to assist in developing the community broadcasting in Mindanao.

As with all of our community empowerment work, we knew we needed to build in commitment of local government. As it turned out, engaging the active participation of LGUs or Local Government Units who provided the required financial counterpart funding and community-based support, immediately caught the attention of government and donor agencies. By bringing UNESCO and therefore support in a conflict situation at the level of the United Nations in 'guaranteeing' project probity, efficacy and fairness, the profile of the Notre Dame Foundation was raised considerably. I was also able to play a role in my diplomatic 'UN Representative' capacity of ensuring the attention of central government and the main donor agencies to what we were seeking to achieve in Mindanao. Thousands of people with literacy problems and their families mobilized to set up Community Learning Centers (the concept we used for extension of non-formal education to indigenous communities on Siberut) in school-less communities, providing land, labour and unused buildings for classrooms. The Muslim community offered their own Madrasah schools as learning sites, while the LGUs contributed benches, desks, tables and blackboards and basic facilities for the Non-Formal Education classes.

Also, introducing community radio into a potentially volatile and religiously divided environment was an inherently risky business. We had to ensure that management of the *process* was done in such a way that ideological division within the radio voice of the communities did not *lead* to division and violence rather than mitigate against it. UNESCO therefore acted in our 'fair witness' role to help develop a Community Media and Education Council (CMEC) around each station, a vehicle for community management and ownership—elected through general community assemblies, and responsible for liaison with local government and the mayor as well as with the community interests, and in particular, for balancing the interests of the Muslim, Christian and indigenous Lumad communities.

The colour of the resulting broadcasting is shown rather well in a description which my Office published in collaboration with the Notre Dame Foundation in 2006 of Radio DXLB-FM based at Lake Buluan and a couple of nearby radio stations:

> DJ Cyber begins his program on dxLB-FM with a jazzy, upbeat station jingle. It is an adaptation of old Filipino-Muslim folk song whose gongs and rhythms have been stepped up.

With his snappy cropped hair and baggy denims, he could be any funky youngster in a radio booth anywhere in the world. So DJ Cyber took to the air along with his co-anchors, chatty DJ Tecla and Lady Miyake, cute and fashionable with chopstick stuck in her French-twisted hair.

But dxLB-FM is not your usual small town radio station. And Lake Buluan, which is what the "LB" in their station name stands for, is not quite your usual town.

Deep in the interior of Southern Philippines' Mindanao Island, the station's concrete blue and white two-room structure stands out in a dusty provincial highway dotted by numerous military check points—telltale signs of the Muslim separatist rebellion that ravaged the area for over three decades. Here DJ Cyber and the girls play their music in between the day's news, farming tips, reproductive health advice, educational commentaries, local government announcements, and Koranic readings. Fans and listeners, including those from hinterland rebel-held areas, send them hundreds of mobile text messages a day, egging them to read personal greetings or play a favourite pop hit. …

The young DJs were volunteers. They attack their jobs with zeal, despite the station's limited capabilities. 'Cyber' they are not (or not yet). Lacking internet access, a motorcycle courier from a national public radio station in Korondal City, one-hour away, starts off before dawn every day to deliver hard copy printouts of the day's news in time for the 7 o'clock sign-on….

Meanwhile … the tanks were rolling past right outside the door, the Abu Sayyaf Terrorists were poised for attack in the nearby mountains … but the terrorists could not depend on any support from the local Islamic Communities on what was broadcast, as these local Islamic communities were now fully engaged and cooperating with all other community groups through the *Community Media and Education Council* (CMEC) around each station.

We built supportive literacy training via these Stations—as I reported earlier, the local literacy rate in the troubled areas of Mindanao was way below the overall rate for the Philippines—at 65.5% of the population. But most importantly, information and knowledge could now be broadcast—backed as the stations were, by integrated community support—even when the terrorists were doing all in their power to suppress it.

Furthermore, a three-hour ride west of Buluan, in the upland town of Upi, rhythmic strings and gongs of tribal music were played on dxUP-FM, another community radio station. In the verdant rolling terrain overlooking the Moro Gulf, ethnic Teduray youngsters took turns with Muslim and Christian broadcasters, reporting news and views. Like their counterparts in Buluan, the DGs intersperse the day's market prices and livelihood tips with jokes and pop tunes.

Among those on board for the morning news and community affairs program at Upi's dxUP-FM is 23-year-old Baimon Abdullah, a dedicated Muslim volunteer who is also a full-time Instructional Manager at the town's out-of-school youth literacy program. She works two slots on the daily radio board: a news program and one devoted to education and values. When classes are out, she is more than willing to fill up five slots on board, or serve as a roving reporter. Her friend, Nancy Lawan of the Teduray community, reports for the early morning livelihood program on tribal traditions—the only radio program in the country aired in her native Teduray dialect.'

As *Initiating Partner*, UNESCO funded the development of the first six community radio sites—at Claveria, Misamis Oriental; Ipil, Zamboanga Sibugay; Jolo, Sulu; Marawi City; Mahayag, Zamboanga del Sur; and Sultan sa Barongis, Maguindanao. Having established the program and its base principles we then placed particular priority on bringing in a wider collection of donor partners and were able to develop the 'mainstreaming' of the project as a component of the Government of the Philippines–United Nations Multi-Donor Program. Under this wider program another 9 community radio stations were established, and the program expanded across a large section of Mindanao Province. We continued to provide on-going but minor support—particularly of advocacy with both government and donors in the Philippines—as our job of catalyzing this development and handing it on as a sustainable community activity was basically done.

Meanwhile, through GENPEACE, *seven thousand people in Mindanao (75 percent women) became literate* between 2000 and 2004; 300 village peace negotiators were trained as well. The power to make these contributions to peace in a post-war zone was fundamentally in the hands of the local communities, however. We simply helped to facilitate a way of engaging this commitment.

Also, quite separately, we were able to be involved in establishing a community-based agreement across Mindanao modelled on our prior success in a nation-wide basic education reform and decentralization program across Indonesia for 36 million children that, as I report in Chap. 16, we were able to extend also to the additional 20% of Islamic Schools previously teaching only Arabic and the Koran, now also teaching basic education and targeted employment skills. As with Indonesia, we were able to establish a deal at across Mindanao where at community level the Islamic Schools expanded their teaching to also include basic education skills in return for the Public Schools adding values and religious studies to their curriculum.

The Danger of Too Much Success

So, our direct support for building education, access to knowledge, and the consequent contributions to peace across the Islamic previous conflict zones of Mindanao, were by now, becoming well known more broadly.

We had already *found out* that lack of literacy and job skills was directly associated with recruitment into the more extreme continuing Islamic terrorist movements, in particular, the criminal group that came to prominence kidnapping foreigners, Abu Sayyaf. In fact, kidnapping for profit was widespread through the province, with gangs even exchanging captives with other gangs at increasingly higher market prices as means of accumulating illicit income. Mindanao was not a safe place to work for us foreigners.

> Indeed, everywhere I travelled in Mindanao, the Philippines Government *required* I be accompanied by a 24-hour two-man armed guard.

Finally, my personal diplomatic and support profile became too much for Abu Sayyaf. So, in 2004, they sent a Hit Squad via Manado and Sulawesi towards Jakarta, specifically to *assassinate ME!* They tossed in the US and Australian Ambassadors as planned extras.

> I had, as it were, crossed into quite another 'diplomatic' territory—in the course of building *knowledge and access to knowledge* in Mindanao.

On receiving a formal briefing from UN Security about this Hit Squad which by this time had reached Sulawesi on their journey from Mindanao to my home city, Jakarta, my Headquarters ordered me out of Indonesia to escape immediately. I chose to travel down to where we had a UNESCO Office I was partially responsible to support … in Samoa.

But the drama did not stop.

As I transited to Samoa through Auckland by Pacific Air, all my luggage was unloaded and replaced with 300 Bibles. So, I arrived in Apia with great religious presence but not much more than a pair of shorts for subsequent formal occasions. Pacific Air generously offered $25 to cover the loss and it took a week before my luggage finally arrived. Prior to the return of my bags, on the first weekend after my arrival, I really did need time-out, so booked the most remote falé, or hut, on the beach at the most remote resort I could find. Jill, my wife, and I, sitting with wooden louvre doors wide open all around—directly over the incoming waves—opened a bottle of celebratory champagne.

Then the CYCLONE hit! Waves through the floor, palm trees flying by. All communication cut.

I was almost praying to be taken back to the terrorists.

Case 2: Banjarsari—Building a Green Urban Village in a Polluted Developing Countries City

On 1st July 2001 I performed one of my more unusual official duties. I *launched* a garbage bin and officiated giving a prize to the designers.

In fact, it wasn't just *a* garbage bin, but a series of bins—green, red and yellow, each signalling a collection point for organic, non-organic recyclable material and non-recyclable rubbish, as well as a push cart used by scavengers for collecting waste of different types from the bins.

We had conducted a competition for the best designs for the kampung or village in the southern part of Jakarta. Because in this developing country's suburb, dwelling sizes were small, rubbish was collected communally by scavengers, and carried to city collection vehicles or locations by handcart. But, established practice was for households to dump their rubbish of all sorts down a chute from their dwelling, ending up on the street where (ideally) a household dumpster was located. Or, alternatively, to dump the rubbish in a common pile on a disused block next door or in whichever river system flowed nearby. In introducing a new waste recycling system, we were therefore introducing a change to habitual behavior of city dwellers, and were well aware that humans being what they are, under an alternate system people would not walk too far from their front door to dump their refuse, so the bins had to be the right size to accommodate the volume of rubbish normally generated from the number of houses that fitted into the typical 'walk convenience' circle. Access to dump the rubbish *in* the bin also needed to be easy, and access *out* for the hand-cart waste collectors had to be accessible for the height and shape of the handcarts. The contest was quite formally judged—by officials of the Jakarta Waste Department, the National Environmental Impact Management Agency, the Indonesian Institute of Sciences together with representatives of the local community and NGOs working there. The winning entry was basically created by welding a few bits and pieces on 44-gallon drums laid on their side and painted. Additionally, we gave a prize for the re-design of handcarts—usually carts cobbled together from found timber and bits and pieces by the very poor scavengers who collected waste as a means of providing a bare survival income. Our designers in this case were the hand cart operators themselves, who came up with a very simple solution to collecting and dividing waste—a moveable wall in the middle of the cart so that the waste collector could take on board recyclable material, push it down to the end, drop the wall and then collect the non-recyclable waste. Organic waste was kept in the village, for that was basic to what the village was becoming—a 'Green Kampung' or 'Environmentally Friendly' Village.

This is the story of Banjarsari, a community where the people learned to live according to the '4R' principles, reduce-reuse-recycle-replant, where streets, houses and every spare crevice of space were eventually covered with growing plants, where a number of small businesses set up based on recycling or medicinal plants grown in the compost produced from recycling, where training was conducted for hundreds of people a year on recycling thus spreading the Banjarsari model throughout many other areas of Indonesia. A year after I launched the garbage bins, with 70 percent of all families in the community now committed to recycling, Banjarsari, our model recycle village, was declared by the Governor of Jakarta to be an official 'Ecotourism Site' of the city.

This story of Banjarsari had its beginnings some years earlier—back in work we were doing on Jakarta Bay.

Since its inception back in 1951 as a base for science cooperation across South East Asia, my UNESCO Office had played a role that was little more than an agency for UNESCO's science activities in Indonesia and across Southeast Asia, all of which were largely determined from Headquarters. The previous Director before myself had started to change this, and expand the functions of the Office to include education and culture—but still very much as marginal activities around our science core without core budget funding. As a long-term *science* office, and in collaboration with the Indonesian Institute of Sciences (LIPI), we had been monitoring the pollution levels since 1985 in Jakarta Bay and out to Pulau Seribu, Jakarta Bay's 'thousand islands'. Needless to say, under the continuing impact of a developing countries city where planners had very little environmental awareness, the level of pollution of the Bay steadily, year-by-year, increased. Apart from uncontrolled industrial pollution, much of the destruction of the Bay was very clearly a product of very careless environmental practices of the people who lived in the city—who used their waterways basically as convenient vehicles for disposal of their rubbish—1,400 cubic meters of garbage being thrown into the 13 rivers that flowed into Jakarta Bay each day. Not only were the rivers heavily polluted: one could find plastic bags and drink bottles tens of kilometers out into the islands. Similarly, potentially recyclable organic waste was also simply fed into this convenient 'sewer': as it decomposed in the Bay, this organic waste threatened to suffocate corals and other marine organisms.

In 1995 after I arrived, we decided to do something about the situation—not just to continue monitoring and alerting authorities about the steady deterioration of their city environment, but to bring local communities in to change things. Whilst at heart our 'Jakarta Bay' program remained a 'science' activity under our CSI or 'coastal and small islands' initiative, its flavour now increasingly called on social science, community development and informal education capabilities. This time we actually did have strong support from our (rather small) headquarters unit set up as a multi-disciplinary team to look after CSI activities. And the key statistic that set us moving in a more community-oriented direction was that *70 percent* of the waste that flowed into Jakarta Bay was organic—its decomposition in the Bay seriously threatening water quality and the survival of marine species, but all of which *could* be put to use if it was only captured and recycled.

We started *in* Jakarta Bay in 1996 on the islands of Pulau Seribu, where the small local fishing communities were having the most direct negative impact on their own coral reefs through careless waste management practices as well as unsustainable harvesting of fish resources through bombing the reefs and through cyanide fishing. As our initial strategy we brought together local fishermen with scientists, teachers, journalists, NGOs, fishing officers and resort owners to launch our 'Save Pulau Seribu' initiative. As the first element in this initiative, we immediately started working with the local island communities on waste management and practical education on how to monitor their own reefs (through simple transect counting of indicator species), and worked out with them the support we could provide to develop alternate income sources with low environmental impact—particularly based on recycled organic waste. Our first target was the production (and marketing) of compost—produced through a variety of techniques including worm farming. We used the island sites also as locations to bring school children from Jakarta for education about the islands, the islands' sensitivity to Jakarta-sourced rubbish, and practical things they, the kids, could do, for example, through recycling paper and developing worm farms for composting. Later in the year, in collaboration with LIPI, the (official) Indonesian News Agency, ANTARA, and NGOs—Friends of the Sea, Kirai and WALHI, I then launched a *clean-up campaign* in three areas of Jakarta—a senior high school, the fishing village of Kronjho Tangerang, and …… the urban village of Banjarsari. We started to develop waste monitoring (also getting the school children involved) and an organic waste action plan in Jakarta—including for waste management at traditional markets—bringing in the local vendors along with scientists, students, and local community members.

Our first pilot project on waste recycling at traditional markets was initiated in 1997 at Bintaro Traditional Market: by the end of the first two months where our job was to encourage local sellers, buyers and managers to participate in recycling their organic waste rather than just throwing it away into the local canals, we were able to achieve a 30 percent reduction in their total organic waste. As we expanded this initiative to another market, the Pasar Mede Traditional Market in South Jakarta, with the attraction to local marketers of *selling* the organic waste as compost, we were able to save a consistent 40 percent of market waste. Children from the local Senior High School SMU 34 were our key agents for change, twenty-four of them explaining recycling to the stall holders and distributing pamphlets. Meanwhile, the Pondok Labu High School undertook to rid their school of paper waste, and started to build serious school income by selling recycled paper through school cooperatives. The school then challenged other schools to do the same thing, setting up a spin-off impact amongst Jakarta's kids. On Pari Island we initiated training in seaweed farming and introduced duck farming (from June 1998)—as alternate income for the fishing families, hopefully to lower the pressure of the poverty stricken families to exploit the last remnants of fish stocks from their own reefs through destructive blast and cyanide fishing practices. Children were quite centrally involved in the duck farming venture, as they were allocated the job of caring for the ducks, collecting and keeping records of the duck eggs produced. We started to work towards fish farming and breeding programs for developing and selling aquarium fish, during 1999 introducing a groper and cichlids fish cage culture to the fishermen of Kongsi Island. And we attacked one of the Pari island's most pressing problems, improving their sanitation system.

In North Jakarta, we developed training for the local women to produce and market fish chips and dried shredded fish (abon). Our approach by now was increasingly inter-sectoral, so, with our education team also coming in to support the social science and coastal scientist teams, we built a demonstration community-based recycling center for paper recycling and composting together with a community education center further upriver in North Jakarta at Kapuk Muara. The centre became a meeting point for the local community to discuss environmental problems and more generally to work towards community empowerment. Although I formally launched the Kapuk Muara Centre in mid-1999, it had been established and was building up community relations for a couple of years already, and indeed was instrumental in serendipitously maintaining peace during the May 1998 riots that rampaged through this northern part of Jakarta.

Quite consciously, we built the Centre right on the border between a predominately ethnic Chinese area and an ethnic Javanese area of Northern Jakarta. As intended, it had been instrumental in starting to forge dialogue between these two communities—in particular at the level of women and youth.

When the rioters came to attack the Chinese in May 1998, the local ethnic Javanese formed a vigilante band that created a cordon around Kapuk Muara and prevented the rioters entering. All around Kapuk Muara, North Jakarta had been burnt, but Kapuk Muara—and in particular its ethnic Chinese residences, remained untouched and no-one was injured or killed as was happening all around the area where over 1,000 people died. The lives of possibly up to 100 people therefore were probably saved in Kapuk Muara. A very important lesson about the power of community building across difference.

So far, all these initiatives were but 'drops in the ocean' for such a vast problem as was posed by the mega-city of Jakarta and its impact on Jakarta Bay. But we were finding that by engaging the press and children (in particular) we were able to start getting the message of recycling out to increasingly broad audiences. However, we did realise the importance of establishing practical on-going community sites to *demonstrate* what could be achieved. And, having established a community waste recycling center at Banjarsari, decided to target this village as our primary pilot recycling village.

One of the major advantages of Banjarsari was that we already had two or three strongly committed *champions* of the idea of turning Banjarsari into a green village, including Ibu Harini Bangbang Wahono, the 70-year old daughter of Dutch-era gardeners, who, as matriarch of Banjarsari's environmental movement became our main trainer, and Ibu Nuning Wirjoatmodjo, attached to our own UNESCO Office as a Senior Program Assistant, and also residing within the village community.

In Banjarsari we went well beyond running training courses towards building up community commitment, with a four-pronged strategy, including establishment of a community-based environmental management committee to make decisions and lead the village initiative, provision of technical inputs to improve the collection of waste, and, perhaps most importantly of all, development of income-generating activities out of the waste recycling process. After the economic collapse of 1997 into 1998 the previous market for *selling* compost that we had been developing in the richer garden suburbs of Jakarta for the poor compost producing villages, started to fall away. So, basic to the Banjarsari initiative was the idea that instead of 'selling' the compost, it would be *used* as fertilizer to generate *more* lucrative income earning possibilities. It was this factor that was most instrumental in our associated actions (the fourth prong of our strategy) to build public awareness and commitment within the Banjarsari community. We put a lot of energy into monthly waste management training programs for women and house helpers, but, at the same time, also maintained an external training program whereby Banjarsari was increasingly seen as a developing model of integrated waste management practice—both within the community itself, and therefore a source of pride, and outside the community, where it was a source of inspiration and diffusion. By 2001, for example, we were conducting 21 external training programs a year in Banjarsari, and had set up a partnership with the Indonesian Boy Scout Organization (of several million young members—previously a compulsory activity for youth under the Soeharto regime) which sent its members to Kampung Banjarsari to be trained in integrated waste management, and then became trainers themselves in their own villages across Indonesia. Meanwhile Banjarsari received 210 official visitors per year and was one of the main sites on study tours we developed for community leaders and students. Indeed, by the end of my UN posting based in Indonesia at the beginning of 2006, there were so many study tour groups wishing to come to Banjarsari that they must register on a waiting list.

The most visible sign of Banjarsari's unique character now was its foliage. The village is located in south Jakarta, directly adjacent to a toll road and one of the main routes to the south of the city, the hot, polluted, jostling, crowded thoroughfare of Jalan Fatmawati. One hundred meters down a side street, Jalan Banjarsari, however, and you enter a new world of green leafy streets, the color-coded bins I launched in July 2001, and every house fronted by potted plants springing up from reused tins or bottles—thriving on a mix of salvaged topsoil and locally made compost: many of the plants are labelled with their name plus traditional medical uses. As a journalist, Djuna Ivereigh, reported in 'ISLAND LIFE' in 2003,

> where space is tight, racks are stacked up for 'verticulture', recalling a verdant Hanging Gardens of Babylon.

One extraordinary house—belonging to resident Ibu Nina, was quite literally a four story tropical jungle, twice winning Jakarta's award for best garden house. (Ibu Nina told me it took her two hours every day to water her 'house'). The ambience of the village now included roadside restaurants, tiny convenience stores, traveling musicians, push cart VCD sellers. The streets were now made of paving stone rather than asphalt or cement—adding to a park-like atmosphere as well as serving the practical purpose of allowing rainwater to penetrate through the cracks, thus reducing the risk of flooding. The village housed a central paper recycling center where young people in particular were engaged in producing recycled paper cards, boxes and other handicrafts, also, a plant seedling nursery, a family medicinal garden—*Tanaman Obat Kelkuarga*—a vacant lot set aside for growing plants used as natural remedies and a central community hall, all of which form concentration points for village activity.

When we converted from the idea of developing income through selling compost to *using* compost to grow plants for profit, we found two main markets, the first was growing and hiring plants to office blocks; the second was medicinal plants. Local champion Ibu Nuning was quoted in the ISLAND LIFE article to demonstrate the importance of this move:

> At first people were a little bored with just sorting garbage. But when they saw they could produce something useful, and they remembered the traditions of their parents and grandparents, that's when the project really took off.

Several small businesses were then established in Banjarsari, marketing medicinal and herbal products; the older women of the village established a traditional medicine-based practice for providing free medical treatment to local scavengers and the very poor who were associated with their community, and in 2004 a local aliphatic doctor moved in, complementing traditional medicine delivery with mainstream treatment as well.

We found, once the genii of possible income from waste was out of the bottle that the people themselves came up with good ideas about how to make money. The youth, for example, picked up on the idea of collecting discarded kerosene tins, painting them with artistic motifs depicting ecological messages and then selling them as waste-bins to the public out on Jalan Fatmawati. The idea took off instantly: for a cost of around Rp10,000, they sold for Rp 75,000. A French tourist who saw them in the first few days put in a (serious) order for several hundred to take back and sell in Europe. We also helped to build marketing bridges, for example, setting up links between Banjarsari and a Japanese Department Store in Tokyo—with the local youth of Banjarsari handcrafting origami objects specifically according to Japanese design aesthetics.

Essence of the 'Idea' of Community Empowerment

The two Case Studies of Empowerment that I have talked about in this Chapter demonstrate the theme of the previous Chap. 11, that is, finding opportunity within challenge by the people themselves—an empowered Mentawai forest community on an island that was previously fast self-destructing, peace and literacy coming out of a war zone in the southern Philippines, and an ecologically balanced village in the midst of a heavily polluted developing countries' city. In all cases of both chapters the underlying dynamic is the same, the perhaps 'unglimpsed' power of communities that can be unleashed to change things for themselves—once the people can *see* the vision and get their act as a 'community' together. Our role as United Nations change agents was primarily to facilitate the opening up of a vision, and knowledge that may be needed to accomplish it but which is not yet a part of the community's repertoire, and the building of initial steps in community organization and empowerment. Often we also needed to become a bridge with the wider world outside the community. This was the case with the Mentawai in building their relations to local and national government; building a bridge to external community radio expertise was basic to our Mindanao GENPEACE initiative; and linking local design of recycled artefacts to Japanese fashion was a necessary step in Banjarsari in broadening the community's market opportunities for recycled products.

It became obvious in every case in my experience though that as 'outsiders' we *had* to be schooled in listening and adjusting—encouraging the community to increasingly take over calling the shots. Usually, the locals knew their own situation better than anyone and had great ideas. We needed to hang in there long enough for the process to mature—in my experience, usually around 7 or 8 years, and to make sure that the pieces were in place to sustain long-term practice. But, then we could, and indeed, should, move on.

In this limited number of Case Studies, I have only been able to touch the surface of our experience: there were *many* other projects which I do not have space to talk about.

There are however one or two additional lessons on empowerment that are worth noting from this wider field.

There was a broad range of entry points. In the Philippines for example, we assisted the people of Palawan Island, Mindanao, to develop an ecotourism industry, where we found one of the most powerful tools for people starting to believe in their *own* ability to develop sustainable income was building connection with them to international community standards and a very simple grasp of science. We helped to build these capacities in developing marine aquaculture, in linking with their own local knowledge to more effectively collect and develop crabs for market, building mangrove walking platforms, ecologically oriented snorkeling and water–sport tourism—including the use of their own fishing boats. Here, simple modification of the boats allowed them to meet international standards and thus serve as tourist boats by day, and as local fishing boats by night. Indeed, in one barangay or community district, what made the difference was learning basic geological knowledge that allowed them to convert a large and inconvenient *rock* on the outskirts of their village into a major eco-tourism site. This was the Tagabinet barangay not far from the main city of Palawan, Puerta Princesa and near Ulugan Bay. The village, located at the edge of the limestone mountains of Puerta Princesa Subterranean River Cave National Park, a World Heritage site, is set at the foot of a very large limestone rock, Ugong rock, that is all that is left after millennia of erosion wore down the cliffs that had previously surrounded it. And the rock is riddled with caves and passages.

The local community knew that this was a potentially great resource, and most of the ideas about developing it into a tourist destination came from them. We supplied them with some essential equipment, key safety design criteria and very basic geological knowledge which formed the basis for their tour-guide spiel. Proudly dressed in bright green uniforms and new safety helmets—supplied by UNESCO under UNDP funding support, assisted by strong torches and arms, they almost literally carried visiting tourists through the maze of passages inside the rock—past fossil stalactites, legacy of streams long-gone, up into steep inclines requiring basic spelunking (or cave climbing) harness. Our field operations guy, Martin Felsted, had shown the locals how to build internal stairways and platforms that met international safety standards. At the end of the passages, one can climb out into the sunshine onto the top of the rock where bonsaied foliage remains in the shallow limestone crevices as unique reminders of the centuries of the Rock's isolation from other ecosystems. For the amateur tourist spelunker this visit was blessed with all the charm of an ersatz Harrison Ford adventure. For the local community however the discovery of how to capitalize on their Rock was enchanting. They were incredibly enthusiastic, and alive with new ideas. And it was they who were in charge of managing their own environment, a carefully controlled eco-tourism site. The locals ran the tour (and directly received the tourist income), not an external 'big tour' operator.

Increasingly, the development of tourist oriented ecologically sensitive activities by the local villagers started to attract visitors—further stimulated by us (UNESCO) establishing a system of unique local limestone ocean caves as a World Heritage Site. But, with local government we did one more thing that mattered. Visitors were initially bussed in after landing in Palawan's capital, Puerto Princessa by commercial interests, and these outside enterprises took the majority of the profits. So, we built a barrier beyond which the buses could not go. From there on, the locals provided all support, guided tours and earned the full profits from their enterprise around Ulugan Bay.

The success of working with the Ulugan Bay communities along these lines was signalled in 2001 when Mayor Haggerdorn awarded me—on behalf of our whole team, the Puerto Princessa Annual 'Mayor's Award'.

At the Centre of All—The Whole Person

At the core of all our work was the vision of a 'whole' person however—where we could perhaps contribute knowledge, ideas, linkages and resources, but where what mattered was engagement of the peoples' true humanity.

We worked in Metro Manila with street children and out-of-school youth for example—our partner being Erda Tech and a beautifully charismatic elderly Catholic priest, Father Tritz, on what became known as the 'Palihan' Project. Our task was to get the 15 to 24 year old kids and youth off the streets and into constructive lives and jobs. There were several key principles of the program—which put together targeted and competitive skills development—including precisely targeted training for *specific* job opportunities that were currently available—e.g. how to make sausages, on-the-job experience, standards that were competitive with any mainstream provider … with values education (for example, of development of self-esteem, work ethic commitment, and basic life skills –setting goals, resolving conflict, dealing with conflicts and so on). At the heart of the program was the principle of 'support always' that is, unflagging support to the youth by the trainers—day and night, together with clear *respect* for the young people. *Discipline* was central. But skills training was not enough. Probably more than anything else what mattered was the fact that the kids felt they were valued and respected as people.

The young people came from some very disadvantaged backgrounds. Many were on the streets full-time; but there was a large group of others who lived in dwellings that were so small that the whole family could not fit in at the one time. Some of the children took me to their houses—built in the alley spaces between city buildings—several stories high but with the tiniest of rooms at each level. The children had to take shifts to go to bed or to have dinner. They were forced to spend the rest of their time out on the street.

To enter as participants in the Palihan project however, the young people had to *choose* to apply, because, as we had decided in advance, their starting point had to be their own commitment to *do something* to turn around their lives rather than be passive recipients of local church or government decision or representation: they *had* to at least show a signal of 'trying', even though most of the young people were caught up in heavy duty trauma or consequences of their lives on the streets.

Having started in 1997, by the time the Palihan project entered its fourth phase—in late 2001, the program was training 200 students per year, and continued to do so thereafter. Of young people trained, 64 percent were working full time; 10 percent went back to high school, and 9 percent were involved in community work. Indeed, our Palihan ex-street children became more attractive to employers than young people graduating out of normal school.

As with anything we ever did with community empowerment however, at heart of what mattered was listening to and engagement of the whole person and the wholeness of the community, not just skill development training or external intervention promoting political change.

We had already realized that this principle of building response that is fully cognizant of the whole person and whole community and its own local culture and meaning lay at the heart of community empowerment intervention by international Development Assistance Agencies such as mine. We had learnt that this lesson of human 'wholeness' applied when our intervention was in response to people confronting major crisis from social or political violence or natural disaster. Importantly, we had also learnt that the lesson of addressing 'human wholeness' applied with equal force when dealing with people embedded in relatively normal life circumstances where our task was to assist the people to enhance previously restricted access to work, income or social opportunity, or where the balance could be strengthened between their productive labor and the sustainability of development.

However, it was the Tsunami of 26th December 2004 sweeping a massive body of water, measured in cubic kilometers, over northern Aceh and Sumatra that proved to us the universality of the message. We found that it was critical to address not only physical needs for food, shelter, and medical support when such a major disaster confronted the community, but also to address the recapture of spirit, human drive and meaning of the person. For there is no will to continue, no spirit to pick oneself up and move on, until the person and their community are able to 'wake up' and again find meaning in having a future vision and are collectively working towards it. Of all the programs we introduced to respond to the 26th December 2004 Tsunami, the most important turned out to be where we worked with local leaders of the Acehnese 'sudhati', or poetry song and dance, to overcome the Tsunami-induced trauma and sense of 'helplessness' that had swept, along with the Tsunami, over survivors, and in particular, the children and youth of the province. As the children 'woke up' because of our local cultural programs in Displaced Persons Camps or Orphanages, so too did their communities.

Confronting the aftermath of the Aceh Tsunami is the focus of my Chaps. 17 and 18. First however, we need to return to the radical transformation of the social and political context of Indonesia for dealing with this crisis six years earlier with the May 1998 Revolution that swept previous dictatorial President Soeharto from power.

13

"Revolution—Lead Up"

May 1998, Indonesia

Dusk in Jakarta on Thursday 14th May 1998 was very eerie and full of foreboding. The evening sky was red, a product of the smoke that had been pouring out of the burnt shells of buildings and cars all day. I climbed up to our roof along with Jill, my wife. Within three hundred metres in all directions, I could see a fire burning. The shopping center at the corner of our street was well ablaze. For the people from the village just at the rear of our house the occasion was like a festival. They formed a chattering procession from the shops past our residence and into their village houses carrying whatever produce they could rescue from the flames—everything from television sets to rice. Apart from them however all was now still. It had been a day of violence and it felt like the city was now resting before again re-erupting.

I had just arrived home from the office in the UN Building mid-town where we had been monitoring the emerging riots, killings, and looting, whilst preparing for emergency evacuation. There were absolutely *no* police or military anywhere in sight. They had totally disappeared. And everywhere … people were out on the streets, in silent witness or in small quietly talking groups … just watching. There was a palpable feeling that something terrible was about to happen, and everyone was simply witness to events beyond their control.

We packed the emergency suitcases, one each, 15 kg maximum, with basic clothes, torch, some food, passport, money, and a feeling of desperation.

The Revolution had begun. And, as we were about to discover, we had a very scary evening in front of us.

Where It All Started

The signs of political turmoil had been building for over a year—since disturbances across the country started to emerge in January 1997, three months prior to the General Election of May 1997, and almost immediately after I had settled back into the Office after sending 108 pigs on their way to Mapnduma in the Papuan Highlands.

Presidential Power

Up to this time the President had ruled with an iron hand, keeping a lid on the first glimmerings of destabilizing movements or opposition. This was a time, it should be remembered, when the distant patrician power of President Soeharto was virtually unassailable, when media was totally controlled—news, for example, being *only* broadcast from Jakarta—16 times a day to the provinces, where there was no investigative journalist capacity outside Jakarta, and even investigation in Jakarta was severely curtailed, and therefore where corruption and political intrigue at local levels simply remained invisible, and criticism of the President a severely punishable offence. Protest was strictly controlled, with immediate arbitrary incarcerations, disappearances and torture that was hidden officially from the public, but widely known and feared.

Meanwhile, President Soeharto manipulated the accepted State ideology of the five principles of 'Pancasila' and its motto 'Unity in Diversity' for his own interest. The Unity Principle had been enshrined in Indonesia's 1945 Constitution, played out in the affirmation that Indonesia was a secular country tolerant of all religions and where all accepted belief in 'One God' but not by any specific religious path—at least on paper. Soeharto made this work in his favour, exercising strong control over any signs of Islamic extremism before they could have any impact whatsoever on his own rule.

> A friend of mine for example, Arief, an ecumenically minded Moslem of impeccable integrity, was jailed 15 times under Soeharto, usually because as a university rector he supported his students. On one occasion, Arief told me, he had gone to the local police station to enquire on why students from his university had been arrested; he emerged again *one year later*.

Additionally, the President's family and a small group of immediate cronies had a stranglehold on the economy, simply moving in to claim a stake in any successful private company they chose, including large multinationals such as

Freeport—with a major goldmine in Irian Jaya, the province now known as West Papua—10% of proceeds heading towards the President's multi-billion dollar accounts—primarily held overseas.

The effect of this corrupt concentration of economic power close to the President effectively removed the Indonesian Economy away from public ownership and accountability generally. Soeharto tolerated this without intervention.

Additionally, as I observed in Chap. 2, Soeharto's authority was legitimated by appeal to the traditional Javanese Spirit World, a power that Soeharto himself strongly believed for he had enjoyed absolute power for so long that he saw himself quite literally as a Javanese King. So too did the people. Even after his downfall and exposure for overseeing massive plundering of the country's wealth by his own family, when Soeharto finally died, the official protocol of his funeral ceremony on 28th January 2008 in Solo, his spiritual home, was that normally accorded in tradition to a Javanese King, not a former civil leader, President or not.

However, it was starting to become transparent to many in early 1997 that there was nothing further from the truth than the official title of the approaching election, the so-called 'Festival of Democracy'. A combination of suppressed information, lack of opportunity for opposition and manipulation of election results would *assure* victory for the Golkar Party, the President's political power base. Democracy itself was on hold whilst the only 'festivals' were of those celebrating the bribes paid to them to vote the right way.

But, even so, the President's men took no chances, and were worried in the lead-up to the 1997 election about emerging signs of contest from Megawati Soekarnoputri, daughter of Indonesia's founding President Soekarno. Suppression of opposition was normally carried out by using draconian laws and a compliant judiciary to seal off impending opposition from pro-democracy activists, trade union officials, students, journalists or other 'troublemakers'. In this case Soeharto's forces chose to intrude directly into Megawati's political party, the Indonesian Democratic Party or PDI to remove her from office as the Party's President—even though the Party was one of three officially sanctioned parties and Megawati's election as PDI Chair at their 1993 Congress was recognized by Soeharto. In July 1996, with backing of the armed forces, Soeharto used proxies to remove *Ibu Mega* from office, replacing her with a stooge, Soeryadi, as the official PDI Head.

Megawati's supporters were incensed. Hundreds clad in the red and black colours and the bull symbol of the party camped out at party headquarters in the central Jakarta suburb of Mentang, vowing not to leave until Megawati was re-instated. Day by day the numbers grew whilst thousands started to appear in street marches that ended up at the gates of the PDI compound where they listened to speeches delivered by the party faithful.

Finally, this all became too much for Soeharto. At 6.30am on Saturday 27 July 1996 the military surrounded the compound. A collection of hired thugs dressed in red and black to project the impression they were Party supporters, then proceeded to hurl rocks and Molotov Cocktails into the compound in a vulgar attempt to prove to the world at large that a large pro-government faction was moving to *reclaim* the PDI Party and its properties. The hundreds of riot police and army officers who were present simply watched. After an hour the riot police stormed the front of the compound whilst Kostrad, the army's elite Strategic Reserve (the force that Soeharto used to topple Soekarno) invaded the rear. Whilst the government admitted there had been a very small number of deaths, according to the Indonesian Human Rights Commission the invasion and hired mob left 5 dead, 149 injured and 23 missing—missing, but never found. Our own information from hospital admissions suggested that the numbers actually killed may have been two to three times as high as even the Human Rights group had estimated for those killed and missing. The Director of my sister organization, the United Nations Development Program, UNDP, Jan Kemp, was there when the attack occurred and told me it was extremely violent, but as the mob swept towards the front of the hall, he was rushed backstage by the organizers and managed to escape.

The anger of the genuine PDI supporters spilled over into rioting that spread out from the compound during the afternoon and into the night—setting fire to buses, banks, and government offices. The PDI then split, with a new breakaway PDI 'Perjuangan' (or struggle) Party separating off from the discredited 'official' PDI Party. PDI Perjuangan (PDIP) increasingly grew into a hugely popularist movement and Soeharto's attempt to demolish his main opposition completely backfired. Soeryadi had no serious political support within PDI so the Soeryadi wing of the party was quickly discredited—gaining only 3.1 percent of the peoples' vote at the subsequent election, a radical fall from the previous 14.9 percent of vote enjoyed by PDI prior to the Soeryadi coup; whilst the attempt to suppress PDI opposition brought the President's anti-democratic actions into high public relief thus *stimulating* opposition from a people who were already restless. Soeharto inadvertently made a martyr and a champion out of Megawati, previously a 'leader' who rarely spoke, was not regarded as particularly good at judging strategy, and who had a very thin track record in public life.

However, the force of opposition that was by now steadily becoming more visible day by day did not gain power on the streets until *after* the March 1997 General Election.

Subtlety of Prior Opposition

For those courageous enough to look, the ways that the President's Golkar Party vote was manipulated, and democracy denied were pretty obvious well before this. And, as with the student protest movement that spun out from Yogyarta's Gadja Mahda University from 1992 onwards, a small number of aware people directly sought to confront the 'unfreedom' of the New Order Government. But in an autocratic regime which ruled with the velvet Javanese glove of non-confrontationist social mores and an ideology of 'unity in diversity' over an iron covert fist of repression of opposition, such a political reality reached nowhere near the surface of public debate.

Indeed, I had found since I arrived in Indonesia 18 months before, that apart from a small collection of brave students, writers, artists, journalists, and activists who ventured out earlier onto the field of protest invariably to the detriment of their own human rights, signals of political opposition remained very subtle indeed.

Perhaps the most elegant form of protest under a repressive regime was what happened in the aftermath of the mob raid on the 1996 PDI Headquarters I spoke of earlier. Leaders of the mob were not arrested and brought to justice, but they *did* appear several months later before the courts. In the most unlikely of alliances, they were supported in a class action case by the Indonesian Human Rights Commission, a group with highly marginalized power to this point.

> The mob leaders claimed that they had been *underpaid* for their contracted services, that is, paid only a few hundred Rupiahs rather than the thousands of Rupiahs promised by the organizers behind Soeryadi. It was a brilliant strategy by the Commission because even with the suffocating level of general censorship of *media* investigation, all court proceedings *could* be published legitimately in the open press. The underpaid thugs apprised the court in enthusiastic detail, appearing not to notice that the activity for which they were stridently seeking equitable settlement, was not quite a fair day's pay for a fair day's work, but illicit and covert payment for violent criminal activity.
> To establish their case for compensation, leaders of the raiding party were led in court through the detail of their preparation and action, e.g.: attending specific police stations to be equipped with weapons and training, briefings by

named individuals, and so on. All of this was reported in the press. As a result, Soeharto's covert strategic violence was exposed to the public in a way that was impossible through normal investigative journalism at that time. This was truly a masterful display of the Javanese way of political shadow puppetry.

At a public level the only relatively legitimate area of protest was to do with the ecology—not in criticism of the official blind eye that was turned to illegal logging, rapacious mining of indigenous peoples' land, or massive development-based pollution, or to the fact that the President's son, Tommy, was the chief importer of tetracyclic lead so there was little opportunity for lead-free petrol to ever appear on the streets. Or that the country's multi-billion dollar 'forestry support' fund had been turned over to Jusuf Habibie, at that stage favored godson of the President and Minister for Research and Technology (later to be President Soeharto's successor, another story) so that he could develop an aircraft building industry—an ill-fated venture of gigantic proportions.

No, protest was more to do with offering greener alternatives. This did not cross the edge into politically pariah territory.

With a platform for legitimacy in UNESCO's mandate to support science and therefore environment assessment and green programs, we started immediately to find ways of turning what for some years had been simply scientific monitoring programs, in particular, of the pollution of Jakarta Bay, into community-based *change activities*—a story I told in Chap. 12. Within my own UN mandate as Resident Director and Ambassador I could not touch the politics directly at that stage for this would have been construed as interfering in the internal affairs of the country. But I could work at the edges.

I reasoned that basic predicates of wider political awareness and transformation could be set in place first through enhancing the peoples' awareness that there were alternatives to the uncontested decisions and actions of a centrally controlled planning system that was actually delivering an environment dangerous to their health and wellbeing … and by implication, their rights. And second, through helping people to see the *possibility* of wider political transformation by directly engaging in change of the status quo even on small and relatively innocuous things. Like on culture—not at the front of the political perspective … but powerful in confronting and developing meaning.

Therefore, working in uniquely 'Javanese' style, some quite elegant forms of protest were already well established amongst performers, musicians and aficionados of the arts. With a United Nations mandate for developing freedom of expression but severely constrained political or diplomatic opportunities in the mid-1990s to pursue this goal in Indonesia, I therefore started within the first year of my tenure to support these guys as they offered something by way of 'backdoor critique' that no one else did.

In particular, a group of musicologists, musicians, performers, their backstage colleagues and students had formed to create an International Percussion Festival. What was special about them was that these were people with real concern for employing culture to empower others, a group that I then worked with for the whole time I was in Indonesia—and afterwards, a group of people deserving enormous respect.

From 1996 a culture specialist/businessman, Siarano Senturi or Rano, emerged as leader of this group, and in my first year looking after UNESCO in Indonesia, 1996, we founded a music and social change NGO together which we called "Sacred Bridge". Rano devoted both the money he made in running a commercial advertising agency to the support of Sacred Bridge as well as enormous amounts of his own time, and became a very close friend. Whilst I co-founded the NGO with Rano, and am still regarded as Founding Patron (e.g.: in 2021 when we ran a major international concert via internet given COVID restrictions, organised by Rano's son, Boo-boo). Rano really was the power behind the force that Sacred Bridge became to the present day in using music and performance to raise awareness and heal conflict and trauma particularly amongst children and young people, yet another story that I will return to in Chap. 18. I brought UNESCO in behind what they were doing—financially and in endorsement, sometimes in the early days feeling, I must admit, some trepidation that we were coming a little close to the edge of Government sensitivities.

Back in the days when Soeharto still ruled, Sacred Bridge's percussion music was, to say the least, creative. Two examples from Performances we supported from UNESCO, both presented by a charismatic very popular gothic motor-cycle style Yogyakarta based musician, Rusdi, who sadly died prematurely a few years ago.

> In the first performance Rusdi's percussion instrument was a *motor vehicle*, a Kejang van, very popular cheap private transport in Jakarta. The 'instrument' was played by five 'musicians' who banged shut the five doors of the kejang under Rusdi's conducting to create the performance and its rhythm, symbolizing in a way that the audience found hilarious the rhythm of taking control over modern life.
> Rusdi's second particularly notable performance the next year under my UNESCO endorsement was to appear on stage before an outdoor audience of 6,000, stripped down to the waist with a heart monitor attached. The

acoustics were turned on at high volume and the rhythm was pumped out by his monitor-recorded heartbeat. With each beat Rusdi added visual affect by opening and shutting a Japanese paper umbrella behind which he was sheltering. Then the band started, quietly as background at first but increasingly picking up the rhythm of the heart and building it into a major musical presentation. subtle perhaps, but symbolizing the significance of the rhythm of the heart within modern life.

More obvious was then the performance immediately afterwards by a group of men dressed in the costume of the Japanese invaders of World War II—only this time, with clear symbolism of the repression and contexts of the present Indonesian regime. Again, though the form of the presentation was uproarious farce which through a subtlety lost on most censors for the regime, conveyed very elegant political protest. This was in 1997 when the ideological edifice of unassailable authority of President Soeharto and his New Order Government was starting to display significant structural cracks.

And we were able to instigate a change to the endemic censorship of expression in the country through supporting the development in March 1996 of the first International Women's' Film Festival, sold to the Government as an appropriate Indonesian follow-up of the Beijing Women's Conference to promote the status of women, and, organized in collaboration with Indonesian film personality, Julia Suryakusuma—firmly committed to women's rights. I determined there would be no censorship whatsoever from Indonesian authorities, i.e.: from the Ministry of 'Information'.

Needless to say, as soon as I informed the Ministry that UNESCO would be hosting this International Women's Film Festival in Jakarta, their immediate response was that *nothing* would be shown publicly in Indonesia without their specific review and approval. What was at stake was censorship of women's right to learn from what was happening elsewhere on their rights around the world. So, I refused to allow any censorship of films that were to be shown. But I sought a diplomatic compromise.

And here was where international diplomacy came in.

So, Step 1: I arranged for local embassies of eight countries to monitor the films selected by informed Indonesian film women, and to assist in diplomatic cooperation with the Indonesian authorities—with endorsement at Ambassador level that any films from their own country would not conflict with local cultural or governmental sensitivities. I backed this with my own guarantee as '*fair witness*' on behalf of the United Nations (my own UNESCO Agency being responsible for UN-wide action, inter-alia, on both Culture and Media) of the acceptability of the international films that otherwise would never be shown.

13 "Revolution—Lead Up"

"Ah", the censorship authorities then responded, "then, unless we specifically approve each film they may not be shown in any public place, i.e.: cinemas or public buildings".

Step 2: Expecting this response, and after much debate with officials of the Ministry of Information, we agreed not to *show* the films at public cinemas, but, having arranged this, at the Dutch Cultural Centre attached to their Embassy, Erasmus House. Apart from minimum age requirements, there was no restriction on *who* could come onto the Netherlands Embassy compound to see the movies.

Back to the Ministry of Information again. "Even if on Dutch property and not on Indonesia's public ground, you may not therefore *advertise* the programs.

My Step 3 response was to agree. Already, the idea of a completely uncensored International Film Program on women and women's rights internationally had generated a groundswell of grass roots communication in social media, particularly amongst university students, artists, and performers. Little general publicity was necessary for the level of public interest to attend became enormous. There had never been an uncensored film festival in the country since the nation was formed.

But the Censor authorities were not yet defeated. "OK, but we must at least *see* the movies before they are shown to the public."

My Final Step: "Absolutely NO! You are very welcome to come along to the film presentations as is anyone else. But, with all the international diplomatic support already in place—including my own personal guarantee as Ambassador of the United Nations Agency responsible globally, my acceptance of not showing films in Indonesian controlled cinemas or halls but on embassy grounds, and avoiding *any* public media advertising at all … here I am drawing the line. Under my implied suggestion of exposure of governmental resistance even against high level international ambassador-level guarantees and total avoidance of public exposure, or being shown in Indonesian premises or advertising through public information … the censors gave up. They, finally, were not prepared to confront the public exposure I had implied if they refused to be reassured by a number of National Ambassadors and myself as Ambassador of the UN for showing films about international culture.

The Festival was shown to packed houses every night. Even Megawati Soekarnoputri—the subsequent President of Indonesia—attended, shown off to the audience as she entered and proceeded to her highly visible front row seat.

Our main achievement was that we had been able to move the censor off his pedestal of total control over everything that entered the country, and showed films under UNESCO's legitimating umbrella that stretched the boundaries of censor-inscribed public Puritanism on the one hand and were politically critical on the other, not of Soeharto, but of other regimes, thereby demonstrating the possibility, indeed the *normality,* of political protest outside Indonesia.

Eighteen months later in September 1997 we followed up in collaboration with the local NGO, the Lontar Foundation, with the Second Jakarta International Film Festival, entitled 'Women in the Face of Change'. By this time the Festival had grown—presenting twenty eight films from twenty countries, ending with a day of short and documentary films and open discussion on film and the role of women in the film industry, in particular as film makers. Our intent was, of course, to signal the empowerment of women and a women's' voice at a time when change of a long-standing repressive social order was in the air. Seven thousand people came.

By 1998, the time when we would otherwise have held a Third International Women's' Film Festival, the change had happened. The student-catalyzed revolution had swept Soeharto from power, and the voice of the people, including women, was emerging unshackled for the first time. And freedom of expression had been released out of its previous imprisonment—as I show in Chap. 15.

Finally, there were courageous authors whose writings had left them incarcerated. One was Pramoedya Ananta Toer, author and left-leaning editor and critic. As a participant in the Indonesian Independence Movement, he was jailed several times between 1947 and 1949 by the Dutch. He was jailed in 1960 for defending the country's persecuted Chinese, then again imprisoned without trial in 1965 at the time when Soeharto seized power and the New Order Government took control. He remained in the infamous Buru Island prison until 1979, and produced a series of four historical novels, *the Buru Tetralogy* focusing on the early 20th Century and the story of characters embarking on the journey from compliance to Dutch colonialism into the fervor of their cry for independence. He read the narratives as he wrote them to his fellow prisoners. For reasons I could not see in the works, the authorities banned the first two of this series; the later two were smuggled out of the country and published overseas. Pramoedya was touted as the most likely Asian author to win the Nobel Prize.

13 "Revolution—Lead Up"

By the time Pramoedya became a concern for me he had been released from prison but was under continuing house arrest. With no advance warning, I was confronted by an enclosure in the diplomatic pouch that arrived from Paris every week, unopened by local authorities according to the diplomatic privilege accorded to United Nations and Embassy missions. The package included a statue awarded as an international literary prize, an Honourable Mention in the Award of the UNESCO-Madanjeet Singh Prize for the Promotion of Tolerance and Non-violence, accompanied by a Letter of Congratulations from the UNESCO Director-General … plus instructions to me as Representative and Director of the Indonesia Office to arrange an official ceremony for handing over the Award.

Literally as I was contemplating how to go about this venture given that the recipient was under official incarceration by the host government, I received a phone call. It was from Indonesian Foreign Affairs. Confidentiality of what was in the United Nations Diplomatic Pouch clearly was compromised somewhere along the way.

> "You are summoned by the Minister's Special Representative", Director of the Division responsible for international organizations—Dr. Hassan Wirajuda, who, as it turned out, later became the Minister of Foreign Affairs when Megawati Soekarnoputri assumed the Presidency. I was to be diplomatically 'carpeted', slapped metaphorically around the diplomatic face for my organization breaking the rules of international diplomacy … according to the Indonesian Government's definition of the situation. The problem concerned Pramoedya.

I arrived at the Office of Hassan to find three stony-faced men staring me down as I entered the room. The other two were the Minister of Education (UNESCO's point of contact) and one of his senior staff. Immediately I was 'dressed down' as Representative of UNESCO for the organization having the temerity of causing severe embarrassment to the Republic of Indonesia by awarding a major international prize to a criminal, jailed for his actions to undermine the State.

> "This constitutes interference in the internal affairs of a Sovereign State", I was instructed.

There was of course an official answer. My response went something like this:

The prize was awarded not by the Director-General or Secretariat of UNESCO, but by an International Jury of people of the highest international caliber and integrity, chaired by Archbishop Tutu of South Africa; the Jury's *membership* had been endorsed by UNESCO's General Conference of all Member States—and *this included Indonesia*. As with all such expert panels the *decision* they came to was not subject to agreement by these same Member States as the panel was independent, not political, and applied the highest competitive and ethical standards in making their choice once selected and set in motion. Member States have the right to approve the membership of such panels and the principles by which they work and decide, but in doing this, sign over authority of decision to the panel. If the decisions were then subject to agreement by all Member States these decisions would invariably be caught up in a morass of debate and dissension, and never be implemented. The Director-General of UNESCO simply passes on this independent judgment to the world community.

This mechanism, I might add, is one of the most important ways within the United Nations System in which issues to do with suppression of human rights can be brought to international attention. In UNESCO's case, for example, international prizes for contributions to media freedom are often awarded through an expert panel mechanism to journalists under repressive regimes. The Award exposes the human rights abuses the person is fighting to change whilst at the same time providing an empowering international profile for the author. Governments that then seek to jail or restrict the freedoms of the Awardee, confront the certainty of international attention and sanction.

After I had been further dressed down with little attention to my justification, I was told very firmly that there was no way in which the Government was going to let me conduct an official public award ceremony for Pramoedya.

I had no choice as a United Nations Ambassador but abide by this enforced demand. BUT, and here lies the craft of diplomacy. One can find other ways.

> Subsequently, I was able to arrange a way of giving the Award to Pramoedya in a relatively quiet ceremony, not in public, but at his residence (where he was in official incarceration) conducted not by me, but a senior UNESCO program specialist from my Office. Whilst press journalists were not *officially* present … and would not have been able to report the event fairly even if they were, we were able to get the information out on Pramoedya's international literary prize into and through the local literary and human rights social media networks anyway.

After the official meeting closed I was taken aside by the Minister of Education and his senior Director for an additional private word. I asked what exactly was wrong with Pramoedya's books that they should be banned. Having acquired the books in Singapore, I had read them all and could find no signs of subversion. The Minister told me firmly that there were subtle signs in the books of the Communist leanings of Promoedya. I wrote his comment down immediately after I left the meeting as it was a classic.

> "Promoedya's communist persuasiveness is deeply hidden and very subtle", he informed me. The people need to be protected. It is when they are not yet educated enough to see the communist assumptions of the plot that these sorts of works are most dangerous.

I am personally still looking for communist leanings in the texts. What I find quite frankly is that Pramoedya simply had a passion for the human rights of all and would not bow to official intimidation for his support of the outcast ethnic Chinese or those associated with the left of politics.

I felt the paternalism that was exhibited by the then Minister of Education was what was most dangerous for the health of Indonesian society, not Pramoedya's novels. But the Minister simply reflected the ways of the Soeharto era.

At that time as a UN Ambassador, it was possible to tiptoe around the edges of political critique and to seek to provide fora that fostered an opening up of these paternalistic anti-human rights assumptions to public scrutiny. However, serious intervention as a UN agency required by international diplomatic protocol to respect the sovereignty of a Member State was not really possible until after 20th May 1998 and President Soeharto was deposed … a possibility that emerged day by day as events catalyzed by the Trisakti University killings a week earlier steadily and irrevocably stripped away the legitimacy and power of the President and with this, the peoples' fear and the media's reticence to report exactly what was going on.

Signs of Unrest Round the 1997 'Festival of Democracy'

Back to the 1997 elections.

Under President Soeharto's regime, all government officials were forced to vote for Golkar, the President's party—with voting performed in front of supervisors in a procedure that required placing a hole in the ballot paper that the voter had to hold up so as to be visible to all. Golkar party officials across the country were paying locals to vote for Golkar, and at the same time, entering advance estimates of the vote levels for their districts and provinces that turned out often to be 'spectacularly accurate'. One estimate that really impressed me at the time came in from the Governor of Kalimantan, predicting that Golkar would capture 96.48 percent of the vote, that is, predicting with an accuracy to two decimal places. Lo and behold, that was exactly the final tallied figure, leading one to be a little suspicious of due process. Out in the provinces the people simply did what they were told or paid for as they had little understanding of what democracy was and the government was certainly not helping them to find out. In the cities and amongst the students however, a broad ranging scepticism was emerging.

Students across the country started to mobilise in increasingly large numbers, calling for democracy and for President Soeharto to resign. With its strongest protest base in Yogyakarta's remarkably independent Gadya Madha University—from which Rector Amien Rais, a Moslem leader, already a critic of the Soeharto regime, subsequently became a key national opposition leader in May 1998—a student movement had emerged initially in 1992. Led with appropriately furtive discretion at the start by a small number of very brave young people, they had confronted a very strong threat of retribution, and a number were jailed, whilst others *did* simply disappear. By 1997 the movement was becoming more open and was starting to bite into public perceptions of Soeharto's unquestioned authority. The Government was forced to tolerate some forms of student protest but limited the impact as much as they could by enforcing a rule that student rallies could *only* be held *on campus*, never out in the streets. As the General Election approached, Soeharto's ability to manage the nation into a sixth 5-year term and his legitimacy, was increasingly and noisily questioned. Amongst the public rumors it started to emerge that the President had lost his *wahyu*, the magic powers thought to accompany a just rule, a concept believed by millions of Indonesians.

There started to be political confrontations on the streets for the first time rather than unproblematic parades of masses of yellow-jacketed Golkar supporters. Now, also out on political parade, though with little hope of significant challenge to the political order, were the red clad PDI Perjuangan supporters (Indonesian Democratic Party of Struggle—of which Megawati Soekarnoputri was head). As I mentioned earlier, Megawati was daughter of the founder of Indonesia, President Soekarno, and later President of Indonesia.

Also, now joining the political parade were members of the green clad Islamic National Mandate or PAN party—of which another (later) Presidential hopeful, Amien Rias, was head. The parties would parade in their colors, led by local small capacity motor cycles so popular in Indonesia, where the driver and pillion passenger would carry their parties' flags and rev the motor cycle engine in a concerted 'vroom, vroom, vroom, vroom, vroom' rhythm. What was dangerous was when the parades met from opposite directions, at which time fighting was increasingly likely to happen. On several occasions in both Yogyakarta and Jakarta when we came across two approaching demonstrations such as these, my driver would simply pull the car into a side street and wait rather than come anywhere near being caught up in events—and I had the additional protection compared to most of CD-1 diplomatic license plate privilege.

And little signs of rebellion did start to appear in the provinces, such as small photographs of President Soekarno in shops, and popular anti-Soeharto sayings were declared more openly like, 'Soekarno made Indonesia; Soeharto made a profit'.

Nevertheless, these were tiny signs, not indicators of a giant political wave that would have been required to counter the Golkar certainties of the May 1997 so-called 'Festival of Democracy' vote. With the General Election in his pocket, the President's own election—in February 1998—was assured, as the President was elected at that stage by Parliament, not directly by the people. The President was very attentive to ensuring the General Election produced the result he needed.

The Double Whammy of Unexpected Economic Collapse

But things did not turn out as unproblematic as the President either intended or hoped.

For, in July 1997 the Indonesian economy was swept into the Tsunami of the Asian Economic Crisis that had generated unexpectedly across the whole region from its economic epicentre in Thailand with the floating of the Thai Baht on 7th July 1997. Nobody seemed to have predicted the impact that the floating of the Thai Baht was to have in opening up Asian currency markets to question. The Baht's value immediately plummeted in value against the US Dollar by 20 percent, and contagion followed. For, although it was generally believed that the region's high growth levels were unassailable, the boom times had injected deep weaknesses into Asian economies—over-speculative borrowing, entrenched corruption, inefficiencies, and complacency. The Philippines and Malaysia were forced to devalue their currencies immediately as the financial disease spread … even into the powerhouses of the Republic of Korea and Japan. The image of the unassailable Asian tigers dissolved overnight. So, when the Asian currency markets were opened up to question by the floating of the Baht, the answers that guided market forces picked deeply into the social and political fabric of Asia as much as into the Region's economies.

Indonesia was by far the most affected economy. It was flawed deeply by political cronyism and corruption, monopolistic practices, and banking and legal frameworks that worked to obscure underlying economic fragility. At the heart of the Indonesian economic collapse lay the foreign unsecured debts of 25 companies, all closely linked with the President or his immediate associates, totaling some $(US)68 billion. Foreign debts could not be repaid, and Indonesia lost all lines of international credit. The Banks were in chaos. Many medium to large-sized companies had either aspired to or owned a bank (there were 200 in total), often treating customer deposits as little more than slush funds for grandiose projects, so now these banks could not sustain the withdrawals customers were demanding. Virtually overnight the wealth of many Indonesians disappeared. The national currency, the Rupiah, went into freefall, dropping from under Rp2,000 to the US Dollar in June 1997 … to Rp6,000 just before Christmas 1997, then Rp16,500 in January 1998 at which time inflation was running at 60 percent. Many goods included imported components, specifically for example, drugs, chicken feed (basic to supply of Indonesia's staple meat), spare parts for automobiles, paper (for newsprint). The consequence was that either the goods were unavailable or too expensive for most people.

The Indonesian economy contracted from 4.6 percent *growth* in 1997 to –12.2 percent *decline* in the first half of 1998. The impact of a shrinking economy on the population was severe, generating a sudden and rapid increase in the percentage of the population living below the poverty line and reducing across the board Government expenditure on social programs. In less than a single year the number of people living below the poverty line soared from 22.5 million or 11.3 percent of the population to 79.4 million or 40 percent of the total population of 202 million people. The unemployment rate for formal employment jumped from 7.7 percent in 1996 to 10 percent in 1997 and spiraled through early 1998 to around 20 percent. The impact on unemployment was probably far higher though difficult to estimate as two-thirds of the Indonesian labor force was either self-employed or in the informal sector. In the construction industry alone 2 million people were reported to have lost their jobs. Although food, drugs and consumer goods were generally available, ordinary people simply could no longer purchase them as the collapse of the Rupiah (to one seventh of its previous value) led to serious erosion in the peoples' purchasing power: per capita GDP plummeted from its July 1997 value, $(US)1,055 per person *by two-thirds*; inflation jumped from 11 percent in December 1997 to 57 percent in the first half of 1998, and was predicted by the Central Bureau of Statistics to reach 80 percent by the end of the year. By early 1998 the Indonesian Statistics Bureau estimated that 80 million Indonesians now earned less than $(US) 4 per month and must survive on 2,100 cal a day, barely two thirds the intake required for a normal diet; 37 percent of all Indonesian children, about 10 million young people, were underweight and suffering from malnutrition. Many parents could hardly afford to send their children to school—where, even in an ostensibly public system, school fees were levied for each child and children were compelled to wear parent-purchased school uniforms.

As could now be readily expected, the political impact was profound. Food riots and looting started to erupt across the country. Law and order was breaking down. And many middle-class Indonesians, the most loyal of Soeharto supporters, started to openly question the New Order Government.

In parallel, Indonesia was affected throughout late 1997 by drought and fires. In the context of a severe El Niño Effect and consequent drought, fires swept through major forest areas of Indonesia, particularly Kalimantan and Sumatra, many of them purposively lit by traditional slash-and-burn agriculture farmers and by large plantation companies clearing semi-degraded forest land for expanded plantings. Again, President Soeharto's financial interests and those of his family were directly implicated. The fires could not be controlled. They set alight to long-burning underground peat concentrations in some areas and delivered severe and at times toxic haze across Indonesia, Malaysia, Singapore, Brunei, Thailand and the Philippines. The fires and drought exacerbated difficulties with basic food supply particularly in Indonesia: rice production was estimated to have fallen by 4 percent in 1997 whilst there was evidence of a sharp fall in output of a number of important cash crops such as palm-oil, cocoa and coffee.

Economic crisis, exacerbated as it was in many rural communities by drought and fires, deeply shook faith of the public in the President's ability to keep control of their economic welfare that up to this point had, in general terms, been quite well looked after.

Interestingly, within the international community, the economic minders didn't see this crisis coming. The IMF had a very limited presence in Indonesia, mainly to monitor the economy and continue the call for

Indonesia to finally abide by IMF's strict monetarist rules in order for the IMF to extend loans to the country—but they were not watching. The World Bank was confidently predicting a secure economic future. The Bank's Director for Indonesia had presented the rest of the United Nations Country Team with a glowingly positive analysis of the Indonesian economy in January 1997 at which point I had suggested that in the context of enormous corporate debt developed by his family and cronies, President Soeharto was old, that there was some political weakness in the system, so questioned what, maybe, just maybe, could happen if the President either retired or disappeared from control. The Bank's Director responded that political factors were irrelevant to the economy's strength. Having some limited background in political economy and a rather more extensive one in sociology I remained rather skeptical of such purist economic claims, but had no real economic evidence with which to counter this World Bank assertion, apart from an abiding fear that a totally corrupt economy was fatally flawed, even if I was not sure how this fault was likely to be played out. In June 1997 we then moved on to the annual CGI meeting, the Consultative Group Indonesia, an international conference held annually for all donor recipient countries, where the major multilateral and bilateral donors come together to develop a collective pledge for the next year of the level of loan they are prepared to offer. I was present at this meeting, held in that year in Tokyo. The CGI was traditionally chaired by the World Bank. Again, the Indonesian Director presented a glowing account of Indonesia's economic strength, with upswinging graphs of projected economic indicator values, calling for confidence in Indonesia's repayment capacity to support increased substantial loans for the next year.

One month later … *one month* … the Indonesian economy collapsed.

By 8th October 1997 President Soeharto recognized he had to do something and called in the IMF to negotiate a bail-out package. His problem was however that the IMF's first 'Package' of reforms hurt the Soeharto family interests directly—at a general level demanding Soeharto accelerate the rate of economic deregulation and attack the widespread corruption and nepotism that had accumulated over the three decades of Soeharto's rule, and at a specific level seeking to scrap his son Tommy Soeharto's ill-conceived National Car project and closing the insolvent banks of his second eldest son, Bambang Trijhatmojo and his half-brother Probosutedo. As Australian journalist Michael Maher observed of the time,

> Soeharto appeared to regard the IMF bail-out package as a bitter pill to put into his mouth but not necessarily swallow.

Soeharto announced the closure of 16 banks, action that precipitated a panic run on the banking system, but he did not seriously push the more general reforms. The strength of the economy continued to fade. Soeharto's 'make-or-break' budget handed down as 1998 dawned was a farce, based on calculations of the Rupiah as worth 4,000 to the US Dollar when it was trading at 7,000 and weakening, and the assumption of a growth rate of 4 percent when the economy was imploding.

Soeharto was finally forced to accept a much more onerous IMF 'Package Mark 2', in which Tommy's tax privileges for his National Car project were removed along with state funding of a number of the massively expensive high tech projects of Soeharto's godson and Minister for Research and Technology Jusuf Habibie—in particular, the building of an Indonesian airplane, the NT 250, a project that had dragged along with very marginal success for years siphoning off money from the major fund that, as I mentioned earlier, was supposed to be devoted to sustainable use and conservation of Indonesia's forests. Subsidies for fuel and electricity were abandoned, the effect of which was to inflame the economic discontent of the poorest of Indonesian society who depended on kerosene for cooking their meals. Not only however did the IMF Package alienate the masses, but the IMF's complete lack of cultural awareness symbolically sent a broadside directly into the President's credibility. The Package-2 agreement was signed live before a national television audience. While the President sat, Michel Camdessus, the Swiss Head of the IMF, chose to stand behind him with arms folded, looking down at the President—quite literally as if he was witnessing a surrender. Folding one's arms in Javanese culture is a sign of supreme contempt.

> The people noticed for this display across a national television audience was a signal of Soeharto's disrespect within the international community, a signal never seen by the people before. He had indeed 'lost his *wayhu*' or spiritual authority to rule.

The economy continued to crash. The package of crises surrounding Soeharto was becoming more and more tumultuous—but, even as his health declined, Soeharto announced his intent to run again for President in March 1998.

Early 1998—Signals of What Was to Come

By early 1998 in the lead-up to the Presidential Election, things were therefore clearly looking bad, sufficient for me to write a Security Memo to Headquarters on 10th February 1998 that said:

(1) There is social unrest in some provinces of Indonesia expressed primarily in sporadic riots targeting Chinese shops and linked to radical price rises of goods.
(2) The causes of unrest are deep and unlikely to be resolved until there is a significant change in both economic and political contexts. Most fundamentally, unrest is associated with disenchantment with the economic impact of corruption at the highest levels of government. Impact is felt directly in the freefall thence uncertainty of the Indonesian currency, the Rupiah; in currently unresolvable foreign debt that paralyzed imports; in galloping inflation; and in radical increase in unemployment and loss of purchasing power. Perhaps most importantly in the Indonesian cultural context, the incumbent President appears to have lost spiritual respect of the people. Increasingly one finds direct criticism of the President and his family in the media that would have been unimaginable 6 months ago.
(3) The situation is well controlled in Jakarta where there is a very significant police and military presence, but less controlled in the more remote provinces, e.g.: of Sulawesi and Flores, where unrest is stronger and military presence weaker.
(4) The critical period is the next two months. A Presidential election occurs in early March; opposition to the current President's continuation in office is legally impossible, yet two main opposition leaders are emerging—causing serious public questioning but not serious opportunity for alternative choice. Consequently, choice of Vice-President is considered critical as a signal of the next regime—with enormous potential economic and political impact, but the President will not nominate the Vice-President until he is formally elected. Business activity is paralysed, and in particular, there is generally recognized to be seven weeks left before all import stocks for the economy run out. It is critical that there is re-establishment within the next four weeks of international market confidence in the Rupiah and in the ability of Indonesian business to pay back foreign debt, and within Indonesia in securing basic food and social security. If these conditions do not occur, and if succession after the incumbent President does not signal a change in elite-interest economics of the nation, the future of Indonesia after the Presidential election is totally uncertain.
(5) The military is deeply woven into national social order and appears to be consolidated. There is therefore little likelihood of a coup, but strong likelihood of serious and unpredictable public unrest—more in the countryside

than in Jakarta. How deep this unrest is likely to be and how continuous is unpredictable at this stage."

As it turned out. I was right in my prediction that we needed to be prepared for sporadic uncontrolled civil violence and economic crime, but wrong in my analysis about the armed forces for there *was* division in the military emerging, though not yet visible—specifically between General Probowo Subianto, hero of our West Papua saga, now increasingly a villain, and General Wiranto, head of the military—a power struggle that would be played out in the impending May 1998 Revolution. Not recognizing this internal political struggle also meant that I was wrong in my prediction that problems would largely lie *outside* Jakarta so we were not likely to face a breakdown in order that could require evacuation from the country.' For the Revolution was not catalyzed by the groundswell of dissatisfaction of the people in the provinces that *was* becoming visible, but by the unexpected murder by military snipers of four students at Trisakti University in Central Jakarta and the directly orchestrated killings and violence that swept through the city thereafter—*at the center of power*, in Jakarta. Unrest did sweep through the country, but its epicenter turned out to be the nation's capital.

The United Nations During Civil Crisis: Being Prepared for Security Breakdown

In my February 1998 Report I then expressed concern that the UN Coordinator responsible for our security and the system itself had left them poorly prepared in spite of the fact that some of us, I guess me in particular, had been calling for tightened UN security for a year now.

The United Nations itself was enormously exposed if order broke down in Jakarta. Our UN Building was located on Jalan Thamrin, the main road between the President's Palace and the centre of town, and was already a main stopping-off point for *any* demonstration heading through the central city, often two or three a day. The UN building was *directly* on the street, that is, with less than two meters separation between the footpath and the office windows. My UNESCO Offices were on the first floor, quite literally three metres from a pedestrian overpass bridge, the stairs for which rose diagonally across my street-facing window, and immediately within throwing range of projectiles from ground level. My own office chair was *directly* over the entrance arch through which any vehicle came into the UN carpark and where all vehicles were searched for bombs. The building itself was a worry too. Gifted to the UN by the Indonesian Government in the early 1970s, it had a rumored providence as purpose built for the American CIA in the late 1960s, with a honeycomb of downward angled cement shutters as an outside frame to a flimsy internal fabric that swayed with alarming flexibility on the few odd times we were hit by an earthquake. In the event of a bomb blast from ground level the shutters would have focused the force of the explosion onto the building's windows and flimsy skeleton and brought the edifice down as a pack of shuffled cement cards adorned by shards of non-safety glass. Meanwhile, the rear escape stairs down to the internal car park would have failed *any* safety assessment and there was *no exit* from the compound out the back and away from the main thoroughfares, even though the rear walls could have been easily breached by an exit gate into a quiet suburban street. Even more alarming, the car park was built over a river that flowed through a wide tunnel *under* the UN compound, and was inhabited by a number of homeless individuals and families. There could have been no better recipe for a disaster about to happen if things went bad.

I had been feeling somewhat insecure about this situation for a year now … and later, unilaterally moved out, but right now we were watching very nervously indeed the impending demise of the President being played out on the streets outside our office windows.

As I reported to Headquarters on 12th February 1998,

> The need to prepare for possible UN response to an emerging security situation has been evident for at least 12 months. … However, the UN system at this stage remains unready to implement a security plan in a rapidly developing emergency context… UNESCO, along with some other agencies, has been requesting since 12 months ago that the UN Coordinator put into place a fully developed plan and tested system of information provision and response…. It remains that the UN-wide system of security response is not adequately in place or tested. As at this date, 12th February 1998—one month before the Presidential election, emergency radio systems have been purchased for wardens and heads of agency, but remain untested; telephone tree information and response systems have been initiated but remain untested—including emergency radio communications; collection points for evacuation have been proposed but not tested or finalized; no final agreements concerning potential evacuation modes have been put into place; proposed consultations with potential national embassy security partners have been proposed but not implemented; a briefing meeting with all UN staff has been held, but guidelines for action and response remain unclear. There appears a general concern amongst UN personnel that further work must be done to ensure security in a developing unrest situation.

For me as a field manager responsible for the lives and safety of the United Nations people who worked for me—with Headquarters support the other side of the world in both real and response sensitivity terms, my first priority was to make sure the staff were OK when things in the country got bad—even if this meant suspending normal operations and practices. No matter how significant our project work was in addressing the problems of underdevelopment, or how much pressure there was from Headquarters to abide by formal rules, my first responsibility was to make absolutely sure that the people under my direct care were safe. Later we could return to our UN job and pick up the pieces out on the streets or in our internal administration processes. But my people had to be safe first.

The UN Coordinator at the time—who shall remain nameless now (and moved on to lesser things)—simply did not care, and ultimately, *he* was responsible for the safety of the whole UN family through Indonesia. Well, actually, he *did* care, but what he cared *more* about was his own image and reputation, against which attention to diverting funding into investments in staff safety was an anathema as was approaching the government for upgraded security of the UN, because he feared he would be seen negatively for his 'lack of faith' in government control of what was going on. He had a career goal in front of him that implied for him causing minimum disturbance in political relations with Government, and maximum attention to ensuring the presented *image* of the United Nations was sustained, in particular, the appearance of the newly designed Entrance Foyer to our common premises. Meanwhile, in spite of constant pressure from several of us, creating an escape gate in the back wall—requiring negotiation with local residents—had been too hard, so we could not get out if invaded from the front street; and whilst the internal staircases were a major fire and safety hazard, no action had been taken to propose forcefully to the Government that they really should provide alternative safe accommodation for the UN, and none of the plans for security or possible evacuation had been put into place.

Consequently, I unilaterally put my own Security Action Plan into place for my own Agency's staff. This plan could look after UNESCO people whilst in Jakarta or the provinces of Indonesia, but, given UN Security rules, had to stop short of the authority to order an evacuation. Fortunately, we had had some practice, so I re-instituted the Security Plan for the Office I had put into place a year before when I had previously been unable to raise the attention of the UN Coordinator to the Security threats we collectively confronted. This time however the situation was looking a lot more serious.

> First we developed a range of sources of information on immediate and impending security situations, including a locally contracted expatriate security

intelligence firm, and contacts I had been able to build up through the diplomatic community, partly as a result of the 1996 engagement with Embassy Military Attachés and Deputy Ambassadors during the hostage crisis we had had to deal with.

Second, we developed a map of *all* staff residences whether they be international or local staff, the Director or a Cleaner, in order to know who was at risk as riots swept through specific areas of the city, and a 'buddy' system whereby *all* staff had a designated alternative residence in *another* area of the city where they could go immediately if security was at risk around their home. (This system turned out to be of critical importance in saving the life of one young Indonesian woman in late 1998 when riots swept through her street and into her house just as she was heading home from the office: re-direction to her 'buddy house' saved her life.)

And third, perhaps most important of all, we instituted a continuously updated telephone tree system, operating 24 hours a day 7 days a week when disturbance was building up, a system that we honed into detailed shape through quite a lot of trials, where we would find completely unexpected gaps would occur through lack of commitment to keep following up after the initial phone call, or people would simply disappear and we could not find them. Within the final system, nominated staff members as you went down the tree from myself as Director and 'trigger', had responsibility to inform a small group of three or four other staff, each of whom in turn had another three or four staff *they* had to notify, and so on. To ensure that we overcame the 'error of silence', that is, where the informant 'tries' but their target person is doing something else, visiting family in their village, or otherwise away from the nominated phone, when we were in 'operating' mode, that is during an impending crisis, everyone on the tree also had to notify the next person up the tree if they left their normal phone access, even if it was to indicate a neighbor or friend's phone via which they could be contacted. The names of any persons not able to be contacted were fed back up the tree to the top, so we knew where there were gaps. And if the uncontactable person had others to notify, their original informant simply took over this wider group as well. Backup to this system was physical contact in the same geographic area (one of the reasons we carefully mapped *all* staff residences in the city) which we initiated when gaps appeared, even if messages were taken on foot by household staff who were less likely at risk on the streets than very obvious expatriates. The last people on the tree phoned the boss to affirm that the message had got through the system. When things were looking risky on the streets, we tested this communication system frequently, particularly as new staff came on board, and we really had to spend a lot of energy on ensuring a real commitment to discipline amongst staff for the system to work properly as a single weak link in the chain of information was critical. We eventually reached the point where we could be assured to get new security information out to all staff at home within around twenty minutes. But I did find that a system like this had to be revivified continuously, or it very rapidly dissipated into disrepair as people become complacent or new staff came on board (an almost weekly occurrence) and were not adequately informed. Of course, I also ran briefings of staff before they left for home on what we knew from intelligence reports if problems were starting to emerge around the city and reminded them of the necessity of maintaining 'tree' discipline.

Having this system in place mattered. We had to rely on our own internal communication system in May 1998 when civil unrest made it imperative to evacuate out all international staff families, then the staff themselves. For the official UN Warden System—whereby individuals were designated by geographic area to act as contact and information points for international staff from *all international agencies* residing in their area—broke down. One reason was breakdown of communication from agencies that were part of the (financial) Bretton Woods group—that is, the IMF and World Bank—with the United Nations System. The problem was primarily a product of lack of advance testing more than anything else. However, what happened was that the IMF staff, a small group at that time, evacuated out of Indonesia at the first sign of trouble, but neglected to mention their intention to anyone else, leaving the rest of us not knowing where they were and at risk as we sought to track down the IMF people who were missing; then the World Bank acted quickly and evacuated their staff, including a substantial number of people who had been nominated as Wardens, thus tearing holes in the fabric of communication that the Warden System depended on. Under severe crisis *all* agencies then had to depend on themselves. Fortunately, by this time UNESCO was well set up to do this.

As with the hostage crisis that confronted me within six months of my entry into the United Nations family, I was again uncovering another face of what it is like to work within the multilateral agency system. Intrinsically we *are likely* to need to deal with quite real danger out in the field. As things get worse, there is *more* need for United Nations intervention, not less, so often UN people are flying in when everyone else is flying out of a country in crisis. UNESCO is not a front-line agency like those that deal with refugees, medical emergency and provision of food—staffed by people for whose courage I normally had enormous respect. But we still are on the ground in uncertain times or destabilized countries and do need to be there quite quickly after disasters, for example, to help re-establish media communications, education and income-earning skills development, preparedness for a return of disaster, and so on.

We could see the civil unrest problems emerging, the lack of preparedness by the UN Coordinator, and were worried. Then, suddenly, the reality of Revolution was staring us in the face.

14

"Revolution—Now"

Suddenly, It's Here!

We could see the danger emerging. As I reported in my last Chapter, we had prepared our own UN people and our protection as well as we could—at least in my own UN Agency. But then the Revolution hit and surrounded us. Suddenly our world changed dramatically.

There was a background.

The immediate catalyst for the violence that forever changed the face of Indonesian democracy in 1998 was the killing on 12th May of four students of Trisakti University, directly adjacent to the Airport Tollway just west of central Jakarta, Elang Mulya, Hafidin Royan, Hendriawan Lesmana and Hery Hartanto. Initial reports were confused, suggesting that amongst the many students seriously injured six had been killed. What was not confused was that the killings had been unprovoked intentional (almost certainly military connected) shootings—bullets literally traveling through walls of buildings, and that the shootings had not occurred in direct confrontation, but *after* the on-campus demonstration was over and the students were starting to move peacefully off the campus. We suspected at that time that the killings were done by snipers (though the police were shy in reporting on what kind of bullets were found) and that the incident was an element in an orchestrated military-based plot, perhaps by rogue forces. But we did not appreciate until later how significant this event was in a major power play that had started inside the military with a jostling for power as President Soeharto desperately clung to his rapidly evaporating authority. Tuesday night was relatively calm. However, a massive student communications and organization exercise was put in place across Jakarta to protest the unprovoked killing of a group of students who were already becoming known as 'Reform Heroes' or the 'Flowers of Reform'.

In keeping with Moslem tradition, the students were buried the next day, Wednesday 13th May. Rallies were held on virtually every tertiary education campus, condemning the killings, and demanding the resignation of President Soeharto. In grief and anger the students spilled off the Trisakti campus and onto the local streets, breaking a long-standing rule of military control that tolerated demonstrations so long as they were held within the narrow confines of the universities. Gathering people off the streets as they went, the demonstrations turned into riots that erupted across the whole city.

We could see things were bad, but we did not fully appreciate how bad.

In an exercise of impeccably misplaced timing, I had arranged for two senior officials from UNESCO Headquarters, Moufida and René, to be in Jakarta on that day to assist me to negotiate with the Secretary-General of ASEAN, Rodolfo Severino, for the development of a high level international conference on *The Culture of Peace*, planned for September 1998, and to be opened by UNESCO's then Director-General, Federico Mayor. Pleased with ourselves for a very constructive meeting and set of agreements, we left the ASEAN Headquarters on the south side of the central area of Jakarta at around 4.30 pm. As we progressed up the main street through central Jakarta, Jalan Sudirman, past the Hilton Hotel and the Semangi Overpass, we were suddenly confronted by the riots. This central hub area is close to Indonesia's Parliament and adjacent to the Catholic University campus, the closest university presence to the Parliament. The streets were littered with rocks, turning driving into a slalom as we navigated a path through them, fully armed military were advancing from the western side of the street whilst students wielding anti-Soeharto placards and throwing rocks confronted us from the other. With bravado designed only to obscure my very considerable fear, I observed to my companions the 'appropriateness' of timing where I had brought them to a war zone to mount a culture of peace campaign. Moushida, with a life's experience of Middle Eastern violence was calm; René, from Chile was actually excited. 'Where are the tanks?' he called, 'This is great! Just like the revolutions we have in Chile'. I got them safely back to their hotel with strict instructions to not go out on the town to public places tonight and my driver headed for my home, picking back routes which sought to avoid the most likely trouble spots.

Meanwhile, I was really quite worried about my wife, Jill. She was returning from medical evacuation to Singapore that afternoon, 13th May 1997. As the morning had started to reveal problems of some sort on the streets of Jakarta I had given the driver I sent out to pick her up instructions to go out very early to the airport to ensure he actually got there in plenty of time as the Tollway past Trisakti University was starting to block with student protests and I was worried he would be stopped and not be able to meet Jill. I told the driver to avoid the direct Tollway from the Airport to the city on the way home but instead to return to our residence via Ancol, around Jakarta Bay and then up the backstreets from North Jakarta to the city, thus avoiding the Trisakti area. Meanwhile I had been unable to contact Jill by phone in Singapore and had no way of contacting her directly now. Unfortunately, whilst the airport was busy there were no sign out there of what was happening on the streets back in the city, so Jill headed for home not realizing that the level of civil unrest was steadily building.

However, it was not long before Jill ran headlong into the riots. As her car approached the center of town from the north, she passed the Presidential Palace, and started to feel very uneasy indeed for the Palace grounds were covered in tanks and armed guards—not a good sign, particularly as the streets were deserted of pedestrians. Not long afterwards, the traffic line suddenly froze. Jill's driver got out of the car to see what was happening, stood up on the door sill and then ran down the traffic line to see more clearly, returning rapidly to tell Jill that he could see soldiers lined up in front, and rioting students. Jill checked it out—just as hundreds of students jumped over the front fence of the University, some throwing Molotov Cocktails across the cars at the soldiers; there was an explosion of gunfire as the soldiers sheltering behind their shields, fired back; smoke started to billow across the street from fired tear gas canisters. Jill jumped back into the car … and phoned me to see if I knew what was going on and how to get out of it

"Get down on the floor" I yelled, and then a moment later, "Where are you?"
"I don't know" Jill responded, "I'm down on the floor and can't see".

At that moment the traffic started to move for the conflict had eased, the students jumping back into the university grounds across the fence. Car by car the traffic queue sped past the confrontation, Jill's driver following suit. Another explosion just as Jill's car passed the epicenter of the fight, making the driver swerve dangerously around the confrontation in the middle of the street. They got past the demonstration—students one side of the street yelling for President Soeharto to resign; soldiers flanking the other side of the street, protected by full sized shields, staring down the students. Twenty minutes later Jill arrived home, a tad unsettled, to say the least, by a close call with serious civil unrest that she had certainly not expected on her return from Singapore.

Even so, we settled, assisted a little by the help of a calming gin and tonic. And we prepared for going out to dinner with a group of Australian friends from the banking, mining and diplomatic expatriate community of the city. The host residence was on the south side of the city in Kemang, a firmly expatriate district where we had previously lived before moving to Permata Hijau, and which was so far quite untouched by the city's troubles. We rang ahead and our hosts said there was no sign of problems on their side of town. Indeed, we confronted no problems on the streets while in transit either there or home.

The atmosphere was calm, a group of eight friends—all senior Australian diplomats or businessmen plus their wives, enjoying a formal dinner accompanied by candles, wine, music, humor, albeit with some serious exchange of experience about what was actually happening out there on the streets. Jill told the group of the terrifying trip back from the airport she had experienced, adding that perhaps this dinner might well be our 'Last Hurrah'. Meanwhile, our senior diplomatic friends from the Australian Embassy kept excusing themselves from the table to answer or make phone calls, receiving the latest news about what was starting to happen on the streets, trying to track down the Ambassador who, at that stage, was lost to official Embassy communication somewhere in the entertainment focused streets of Bangkok, and as we found out later, our Australian diplomat friends were starting to prepare for the possible rapid evacuation of Australian Embassy families. However, they kept things pretty much to themselves in the interests of 'internal Embassy security'. So, dinner progressed relatively unproblematically through all three courses and coffee, and any serious questioning of the idea that maybe the city as a whole was *really* unsafe was brushed under the table. Meanwhile, the Jakarta environment was misleading—largely because it is a city of many faces, all existing alongside each other—modern life adjacent to traditional villages, ethnic group concentrations in separate areas, university epicenters of protest scattered through the city's urban fabric but with locally focused impact. Therefore, there could be major unrest in one part of the city, but total calm everywhere else with the violence seemingly localised at a safe distance. The real problems were emerging as we subsequently found out, on the north side—and did indeed spread, but in the south, it was business as usual.

We arrived home safely and without incident and went to sleep.

But the next day we realized that the evening dinner had indeed been what Jill had called our 'Last Hurrah'.

For the next day, Thursday 14th May, the situation on the streets *generally* started to deteriorate rapidly. By evening, our embassy colleagues were starting to be evacuated out of the city, our business colleagues were looking for exit flights, and the city was ablaze.

In the morning however I had gone to the Office as usual, thinking that the city may be confronting some demonstration and traffic problems but not that these could be life threatening. Jill went out to stock up on essential supplies in case we had to shelter at home and stay off the streets. Then the information about riots and anarchy started to come in via our security sources and phone contacts. The United Nations Building was located on the main street between the center of town—the traffic circle bounded by the British Embassy, Hotel Indonesia and the Mandarin Hotel … and the President's Palace. The demonstrations were now crowding down this street right in front of our office windows. By 11.30am it was clear to me that the city center was likely soon to be totally blocked with demonstrators and possible riots, so I cancelled all appointments for the day, ordered the Office to be closed and sent the staff home, calling into operation our own internal security system that we had put into place a year before when we started to confront civil unrest and street disturbances around the General Election period.

The UN Country Team met to consider our collective action… and the official Security Phase we should declare. We upgraded our previous Phase 1 to Phase 2, meaning that offices close and caution is exercised …. but not yet extending to evacuation. And at 1.30 pm, as I ensured the last person from UNESCO had departed, I left the UN building… just in time as it turned out, for shortly afterwards the central business district of Jakarta was entirely blocked by rioters and no one could get out.

By the time I reached the end of my street, the local supermarket and shopping center on the corner had been attacked and were well ablaze, with looters raking through goods saved before the fire. My driver was able to get past them reasonably easily as the mood of the crowd, many celebrating the 'liberated' goods of the destroyed shops, was more festive than aggressive by this time.

I arrived home a few minutes later, this was Thursday 14th May, and immediately wrote my Security Report and faxed it to Headquarters notifying them that I had closed the UNESCO Office at 11.30am that morning because of the increasing anarchy and danger on Jakarta streets, along with notification of the Security Phase 2 decision of the UN Country Team.

I contacted René and Moufida, my official UNESCO guests from Paris, and suggested they keep a very low profile for the day and investigate early flights back to Europe.

Then Jill and I bunkered down for the evening—aware of the best advice for handling the security problems associated with major civil unrest, that is, make sure you have food, water, enough scotch or gin and tonic, and an ongoing subscription to the pay-TV channel. That is, *stay in your residence!*

Amongst my other duties however I was the UN Warden for the suburb, Permata Hijau, and this near western side of the city, the district within which we lived. What this meant was that I was the contact person for *all* UN personnel within the district, needed to provide all of them with ongoing information on what was happening, manage their safety, and possibly in a worst case scenario, coordinate their personal evacuation. It was not long before the phone calls started. As I reported earlier, the local shopping center was ablaze, and the looters were on the streets. We all knew this. What was more worrying was that several of my UN colleagues phoned in to say that there was a rumor around that the mobs were coming, and people should get out in front to protect their houses. At that stage this was just a rumor—and in situations like this in Indonesia, unsubstantiated rumours explode across public consciousness. So we weren't sure how seriously we should take it. The standard advice about what to do in civil unrest was 'stay at home off the streets'.

I checked with our security sources: all they could tell me was that they too had heard the, rumors, adding some detail however: according to rumor, the mobs were apparently gathered in the near southern area close to the retail shopping 'Block M', a few kilometers down the road from me, had trucks available for transport, and may well be looking north, targeting Permata Hijou where I lived because it was largely an ethnically Chinese middle-class area, and these guys were hitting on the Chinese. At the time I could not confirm this.

I later discovered that the mobs, which *were* quite real, were constituted from gangs from Timor and North Jakarta put together and paid by Probowo Subianto (now promoted since his involvement in the West Papua hostage crisis to *Lieutenant* General) in a political move to gain power against the head of the military, General Wiranto—one of the many stories I will return to shortly. My experience at the time was that there was a *rumor* around that we were all potentially threatened by the impending arrival of a mob that became popularly known as *Probowo's Ninjas*.

I rang around to all of my 'charges' for whom as Warden I was directly responsible. I told my colleagues that in case there was a problem, other peoples' property was not a priority and it was not a good idea to confront local mobs as a lone expatriate if in fact mobs did arrive in their local neighborhood. Given that the UN Coordinator—responsible for overall UN security, as I observed earlier, had not put any serious security preparation into place, the UN at this stage had no collective exit transport system available—given in particular the unexpected situation and the complete absence of military support for the UN that would have been necessary to send in secure vehicles. So, I had no UN-supported means to get them out anyway: if they judged themselves unsafe, they might consider getting out *now* to a city hotel and we could reconsider things in the morning.

Jill then talked with the servants. Mul, our main pembantu or house staff, declared nonchalantly that all the local residents had already left the street, and we were actually staying there almost alone. This was entirely new information for us. I checked out my two so-called 'Security Guards' or Satpans. Both had changed into civilian clothes in order to not be recognizable on the streets and were exiting through the front gate. So, I had no Security Protection any more, except my Tibetan Spaniel, inherited from a UN colleague who had previously rented the house before me … a totally brave, and committed canine warrior, but only 40 cm tall, not quite adequate to fend off attacking men with guns and fire sticks. We did become, as it were, a tad worried. But we really did not believe that we were in serious danger that night.

By now it was actually quite late in the evening, so, albeit with some disquiet, we decided to stay—in line with the basic security advice that the safest place in the midst of civil unrest usually is at home.

Escape

I went to bed. Jill watched TV. Having taken a double dose of sleeping tablets to ensure she could go to sleep given a rather tense and highly eventful day, she was waiting for the relief of induced sleep to overwhelm her highly active mind. But suddenly, she was vibrantly *awake!* … though distinctly disoriented. A car next door had noisily come to life. She walked out onto our front balcony and saw that our ethnic Chinese neighbor was still there, but revving up the motor of the family car, a fully packed Kijang van, before departure of his family out the compound gate. It left. But he stayed, flanked by his two attack Rottweiler guard dogs. Jill woke me, and I called over the fence to ask what was happening. Our neighbor responded, "*the mobs are coming, my family has left, but I am staying here with my dogs to protect my house*". Meanwhile he had raised an Indonesian flag on a rapidly erected pole at the front of his residence—a sign that he hoped was going to work against the invading anti-Chinese hoard. Jill, with sensible judgment asked, "Can you give us an

Indonesian flag as well?" We did have a flagpole. He obliged. And we raised the national flag at the front of our property to signify support for Indonesia, keeping the UN flag also in sight of the street, but in full awareness that most thugs in a village-level recruited gang would have no idea what it meant.

And, now for the first time *really* believing that the mobs were coming, we decided to go. I called around my local UN colleagues to suggest they followed suit. This was by now 2.00 am on Friday morning, 15th May. I called the Hilton Hotel and made a reservation, even though this was very late at night.

Jill finished hurriedly packing her bag, by now in that zzzzzzzz zone that accompanies an extremely tired and sleepy brain after you take a couple of sleeping tablets but find you simply *must* stay awake, so your eyes are riveted open while the brain is in neutral. She did not get back to the house for two weeks—as we were forced to evacuate out all UN attached families to Singapore the next evening and things didn't settle down enough for us to feel confident bringing families back for that long. When Jill arrived finally at the Singapore hotel we had reserved for UN dependents, she opened her bag to find a very strange collection of clothes—single unmatched shoes, the formal evening dress she had worn the previous night to the Last Hurrah dinner, and basically anything else that had been within reach at the last minute.

We had dismissed her driver after dinner. My official drivers had gone home long ago. So I had to drive. We jumped in the car and headed down our street—lights off so as to be as invisible as possible, threading our way through the rocks, burning buildings, dropped loot, and people who were ambling around basically enjoying the dramatic late-night show. At this stage the mobs had not attacked but we could hear rumblings and yelling in the distance that were very disquieting. Jill was wearing an Indonesian shawl over her head, but there was no disguise that could change my distinctly western appearance.

As we rounded the corner from our own street we passed a very odd couple. The woman was dressed in traditional Indonesian sarong and shawl, her face entirely covered though her body was rather portly when measured against most Indonesians; but the man was the one who stood out—well over six feet tall, a giant amongst Indonesians, and dressed as an Arab. Whilst curious we were in no mood to stop as at this stage, we were really not sure we were going to make it out of the area through one of only two exit streets before it was blocked by screaming machete wielding mobs of young village men. Some weeks later, after the crisis had passed, we found out who this strange couple was. The Deputy of the South African Embassy and his New York born wife lived just around the corner from us. It was them. Their staff had also told them that the mobs were coming, and they had to get out, but that it was far too dangerous to drive. So, they donned the best disguises they could muster and hit the street on foot. They made it to around a kilometre from their residence before they had a very serious change of mind as the mood on the streets was very alien and surreal. They went back home. Fortunately, their residence remained untouched so they were safe for the night.

Around thirty minutes later we arrived at the Hilton Hotel, a good security choice as it was set in very substantial grounds, so the buildings were reasonably well protected from the street. The Hilton also was the largest hotel in town and had a helicopter pad allowing at least the possibility of direct escape if necessary. Our hearts were pumping at an alarming rate, I was in a lather of sweat. But the wave of relief that swept over us as we were finally admitted through the gates into the hotel grounds was profound. But we still had to get a room. It was by now 3.00am on Friday morning.

As I drove up to the entrance foyer of the building a very stern security guard told me we could not stay as all 1,200 rooms of the hotel were now fully booked with people escaping the violence. The place was in lockdown, the atmosphere as we arrived was like entering a war movie set, extremely tense at the entrance, scared-looking refugees everywhere with as much luggage as they could carry, a sense of turmoil and danger close by, and with the external security staff protecting the hotel and sending anyone without reservations on their way to who knows where. Even claims to have made a room reservation were treated with general disbelief. Fortunately, I had taken the precaution of recording a reservation *number* when I called ahead. The room was still empty, and I had the added advantage of being in a senior diplomatic vehicle. After we were finally admitted as legitimate guests, I was even able to park our car right next to the entrance foyer in the parking spaces reserved for CD1 and CD2 diplomatic and VIP vehicles. We collapsed into an immensely welcome and comfortable bed around 4.00 am—16 floors of secure hotel separating us from the danger of the streets below.

When we awoke the next morning, we could see from our 16th floor window fires and smoke across the whole of Jakarta, particularly to the north. I decided to set up office in my hotel room, acquired a fax machine and extra telephone, and started to contact my UN colleagues as well as phone around to make sure our UNESCO staff were OK. High on my agenda was getting my two Paris-based visitors out of town in a hurry. Both Moufida and Rene made it to the Hilton at 3.00 pm, a good staging area as it was not only relatively secure given the size of the grounds, but also directly on the route out of the city to the airport—a considerable advantage under normal circumstances given Jakarta traffic congestion. After a truncated debriefing I found them a car and driver and sent them out to the main international airport. They got through, even though they then had to wait until early the next day before they could catch their scheduled flight out. However, by the time that Moufida and Renée arrived at the Hilton we had serious doubts about the safety of the main airport road so I got them to the airport via the coastal Ancol route, not by the direct Expressway. It turned out this was a fortunate choice because as the day progressed the airport expressway itself became increasingly dangerous. Mobs from villages on the way to the airport started to block the road, ostensibly looking for ethnic Chinese escaping or in some cases, to extract an informal toll. Not long afterwards the killings started and the road became impassable. We had to get people out by a different route now.

My Security Report to Headquarters the previous afternoon had summarized the situation at that stage, a time when we thought that only 10 or so people had been killed on Wednesday, but had little knowledge of quite how serious the situation was as the evening of Thursday 14th May approached:

> Following the killing of 4 students—who appear to have been *on* campus—by the military on Tuesday 12th May, 1998, the security situation in Jakarta has seriously deteriorated. Rallies are being held on virtually every tertiary education campus, and in spite of strict warnings by the police, are spilling into the streets, where police and military personnel are attempting strict control by force. The rallies are now linking with wider community groups off campus. Meanwhile, mobs have taken the opportunity to start looting and burning. Consequently, riots and fires are starting to occur across wide reaches of the city, including burning of petrol stations, vehicles, and shops. Some shops have been looted; most are closing. Movement around the city is seriously restricted along key routes—including to the airport—by either rioting or serious traffic problems. There is a strong military presence, but in some areas police control of the mobs appears to be failing. Ten deaths were reported for yesterday. Since 10.00am today, Thursday 14th May 1998, the situation has again deteriorated; many people are on the streets, serious fires are occurring across the city, including the burning out of major shopping malls; there is a mood of fear and apprehension generally. There is an expectation that further problems may arise when people leave the mosques following Friday prayers tomorrow....

In fact, we did not appreciate at that point just how bad the situation was, particularly in northern Jakarta, a largely ethnic Chinese area, where uncontrolled mobs and gangs of black-dressed 'ninjas' were sweeping through the streets and residences, looting, killing, and raping as they went, and setting alight to what was left.

The Chinese Citizens Issue

It was no accident that ethnic Chinese were targeted for they were the perfect scapegoat for evoking crowd anger. The Chinese had become firmly entrenched as middlemen during Dutch occupation of Indonesia, a role they continued to play thereafter. However, this role of a tiny minority of the population generated widespread resentment because of their alignment with colonialist Dutch interests and because of the wealth they had been able to accrue as a result. Furthermore, previous President Soekarno encouraged the Chinese for his own interests—in particular, building the PKI Communist Party and its support that spread widely across Indonesia. With the overthrow of Soekarno and as one means of shoring up his burgeoning authority, Soeharto directly attacked the PKI as he was coming into power, spreading a pogrom across the whole of Indonesia that co-opted the people into the killings and swept up whole communities into payback against not only Chinese but anyone against whom a debt of revenge needed to be settled. However, the Chinese were the prime targets, to the point where the Non-aligned Movement sought to intervene to moderate Soeharto's excesses.

But it was not only the immediate violence that left a long-term stain on Indonesia's treatment of ethnic Chinese. In the name of national security against Communist threat Soeharto moved to seriously constrain the human rights of ethnic Chinese within wider society from then on—no matter what their political convictions might be. Chinese script was banned. Ethnic Chinese could not hold government, teaching or military positions and even after five generations were not automatically Indonesian, having to register at birth and *apply* for citizenship.

This anti-Chinese action was a curiously cynical political shadow play given that the economic wealth of the Soeharto family was deeply woven into business alliances with Indonesian-Chinese interests. The First Family was surrounded by a coterie of Chinese tycoons, the so-called *cukongs* or big-time financiers, who were central in funding and organizing the Family's wealth. For example, Liem Sioe Liong, Indonesia's richest man, Eka Cipta Wijaya, Progo Pengestu, and particularly Muhammad 'Bob' Hasan—the Soeharto family's 'Mr Fix-It' and Soeharto's main golfing buddy. Soeharto's wife, Madam Hartinah *Tien* Soeharto, led such heavy nepotistic involvement with the Chinese cukongs that she became popularly known as *Madam Ten Percent*, a reflection of the commissions she extracted from her proximity to the President. Alignment with Chinese interest was Soeharto's privately enjoyed play, ideally, not too exposed to public scrutiny.

For the public, the situation for ethnic Chinese followed a very different script. Excluded from other means of social or economic advancement, the Chinese communities had little choice but to run businesses: though only 3.5 percent of the Indonesian population, they therefore owned nine of the top ten business groups and controlled 80 percent of the assets of the top 300 groups; thirteen of the top 15 taxpayers were ethnic Chinese (whilst the other two were Soeharto's sons, Bambang and Tommy). In the context of their wider social exclusion, ethnic Chinese also tended to reinforce their own cultural separation from other Indonesians and were widely regarded as maintaining exploitative relations with their employees. Additionally, under the implicit endorsement of Soeharto, collusion of Chinese financiers with local officials and the military was commonplace. One key result was the expropriation of land at trivial prices from peasants for development, for example, of housing estates and golf courses. The locals, the *pribumi*, or 'sons of the earth' often ended up landless, unemployed, and as very poor immigrants into the cities burning with deep resentment against *all* Chinese, not just the rich who had taken their land through corruption and collusion with local officials. Meanwhile, as the New Order regime started to come apart at the seams and the people were confronted by suddenly grinding poverty, the association of the wealth enjoyed by Soeharto, his Family and other leading figures of the regime with Chinese businessmen further fueled the anger the people felt towards Chinese in general.

Rioters on the streets of Jakarta in May 1998 therefore associated ethnic Chinese with hoarding, profiteering and exploitation—even by the Soeharto elite. In the context of public anarchy and the disappearance of law and order off the streets it was easy for provocateurs to light a very short fuse of anti-Chinese sentiment.

As we subsequently learned, one thousand one hundred and eighty eight people died, a number of whom were looters caught in fires that were intentionally lit in North Jakarta's shopping malls and markets—areas that were often characterized by very closed-in narrow corridors between shops, crowded with boxes and extra goods to be sold and very very hard to exit quickly. But most killed were Chinese. As many as 468 (mainly ethnic Chinese) women were raped. The official statistics on destruction were mind-bending, 2,547 shop/houses, 40 malls, 1,819 stores, 383 office buildings, 535 banks, 24 restaurants, 15 markets, 12 hotels, 1,026 houses, 2 churches, 11 police stations, 1,119 cars, 821 motorcycles and 9 gas stations were damaged or burned in the riots—the worst riots ever experienced in Indonesia since the anti-communist pogrom that was associated with the rise to power of

Soeharto over thirty years earlier along with the reputed murder of up to between a half to a million people across Indonesia.

On Friday morning 15th May, we did not know all this, but the reports of violence were becoming increasingly alarming. My UN colleagues and I now fully realised that we had to get the families of our international staff out of harm's way as quickly as possible.

Given the lack of due diligence in preparing for such an event by the erstwhile UN Coordinator, we were very much on a back foot arranging exit transportation, in particular, as we now could not use the main international airport.

Increasing Pressure to Evacuate All Families and Staff

Quite frankly we were very lucky. The World Bank, by this time already set up with well-equipped offices in the Hilton Hotel, was instituting a major evacuation plan for its families and non-essential staff. In conversation with the Bank's Director, the UN was able to arrange a serendipitous plan that was tied to the coat tails of World Bank arrangements, that is, to hire the same charter aircraft that the World Bank was using to get their people to Singapore. The problem was that we had to wait for the Bank to fly its people first and for the plane to return for a second load.

Nevertheless, we managed during the course of the day to contact all UN families and get them to the United Nations Building, our staging area, by 6.00am the next morning, Saturday. They boarded buses traveling in convoy, not to the international airport but to the military base, Halim Airport, where two years before, our abducted staff, Martha and Mark, were flown in after escape from West Papua. We wanted to get the UN families to Halim as early in the day as possible as the city was still quiet, but the cycle of violence was likely to heat up later as the day progressed, particularly from around 11.00am or so onwards. The families got through to Halim Airport without any major problem—except that the lead car got lost, had to leave the direct Expressway in order to turn back, so, to the heart-stopping disquiet of the evacuees, took the entire convoy in a long journey on and into the small back streets of the suburbs well beyond Halim before the bus drivers could find a way back onto the Expressway in the opposite direction and back to the airport.

The families did not then have an easy day. There were lots of children and not much for them to do. The departure lounge was geared up for spartan military travel, was small and stuffy, devoid of comforts. Food and drink were scarce. The worst thing was that the families had to wait until 3.00am the next morning, Sunday 17th May, before they could fly. After dropping the World Bank evacuees off, the plane was seriously delayed in Singapore and did not get back to Jakarta to pick up the UN families until 20 h after the families left the UN Building. But they all got to Singapore eventually, accompanying the morning sun into the city—totally fatigued, in shock, and into the scarce accommodation that could be arranged for them at the very last minute by UN officials who had flown down from Kuala Lumpur. Some evacuees still were forced to sleep in the lobbies of the hotels until rooms could be found some time later.

It was two weeks before the evacuees could come back to Jakarta.

Meanwhile, on Saturday, after waving goodbye to Jill and the other UN family members, I spent the morning in the UN Offices, planning operations with the UN Country Team, gathering as much intelligence as we could. Given the danger in some areas of the city, five of our own staff by this time were billeted in their allotted 'buddy house'. I contacted all international staff overseas, and found ways of extending their missions so they did not have to return until the situation was clear. And then I left the Office around 11.00am before the riots were likely to heat up too much and block the streets. I met a colleague from the World Bank to discuss the evacuation arrangements, and then checked out of the Hilton at 2.00 pm in the afternoon to go back to my Residence in Permata Hijou, figuring by this time that the violence had swept past, and the house was relatively safe, and having checked very carefully with our intelligence sources that the access routes were OK.

On the political front, President Soeharto during these few tumultuous days had gone through a series of 'shadow plays' seeking to quell the public disquiet but clearly at this stage not appreciating just how serious the situation was for him. On an official visit to Cairo on the day the riots hit Jakarta, the President had been quoted by *Kompas*, one of the most reliable daily newspapers in Jakarta, as being prepared to resign. However, on the Friday morning when he arrived home, he denied ever making this statement, but now offered the olive branch of being prepared to resign *if* the people had lost faith in him. Meanwhile, as riots spread to Surabaya and Solo and other Javanese towns, the government cut fuel and electricity prices, an initial precipitant of public unrest following the 70 percent price hike introduced on the previous 4th May (a socially uninformed requirement, by the way, imposed by the IMF ostensibly to make the Indonesian economy internationally competitive). The next day, Saturday 16th May, Soeharto stated he would reshuffle his cabinet and was willing to 'abdicate', though with the significant qualifier, *consistent with the constitutional process*. As far as the people were concerned, in particular the student leaders of the burgeoning protest movement however, these offers meant no more than window dressing for Soeharto to maintain substantive power but appear compliant to the peoples' wishes.

I had a quiet evening at home, but not a relaxed one.

Next morning, Sunday 17th May, I called in Jill's driver and took a trip around the local shopping centers to stock up on food, water and petrol before panic buying exhausted all supplies. I took the precaution of getting back to the house before 11.00 am, the 'magic' hour for riots to start.

One interesting sidelight on the panic buying sprees that did follow was the *one* commodity that became totally unpurchasable in Jakarta over the coming weeks was *tonic water*. We had to assume that the expatriates were whiling away their time off the streets with a surfeit of gin and tonic. Meanwhile however the poorer locals were suffering quite seriously as prices of staple foods escalated rapidly.

On Monday morning 18th May I went to the Office—around 7.00am. Staff came in on a voluntary basis dependent on their own judgment as to whether it was safe for them to travel from their particular suburb to Central Jakarta.

As the day progressed, we watched the start of the political fallout from the riots blow across the face of the city. It was becoming clear that the command that Soeharto had previously taken for granted was rapidly slipping away. Soeharto started tough, planning as part of his promised Cabinet Reshuffle to sack the Commander of the Armed Forces, General Wiranto—largely as a signal of his power to the Armed Forces faction in Parliament who had been threatening support for a Special Session of Parliament to dismiss Soeharto. More disturbingly for the inner elite and the students was Soeharto's intended promotion of Lieutenant General Probowo, his son-in-law, to Deputy Commander of the Armed Forces, a post that clearly was a temporary stage for launching Probowo as head of the military.

Even by this stage, Probowo was widely believed to have been behind the deaths of the students at Trisakti that had precipitated the crisis in the first place. Soeharto was away in Cairo, and it was popularly believed that Prabowo orchestrated the killings and riots in order to show how ineffective Wiranto (Head of the Military), was in controlling them—a plan to replace Wiranto under Soeharto instruction.

Meanwhile, Wiranto was widely respected for the way he handled the riots, so the political elite had had enough of the damage they could see working its way through the economy, and shook off the mystique that had maintained

Soeharto in unassailable power. Soeharto re-read the situation, saw Prabowo's self-promoting deviousness, and brought in Wiranto for support.

The leadership of Parliament gave permission for the students to use the House as a site for anti-Soeharto student demonstrations that were planned to coincide with testimony to a Committee by Amien Rais, Head of the Moslem Muhammadiyah organization. Tens of thousands of students arrived, to be escorted into Parliament by academic leaders and former military officers including the previous Minister of Defence, Edi Sudradjat. Late in the afternoon the Speaker of Parliament announced a plan to consult the factions towards a request for Soeharto to resign.

By nine o'clock in the evening, Wiranto gave a press conference, now speaking *for* Soeharto, calling for a Cabinet reshuffle, asserting the constitutional illegality of sacking Soeharto without a full Plenary Session of Parliament, commanding the Armed Forces to put down anticipated demonstrations in two days' time on National Awakening Day.... and calling for a Reform Council to be established. Soeharto was shuffling through his shadow puppetry.

It had been a day of intense political maneuvering. Nevertheless, the schedule of diplomatic functions remained untouched. The Ambassador of Norway hosted the celebration of Norwegian Constitution Day at his residence early in the evening. I attended then went to a farewell dinner hosted by a good friend, the Ambassador of Slovakia, Peter Ambrovic, and his wife Eva, along with a group of other diplomats. While we feasted and swapped stories of the latest happenings on the streets, the city became increasingly tense for an impending confrontation.

By Tuesday even Soeharto could read the signs, albeit somewhat unclearly. He offered to step down—but on *his* conditions, that is to maintain his own control over the reform process and elections. The students accepted nothing short of full resignation, and shouted this from the roof top of the Parliament itself. Meanwhile, Soeharto had met with nine key Muslim leaders in the morning and offered to resign in due course after new general elections sometime in the future. Again, in the evening Parliamentary leaders called on Soeharto to resign.

Meanwhile, we were also increasingly concerned that Amien Rais, at that stage a front-runner in pushing the anti-Soeharto reform agenda, had announced that to force Soeharto's hand, he would lead a *major* street rally of perhaps a million people from Monas Square near the President's Palace early on Wednesday morning 20th May. This action was harbinger of direct confrontation between an embattled President and non-compromising students, a very dangerous situation. What particularly disturbed us was that such a massive demonstration against an unmovable President was going to hit the streets in the midst of immensely volatile civil unrest.

As a UN Country Team, we decided it was time to evacuate all international staff and give local staff the opportunity to get out of the city if it was safer for them—as it often was, to go back to their home villages. Two female staff in my Office who *looked* Chinese, even though they were not, were particularly at risk, and had already been threatened in the streets, and were, by now, very scared. I agreed for them to go immediately out to their homes in the provinces. The UN team also agreed that it was time for those who were left after the evacuation, that is, the 'essential' Heads of Agencies, to move out of their residences and into the same hotel. This was the Sari Pan Pacific, diagonally opposite the United Nations Building, offering us the opportunity to dash across the road to our offices when things were safe, but otherwise to stay as a team in a place that was hopefully going to be reasonably well protected. After a very rapid trip back to my house for essential clothes and toiletries, I checked in with my UN colleagues to the hotel at 2.30 pm in the afternoon. We turned our attention to rapidly organizing to get *all* international staff to the UN Building at 6.00 pm and onto buses to Halim and evacuation. By now, we had the system reasonably well organized and had a local Mandala commercial airline charter set up. We did not want the staff to still be in Jakarta in the morning when we feared major civil violence could erupt. And indeed we made it. The Mandala flight departed Halim Airport at 11.45 pm that night.

In the meantime I had had a quite extraordinary experience that I reported back in Chap. 2 of just how far away our Headquarters was from a sense of reality of what we were then facing on the streets of Jakarta—when I had finally been able to get a phone call through the highly congested phone lines to Paris and was setting up administrative arrangements for local staff to be paid until things settled down again—in the midst of an evacuation with riots sweeping past the UN building and murders happening just outside my window.

As I reported back in Chap. 2, the Paris finance officer, looked at her watch and said to me, "My Goodness its 6.00 pm. It's time for me to go home and not be late for dinner", then immediately hung up, putting everything on hold until she came back to work the next day. UN staff lives were on the line in Jakarta.

The experience left me with an indelible sense of the wide cultural rift that had to be bridged within UNESCO to draw the organization's central Parisian administration into real support for our field operations, a concern that became of paramount importance to me later, when from late 1999 onwards I took over responsibility under the Director General's authority, to develop UNESCO's strategy through leading the reform and decentralization of the entire UN organization globally. I will demonstrate the pain involved in crossing this UN cultural bridge when I get to the Decentralisation Story in Chap. 21.

As the international staff later left on the buses at 7.00 pm. I remember the feeling, after waving them goodbye as the bus left on the street outside the UN Building, 'Why am I here?' 'What will the morning bring?'.

Several Heads of UN Agencies but not all, did stay Not being able to get back to our homes, we had, as I mentioned earlier, booked a room each in the Hotel diagonally across the road, the Sari Pan Pacific. To calm that distinctly sinking feeling we all felt, we did what any sensible person does in situations of great stress. We retreated to our hotel bar for a drink, together, in the interest of feeling mutual support. The hotel was the nearest one to the Presidential Palace, so the only other guests were CNN and other international reporters flown in to report.

The Indonesian military on the other hand pushed the city into lock-down mode. Heavily armed military personnel deployed tanks, armored vehicles and razor wire to seal off all streets leading to the National Monument Square, Monas, where Amien Rais's planned demonstration march was scheduled to commence.

Indeed, the situation could have got a great deal uglier than it in fact did. We learnt the next day that at 4.00am on Wednesday morning 20th May, General Probowo, by now strongly distrusted as a renegade force in the city's anarchy, phoned Amien Rais, informing him that he was going to turn the march into 'Tiananmen Square' if the people came out onto the streets. Amien Rais was appalled and had no reason *not* to believe him given Probowo's already demonstrated involvement in the city's violence. At 5.00 am, Amien Rais cancelled the march.

Our newly adopted home, the Sari Pan Pacific Hotel was located on the route of the march, on the main road through the central city, Jalan Thamrin, indeed the closest hotel to the President's Palace and Monas Square. For us, our choice to be in residence was a product only of its proximity to the UN Building. For the international press however, this was the place to be to report on emerging events of the next day. CNN, amongst other news teams, set up cameras and broadcasting facilities on the roof where they had a clear view of where the march was to go. It then became a strange double take as we breakfasted next to the internationally famous TV journalist glitterati who had flown in for the emerging events, then went up to our rooms to watch on TV their broadcasts from on the roof of the same hotel—right above our rooms.

We awoke to greet the next morning, Wednesday 20th May, in severe trepidation. We really did believe we were in front-row seats for major street conflict. And our hotel had a major security problem. There was no rear exit from the hotel grounds, so the only way to escape potential invasion by the mobs was *through* them out onto the front street. Overnight the street had become packed with military, razor wire entanglements, tanks and weapons. But the streets were otherwise totally deserted, as if aliens had removed the entire population to a parallel universe.

We watched!

Nothing happened.

Then, seemingly out of nowhere a small group of a half dozen Supreme Court Judges appeared—in full magisterial splendor of their robes, *marching* south down Jalan Thamrin towards Parliament. No one else, just the judges. It was quite surreal. The military did not move but remained watching impassively. The judges proceeded past, and unchallenged, marched on to Parliament where they addressed the students. Now Members of Parliament from the President's own party, Golkar, voted to call a Special Session of the MPR to remove Soeharto; fourteen key Ministers met and agreed to inform the President that they would not serve in his Reform Cabinet. By evening Soeharto could finally see he had nowhere else to go but resign, and instructed his State Secretary Sadillah Mukrsjid and legal expert Professor Dr Yusril Ihza Mahendra to draft his resignation speech. The President met with Wiranto. He also met with Jusuf Habibie, his Vice-President since the March Presidential 'election'.

Resolutions Emerge

These meetings, it turned out, were pivotal to the future of Indonesia. As I was informed by Palace insiders, Soeharto offered Wiranto the Presidency, but Wiranto declined, saying that he could not expect international credibility if he took over civilian power as the previous Head of the military. Wiranto did undertake to guarantee the safety of the President and his family in the event of Soeharto resigning. But Soeharto did not want Habibie whose previous elevation to Vice-Presidency by Soeharto was more than anything else an exercise in 'puppetry', blocking anyone of any real power from the implied legacy of Soeharto's rule. Indeed, Soeharto had stated publicly on 19th May that a Habibie presidency could lead even to civil war. Nevertheless,

Habibie apparently claimed his right to the Presidency from Soeharto who remained impassively resistant when they met in private. Habibie increasingly became agitated and pleading, finally erupting in a temper tantrum, crying and demanding to be anointed. Soeharto remained implacably distant and unmoved until finally he gave in and said to Habibie,

> All right, you can be President. But you will never speak to me again.

And from that meeting to the day of Soeharto's death in 2008, they never talked again, though Habibie *did* visit Soeharto on his deathbed shortly before he died.

There was palpable tension between Habibie and Wiranto thereafter as well. A quaint public demonstration of the tension occurred at the President's Reception for the next National Day on 17th August 1998, an event always held in the State Palace and gardens for the Indonesian elite and senior diplomatic corps. Under Soeharto this annual opening up of the Palace was a formal and serious affair—although it should be added that Soeharto kept the best bar in town.

Habibie had bowed a little to Moslem protocol and reduced the bar offerings from the best scotch to beer (by Megawati's Presidency, the occasions had become entirely alcohol free), but, at the same time, he introduced a levity into the occasion that the local elite found appalling. As I reported back in Chap. 3, Habibi set up a band on the steps from the palace down to the garden so he could show off his singing ability to the guests, and, after inviting Wiranto to accompany him, hid the words, causing Wiranto severe embarrassment.

More significantly in my own experience was an occasion just over a month later, on 26th September 1998 when I was fulfilling one of my UN diplomatic tasks to get the Presidents of the countries for which I was UNESCO Representative, at that stage Indonesia and the Philippines, to sign the Ocean Charter developed by UNESCO as a high level acceptance of the principle of international cooperation to guard the health of the planet's seas.

> In Indonesia, through some advance diplomatic work, I had been able to develop strong support from the Navy, and the President agreed to put on a major show in Manado, the capital of Sulawesi.
> I pick up this story in Chap. 20, so here will only observe what happened between Habibie and Wiranto.
> During the preparatory ceremony with President Habibie on land before embarking on the Presidential Ship, I was sitting with General Wiranto in the front row alongside myself, and Canadian Ambassador Sunquist. Wiranto

started chatting to us, and continued to talk through the whole of Habibie's Presidential Oration, paying no heed to our attempts to focus back on the main event. Later, after President Habibie had signed both the Ocean Charter with me, and a nationally focused equivalent, the 'Bunaken Declaration', and when Habibie was leaving the stern of the ship on a helicopter, the collective naval establishment were all standing to attention and saluting. I was standing next to General Wiranto. As Habibie appeared on deck, Wiranto turned his back to look over the side of the ship and refused to salute. Wiranto was not alone. Even Habibie's own Palace and protocol staff tended to treat him as a lightweight load they bore rather than a national leader whom they revered and served.

On Thursday 21st May 1998 at 9.05am President Soeharto resigned in a 10-min ceremony, witnessed on National Television, by the nation. Habibie was sworn in for the remaining five years of the Presidential term. Few believed he would not be swept aside before this for there was overwhelming opposition to Habibie from the students. Habibie was however a Moslem, a card played out in the political events of the next day.

Meanwhile, General Probowo was on the skids. His future was plummeting along with that of the President. It was becoming abundantly clear by now that Probowo had been purposively creating chaos on the streets in a power-play against General Wiranto, with the intention that the crisis would be severe enough, and Wiranto not able to handle it, to justify President Soeharto stepping in to declare martial law, thus maintaining his Presidential position, and promoting Probowo as new Chief of the Armed Forces.

The street riots had been orchestrated by Probowo, pursuing a strategy of discrediting Wiranto for his inability to control student demonstrations and civil unrest. So, Probowo had a strong interest in bigger and bigger riots, the bigger the better, that he, using Kopussus and Kostrad troops, could restore to order, thus proving Wiranto's incompetence and his own hero status. It was therefore no accident that, as was alleged, Probowo permitted the shooting by his own troops of students of Trisakti University to catalyze thence inflame civil riots, and was rumored to be behind the subsequent violence of organized gangs who swept without constraint through the city, in particular, its ethnic Chinese quarters, including the suburb where I lived.

But Probowo's strategy was unravelling. As further action after the major riots had started to calm down, Probowo had sought, two days earlier, to destabilize the student movement in Parliament by bringing in, under protection of his own Kostrad troops, his 'Pancasila Youth' thugs. These thugs had been the perpetrators of the mob riots and killings on previous days. Now, immediately after Habibie's appointment, Prabowo was instructed to reduce the numbers of Kostrad troops he had brought into the city. What was Probowo's reaction? He disobeyed. He brought in *more* of the 22,000 Special Strategic Reserve Command troops under his direct command.

That evening, an agitated Probowo arrived at Habibie's Residence, dressed in battle fatigues, equipped with a hand gun and accompanied by 200 troops and one of his key supporters, Major General Muchdi, Commander of the very powerful Special Forces, Kopussus. Fortunately for Habibie, Probowo was intercepted by a senior military official accompanying the President who, after a tense stand-off, finally persuaded Probowo to remove his gun before seeing the President, thus defusing a potentially very dangerous confrontation.

Probowo angrily criticized Wiranto and demanded that Habibie reward him, Prabowo, and not sack him, pointing out the favours he had done for Habibie, in particular, his plan to bring in a gathering of Moslems to Parliament the next day to evict the students. Probowo finally left. Habibie, severely shaken by what would appear to have come very close to a military coup, immediately moved out of his residence to stay in the better protected State Guest House in the State and Merdeka Palaces complex.

The next day, Friday 22nd May, Probowo was sacked from his powerful Kostrad post.

> As a side note here for you, the reader, it is helpful to note that I am not reporting just from news. I personally knew Prabowo as my military counterpart in 1996 when, as I talk about in Chaps. 5 and 6, in 1996, I was involved in negotiating the release of two of our own UN staff and others from being taken hostage by the OPM Freedom Fighters of West Papua. Prabowo's girlfriend, Tamara, quite separately, was also a friend of mine—linked to my own UN mandate through her responsibility for a heritage house in North Jakarta. And I knew Habibie as he had been my counterpart previously. Prior to my joining UNESCO full time, he had been Indonesian State Minister of Research and Technology, when with an Australian team I led, we negotiated Australia's inaugural science relations with Indonesia in Jakarta in the early 1990s.
>
> I also had built good relations with several key people *inside* the President's Palace and senior administration, e.g.: Ali Alatas, Minister of Foreign Affairs through several Presidencies, including Soeharto and Habibie. On the social side of my 'diplomatic' life in Jakarta, my wife, Jill, and I, were accepted into an elite social scene of politicians and the wealthy … and indeed, I won a dancing contest in this group against Ali Alatas—who, amongst other things, invited me to his house for dinner several times … along with his wife and absolutely identical *single* twin sister, who both lived there. Behind the hand rumors were colorful.

As a next step in his attempt for power, Prabowo was planning to get Moslem youth to evict the students from Parliament. I did not know this. But, in both my UN role and as a previous Sociology Professor committed to participant observation, I decided to go down to Parliament to talk with the students, to better understand their action, and potentially see if the UN may have a legitimate role in assisting their call for justice.

When I arrived and started talking with a few of the student leaders ... I was a little surprised by their nervousness.

Impeccable, and unfortunate timing. In line with Probowo's plan, hundreds of Moslem youth did spill out of the mosques and into the grounds of Parliament, behind pro-Habibie banners, prepared to fight. An intense confrontation built up. It suddenly became clear to me, as both a non-Indonesian *and* UN diplomat, that this was not a good place to be. I had my very streetwise driver, Lukman, with me (had got me out of a few difficult situations before), so left my student consultations behind—with apology, and came out to my car.

We confronted a very large crowd of Islamic youth approaching through the gates into the Parliamentary grounds intending to attack and force the students *out* of Parliament. I just happened to be in the way.

> I had been rather nervous when evacuating everyone else and escaping the Revolution.
> This situation seemed even more directly dangerous.

At that moment ... the 2.45 pm Call to Prayer was broadcast from the Minarets of the nearby Mosque. Immediately, *all* the Moslem youth stopped, turned around, and returned to the greater good of worshipping Mohammad. I have never been more thankful for the benefits of religious belief. Lukman and I escaped without problem. It felt appropriate afterwards for me to quietly tell my friends in humor, "I was saved by God."

Meanwhile the students had been very busy on the phone. With support from Jakartans, other students and parents who then started to flood into Parliament to demonstrate solidarity with the student protestors, the student numbers swelled, and they peacefully regained control of the building and grounds. Seeing this new situation after finishing their time of worship, the Islamic youth did not come back.

The armed forces called on the students to end their protest. Habibie publicly announced his Reform Development Cabinet which reappointed twenty Ministers from the previous Cabinet and added sixteen new Ministers. General Wiranto commenced an incredibly complex job of separating out and removing from power Probowo's supporters in the military, confronting for the first time Moslem politics when he, a Christian, realized that his own critical supporters were Christians not Moslems at a time when Islamic politics was starting to be played out on a highly volatile national stage.

In the evening of Saturday 23rd May the 5,000 students remaining in Parliament were quietly escorted by the military out of the Parliamentary complex. It was rumored that Probowo was still not finished and, with armed troops still loyal to him, he confronted buses as they passed under the nearby Semangi overpass. Navy marines, who had already developed a reputation amongst the students during the previous week's events as the 'good guys', were protecting the students and stood up to Wiranto-led troops. They finally managed to get the buses moving again to safety. But it was close.

The Revolution was over!

15

Revolution—Aftermath

The Shifting Face of Trouble

During the decade I served in Indonesia, we had to move our focus of security preparedness almost continuously. Fortunately, after the trauma and some near-escapes in the May 1998 events, the United Nations did start to provide significant security support—with permanent ex-military security officials from the UN's Security team from New York based both in the city and through provincial trouble spots where UN teams were operating, with accessible budgets for building protection and home security support, and so on. And the UN Coordinator who had been in charge as we approached the May 1998 revolution was recalled to Headquarters in New York late in 2000 to be replaced by a person with a clear mandate and commitment to ensure staff safety, a tall gangly and very committed Swede, Bo Asplund.

After seriously oppositional street demonstrations first appeared in 1997 as the grip of the Soeharto New Order government loosened its control of the populace, street protests continued after the Revolution, gaining momentum as we headed towards the first democratic elections of June 1999. As before, the street demonstrations invariably stopped off at the United Nations Building, no matter what the issue, and we did become used to dealing with at least one or two demonstrations a day. Some were peaceful, particularly those of the students. Some were quite violent, particularly those where many of the demonstrators were hired for the day, usually village lads bussed in for the occasion and contracted for the cost of a meal and a few Rupiah cash to join demonstrations that often conflated an unusual mix of causes and were rarely even understood by those on contract.

We discovered a rhythm to these demonstrations and learnt to adjust office activity accordingly. Demonstrators during this phase in Indonesian political life got up late and didn't get organized until around 11.00 am, usually going home around 4.00 pm. For UNESCO staff members this meant that getting to work was not a problem; getting home could be if the demonstrators were unusually vigilant; and making appointments around the middle of the day that required somehow getting out of the UN compound could be next to impossible. Meanwhile, we were being 'looked after' now, that is, after May 1998 onwards. In the carpark at the rear of the UN Office, at around 9.00 am every day, sixty to eighty police would arrive for the daily anti-demonstrator shift, shuffle around unpacking riot shields, weapons, and lunch boxes, and then while away their time in collective karaoke singing. Every day we were 'entertained' while we worked by sixty singing policemen, reminiscent of the caption of a British comedy show.

Occasionally there was shooting. Occasionally people were seriously wounded. UNESCO staff, being on the first floor above the entrance had a front-stall view through the slanted cement shutters that formed something of a shield against the rocks, eggs and other light projectiles thrown at times in our direction. But we had to institute a standard procedure of moving people away from the windows to the back of the office as we heard the more violent and noisy demonstrations coming down the block.

There was an occasional lighter side. One day shooting started, into the air, and we moved the staff to more protective cover deeper inside the office in case things grew worse. But then we noticed the only casualty. A random shot in the air had punctured the 4 m high blimp of Ronald MacDonald sitting on the roof of the hamburger outlet across the street from the UN Building. He slowly subsided with an exhaust venting sigh into a rubber puddle. Some of our staff were noticed applauding the symbolic collapse of capitalism … Ronald was plugged and re-instated to his commanding position overlooking demonstrations targeting the UN Building by the next morning, so capitalism did not rest for long.

The UN Building acted more as a convenient source for attracting international attention than anything else through 1998 into 1999, but from August 1999 onwards when the East Timor autonomy issue moved center-stage in Indonesia, the United Nations started to become the consistent central target for groups speaking *against* outside international intervention that was seeking to stop the militia killings in and around Dili. It was quite extraordinary how easy it seemed to be for political issues to be redefined in the public mind by covert interest groups into quite absurd antagonisms. In the case of East Timor, for example, where as Indonesian militia were engaged in uncontrolled murder, opinion on the streets in Jakarta blamed the United Nations—plus Australia in particular as the first country to bring in peace keepers—for interfering with Indonesia's sovereignty and dignity.

Whereas previously local ethnic Chinese were at risk in Jakarta, and subsequently in Indonesia's Eastern Provinces particularly, Christians or Moslems also, depending on who ruled the local communities, a new phenomenon emerged through 1999 in a practice of 'sweeps' through the streets by gangs. Individual expatriates started to be accosted at bus stops or while walking, questioned about their country of origin, intimidated, bashed, or chased. As a highly obvious Caucasian expatriate, it was wiser to learn to be Nordic rather than Australian during the Timor crisis and to speak with a thick European accent when confronted. As we moved into the 2000s and the focus of attention redirected increasingly towards action by extremist Islamic groups and attempts by some to bring errant 'Westernized' activity under more Shariah Law style control, like late-nightclubs and duty-free liquor outlets in particular, these gangs became more violent, raiding or intimidating patrons, but at the same time engaging in criminal activity themselves, stealing wallets and threatening people with physical attack.

Meanwhile, the bombings started. At first these had nothing whatsoever to do with Islamic extremism. Instead, the bombing of shopping center crowds and of the World Bank Building—from its subterranean car park, were the work of either corrupt figures in the financial world seeking to intimidate, in particular, as later convicted, Tommy Soeharto, the ex-President's son, or shadowy interests seeking to destabilize the emerging democratic process. Two bombings in 2000 (killing 17 people between them) occurred just before ex-President Soeharto, after his fall from Presidency, was supposed to be appearing in court to answer corruption charges. The Head of State at the time, President Abdurrahman Wahid, bitterly complained that his opponents were using terrorist tactics to destabilize his reformist government. Meanwhile, in what was most likely an attempt to deflect attention sideways from the real culprits, the Acehnese Independence Movement, GAM, was blamed initially for a number of these Jakarta bombings, but in fact was unlikely to have had anything to do with them.

But whatever the politics behind the bombings, within the UN System we did have to recognize that new parameters had entered our security equation. We set up standard advice, particularly for expatriate staff, to avoid shopping malls during the most crowded mid-day times, to avoid nightclubs, and be forever vigilant about errant packages in dark corners. We booked international visitors into quiet hotels owned locally and advised them to avoid getting a room overlooking the front of the building. But we still had to go about our daily business.

Two of our international staff were subsequently caught up in bombings.

In one of these bombings—of the Jakarta Stock Exchange on 13th September 2000, Philippe, leader of our Culture team, came incredibly close to being killed. He had arrived back in Jakarta only a few weeks before with a significant limp, after I had him evacuated from Dili following a very nasty accident when clambering over the wall of a World Bank house from which the night guard had taken himself off on evening leave and the local Bank officials had yet to give Philippe a key. Philippe was in the Stock Exchange Foyer when the bomb went off.

> The Foyer is fronted by a wall of glass. Philippe fortunately, by sheer accident of timing, had finished his meeting upstairs in the World Bank offices, descended to the Ground Floor Foyer and was about to enter the basement elevator at the rear when an enormous percussive force set up waves across the floor and massive glass shards and marble speared from 10 metres above into the tiles and any people unfortunate enough to be underneath.
> Philippe got out of the building through the escaping crowd, deciding as it was hard for him to walk because of his previous accident in Timor, to go down through an outside entrance to the basement car park to rescue his car from the second level down. As he passed through level 1 he was knocked to the ground by a second enormous explosion down at the second level of the basement. Disoriented but not seriously injured, Philippe got up and out of the car park, which by now was rapidly filling with acrid smoke.
> The main access road outside, Jalan Sudirman, already packed with traffic, turned into chaos as black smoke belched out of the underground ventilation system at ground level and across the street. Access even for rescue vehicles was extremely difficult. Philippe was able to get through on his mobile phone to me to tell me what had happened and to ask for help.
> Having established that Philippe was not seriously injured but mainly having difficulty walking, I called out the United Nations Security Officer immediately as I had no authority to cross the emergency police line that was forming around the building. The Security Official immediately embarked on the journey from the UN Building to the World Bank, but was significantly delayed by the traffic. Again, my lack of faith in the UN Coordinator of that time (before Bo arrived), still the same one who placed security down the list of priorities, was reinforced. The Coordinator was scheduled to travel to New York the next day to report on the current situation in Indonesia and after 30 minutes or so of the Safety Official being on the road, phoned him and commanded him to return to the office to complete his briefing on the current security situation and *not* to assist Philippe. We were not impressed by the UN Coordinator's assertion of priorities, of personal image in the system rather

than welfare of staff. But this, as I found over ten years in the United Nations System, was an inherent tension in a human organization in which personal careers are sensitive to the appearance of serving idealistic system goals, and in particular, one's politically anointed bosses who are designated to uphold the Member States' belief in the organization.

Philippe had to find his own way out of the chaos, and got home by taxi.

Meanwhile, fifteen people had been killed, mainly drivers who had been waiting down in the subterranean car park. Fortunately, Philippe had driven himself to the appointment that day as our three official drivers were already committed, so we did not have a UNESCO driver on stand-by underground, who would almost certainly have been killed. When our staff went back to extract Philippe's vehicle the next day, we found it had been sheltered by a concrete pillar and although blanketed in soot and dust, was virtually unscathed.

Jan, another international staff member, was also in the Jakarta Stockmarket Building, but escaped unharmed.

We now realised though just how close we were traveling every day to serious threat, so we had to start taking precautions against a new form of violence—bombings and terrorism. The most basic problem was that the United Nations simply could not allocate the kind of budget that individual embassy missions could provide to protecting themselves. Consequently, whilst the Embassies started to bombproof their offices and purchased reinforced steel-shelled vehicles, we could only afford to place plastic anti-blast film on our office and car windows, and keep as low a profile as possible. Later, when the security threat moved again, this time with extremist terrorism personally targeting international officials—particularly those from the USA and Australia after the 2001 bombing of the World Trade Centre in New York and America's subsequent invasion of Iraq and Australia's endorsement and involvement, quarter million dollar armored BMWs became the de-rigor car of choice for the most exposed national ambassadors. But, all we in the United Nations could do on UN budgets was to renew the bomb-blast plastic sheets on our car windows.

With this new post 9/11 phase however, we did have to move into a rather more defensive posture in getting about in the streets. As Head of Agency and therefore official Representative of the UN, and by nationality a senior *Australian* diplomat, I was potentially at risk and introduced a number of procedures, like varying times to and from work, and the route I took, keeping a very watchful eye on being followed. By this time I had moved our Office out to a quiet suburban location and I had our security guards trained in counter-surveillance so they could keep a careful eye on suspicious movements around the area where we worked. But the bombproof BMW remained a distant fantasy!

At that stage I also discovered that a captured terrorist list targeted my own home as well, the Hilton Hotel where I had rented our residence in an apartment tower in the grounds after we moved for security reasons *out* of our residence in the suburb of Permata Hijau following its attack by mobs in May 1998. For a while there I was feeling particularly embattled.

With the Bali Bombings and the two really serious bombings in Jakarta, of the Marriott Hotel on 5th August 2003, and a year later (subsequent to the 12th October 2003 Bali Bombing), the Australian Embassy—at 10.30 am on 10th September 2004, a number of my friends in the diplomatic corps had extremely narrow escapes.

> The Ambassador of Lebanon had intended to lunch in the café at the front of the Marriott Hotel – a favored place for diplomatic social dalliance given its proximity to one of the main Embassy areas – but arrived to find the last table had been taken. He quite literally had walked just around the pillar separating the Foyer from the staircase to climb upstairs when the Kejang van arrived with bomb and the explosion blew out the entire Foyer and Restaurant and sheared off the facia of the front of the hotel.
>
> The bombing could have been a lot worse but for an attempt at economic parsimony by the terrorists. They had purchased the cheapest Kijang van they could find, figuring its future life and maintenance schedule were distinctly short, and, laden with the weight of the bomb, the driver was unable to get it up the full length of the hill to the foyer entrance. As the van stalled halfway, the driver fled and the bomb was remotely detonated by watching back-up terrorists, killing one of their own, but sparing the Marriott Foyer from a fully direct blast.
>
> I saw the Lebanese Ambassador when I sat next to him the following day at a Session of Parliament we both attended. He had trouble hearing and was still pretty shaken, but, as he said, by the Grace of God, he had remained uninjured whilst people on both sides of him were killed.

When the Australian Embassy bomb exploded eleven months later, the Ambassador of Australia at that time was sitting in his office at the front of the Embassy. The mission had recently upgraded their security though the building was intrinsically still too close to the street to be fully protected. Amongst their precautionary measures a new four meter high perimeter security fence of 5 cm diameter poles had been erected, at the tops of which, sharpened one meter pipes were welded on at a 45° angle facing the Embassy building, making it all but impossible to clamber over. However, with the explosion these extra security pipes turned into missiles, blown at enormous force off the fence and into the embassy walls and windows. Fortunately for the Ambassador his window had been seriously bombproofed not long before with 5–8 cm thickness of bulletproof glass. The fence-top missile blew straight into his window travelling at head level for the desk where he was sitting, spearing through, but held by the security glass just a few centimeters into the room. I visited him shortly later and he showed me.

Meanwhile, directly across the road from the Australian Embassy, the Greek Ambassador, a close friend of mine, had walked moments earlier out of his Embassy Office in the Plaza 89 Building overlooking Rasuna Said, the street where the bombing occurred, to dictate a letter to his secretary in a room to the rear. Glass from his office windows sheared across the room at up to head high level embedding into the rear wall; a human torso was found blown into the tree directly outside his shattered window … but Alexis survived, shocked but quite uninjured. Indeed, that night, we had dinner at the Ambassador's residence, and his wife showed us Alexis's briefcase which had been sitting beside his leg before the Ambassador walked out the back. The bag had been severely scarred by shards of flying glass.

We were in a staff meeting in our UNESCO offices when this Embassy explosion occurred—around 5 km away. We knew immediately as our own building shook that there had been a really big bomb blast, and shortly afterwards a pillar of smoke in appearance not unlike those associated with a nuclear blast, spiraled into the sky above Jakarta.

Fortunately, by that time, I was in our new Offices in Kebayoran Baru, not the common premises of the United Nations Building on Jalan Thamrin. I had taken that decision to move out eighteen months earlier. It had become increasingly clear that, under the overall security management of the then current UN Coordinator, we were going to remain in an immensely exposed position to outside attack, in an intrinsically unsafe building with no viable means of easy escape. With my staff I developed a visual power-point presentation on how serious this risk was, including a map of how much of the UN would be obliterated by a bomb of the proportions that had exploded on 5th August 2002 in Bali's Kuta Beach shopping and entertainment district, killing 91 people.

The presentation made no difference to the UN Coordinator although several other Agencies increasingly became concerned. However, it did allow me to convince my own Headquarters to bankroll a move to a new location. We found a large house in a suburb that edged the south side of the central business district, close to the Ministry of Education with which we dealt continuously, and easily accessible to the rest of the city. The area, Kebayoran Baru, was populated with numerous diplomatic residences which meant reasonably attentive security staff in most nearby streets. Indeed my own chosen Office building was previously the residence of the German Ambassador. We did the basic renovations necessary to turn the house into appropriate office space and unilaterally moved out of the UN Building in April 2003—to the relief of all my staff, now a complement of around 70 people strong. Other UN Agency officials visited and looked longingly at the quiet tree lined streets, the feeling of a cohesive office in one large house, and the anonymity of living well away from the central Jakarta symbol of the UN System. But they chose to remain in the common premises. My newfound Office residence had two flag poles out the front, but we did not raise the UN flag, advertising our presence only by a small UNESCO logo next to the front entrance gate.

And then, just three weeks after I moved us out, the bomb went off at the United Nations Building on Jalan Thamrin. It was not a big bomb. It injured two unfortunate people on the street, but no UN officials were hurt. Almost certainly it was a 'protest' bomb from remnants of a local terrorist cell of Jemiah Islamiah some of whose leaders had been arrested that day. However, it was clear even though the bomb was small that the target was still the United Nations.

Immediately, a particularly belligerent financial officer from my Headquarters who, from the distance of Paris life could see no need for the moving expense, was silenced, while I was congratulated by the other administrators for security perceptiveness, and the rest of the United Nations Agencies in Jakarta became very restive indeed about their enforced location.

It was only five weeks later that the United Nations as an entity was very seriously targeted, with the bombing of the UN Building in Baghdad in June 2003 that I mentioned in the last chapter, and the killing of a number of staff including the UN Secretary General's Special Representative, Sergio de Mello. Immediately, the UN office in Central Jakarta was ordered by United Nations security officials in New York to be closed and alternative accommodation to be found. Three floors of a nearby office block were rented and all remaining Agencies moved out—under duress, and with little time to seriously explore more congenial office space. This was one of the times when my own staff were totally delighted with a decision I had forced into priority action just a couple of months earlier.

And the previous common premises UN Building remained uninhabited on Jalan Thamrin, Central Jakarta, the UN flag flying overhead, with no function but as a decoy to anyone seeking retribution to United Nations employees, but who have not looked up the current working address.

What Next?

The May 1998 Indonesian Revolution had been twelve very tense days of history-making change. Over the subsequent decade the students' initially explosive enthusiasm for democracy that had brought down Soeharto's 32 year rule slowly eroded as they confronted the reality of a political culture that moved against the nation's deeply entrenched elite self-interest with glacial slowness, and a series of Presidents who failed to deliver ... until finally there was a glimmer of real hope with the election in 2004 of President Susilo Bambang Yudhyono. The reform movement *did* spill over into the business world targeting corruption and nepotism, although with much less long term success than hoped for. Islamic politics had entered the national arena and continued to exercise increasing influence over events .... But these had been 12 days that shook the world.

In 2009 there was a postscript. The specter of a return to more authoritarian rule remained hanging in the political air. For after being sacked from the army by a military tribunal led by General (later, President) Susilo Bambang Yudhyono for, amongst other violence, the kidnapping and torture of nine democracy activists during the events of 1998, and after remaining in the political wilderness for a decade, General Probowo Subianto had moved directly into politics. Supported by the largess of his billionaire brother, Hashim Djojohadikusumo (who lived just down the road from me in Permata Hijou), Prabowo formed a political party, the Great Indonesia Party, which claimed a membership of 10 million people, each of whom was rewarded with a one-year life insurance policy on signing up. Probowo led his party, Gerinda or Gerakan Indonesia Raya, to compete in the Indonesian National Parliamentary General Elections of 9th April 2009. He claimed to be standing as a champion of the rural poor and as a decisive leader. He was not shy in pointing out that whilst he did the hard yards as a combat officer, President Yudhyono was only a desk officer. Probowo remains barred from entry to the United States because of his record of human rights abuse .... but, given his well supported call to the rural masses, he was a credible candidate, with his party gaining 4.3% of the national vote. Interestingly, the party led by Probowo's military opponent in 1998, General Wiranto, Hanura or Partai Hati Nurani Rakyat, also sought election, and came in close behind Probowo with 3.6% of the national vote. The militarists directly involved in the 1998 violence were therefore now supported by 8% of the people who wanted *firm* military-style leadership. Indonesia was playing on the edge of return to more authoritarian rule 11 years after the fall of Soeharto.

Briefly bringing the Prabowo story up to the present, 26 years after the fall of President Soeharto, return for Indonesia to authoritarian rule is even more likely. Prabowo, now with at least $(US)127 million in personal assets, and Defence Minister under President Joko Widodo until now, was the prime candidate to win the current election to become President of Indonesia when results were announced on 20th March. He had more than 50% of the currently counted public election vote on 14th February 2024, and was appealing to the high proportion of voters who are young and who have little knowledge of what happened when President Soeharto was deposed in May 1998. Prabowo has had a make-over to fashion the current 'cute grandpa' image he has crafted on social media. He has never faced trial for major human rights abuses in 1998 though some of his men were tried and convicted and even the military forced Prabowo's exit from the military through a dishonorable discharge.

From our own position in UNESCO, we had confronted serious test of how the United Nations could respond to protect its own staff during major civil unrest. At the same time however, we had been sitting at a vantage point in the midst of the action where we could clearly see the extraordinary complexity of the country's political and social make-up increasingly revealed as three decades of autocratic rule were abruptly unraveled. This understanding was critical in our ability to then deal with subsequent events and in drawing the international community in to assist Indonesia's flight into freedom.

Increasingly as the climactic 10 days of Revolution receded into history, we found that the change that had been written over Indonesia's political landscape opened up extraordinary *opportunities* for us to assist in the subsequent pursuit of democracy and openness in a society denied these rights for three decades. In particular, the shackles of freedom of expression had fallen away day by day as the revolution progressed. By 14th May the Department of Information had dropped the barriers to foreign journalists entering the country and film of the events was no longer vetted prior to its international broadcast through satellite feeds. By the time that Jusuf Habibie was sworn into Presidential power, this newfound freedom was not going to go backwards .... but the country was ill prepared to cope with what freedom of expression really meant. The nation was still deeply plagued by financial crisis and spreading poverty, and by a long-standing politically enforced ignorance.

On behalf of UNESCO, we were able to assist in very meaningful ways in opening up the voice and knowledge of a nation that had so recently tasted freedom, and in dealing with the ethnic and cultural conflicts that accompanied the transition—identifying and capitalizing on opportunity in the midst of the deepest of crisis and challenge.

The one benefit of Revolution is that suddenly everything is thrown into the air … and can come down entirely differently from what existed before. As a direct result, within three weeks of the Revolution, having previously worked hard at establishing links into all levels of government, I now had access to the new Ministers and Senior Officials who were handling the uncertainty and thus, we were able to make major change happen on behalf of the UN—particularly from total censorship to fully open media freedom, and converting basic education for 36 millions of Indonesia's young from centrally controlled rote learning of what the Regime wanted people to know, to community-based open and creative education across the whole country.

At heart, being *directly* involved within the society and communities and in personal contact with key players in the events, meant, as a UN Ambassador and Change Agent, my staff and I could intervene and help guide Indonesia into a new future.

This is the story of following Chaps. 16 and 17.

16

Opportunity Out of Challenge—Opening up Media Freedom

Opportunity—A Time of Change

President Habibie, Interim President after the May 1998 fall of previous long-standing President Soeharto, made a curious choice in selecting his incoming Minister of Information. This was to select Mohamad Junus Yosfiah, a retired military general, previously as army captain, the field commander of 'Team Susi'. He and his team were allegedly implicated under orders from central military authorities in the killing of five Australian journalists at Balibo in East Timor after they had surrendered, the action apparently taken in an attempt to hide Indonesia's illegal intrusion into the territory in October 1975. Junus was later referred for war crime prosecution by the NSW Australian Coroner's Court in November 2007, a judgment it should be pointed out that is still rejected by Indonesia's Ministry of Foreign Affairs.

As incoming Minister, Junus's task was to convert a Ministry that had been the chief architect of censorship under President Soeharto into a Ministry that was now responsible for *opening up* freedom of the press and freedom of expression. The Ministry was staffed by 50,000 people, each of whose job was basically to suppress anything that might threaten government credibility and image. Strict controls remained in place. News, for example, was broadcast from Jakarta 16 times a day, syndicated to the provinces, but not complemented by any local journalist investigative capacity.

Both the Ministry and the media itself were poorly prepared for the new awareness that was suddenly thrust upon them by events of the May 1998 revolution. And, in charge of the transition was a man whose reputation was allegedly forged by brutal suppression. I was distinctly skeptical of UNESCO being able to work with Yunus and this Ministry to follow our United Nations mandate of opening up freedom of expression around the world.

Nevertheless, along with one of UNESCO's key media specialists, Jayaweera, at that stage based in Kuala Lumpur, I arranged an appointment to see Minister Yunus three weeks after the explosion of the May 1998 revolution had subsided.

I was surprised. I found myself talking with a man who gave off all the right signals of being entirely committed to now opening up Indonesia's media. And as I discovered over the next year, this commitment was entirely genuine, even to the point where he opposed President Habibie's cautions in pushing forward the new press freedom plans into Parliament and having them approved.

With continuous and committed support from Jayaweera and highly professional UNESCO Headquarters' Communications-Media personnel, we therefore immediately started to put into place a program of support—for the development of new laws of press and media freedom, for the training of journalists in dealing responsibly with the new open media world in which they were suddenly now operating, and we started to build a network of independent radio stations through the provinces dedicated to investigative news.

After 32 years of tightly constrained freedom of expression the Indonesian media situation presented us with some real challenges. There was a small number of courageous journalists and editors who were committed to freedom of expression, most of whom had paid dearly for their actions, with various sentences of incarceration or actions of direct intimidation. Some journalists had paid with their lives. The press in general however had adopted the spots of corruption that characterized Indonesian 'official' society generally. 'Envelope journalism' as it was commonly known, was normal. That is, journalists were paid through the person or group who wanted to be reported positively quietly slipping them an envelope of money. So, of course, the journalists told *their* story rather than reported in an investigative or disinterested manner. He who paid the most received the best press coverage. At absolute minimum, a press conference *had* to be accompanied by food and drink. On the other side of the camera or microphone we also found that politicians in general were not used to the possibility of facing exposure, so any journalist who was critical was highly likely to find themselves confronted by quite direct intimidation. Indeed, in the early 2000s, one particularly powerful local politician hired gangs of thugs—hiding under the mantle of 'concerned members of the community'—to intimidate journalists quite directly and to invade and vandalise the newspaper offices that were investigating his corrupt city development practices. Politicians in general were not used to facing negative public scrutiny. Consequently, we commonly saw, even from each of the Presidents following Soeharto, a call for journalists to be 'professional'. The overt text of such a call was entirely appropriate: there was a long way to go in the development of responsible journalistic practice and ethics. The subtext however, the 'real' story, was a call to not criticize *them*.

And remember, the Ministry that was now charged with the responsibility of opening up freedom of expression, the Ministry of Information, was staffed with officials whose entire job up to this point was suppressing or providing 'spin' to information about the government and its actions.

We very quickly learned just how deeply the Ministry culture had been inscribed with values of not letting go control of what people talked about. For example, after we had obtained agreement from the Minister over a series of meetings for UNESCO to assist the Government to develop a new Press Law as part of the new Democratization Reform Agenda, we established a small steering group to guide the process. We met alternately in the Ministry Offices or the UN Building with me as Chair—again, the 'fair witness' role that the UN *can* play. Minister Yunus had accepted the idea that the group would consist of half of government officials charged now with developing freedom of expression, whilst the other half were to be the most respected *independent* journalists in the country. The principle was fine. But the Secretary-General of the Ministry, who was on the Committee as Co-chair, *insisted* that the Ministry knew the media situation better than anyone in the country, so *they* would choose the best independent journalists. It took a while before I could get him to agree with the stance that we were certainly *not* going to move from, that the whole point of 'independent' journalists is that they are *not* the journalists that the government finds most comfortable, but had to be nominated by the journalistic community. The resulting steering group was formed, comprising three very courageous and highly respected genuinely independent journalists—two of whom had spent time in jail under Soeharto, a matching group of government officials, and a couple of people from UNESCO—a technical advisor and myself. As the Steering Group dynamic developed, we had many 'interesting' debates as the Ministry officials were prevailed upon to steadily clean out their bureaucratic cupboard of their media-suppressing habits. We eventually had a very steering effective group that carried the respect of the journalistic community with them, as well as the authority of government—two absolutely essential conditions if we were to make serious inroads towards freedom of expression.

However, we did have to move quickly to 'socialize' the various government and non-government communities with the 'idea' of freedom of expression, why it was so central to an emerging democracy to establish a generally supportive climate to the free flow of ideas. We needed external stimuli and assistance from outside Indonesia, but also for Indonesian politicians and people to fully 'own' the laws and new practices we were assisting the country to adopt. We therefore decided to bring in a strong 'Needs Assessment Team' to review the media situation in Indonesia and to recommend on what should be done about it. Minister Yunus agreed. To increase the credibility of the team we decided that the leader had to be very highly respected internationally but also to come from a developing country rather than from London, New York or elsewhere within the advanced country media communities. We chose Cushrow Irani, Executive Manager of the highly respected Indian newspaper in Calcutta, *The Statesman*, who had also served previously as Chair of the International Press Council under UNESCO. The team arrived in July 1998, just 2 months after the Revolution, and met with a wide cross-section of people including Government officials, the Minister of Information, prominent figures in the media and a large number of editors and journalists. We wanted not only to survey the needs, but also to use the international prestige and experience of the team to help socialise the idea of freedom of expression, and allay fears amongst politicians and officials of a suddenly unleashed rampant and irresponsible press.

We were also very aware that a number of foreign countries which prided themselves on their own democratic principles and openness of the press were champing at the bit to introduce their own programs (and ideologies) into Indonesia's new venture towards an open society. Strongest interest came from the USA, Britain, Canada and the Scandinavian countries. This situation provided opportunity, but it also promised potential problems—as programs duplicated or interfered with each other, whilst any early stains of ideological intrusion could well destabilize the whole enterprise. UNESCO was however recognized by all as *the* multilateral agency that really did have an independent mandate to develop freedom of expression throughout the world in line with one of the most basic principles of the United Nations Charter, Article 19. We therefore formed an international Donors Group—representatives of the countries which wanted to provide assistance to Indonesia's burgeoning media industry and its independent investigative capacity. Whilst I did not necessarily want us to do the whole job ourselves, I certainly did want to ensure we knew what each other was doing, and seek to coordinate. As it turned out, the USA did choose to take their separate way—although we did maintain good liaison, in particular through a US-supported

NGO, *Internews*. But Denmark (in particular), Britain and Canada, worked primarily as partners supporting their programs under the multi-lateral 'fair witness' coordinating and implementing umbrella of UNESCO. We were able to set up agreements where each played different supportive roles. Denmark funded and directly cooperated in the development of an independent local radio network through the country; Britain primarily supported training, the development of broadcasting law and the strong attempts we made to legitimize and disseminate community radio stations; Canada was particularly helpful in supporting the many conferences and public events that were needed to both draw the journalistic community together in a new and more professional media environment, and to keep the *idea* of freedom of expression as a non-threatening essential plank of democracy in full public view. We had further minor support from Switzerland, Australia, and several other countries. Particularly though, the Danish Ambassador had developed trust in UNESCO after the support we provided—without asking for remuneration—when the Papuan Highlands water project funded by Denmark ran into problems due to supplied equipment not being of the notified size needed to be carried into jungle by human bearers. He responded immediately therefore when I came to him looking for funding for our media initiative and he remained our fully committed long-term central funder for our post-revolution radio network program.

First Steps—Development of a New Press Law

Minister Yunus set to work quickly—in particular, radically simplifying the 20 or more repressive conditions that had to be met and previous longtime delays in obtaining approval for anyone establishing a new private radio or newspaper venture. Twenty conditions were condensed into just four, and these referred to economic viability and accountability and station technical requirements, but *not* to views or political positions expressed. The Minister affirmed a guarantee that any application would be dealt with in three weeks, so the numbers of radio and press outlets suddenly expanded dramatically across the country. He also immediately accepted the recommendations of Cushrow Irani's Needs Assessment Team, and ordered his Ministry's full support for the actions which followed—in particular, development of a new and empowering Press Law. Originally Yunus wanted to combine Press with Broadcasting Law and shepherd a joint Act through Parliament. However, it became very clear to us quite quickly that to combine the two laws was going to be a mistake. There were many very powerful commercial interests in Broadcasting Law—in particular for the freeing up of opportunities for expansion of TV across the country, and serious unresolved debate between different Parliamentary factions about conditions that would minimize potential foreign influence. Press Law was much lower down on the horizon of official paranoia, and models for drafting the Law to abide by solid international standards were readily accessible—such as from South Africa and India and some of the newly emergent post-Communist states in Europe. To attach this Law to Broadcasting Law could well mean its dilution and delay. Yunus did finally agree.

We then put together a team to draft the Law—under guidance and monitoring of the Steering Group I mentioned earlier. Chief architect was Toby Mandel from the London-based NGO called "Article 19", named after the Article in the United Nations Charter that deals with freedom of expression. Toby was Article 19's legal expert with very considerable experience assisting newly emerging democracies to put new Press Laws into place. Along with the international and local media experts we had brought together into a UNESCO team, Toby worked with the nominated Ministry officials quite literally day and night for a month to put together the final Press Law draft that was arguably one of the best in Asia—though with one flaw that we could not get changed as the Law moved into the realm of Parliamentary political debate, that is the superordination of Criminal Law over Press Law in dealing with cases of libel and defamation. *In fact* it was within the discretion of the trial judge to choose which law to apply even though Criminal Law was normally to have precedence. The problem was that given this discretionary condition, trial judges could be bought off by wealthy litigators—and often were. Or alternatively, they were simply unfamiliar with the new law and its mediating rather than litigation intent and favored the legal system and precedents with which they were familiar. As we expected, this condition opened up the possibility of serious intimidation by corrupt officials or developers who used the criminal penalties to intimidate investigative journalists rather than have matters brought before a mediating Press Council.

Minister Yunus fought strongly for the Law—with all the new-found freedoms it promised. And there was, as I mentioned earlier, a genuine fear from many politicians and officials that really reflected a lack of faith in democracy itself—that is, a fear that journalists needed to be under some forms of official control else they would act 'irresponsibly', that is, report perhaps too critically. President Habibie, having risen to the position of President by virtue of Soeharto's downfall, was cautious. He expressed concern about possible irresponsible influences in the media, and called for guarantees of professionalism. As an engineer, he saw these guarantees lay in extensive professional training, indeed a degree course. In the context of Indonesia this could not work as a *condition* of being allowed to practice as a journalist, although we fully realized that a major effort did need to be injected into training as the investigative and professional capacity across the country was still very poor. The problem with Habibie's proposed condition was that the majority of the country consisted of poor rural communities. They would probably *never* acquire local journalists if the journalists had first to complete tertiary level training and accreditation. Yunus stood up to Habibie as well as to a number of his more suspicious Cabinet colleagues, and won.

The new Press Law was approved through Parliament in August-September 1999, just at the time when the East Timor plebiscite violence and crisis occurred. The new Law facilitated more open reporting of these events in Indonesia.

It took another 3 years of debate and amendments however before a new *Broadcasting* Law finally was passed by the Indonesian Parliament—in November 2002. To assist in this process, we assigned a small UNESCO team we employed of local journalists to work with the Parliamentary factions and to try and maintain some steerage in the development of the Law—in particular, to overcome the fear of 'letting go' the licensing process from official government hands into those of an independent regulating authority. This objective was achieved so the new Broadcasting Legislation established an independent regulatory body for the broadcasting field—at national level, the Komisi Penyiaran Indonesia Pusat (KPIP) or Central Broadcasting Commission, and at provincial level, the Komisi Penyiaran Indonesia Daerah (KPID) or Provincial Broadcasting Commissions. The objective of the Commissions was to ensure that broadcasting through the country is managed democratically, fairly and transparently—principles that previously did not guide national broadcasting practice. The Commissions were launched a year later—in December 2003, but poorly equipped and with limited knowledge about how to go about their tasks, for example, preparing a broadcasting code of conduct, assessing applications from broadcasting organizations for frequency licenses, issuing frequency licenses and monitoring the utilization of these frequencies. It was UNESCO's role then to help strengthen this new broadcasting steering mechanism, so we found support from the British Government and commenced training in consultation with KPIP and KPID in the four areas, Medan, Palembang, Pontianak and Jakarta.

Building Investigative Reporting Through the Country: Powering a Local Radio Network

The other key recommendations that arose out of the 1998 Needs Assessment Report of Cushrow Irani targeted upgrading the professionalism and investigative capacity of journalists to support the burgeoning post-May 1998 democracy movement. Under the repressive regime of Soeharto's New Order Government, very few journalists were trained or experienced in investigating and publishing 'free, fair and accurate information' as distinct from the government line (or that line which best suited the financial 'envelope' that was usually handed out for good-news reporting by those running press conferences), and the population of journalists through the country anyway was very sparce, the particularly in the provinces where they were often very isolated. The Irani Report therefore highlighted the training of journalists and editors to promote professionalism as well as networking to capitalize on whatever capacity already existed to reach the isolated members of the journalists community through exchanging information and experiences.

In response, we decided to put a major effort into the training and networking of journalists attached to local *radio* stations. Reason: radio reached more people than either the print press or TV, particularly outside the cities. And we also realized that networking could play a very important role in developing a sense of professional solidarity between the previously isolated journalists across the far-flung archipelago as well as contribute to their safety, most importantly for journalists likely to be most at risk, for example, in the war zones of Aceh, the religious conflict and violence areas in the eastern islands and the areas where greatest illegal exploitation of natural resources was going on, for example in Irian Jaya (West Papua) and Kalimantan.

However, a quick survey of the existing stations told us that we needed to do rather more. Many, indeed, most, of the 769 private radio stations, basically provided a broadcasting platform for local 'dangut' or pop music, and had very little capacity or interest in news or local investigation. Up until now, it had been rather dangerous to try to develop such a capability. To build a demonstration network we therefore needed to go further than just train and bring in networking. We needed to *transform* local radio stations through the country away from their current broadcasting repertoire towards a more news-oriented capability. With strong support from Denmark we therefore embarked on a program to build a local radio network through the country and to assist the stations to acquire the equipment, skills and management they needed to undergo this conversion. If we were going to develop a network, we also had to ensure they had access to adequate computer and internet equipment as well.

With the help of key local radio journalists, we therefore selected (initially) 19 private radio stations that both had a good reputation for professional broadcasting and were prepared to move in a more investigative news oriented direction if we provided support, for example, of funding for new outside recording and broadcasting equipment, new computers, support of additional journalist staff (over an 'introductory' period), and of course, training. The selection criteria were actually quite strict and monitored and over time we handed over all decisions about new members of the network to the Local Radio Network itself and assisted them to become increasingly engaged in *monitoring* the performance of all network members. We did have to 'evict' a few stations early in the piece because they had *not* kept their promise to upgrade investigative journalist capacity, or because they had become associated with particular political interests that were biasing their news reporting. These decisions were made by the network once it was well established because *they* took pride in their 'professionalism' as base criterion of membership, recognizing that they could not afford to be associated with errant members whose indiscretion would effectively bring the whole network into disrepute. By the end of 1999 we had 25 members of the network, and by 2001, the network stabilized with 30 members.

The internet-based networking was probably the most important ingredient of the mix that allowed the Local Radio Network for Democracy, as the group eventually decided to call itself—to evolve into a self-sufficient and empowered group—following its inauguration as a 'Local Radio Meeting Point'. UNESCO provided the computer server and home page, and acted as a clearing house while the network was establishing. Through this mechanism radio stations could exchange stories with any other radio station across the group. There were two key results of this strategy. The first was that we were getting somewhere around 45–50 news stories being lodged on the site and exchanged each day, so the stations immediately had access to massively increased current news sources. The second result emerged, and that was to promote some level of safety for radio stations confronting intimidation or intimidating local conditions. For example, during the period of special military rule in Aceh, two of the stations were confronted by quite direct intimidation—with shadowy characters just appearing at the station and brandishing guns after some news was broadcast that they objected to. The stations immediately put this information onto the internet so the acts of intimidation were reported across the whole country though not locally. Similarly, when stories were too 'hot' to broadcast locally, they could be lodged on the site, and were often broadcast in a province remote from the immediate danger: but the message got out. Additionally, our own UNESCO media communications staff could continue to monitor what was going on both at specific local stations as well as in the interchanges that built up as the network matured. And, of course, we used the network as a vehicle for distance learning on journalistic methods as well as technical instruction—giving us access to training nodes across the whole Indonesian archipelago.

To back up our role as driver of the network's development, we also built a mini sound studio within our UNESCO Offices in Jakarta. Given our limited levels of funding this was a bit of a chewing gum and wax style of improvised sound recording. But it was adequate, kept out the street noises and allowed us to record with digital audio capacity and professional recording standards. Our main objective was to enrich the resources available to network members through producing radio programs of interest to them and which they could access and use free. Our charge for groups, including the UN itself to use the studio, for example, for awareness and promotional campaigns, was a mere Rp400,000 for a manned 8-h session, approximately $(US)40 to $(US)50. Our first recorded broadcasts included an anti-corruption public service announcement or PSA by the Indonesian Corruption Watch (ICW) organization; a PSA and talk show by UNIFEM, the UN Agency dealing with women's empowerment; and a PSA produced by a coalition of NGOs promoting freedom of information—our next target for legislative change after broadcasting law. Each of these awareness PSAs and programs was then immediately available to large audiences across the whole of Indonesia through the network.

In my experience, 'virtual' networks and communications often do not work if that's all you do. I had found this already with teleconferencing when in my previous Sociology and International Science and Technology (S&T) Cooperation position based in Australia before joining UNESCO full time. People have to meet at a face-to-face level as well in between. And then the teleconferencing will work as a vehicle for real exchange of ideas and opinions which otherwise tend to degenerate into more formal giving of orders or 'instrumental' information. When UNESCO established the Task Force in Headquarters to meet and develop responses to the Tsunami disaster that hit the Indian Ocean out of Indonesia on 26 December 2004, they also established regular teleconferencing with each of the Field Directors responsible for geographic areas affected by the Tsunami—one in India, one in Sri Lanka, one in Thailand, and myself in Indonesia. But the group, protected by we, the Field Directors, was anonymous publicly. We were using auditory, not visual interaction. You can't sense the meeting and the people and informal power plays that basically constitute the dynamic of the way a meeting-group develops over time. Meanwhile, we the Field Directors were basically invisible from Headquarters. On one particularly notable occasion, a highly enthusiastic staff member responsible for raising external funding in Headquarters launched his plan, but presented it entirely by powerpoint—which, without visual connection, we, in remote locations, could not see. He had not bothered to send out any information in advance. Each of us, the Field Directors, did spend time in Headquarters and attended the Task Force meetings where we had the benefit of face-to-face interaction, and this did allow us at least a bit, to establish our credibility (not possible in the virtual communication world) our *presence,* or to experience the subjective feedback that allows you to locate yourself within group dynamics. When we had the chance to participate directly in the Paris meetings, we also developed a feeling of how the group was operating and where it was going—again, not possible outside the subjective observation and understanding of the group's dynamics.

Sometimes the technology gets in the way as well. I remember a notable teleconferencing problem I confronted in my previous life as an academic S&T policy advisor to government in Australia. We were linked into a national hook-up across six States with the Minister of S&T of the time who was participating from Canberra—on this occasion with visual as well as auditory access. But the technology was set up to control the sequencing of interactions. That is, the camera selected for network broadcast from one of the seven sites was triggered by an intervention—making sound—coming from that site. At one stage the Minister was outlining his own policy ideas when a member of the Queensland Panel decided to wander off to the side to get a cup of coffee. He was rather noisier than he expected, triggering the camera in Brisbane. Instead of the Minister's serious policy intervention, we were all entertained with the image of a poor furtive coffeemaker in Queensland, suddenly and unexpectedly being exposed.

Back to the point of these digressions. We needed to do more than just build 'virtual' relations between the members of the evolving Local Radio Network, so supported 'real' network meetings on a regular basis, plus annual Workshops on journalistic response to key current events or issues, for example, democratic elections. In other words, we needed to build the personal solidarity of the group. As people got to know each other at a personal level and to hear and feel what they were saying, the 'spirit' of the group evolved along with their quite genuine sense of pride in being included in the group—of critical importance in maintaining commitment to the group's professionalism objectives.

Additionally, we needed to help the local radio stations to develop *income* out of their new status as news broadcasters. Therefore, in 2001, with funding from the British Government, we brought in an international expert from the UK, Graham Mytton, to work through the regions of Indonesia with the network to lead the development of training and introduction of a system of audience research. We backed up the training with publication in Indonesian of two key books on audience research to provide an ongoing resource. Again, such systematic feedback of radio station reach and impact simply did not exist outside Jakarta and one or two other main cities. We reasoned that if the stations could *show* they had reach in their broadcasting then it was very likely to be a major factor in attracting commercial sponsorships and advertising from local business. This worked. Additionally, the status of the network as a 'Local Radio Network for Democracy' placed them in a box seat for accessing either government of multilateral donor funding (principally, UNDP) to broadcast information about democracy and the election process as democratic principles were increasingly bedding down across the country. Indeed, because the network gave guaranteed and professional coverage to millions of people outside the city concentrations, we were also able to launch (funded) public awareness campaigns across the whole of Indonesia, again, a continuing source of income for network members.

As a consequence, by 2003 the network was independent and self-governing. We also had been able to develop from a mature and respected base, collaborative relations with other networks, in particular, ISAI's 'Radio 68H', an internet news agency, and the US funded 'Internews' network group. We still continued to provide annual workshops and general training. But the baby was now grown up, even to the point that when disaster struck one area and the local radio stations there, the others would pitch in to help them out of the disaster. This support was of critical importance in getting the four radio stations we had supported in Aceh back on air quickly after the Tsunami swept them out of existence at the end of 2004.

Community Radio—Good Idea, but …

Meanwhile, one of our hardest battles was to introduce *community* radio as a component of Broadcasting Law, a media tool we had found invaluable in the southern Philippines and Timor Leste.

In the southern Philippines, under our 'GENPEACE' program that I talk more about in the next chapter, community radio provided the vehicle for drawing potentially opposing community religious groups together with local government in a highly successful venture to expand literacy training, particularly for women, and the training of peace facilitators at village level. In Timor Leste, we introduced community radio to the most remote areas of the country to facilitate the education of local communities about democracy (as no other media could reach these areas) in the months leading up to Timor Leste's first democratic elections.

In Indonesia however, we found the idea of community radio met with strong suspicion from the country's officials. The view most frequently expressed was that a community radio could far too easily be taken over by a religious or otherwise ideologically minded group in the community and used to foment violence or to proselytise. This clearly was a danger. Indeed, the extreme Moslem group, Laskar Jihad, that had swept into Ambon and create violent opposition to local Christians *did* start an illegal local community radio station and *did* use it to preach radical Islam and to enflame local conflicts.

We dealt with this issue in the Philippines by ensuring the development of a Community Media and Education Council (CMEC) around each station, elected through broad-based community assemblies as a vehicle for community management and ownership, for liaising with local government, and in particular, for assuring against bias from one faction over another. Standing in the background, the UNESCO imprimatur meant we kept an eye on things, and were seen to be watching, as 'fair witness'. So, we knew from experience—obtained, I should emphasize in potentially highly volatile conflict zones—that it was possible to avoid ideological bias and to promote a local voice that empowered governance rather than sowed seeds of dissension. But we also noticed in Indonesia that whilst we were constantly confronting resistance to formally permitting community radio to develop, the Laska Jihad station was allowed to continue operating without restriction. It was, we believed, meeting a covert interest of some military connected people to destabilize the local community for political ends. The real reason, we believed, that community radio generally was viewed with suspicion, was that, at this early stage of democratization, the military and many politicians were afraid of providing an open media channel to local increasingly empowered communities which, given this opportunity for a public voice, may well, as far as the opponents were concerned, act to make the government of the day uncomfortable and stimulate disunity during troubled times. The country was still afraid of what democracy may deliver.

We tried hard—in particular to legitimize community radio and remove the fears amongst those in power about the danger of dynamic two-way public interaction through community radio. We translated into Bahasa

Indonesia and broadly distributed the main reference work that UNESCO published globally on community radio, "The Community Radio Handbook" by Colin Fraser and Sonia Restrepo Estrada, a book that discusses what the key characteristics of community radio are, that deals with legal and technical aspects, and what must be done to establish a community radio. The book features case studies from UNESCO's worldwide experience, including in Kenya, Ghana, Bolivia, Nepal and the Philippines. We held seminars on community radio in Jakarta and Yogyakarta which targeted parliamentarians and the Indonesian Government and sought to help them understand the real benefits to public awareness that could flow from legitimizing community radio. Our UNESCO team spent many hours talking with parliamentarians, and I had many meetings with Ministers and influential politicians to promote the idea. A succession of Ministers of Information eventually promised that we could start some pilot test community radios. But, when it came to practical steps to put the idea into practice, we could never quite get the final approvals.

To the time I needed to move on from my UNESCO responsibility, this battle for community radio had not been won, for the Indonesian Government had steadfastly resisted its legalization. So, given the importance in fostering community empowerment and education through media and ICT access, we needed to be creative, whilst still working within the national legal framework. Consequently, from 2003, under the guidance of Arya, leader of the Indonesian UNESCO communications/media team, we started developing "Community Multimedia Centers" (CMCs). The CMCs combine radio stations with tele center facilities such as computers and internet. In other countries in Africa, Asia and the Caribbean where UNESCO has already established 40 of these Centers, community radio stands at the core. In Indonesia, we built the CMCs around local private radio stations for example, Radio Tuah Suara Murni in Lubuk Paka, North Sumatra, Radio Suara Dermaga Ria in Sekadau, West Kalimantan, Radio Rona in Kendal and Radio Pragola in Pati, both in Central Java. The Centers were used by students for homework and training in accessing internet, but also offered 'radio browsing', programs where listeners could request Internet content to be broadcast on radio. Most importantly the CMC program brings communities into a direct relationship with the local broadcasting media.

We therefore had not been entirely successful in building the voice of the people as deeply as we wanted into the democratization reform process. However, in the post-Soeharto period, a lot had happened to open up freedom of expression. In the midst of challenge, the May 1998 revolution, we had discovered extraordinary *opportunity*.

A Way to Go

I made the following observation during my Closing Speech at the President-hosted celebration of World Press Freedom Day, 2000, which we held in Jakarta:

> Indonesia was well prepared by the New Order Government of President Soeharto until May 1998 for *rumor*. Through regulatory licensing of those who were allowed to speak or broadcast, direct censorship and indirect threat, investigative reporting on human rights abuses or of KKN – the acronym for corruption, collusion, and nepotism *(for those at this dinner from outside Indonesia)* - was suppressed as was the freedom to express opinion, informed or otherwise. News coverage was fully and centrally controlled. Reports broadcast through radio in the provinces were directly fed from Jakarta 16 times a day, so there was no capability to investigate or report locally. The first result, as President Abdurrahman Wahid, said during this morning's Opening Ceremony, was that people learnt to communicate in what the President called '*circle language*', to say one thing but mean another. The second result, as was demonstrated so vividly and violently from May 1998 onwards has been the driving force of rumor in mobilizing riots, razing houses, and killing people identified by the mobs as somehow different. Rumor that was in many cases intentionally distorting, unsubstantiated, or which blew minor incidents out of proportion. An example … the *fact* of a rock accidentally thrown through a Jakarta Mosque window in the midst of a fight between rival car-parking gangs which became a *rumor* of intentional arson by Christian forces attacking Islam, and led to the *real* burning of four churches. During the period in and after May 1998, rumor would sweep through cities with alarming speed, fed by emotion, fear, interest and salacious attention to be noticed rather than by even a moment of reflection on facts. And the result was anarchy, senseless killing and long-term distrust and hatred between communities that had lived comfortably together as in the Molukus for generations.
> Where there is no source of reliable and disinterested information that the people can trust, a society is forced to *feed* on rumors, an open doorway for *mis*-information and intentional *dis*-information, and the social destruction that we have witnessed can so easily follow.
> This was the consequence of the suppression of a basic human right, the human right that is most frequently and most widely violated, in war, or in peace, in conflict situations and even in post-conflict countries, the one human right that forms the most 'dynamic cornerstone of democracy' - to strengthen *old* democracies, to build *new* democracies … *the human right to freedom of opinion and expression.*

In the year 2000—when I made the remarks reported above—we were just 2 years into the growth of a new tradition of freedom of expression in Indonesia, but we thought we were getting somewhere. Indonesia was the latest country to have gained press freedom. Newspapers, radio and television had increased in numbers and the media were increasingly active and critical. I was therefore able to convince the Government and President of Indonesia, at that time Abdurrahman Wahid (popularly known as Gus Dur), to host the international celebration of World Press Freedom Day—an event we organized in collaboration with the Southeast Asian Press Association—at the Presidential Palace and the five-star Hotel Peninsula in Jakarta. To stage such an event in Indonesia just 2 years earlier would have been inconceivable.

The event highlighted however the knife-edge on which the country was still poised.

On the one hand, the event was successful as a proud celebration of achievement. Indonesia *had* put into place legislation which arguably gave the greatest freedom of expression to press and the media of all countries in Southeast Asia. As I observed in my Opening Speech that morning before the President:

> This (new Press) Law is strengthened by the recognition it contains that press freedom is perceived as a *basic right* for citizens. The Law states for example, 'the press is free from any forms of prevention, prohibition and or pressure so that the public right to information is guaranteed'. The Law further states that the press is free from censorship and is not subject to publication and broadcasting bans. These are achievements to be cherished now against pressures to backtrack.

On the other hand, however, there remained some very worrying signs. Those at the Seminar, including the President, were aware that at that time too many stories still reached the front-pages of newspapers unverified, often building on random rumors, sometimes even extending into pure fiction. This was not too surprising as responsible reporting was an entirely new concept and not too many journalists knew how to do it or what acceptable standards were. However, lack of skill or, in some cases, ethical sensitivity, had led to situations where the press and media *ignited* the existing local and regional conflicts rather than contributing to mutual understanding and tolerance. Furthermore, there was a growing number of incidents where mobs attacked press and media buildings—a sign that the audience was fully aware of, this mismanagement of responsibility stimulating violent reaction (although, we also knew that in some cases, the violence of the crowds was engineered and paid for by corrupt officials who were seeking to escape critical public scrutiny). Even so, most of these physical attacks were rooted in a lack of understanding amongst the people of the (critical and responsible) role of a free media and press in a democratic society.

Still, far too many journalists practiced as 'normal' the 'envelope journalism' I spoke about earlier, that is, to discretely receive money from their interviewees for giving the right spin to their report, and the practice remained deeply rooted in the ongoing, and at times aggressive, self-interest of some within the journalistic community. In one case we knew about, a newspaper journalist initiated an investigative report into the bribe-taking practices of his own colleagues. He ended up having to take his family into hiding following death threats from those colleagues he had investigated.

Even by the time I retired from my UN position based in Indonesia at the start of 2006, there was still a long way to go, although the situation then was a quantum leap forward from what existed prior to May 1998 when there was virtually no local investigative capacity or commitment through the country and central government ruled freedom of expression with an iron fist. Still, some politicians, officials and commercial interests *feared* exposure, at times with good cause as corruption still crept quietly in the shadows—even though not in the full light of the bureaucratic day as was the case under Soeharto. Cases of intimidation still did occur along with predatory use of defamation laws under the *criminal code* to suppress reporting. As "Reporters Sans Frontières" (RSF, or "Reporters Without Borders") noted for 2008, the criminal law on defamation was used by the Supreme Court to sentence *Time Asia* magazine to pay damages of $(US)100 million to former President Soeharto for "harming his reputation and honour"—after the magazine reported on the transfer of $(US)73 billion of embezzled money by the Soeharto family from Switzerland to Austria—a case however that was probably dropped permanently now with Soeharto's death in January 2008; one journalist was imprisoned for 6 months on defamation conviction after he accused the executive director of a newspaper of sexual harassment; another, from the daily *Koran* newspaper faced prison after 'insulting' the office of the prosecutor general by claiming it had intervened to ban a scholastic book. Although the choice of which law is to be applied to defamation cases was subject to the discretion of the judge, Press Law in practice remained generally subservient to Criminal Law and we were never able to get corresponding changes to the Criminal Law code to be made to remove this threat. However, there were small signs of light. Erwin Arnada, editor of the Indonesian edition of *Playboy*, was acquitted in April 2008 of publishing indecent photos, the judge rejecting the complaint on the grounds that it should have been lodged under the Press Law. Extremist Islamist groups however demonstrated throughout the trial and made death threats against Arnada. RSF concluded in their 2008 survey that whilst threats also occurred on occasion to protection of sources, "investigative reporting is gradually gaining ground". Indonesia had crept up a little in the latest Press Freedom Index determined by RSF at the time, from 117th place in 2005 to 103rd position in 2006—out of 168 countries. There *was* now healthy public debate about what freedom of expression implies—unheard of just a decade before.

UNESCO continued to bring concerns about media freedom into the public arena through promotion of events such as World Press Freedom Day, and high profile seminars—not just in Jakarta but throughout the provinces as well, particularly targeting influential groups such as parliamentarians, attorneys, judges, lawyers and the police force. Meanwhile, given that investigative reporting only opened up as a *possibility* in the late 1990s, standards of professionalism and journalistic ethics were not yet solidly enough in place to ensure the proper use of media freedom by the media itself. Our UNESCO team developed more than 50 training programs from 2000 until the end of the time I was in Jakarta in December 2005, addressing journalistic ethics, investigative reporting, as well as focusing on how to handle specific reporting issues around elections and reporting more delicate issues, such as HIV/AIDS and conflicts involved around sustainable development vs. illegal but connected forestry interests. However, we still must remember that Indonesia is a vast and complex country without a tradition of responsible journalism—until very recently.

Consequently, the journey had started—opportunity arising out of the severe challenge confronted by the events of May 1998 when President Soeharto and his New Order Government fell from power and Indonesia embarked on the tortuously slow path towards free and open democracy.

Indeed, attention to the role of the new and more open media played a critical role in *preventing* riots and unrest as early as at the time when the *first* democratic elections were held—in 1999. The *problem* was that at that stage in the evolution of Indonesia's democratic process, a conflict remained between a wholly new free popular election process and the Presidential *appointment* process which, no matter what the people voted, remained in the hands of the parliament.

A popular election had delivered the daughter of the founder of modern Indonesia, President Soekarno, Megawati Soekarnoputri, as the clear winner. However, the President in 1999 was not formally *elected* by popular vote but by Parliamentary representatives interpreting the popular vote according to party political interests, never a problem before as President Soeharto had the Parliament rigged in such a way as to make election of anyone but him impossible. (I should also note that since 1999, the system has changed: the current President is elected by direct popular vote, providing him, or her, with an immensely stronger defense against potential Parliamentary impeachment sanction.) Back in 1999 the intrigue of a newly empowered Parliament was engaged when President Habibie, the interim President after Soeharto, decided to run for President, but there was general disillusionment with his performance so that his 'accountability speech' to Parliament was rejected by vote—thus removing him from electability as this action was tantamount to impeachment. Parliament then elected Abdurrahman Wahid, the religious leader, to be President, passing over Megawati, even though she had the peoples' support. Tension started to build. A vote was then held for Vice-President. There were three candidates, Megawati, General Wiranto—the head of the military, and Hamzah Hass, a distinctly self-interested Islamic leader. Megawati initially refused to be nominated for Vice-President as she feared yet another embarrassing defeat at the hands of the parliamentary factions. I was present in the room along with the other ambassadors and international representatives observing the election process. And the tension became palpable as we could hear the rumblings of the crowds that had gathered outside the parliamentary doors, many of them Megawati supporters, now starting to become very angry, having just learnt that the popular will of the people had been denied by the parliamentary factions. Wiranto saw the signs and graciously withdrew from election to make way for Megawati. Hamzah Hass, on the other hand, refused. We could all see that if Hass was elected over Megawati, and in particular, if the people believed this was by veiled sleight of hand of the parliamentary election process, we faced the prospect of major civil unrest through the whole country. The election process started, conducted with meticulous attention to checking and rechecking publicly each vote, as it was passed around a large central table past eight to ten scrutineers. The election process therefore proceeded with glacial slowness and the tension built as the result swung in either direction depending on which faction group was voting. Finally Megawati was elected. Compared with her being the President, election to Vice-Presidential status was a compromise, but a necessary compromise, given the enormous tension surrounding the result. My diplomatic colleagues and I breathed a very heartfelt sigh of relief.

What remained important though was that the people believed now that the parliamentary election process was fair and above board, for they had believed up to this point in the simple truth that their new-found democracy actually meant that the will of the people would now for the first time determine who led the country. And they were now both confused and feeling distinctly ripped off. It was here that the (new) role of the media turned out to be quite critical in avoiding the riots of dissatisfied voters we all feared when Megawati failed to be elected as President. Those guiding Parliamentary protocol had been careful and brought the media in to ensure full transparency of what was going on. What mattered was that for the first time each vote was counted one-by-one in full public view, with full TV and radio coverage bringing the *process* to the many million people of Indonesia. Transparency and immediate broadcasting was almost certainly the major factor that held back public protest to quite limited unrest. Political sentiment boiled with Megawati's rejection, but it did not boil over.

What we saw through the years from 1998 to the time I left at the end of 2005 was a general awakening from the long sleep of autocratic rule that had been stamped on the country over the previous 32 years, and the sentence of ignorance that had consequently been imposed on the nation's people. What we saw emerging as we travelled around the country and engaged with local communities over this 7 year period, even though still in its infancy, was a new culture of the people, empowered by transparency of information and freedom of expression, core roots of democracy. This new cultural order was evident in the steady development of a new-found release from the peoples' previous reticence to speak out as faith in democratic reforms started to spread through the villages, and people realized that for the first time they actually had a voice, perhaps small, but still, a voice that was previously entirely suppressed. For us, the development of a strong and open media remained of critical importance though for we so often saw the insidious and dangerous power of rumor persisted, sometimes mischievously created, or simply arising in a contagion of compounded error. Apart from the rumors that split apart Moslem and Christian communities so frequently after May 1998 when a number of interest groups (some with shady military connections) continued to promote civil conflict for their own religious, political or economic benefit, we found similar problems in times of natural disaster. For example, rumor fueled very dangerous panic in Meulaboh and Padang in the days after the December 2004 Tsunami when a mistaken rumor of a tsunami triggered mass panic as people ran away from the ocean. In the case of Padang, the rumor started and spread rapidly when a man noticed the ocean height had changed and thought it signaled an approaching wave when in fact it was simply the normal ebb and flow of the tide. Having an informed media available and trusted by the people shifts the onus of truth from street rumors to authorities who can dismiss or affirm the peoples' fear. For this reason, we moved quickly into Aceh very shortly after the Tsunami struck, amongst other things, to provide surviving radio journalists training in how to deal with a scared public—in particular, handling authoritative information that guided people to food, shelters, and to locating their relatives.

Meanwhile, the events of May 1998 and the preceding economic collapse that had led to revolution and the society and its governance being thrown in the air, led us to new opportunities as things started to resettle to inject change and thus help lift the wider sentence of ignorance that had been cast over Indonesia's education of its people, to turn around a highly centralized and authority-based practice of the previous era and relate education to the newly emerging empowerment of the communities themselves.

17

The Time Was Right—Basic Education Reform

Discovering Local Commitment to Education

Indonesia's May 1998 Revolution was precipitated by interacting flaws in the nation's political-economic system: an economy unable to respond to international financial crisis as its resilience was seriously eroded by concentrated high level corruption, and a regime that had outworn the credibility of its rule by overt and covert coercion. The consequences were likely to be particularly tough for people living in remote rural areas—whose lives and livelihoods had been further impacted by prolonged drought and forest fires. As a United Nations team of Agencies, we knew we needed to build a concerted UN-wide response, realising for example, that the number of people living below the poverty line had almost doubled from 22 million to 40 million from 1997 to 1998 as the economic crisis hit. But we had very little hard information to tell us what was happening at grass roots levels. Consequently, we formed a high level 'United Nations Inter-Agency' team to conduct a 'Field Assessment of Economic and Social Crisis in Indonesia'—focusing in particular on the poorest village communities we could find. Our opening case study took us across to the poorest villages in the most remote province of Indonesia, Kalimantan (or Borneo) in the far East. Comprising the Heads of all relevant Agencies, our team arrived in East Kalimantan on 23rd August 1998, and accompanied by local Indonesian officials, set off to explore what was happening in some of the more remote rural communities.

The situation across all village areas was similar. The people were confronted by extreme difficulties following two failures in rice harvest due to drought—their last crop being brought in 18 months previously. Fires had destroyed cash crops for peppers, rubber and corn. Short-term employment in towns was becoming increasingly hard to access. And the price of rice was increasing whilst subsidized rice from the central Government was yet to arrive, even 3 months after the program was to have started. The villagers were close to the end of their resources and very vulnerable to another crop failure.

But the level of resilience in handling the crisis at a personal level was quite extraordinary, an observation that changed our understanding of how the impact of the economic and political crisis was distributed through the country. Some income was maintained through taking casual jobs in town, selling goats, growing small cash crops, harvesting rattan from forests in order to make furniture, harvesting reeds for matting and mattresses, and so on. Indeed, although radically affected by drought and natural disasters, where village people could rely on a flexible agricultural food and economy base—even harvesting from the forests—they were in general insulated from the main impact of the wider economic crisis and in a better position to cope than many poorer people living in cities.

Most strikingly, even with their livelihood resources dwindling towards almost nothing, the people in general maintained a high level of commitment to keeping their children in school. Two examples:

> Lamri, a farmer near Tanggarang, had run out of stored rice in June 1997, had survived by taking small jobs in Tanggarang at Rp7,000 or $(US)0.70 per day (at the exchange rate current in 1998 when we conducted our assessment), renting out some of his land, harvesting cassava and taking rattan from the forest, and selling his (and his daughter's) five goats at Rp250,000 or $(US)25.00 each. His family ate a mixture of cassava and rice. However, he continued to pay for his daughter's schooling in primary school - at Rp12,000 or $(US)1.20 per month.
>
> All five hundred and fifty families of a village near Kota Bangun suffered much the same level of economic impact and poverty. However, together, they maintained fifty of their children at a local university, where enrolment fees were Rp120,000 or $(US)12.00 each.

Commonly, what I found was that although at a national level, drop-out rates of children from school increased by a factor of three, from 2 to 6%, as family livelihood resources dwindled towards almost nothing, the families would do all they could to *maintain* their children in *the level of school where they were enrolled*, that is, primary, or junior secondary, and occasionally tertiary, but when their family income hit the wall, the parents would not be able to handle the jump to the next level, that is, from primary to junior secondary, for example. And besides, the children were a labour resource at home, able to help with gathering forest products, bringing in the crop, weaving, and so on, that is, as a source of additional income.

What was inspiring at the same time however was the way that the communities came together, as with the village near Kota Bangun, to support their kids' education—even under the most dire economic circumstances. But the parents were not involved in the schools or the decisions that were made, usually centrally by government, about their children's education. It seemed to me that we were missing an enormous opportunity.

Therefore, along with this recognition of courage and commitment to education at village level came the germ of an idea: let's *build* these ties between local communities and their schooling of kids, so the communities can be stronger in keeping their kids in school and having a serious voice in improving the quality of their children's education. In retrospect perhaps the idea is pretty obvious. At the time though we had been playing around the edges, not unlocking the key, and we had no idea of just how much work was involved in converting the current national system that was nurtured— by philosophy, organizational culture and even access to additional corrupt finances for senior officials—by *centralized* policy.

Officially, as was the case generally in Indonesia, as the shackles of the Soeharto era were cast off, official policy increasingly extolled decentralization, a policy that promoted principles of democracy, community participation, equity, justice, recognition of diversity among regions and the need to strengthen local governance, and which was formalized in two 'Decentralization Laws' Numbers 22 and 25 voted through Parliament in 1999. decentralization Policy directly aligned with the idea of local community-based education engagement. But to implement decentralization seriously required turning around the large and committed juggernaut of the State apparatus. Resistance was built into the floorboards of every organizational platform with which we could work.

In response to the double political and economic crises, serious financial intervention was already starting to flow by mid-1998 from the World Bank and other multilateral funders. The funding was in the form of scholarships to very poor children and block grants to schools—*administered*, as one might expect, *through the central government system*. But it was clear that neither of these funding mechanisms was sustainable in the longer term. When the money ran out, the people would be back where they started. And very little was going to be achieved, including with even establishing a basic platform for decentralized decision about what to do next. This, the Social Safety Net or SSN project was however important in helping people get through the crisis. It lasted from its inception in 1998 for 5 years. When the SSN project terminated in 2003, it was demonstrated that the poorest 40% of participating children had gained 63% of the scholarships while the richest 40% had acquired 18%, so whilst the help did not end up entirely in the hands of the poor who most needed it, overall performance wasn't too bad. Getting past the crisis was one thing though; long-term sustainability was another.

If they, the parents, could take the responsibility however, and actually be involved in *helping* the school, maybe we could catalyse the development of a sustainable long-term system that would even manage to thrive when things got tough again.

Thus, was born the 'Creating Learning Communities for Children' or 'CLCC' program we collaboratively introduced, an initiative that ended up before I left my Indonesia-based UN job in 2006 as national strategy across the whole of Indonesia backed by many millions of dollars in development assistance to put the transformation into place. The financial sustainability key we recognised was that whilst it does take very considerable financial inputs to *turn around* a nationally centralised rote-based learning system in such an enormous and complex country to a local community-linked open education enterprise, once introduced, the cost of continuation is no more than the cost of education under old ways. The idea caught on to become a wild fire. Once introduced, a CLCC school never returned to the past and usually served as a model for local grassroots copying. Teachers, parents and the children loved the idea of working together in the education process.

Charting the Way

UNESCO had already tested some of the ideas for putting such a community-centred education system into place.

Planned in 1995, funded by UNDP, collaborating with ILO, the program was implemented under our guidance by the Ministry of Education and Culture, from June 1996 onwards. Final results indicating what had really been achieved were just starting to flow in as we started to look towards the future. We had been assisting the government to develop and introduce more locally oriented education materials, but found they were coming across the same blockage country-wide, lack of decision-making capacity at local levels *within* the schools—particularly at the level of Principals and Head Teachers. The test project therefore sought to answer the question of how to develop the school as a local decision-making entity, our 'Managing the Delivery of Local Content Curriculum' or MDLCC project. We worked with 36 schools in the poorest areas of the three poorest districts in Lampung Province, South Sumatra, introduced micro-financing to assist the young people to use their newly acquired skills to develop local enterprise. We also needed to provide lots of training for Head Teachers and Principles as this was a totally new approach to making their teaching relevant.

What the project primarily achieved was to establish a carefully tested model and curriculum materials for the Government to scale up to more general application. More importantly though, the project opened the door for the CLCC project as it showed us just how much work had to be done to develop managerial capacities at local levels for *any* local community oriented schooling system to be put into place.

Furthermore, we had also been assisting the government on general literacy development in poor communities; and in design and support that brought together eight Ministries, including Health, Agriculture, Trade and Industry, Home Affairs and so on, along with Education and Culture in a coordinated Distance Education program generated out of Indonesia's Distance Learning Network (IDLN). As a specific hands-on approach to local skill development for poverty alleviation we had introduced a test of continuing education linked with income-generating activities for low-income families in Karadenan village, Cibinon sub-district, Jakarta. Together, these elements helped us see what now had to be done.

Our first step was of course to assess what was the real scope of the problem with which we were dealing. Consequently, immediately after my Kalimantan mission, we introduced a 'Rapid Assessment' of the impact of the economic crisis on education across Indonesia', again with support from UNDP, implemented under our guidance by the Ministry of Education and Culture, and this time, also in collaboration with UNICEF. Reporting by December 1998, we found, perhaps as expected, an alarming level of 'dropouts' of children at the end of primary school and very few new students enrolling in Junior Secondary Schools.

We clearly needed to move quickly rather than just continue to study the situation. So, we started—with a final pilot in an area of the overall plan where little had been done before, the strengthening of the capacity of parents through Parents Associations to support the schoolteachers in management, financing, monitoring and in the teaching–learning process.

A Momentary Aside on Accessing Money and the UN System

I had to raise the money to start. This was an opportunity that arose out of immediate crisis and was not foreseen in the normal UNESCO planning process that had been put into place 2 years earlier with the blessing of all 190 Member States. And besides, UNESCO's overall activities budget at that stage stood at somewhere near $(US)500 million, about level with that of a medium-size developed country's university.

UNESCO is not a Funding Organization, but a Specialized Technical Agency, a mantra I have been drawing to the reader's attention for the whole of this book so far. I'm actually not too sure in its pure form that this separation between funders and experts in multilateral organizations is all that helpful any more. It worked within the UN system when the roles and responsibilities of agencies were clearly defined, and UNDP really was largely a UN-wide 'bank' accessible for the Agencies focusing on technical expertise in specific areas—health, children, industrial rights, and so on, to draw from. But the international funding context has increasingly tightened over the last few decades, so what we found is that those that have the mandate to raise money for development implementation—in particular, UNDP and UNICEF, increasingly take charge, even though the best technical expertise may be elsewhere. In parallel, the Bretton Woods institutions, in particular the World Bank, had moved increasingly into the territory of the specialized agencies—usually with *hired* international consultants to fill in the expertise gap rather than in-house and local expertise. Those with the cash had tended to become increasingly self-referent in their reliance on expertise … and colonizing of the mandates of 'technical' agencies.

I should also add that I do not believe the Specialized Agencies should, or are kitted up to take over long-term development implementation. This requires an order of magnitude shift in logistical capacity. But Agencies like UNESCO can move quickly in developing new ideas and making sure they work *before* they become enshrined in long-term high-cost development models. The constraint of large funding and longer-term development assistance is that usually this requires a much more elaborate government agreement and approval process through Planning and Line Ministries. UNESCO's front line of relationship with government at field level is through what is usually called a 'National Commission for UNESCO', a government supported body *required* as a condition of joining UNESCO, that draws together the *numerous* government Ministries which UNESCO's mandate serves—across education, science (including environment), social science, culture, media and informatics—with civil society inputs. Approvals, support, and influence through a range of government Ministries is then very much more flexible than it is when embedded in a formal planning and approval process. So, we could come up with great new ideas—and here being a 'technical' group working across nearly 200 countries really does make a difference, that is, in knowing the latest pilots or ideas that seem to have legs. And as far as I was concerned, our job was to test the ideas, and carry through these tests to all the stages of implementation that were required to really make the idea work in practice, make sure long-term funding and political support was in place, and then .... *hand the project on!* In particular for anything to do with community development this process may need to take several years. But there is a clear final line drawn in the sands of time, where large scale implementing agencies should take over. It's just that the 'big guys' are not in the same position to come up with and quickly trial the idea in the first place.

The lines of mandate and agency were still running a moving battle however within the multilateral community. One of the most fundamental problems that lies at the heart of enhanced inter-Agency *cooperation*, a desideratum of both the governments that fund the United Nations, and of the UN official line as well, lies in the structure and culture of the Agencies themselves. As was particularly the case for UNESCO, Headquarters of UN Agencies generally tend to be somewhat insular, even in strongly field-oriented Agencies such as UNICEF, WHO and UNDP. Headquarters tend to be complete and well populated worlds of like-minded officials and experts needing to prove themselves to their political Member States, where business is focused strongly on the Agency and its performance, and where expectations, career goals, and evaluations—are to do with Agency performance rather than wider cooperation. Multilateral financial organizations like the IMF and World Bank, members of the so-called Bretton-Woods institutions, have an additional problem. They are accountable *only* to the 26 or so advanced industrial countries that form their governing bodies. Consequently, the Board of the World Bank includes *no* developing countries. While ostensibly pursuing a mission to support the world's debtor countries, what they are offering is soft loans rather than untied assistance and the shots are called in reality from the distance of well-paid officials and the politics of rich country interests. Institutional cooperation across the UN-Bretton-Woods boundary can be problematic, in particular, as the level of finance available on a loan basis, in particular from the World Bank, is orders of magnitude above what the UN can afford to give. The result not surprisingly is that he who has the money calls the tune, further skewing overall development objectives towards the perspectives and culture of Washington and western industrial ways of doing things.

Where cooperation works between UN agencies is *in the field* where the teams of all Agencies are relatively small, in close contact with each other, and where Agency Heads meet frequently—both formally and socially—in pursuit of whatever national crisis or goal is currently confronting them *as a group*. I personally found that cooperation with the World Bank fundamentally depended on the openness, perceptiveness and clout in Washington of the specific local Country Director through whom Washington perspectives were channeled and the atmosphere of either arrogance or care the Director fostered amongst his or her own staff. Usually however, the UN remained financial supplicants rather than equal partners.

The consequence of all this for the development of the newly conceived CLCC program was that we had to raise the money in an environment where my own Headquarters bureaucracy had its eyes (and systems of support) turned more inwards towards ongoing Headquarters-led global initiatives than to urgent response to a 'remote' field-defined priority, and where cooperation with other UN Agencies and bilateral development assistance agencies *at field level* made a lot of sense—for we had a common and urgent goal. We were all collectively seeking to deal with the same national political and economic crisis. Mobilising funding and developing partnerships, by the way, was a task that in general, occupied probably a quarter of my direct managerial time, and formed the backdrop to *all* initiatives my staff and I worked on together. Overall, to do the job effectively, I generally needed to raise around four times the funding allocated to me via Member State agreement each 2 years and the consequent Regular Program budget.

Serendipity played its part.

I mentioned in Chap. 13 that in the middle of the May 1998 Revolution I found myself in the paradoxical position hosting two colleagues from Headquarters, René and Moufida, while we completed final negotiations with ASEAN about jointly hosting a high level International Culture of Peace Conference scheduled for September 1998 ..... and then having to orchestrate René's and Moufida's precipitous escape from a rapidly deteriorating situation of civil unrest. Well, the Culture of Peace Conference came off successfully in September, bringing with it UNESCO's Director-General, Federico Mayor, to launch the occasion in Jakarta in cooperation with ASEAN.

Every Director-General had his or her own personal style. They all necessarily are highly political animals and usually love to come to a country

17 The Time Was Right—Basic Education Reform

bearing gifts. The problem in Federico's case was where the money for the gift was going to come from. Often the organization's Sectors had to do financial handstands to find the backing that had suddenly been newly committed. When he came to Indonesia however it was abundantly clear that the country was still in major crisis and Federico Mayor wanted to help—particularly as the organization's commitment to fostering a global 'culture of peace' had his strong personal stamp on it, and here he was in Indonesia for a major Peace Conference at a time when the country was reaching forwards to newfound principles of democracy out of major civil violence. I should add, the benefit of having the Director-General visit the countries for which you were responsible as his official Representative was that one had the chance to spend significant amounts of time with him, or her, while we drove to the next official engagement, or while briefing, or even occasionally while just sitting together and waiting. And one could show the Director-General what was actually going on. When a Field Director visits Headquarters, it was often very difficult to arrange any time to be fitted into the Director-General's overburdened schedule, and if possible, a 'long' meeting rarely lasted much more than a quarter of an hour, most of which was probably going to be spent with the Director-General telling you of his latest key priorities and what he expected of you as his Representative out in the developing countries world remote from Paris.

Having been already well schooled in never letting an opportunity go by for asking for money, I took Federico to meet with the United Nations Coordinator (appropriately briefed to say good things about UNESCO) and with the other Agency Heads, where we talked about our joint assessments of the impact of the political and education crisis. Our conversation swung rapidly to education and to the germ of an idea about developing a community-based system. Federico immediately gifted my Office $(US)150,000 to prime our project development pump. We started straight afterwards with the design and implementation of the pilot on strengthening parent involvement that I mentioned earlier.

I had found that to raise money from other Agencies it was always important to have some yourself, to show commitment and to stand somewhat taller as a supplicant. It made a lot of sense to collaborate with UNICEF. They had a presence in their own field implementation offices through the country that UNESCO could never aspire to; whilst we had a capacity in expertise in developing education innovation, training and monitoring that could help UNICEF a great deal. Fortunately, I had a very good personal relationship with the Indonesian Director of UNICEF, another Stephen, Stephen Woodhouse. I brought the project to him, and he immediately agreed to match the UNESCO Director-General's funding.

We now had some substantial funding in place, $(US)300,000, and could start being serious.

The one thing I felt was absolutely critical however was that this was not going to be just an 'education' project. Whilst there were absolutely fabulous innovations emerging from education expert dialogue, there also tended to be a mind-set that focused on the process of pedagogy and 'educating' rather than on building community engagement. I insisted that our project was both an education and social science-based activity. This criterion turned out to be critical.

We then settled in to design where to go. UNESCO had a limited Social Science capacity, none of which was officially located in my Office amongst regular program staff. I had had to make do by hiring young people trained in social science where I had appropriate contract money, but mainly take the responsibility personally—having been a Sociology Professor myself for over two decades before joining the UN. There were several players in developing the design, in particular, my own Education Specialist, Ayako, and UNICEF's Yoshi, along with both our local Indonesian education support people. The design we came up with had three legs to stand on.

> The first leg was school-based management – train the local principals and teachers in managing their own school, get the community involved, make the finances transparent, for example, through reports on a large white board of where the money was coming from and going, a fundamentally new principle compared with Indonesia's previous rather more hidden ways.
> The second leg was community engagement – not just getting the parents to come to meetings, but training them, for example, in management, in education; encouraging them to assist the school with whatever capacities they had, for example, in school repair; and assisting them to complement the school education process with external tutoring and quality time with their own kids. Most importantly the parents were now involved in seeing how the school operated, where there was a gap in money that could be shown to obviously matter, they now started to be engaged in looking for a source of the finances themselves.
> The third leg of the design was 'joyful learning' – turning the classroom structure around from forward facing rote-learning promoting desks to project clusters of desks and chairs; building a library resource, no matter how limited; training teachers in new ways to engage the children in creative activity.

The combination of these three legs gave us a very strong design stool as platform for making community engagement work. At heart however was the fundamental transformation at government and institutional level to *decentralize* education management. At this stage, *everything* was centralized.

First Steps

We initiated the project in our first batch of 64 general and Islamic 'test' primary schools in early 1999 in three Indonesian provinces, West Java, East Java, and South Sulawesi. One key design criterion for selecting the initial target sites was that we had a local UNICEF Provincial Field Office nearby and could therefore provide more serious back-up and monitoring as we tested our new model. We divided responsibilities between UNESCO and UNICEF according to our respective strengths. UNESCO was responsible for agreed project design, funding, and supporting the National Project Coordinator and three Provincial Project Officers, for review of similar previous projects and other back-up activities such as the development of a Training package, national-level Training of Trainers (TOT) and technical assistance that brought together the social science/community and education elements of the enterprise. UNICEF, on its side, was responsible for field-level activities at provincial and district levels, monitoring and related activities of the Provincial Project Officers, activities at school clusters and school levels, and provision of block grants to the participating schools. We had negotiated full support from the Ministry of Education and Culture at its most senior levels. Given their new-found commitment to decentralization they were delighted to try out this community-oriented experiment. To concretize this cooperation commitment, we set up Task Forces of relevant government officials and representatives of NGOs concerned with education. It was their job to coordinate and supervise project implementation in the existing school cluster system. Although we were maintaining a strong guiding hand and keeping a very careful eye on things at the start, we were already conscious of the need to bring in 'participation' and ownership of those who would have long-term responsibility for national implementation. For it was they who would eventually carry the responsibility for dissemination and replication of the ideas we were testing, and therefore, the project's long-term sustainability.

There were several hard parts—particularly as managing their own affairs was a completely new idea for many of the local school principals and senior teachers who up to this point had rested behind the highly centralized controls and directions that emanated out of Jakarta, and who had little experience of encouraging community engagement in the education process. Training in new ways was therefore an essential ingredient for even getting the project off the ground. At the start we targeted this training out in the field at local school levels, but over time we realized that we had to do serious work right back up through the entire national system to Headquarters of the Ministry for, as with all organization cultures that are embedded in the past, it turned out to be very hard for many to even know how to 'let go' of centralized control and to work out what new systems had to be introduced from the very top right down to the classrooms in the most remote of Indonesia's Provinces. Control from the center under the old scheme was complete—even down to the purchase and distribution of pencils to schools in the most remote of jungle environments in West Papua. Indeed, at senior levels in Headquarters there were many good reasons to not let go. This was not obvious at first. But as the project increasingly needed to pay attention to releasing local schools from the iron stamp of totally centralized authority through fostering the decentralizing process right back into Headquarters we started to realize that decentralization was a significant threat to the most senior officials. For decentralization meant the signing over to others of the authority to sign for the millions of dollars that flooded through the senior echelons of the Ministry to the Provinces and local schools systems from the World Bank and other development assistance agencies. We did come across examples of deeply seated corruption attached to control from the center of this money flow—where small percentages of large amounts would drop off along the way. But, perhaps more importantly, letting go of the money trail also meant letting go of apparent power and organizational arrangements that both expressed and supported this power and were deeply embedded into existing 'safe' patterns of management. Eventually, as we obtained serious funding for project implementation—from 2002 onwards in particular from the support of New Zealand and later, Australia—we built a UNESCO sponsored team inside the Ministry itself so we could work alongside and support the Ministry quite directly in this transformation.

Of course, we could not do all the training ourselves and had to develop a 'multiplier' effect into our design as rapidly as possible. After all, as the final target of change we were addressing a school system that in 1997 was seeking to reach 29 million elementary school children and nearly 10 million junior secondary school students. So, we focused on the 'Training of Trainers' our TOT component. By October 1999 we had developed our first Training Package for teachers and principals and went out to field test it in rural schools in Pandegland, West Java. As always, we learnt a lot from the gap between theory and practice and used the subsequently revised 'package' as

17 The Time Was Right—Basic Education Reform

the basis for our first Training of Trainers sessions held in Mojokerto. Our students were the National and Provincial Government officials and NGOs in education from Mojokerto and the three pilot sites whose job was then to go out to train grass-root level school headmasters, teachers, Parent and Teacher Associations (PTAs) and community leaders in their own localities. We found that a particular strength of the training program was that the key stakeholders did their training together rather than separately. For this led to greater understanding between the different groups and greater transparency of the whole process. It was a design principle of building trust into the project.

But the hardest part to deal with at first was just what strategies were going to work to bring the communities into a whole new engaged relationship with their local schools. We quickly learned however that the communities were ready waiting for the opportunity, and that there was an enormous empowering potential in aligning school-based management internally with community involvement externally. To assist the local principals, teachers, PTA, and community leaders to see how they were doing we developed a Manual of Indicators and Guidelines that allowed them to analyze progress in participation and more clearly identify the varying roles they each played.

A key innovation was the planning and budget whiteboard! The school principal would write up the flows of school finance on a whiteboard that he or she would then display to the assembled parents and citizens as the basis for developing school plans by the community and school together— never tried before. The whiteboard budget and plans remained on display. There were two important effects—the introduction of transparency into allocations of funding for the school—of considerable importance in minimizing the temptation of corruption at local levels, and provision of the chance for the community to see where there were gaps that perhaps they could do something about themselves. Indeed, by the end of the first project period, 2000, many schools reported sharp increases in parents' monetary contributions. We complemented this school-based management principle of the whiteboard with small block grants to the schools for them to actually have some money that they could manage, thus introducing a fundamentally empowering factor into engaging communities into their children's schools.

It was also important to show parents and community leaders what they could do. We therefore introduced training in assisting the school with maintenance and in teaching, promoted the development of out-of-school tutoring sessions managed by parents, and perhaps most importantly sought to change the culture of education at home— by encouraging parents to turn off the TV at night and talk with their kids about what was going on in their schooling. Meanwhile, the introduction of AJEL, 'active, joyful and effective learning' started to make a highly visible difference in what happened at school. Children no longer sat in rows learning by rote, but at small project tables. Even with miniscule resources, tiny library corners were established, and children were encouraged to do things for themselves, to be creative, to learn by doing rather than by listening and copying. The parents could see the effects in their children's' faces and excitement and were enchanted, becoming increasingly committed to strengthening what was for Indonesia a new way of promoting primary school learning. And primary school is a lot more basic to what education means particularly in rural communities in Indonesia than in most countries of the West. At the time we were developing this CLCC project, 30% of children 18 years of age and younger who graduated from primary school either did not go on to junior secondary school or had dropped out. Of the poorest 20% of the population the proportion of young people with only a primary school education was nearly 50%. So many in Indonesia, particularly amongst the rural poor, had no experience of education beyond these first few primary school years.

By the end of the initial 18 months implementation period late in 2000 we had extended the project to cover an additional Province, East Indonesia's Nusa Tengara or NTT Province, whilst the number of schools we were working with had extended to 95. At this point we established an independent external evaluation of the project led by two international consultants with a lot of school-based management experience internationally. The evaluators found that the school-based management initiative had helped to create a new atmosphere and sense of responsibility in school management—more open administration, better informed and capable decision-makers and the capacity of the school to self-evaluate. Meanwhile, AJEL had improved students' motivation, extended learning hours for extra tutorials, helped reduce absenteeism, repeaters and drop-out—thus leading to improved learning. The teachers could see this too. The evaluators therefore found a new attitude emerging amongst teachers to their work, higher levels of motivation and an increased sense of professionalism. The openness and transparency encouraged parents and community participation and the building of trust amongst the key stakeholders.

The education process was therefore being quite fundamentally transformed. The CLCC project was sized up against recently developed criteria of 'public good' in education policy and passed the test in each of the six values-based criteria: equity, access, choice, growth, efficiency and harmony. But whilst a better learning process is highly desirable, this is not an end in itself. Rather, what matters is how the students improve. And they did. Even by the end of 2000 there were clear indicators of progressively higher test scores of learning progress of the children involved in CLCC schools.

Moving on to a National Program

Through 2001 the Government of Indonesia fully committed to the CLCC initiative as the cornerstone of the government's efforts to raise the quality of basic education in Indonesia's new decentralized and democratic environment. The Directorate of Primary Education within the Ministry adopted CLCC principles as the Government's official policy and the program was now fully a joint program between UNESCO, UNICEF and the Government, having moved well beyond its initial status as an experiment led by UNESCO, supported by UNICEF within a framework of government approval. Indeed, the CLCC program bedded in beautifully with the wider initiatives the Indonesian Government was taking to decentralize education. By now the majority of funding for basic education was delegated to districts and increasing amounts were allocated directly to the schools. School committees had been established as official policy and District Education Boards established to provide more local overview and to lobby for proportionately higher education expenditures in District level government budgets. All of the Provinces and Districts that were involved in the CLCC program had allocated substantial funding to disseminate the program in their areas, and a number of bilateral donors were becoming very interested. Within another 2 years, and with the CLCC model firmly in hand, government introduced a new Education Law (No. 20) ratified in 2003 which firmly located the CLCC model as official policy, with principal responsibilities for management and resources for the delivery of education now, as a matter of law, to be transferred to lower levels of government, including to the schools themselves.

What we then started to find was that we were having enormous difficulty meeting the emerging demand. By 2004 we had trained 4,000 practitioners in CLCC principles and methods, but the demand was accelerating. Coming from the grassroots rather than from central policy initiative as such, parents from nearby non-CLCC schools started trying to move their kids to the new-wave schools; teachers in non-CLCC schools were clamoring to bring the innovations to their own school environments. Both UNESCO and UNICEF therefore committed to continue and to build the program. We were on a roll. But again, I had to find the money.

Through 2001 we found enough funding for steady expansion and reinforcement of the schools we had been working with already—extending the project now to 124 communities in 7 districts in the 4 provinces we had targeted. By the end of 2001 we had been able to generate considerable interest in New Zealand—backed up by evaluation teams that came up to Indonesia and my own visit to the relevant New Zealand officials in Wellington, New Zealand. New Zealand committed just over $(US)3 million to expand the project over the next 3 years to 1,000 communities and 6 provinces. By New Zealand's own aid criteria this was a very strong commitment. We signed off on our New Zealand partnership in May 2002. Now we were really cooking. Furthermore, both the World Bank and Asian Development Bank committed to introduce the CLCC approaches into some of their own very well funded Basic Education initiatives.

I retired at the end of 2005, blessed with the realization that the CLCC initiative really had made a difference.

Before the advent of the CLCC program, the resource envelope dedicated to school-based management and decentralized school management in Indonesia was negligible. The New Zealand Aid (NZAID) commitment of $(US)3 million through 2002–2005 allowed the initiative to bed in strongly throughout Indonesia and stimulated the interest of both the Indonesian Government and the wider donor community in CLCC principles—most commonly known through Indonesia as the MBE or school-based management movement. Funding was provided by Australia's AUSAID through UNICEF of $(US)2.7 million to expand the CLCC program through an additional 13 districts across 7 provinces, and separately, added another $(US)5 million to expand the MBS principles ('manajemen berbasis sekolah', the acronym being SBM when translated into English) to an additional 3 districts in one province; private sector funding of another half million US Dollars allowed the CLCC program into an additional 6 districts across 3 provinces. And the Indonesian Government committed (US)1 million, and USAID committed (US)10.1 million from the national budget over the 2002–2004 period for support of MBS in 20 districts across 2 provinces. The program now was setting the pattern for basic education across 42 districts of Indonesia. The European Union was preparing to commit very substantial funding, and NZAID, having reviewed the program's development, decided to fund a second phase of the CLCC program from 2007 to 2009. Perhaps most important of all, as a signal of the grass-roots fire that CLCC had lit, by the end of 2005 local governments undertook to use their own budgets to scale up the CLCC program to schools other than the 1,500 or so covered by our own direct support—expanding the total number of participating schools to 3,364, whilst the central government used the model to support a school cluster in every province in Indonesia.

National coverage is only however a context for the children receiving a better education. The final proof lies in improvement in the children's educational achievement. Our own assessments across a sample of 41 schools showed consistent improvement in reading, writing, maths and science performance. Scores for reading in the earliest days of schooling—Grade 1, for example, improved over the 2 years from 2003 to 2005 by 16%, and Grade 5 science by 12%. NZAID complemented these data by their own independent assessment, using a sample of 24 schools and visiting every CLCC province. NZAID concluded in the second half of 2005,

> The quality of learning outcomes is positive; school-based management processes are being progressively embedded in the governance and management of CLCC schools; and there is strong community commitment to their schools.

The difference to pre-CLCC days could mainly be felt however in the classrooms. Instead of sitting passively in rows for delivery of rote learning, the students were now engaged, sitting in small groups around tables and involved in open-ended and creative learning tasks such as investigative assignments in science and social sciences, actively presenting poems and stories in their own words. The students were now surrounded by classroom walls covered in displays of their own work, and able to explore basic library and resource collections for themselves. Whilst Soeharto's New Order Government had exercised dictatorial control over the people, what people officially knew and what children were taught came, along with the management of educational resources, from the center. Now, decentralization of thought followed decentralization of management and control right into primary school classrooms and into a newfound encouragement for children to think for themselves—a basic cultural tenet of democracy.

By the time I retired and handed on responsibility for the program to my successor at the end of 2005, the program was directly supporting 1,496 schools in 40 districts across nine provinces, local government supported introduction of 'School Based Management' further so the overall number of participating schools was 3,364 whilst central government was using the model to support a 'school cluster' in every province, and was now the guide for other major funders of education nationwide. After 2009 UNESCO was expected to steadily withdraw from the CLCC initiative, having finished our part of the job, that is, testing the idea, making it happen and securing its support and national ownership for the long-term future. The 2006–2009 strategy, developed in 2005 was planned primarily as a transition—building capacity and ownership within government and at local levels to continue the job for themselves. It was for this reason that we built a UNESCO-Government team inside the Ministry of National Education in order to work directly together to command this transition process.

Opportunity out of crisis! The CLCC program reinforced a fundamental lesson for me of how one should try and see when as a change agent one is searching for a path towards a better deal for the people through the massive problems associated with underdevelopment and civil crisis that continue to characterize much of the Third World. At the heart of this path is provision of the stimulus and initial resources to help people to empower themselves.

Including the Islamic Factor

But there was more to do.

Whilst things were going well for the national education system, we also recognised that targeting CLCC in the national education system alone was not enough. In fact there was in many ways a bigger problem elsewhere.

The national school system covers only 87% of school enrolments in Indonesia—under the auspices of the Ministry of National Education (MONE). The other 13% of children attend Islamic education schools, or Madrasah (Arabic for 'school'). These schools are administered under the separate Ministry of Religious Affairs (MORA) which as a religion-promoting Ministry included education within its larger portfolio of concerns, but, with a highly centralized system of administration, had little interest (or intention) of seriously cooperating with the Ministry of National Education on decentralization and sharing of educational budgets and objectives. That is 6 million children (according to 2004–2005 figures) were likely to be excluded from the CLCC and MSB initiatives. Here lay a significant series of educational problems. We wanted to do something about them.

Madrasahs have a long history in Islamic education, the first of such schools being founded in Baghdad in the 11th Century AD. Whilst in Indonesia the Madrasah formally follow the national curriculum, and students sit the national exams, also being able to transfer to national schools, the main emphasis of the Madrasah schools is religious—following the original traditions of teaching classical traditions in Arabic linguistics and the Koran through a lecturing pedagogy and rote learning. Ninety percent of Indonesian Madrasah were funded privately—from benefactors, Islamic Foundations, or the local community—but funded poorly. A direct result was that teachers were paid poorly as well, so 83% of elementary school teachers lacked undergraduate degrees and only 2% had a degree in core teaching subject areas whilst 73% of elementary school principals were unqualified, a figure that remained at 37% in junior secondary schools. However, Madrasah largely provided education that would otherwise be too expensive in the national school system for the very poor—particularly in rural communities. According to the Asian Development Bank 84% of the parents of Madrasah students had incomes below the regional poverty level.

Indonesian Madrasah—administered as privately funded enterprises under a religion focused Ministry, therefore offered poorly resourced, poorly taught, religion-focused education largely to poor families. Not surprisingly the children performed badly in general education subjects: in the 2006 National Exam for example, Madrasah students trailed national school students in student performance in almost all subjects in almost all provinces. Students from Madrasah tended also to graduate with very poorly developed technical and job-related skills.

It was not however the case that the schools resisted the possibility of improvement or, for that matter, the introduction of more secular elements into their curricula. What mattered was maintenance of the ideological and moral character that Madrasah supporters associated with the strong Islamic philosophy of dedicated Madrasah schooling. So, introducing change was a question of balance. We therefore did not wish to threaten the religious character of the education, just complement this with a better general education.

Indeed, UNESCO had already conducted some quite significant pilot work under a $(US)820,000 UNDP grant—from 1988 to 1996—introducing vocational education into eight Madrasah Aliyah (or high schools). I had come into the Indonesia office in the last couple of years of these trials so could see the results of what we had done. Training was in areas like motorcycle repair, computer skills, welding, tailoring and secretarial skills to which were added training to turn 'job seekers' into 'job creators'—entrepreneurship training (bookkeeping, marketing, management, procurement, stockkeeping and so on). We had found it was particularly important to align the skills taught with the specific job environment surrounding the school—a lesson we put into practice in a number of other initiatives we later put into practice—in the vocational training of girls in poor communities who were dropping out of school in Indonesia, and in the training and development of employability of street children in Manila. We did discover a very important lesson in our initial Madrasah pilots in Indonesia—that if the training was specifically targeted enough and complemented by wider managerial skills development, it tended to have a ripple effect. Of the 1,600 students included in the Madrasah Aliyah project, most graduates gained employment or were able to set themselves up in a business of their own, often training other members of their family in the skills they themselves had learned, for example, in tailoring.

A story from the project that was reported by the project coordinator in our UNESCO Jakarta Office 1995 Annual Report shows what happened:

> Herlina graduated from the dress-making course in 1990. She purchased a second-hand sewing machine and started in a backroom of her parental home. Things went well and a year later she asked her friend Henny, who graduated from the same course to join her. They bought a second sewing machine from the profits Herlina had made. But the room was too small. They rented a nice room in a big house from a relative, gained experience and their products became nicer and nicer. Yet a year later they asked Herlina's cousin Ahmed who was not formerly trained in dressmaking to join them. He is now undergoing on-the-job training, taking the simpler jobs to start with. Their total income reaches up to Rp. 500,000 per month.

So, we had experience of working with the Madrasah before—introducing a more secular and skill related flavor to what was otherwise highly focused religious education, and producing positive self-generating job prospects for Madrasah graduates.

We also had experience of working with the Ministry of Religious Affairs (MORA). The Ministry was supposed to cooperate with the Ministry of National Education (MONE). Under the National Education Law 20/2003 formal integration of the Madrasahs into the national education system was legislated, a policy that was backed up by a subsequent specific Parliamentary directive to both Education and Religious Ministries to formulate a common policy and strategic framework for national education development by the end of 2006. What we had realized however was that this cooperation was not going to be easily forthcoming—primarily as MORA was not at all keen to let go of their economic and ideological interest in full control of the Madrasah system—and all Ministries in the Indonesian government anyway are basically fiefdoms with high bureaucratic walls to defend against invasion from without—that is, cooperation across Ministerial boundaries that threatens absolute control of the territory and budgets. Consequently, the two Ministries met many times to develop a cooperation agenda through 2004 and 2005, but by the end of the time I spent in Indonesia in 2005, had still to work out an agreement.

In the meantime, we worked directly with the Ministry of Religious Affairs—but introduced the principles we had been developing for the CLCC program in cooperation with the Ministry of National Education. As international 'fair witness' we sought to help with building the 'bridge'. As with the CLCC program, the principles of 'active, joyful and effective learning' (AJEL), school-based management and community participation sell themselves—as students, teachers and parents start to see the enormous difference to the education experience that follows. Under a project grant from the Director-General of UNESCO, in the course of 2 years—2003–2005—we were able to transform 45 Madrasah Ibtidaiyah (elementary) schools in Magellan district, Central Java, Mojokerto district in East Java and Gowan district in South Sulawesi—including training of all the school principals, school committees, and 225 teachers, with a wider ripple effect built in with the training of 25 'Master Trainers' who could keep the initiative running after we had pulled out.

There were a few keys to success that were quite critical in making these sorts of changes work towards more open and transparent education in the Madrasah, a traditionally quite closed and rote-learning based system. The first was to use existing mechanisms and structures so that innovations were bedded into a familiar organizational context. Second, the Madrasah schools are generally poor, so sustainability of our intervention required making the change affordable by the local community after we moved on. For example, we provided a modest block grant of Rp2 million (equivalent to $(US)225) to provide a base for the school communities to plan and finance school activities—but it was entirely realistic that in future the local communities could raise an equivalent amount. Second, we honored the religious value of the Madrasah School System, so did not focus only on building strength in mainstream literacy and numeracy skills, but, in cooperation with experts and practitioners, re-jigged the religious curriculum into a more active and joyful learning experience. And we sought a balance across the communities. In these pilot projects where we were opening up Madrasah to more joyful, participative and mainstream education, in parallel, we also introduced AJEL-friendly religious curricula in national schools. The Madrasah communities therefore could see that we were not just targeting them to reduce the importance of religion within schooling but were seeking to *strengthen* the values-based elements of education generally at the same time as we were helping the Madrasah more firmly into the mainstream where their graduates, with greater literacy and numeracy capacity, would also have a much better chance of getting jobs.

Meanwhile, across the water, in the troubled southern province of the Philippines, Mindanao, the message had spread that we were having some success in 'mainstreaming' Madrasah education in Indonesia. At heart of the 'idea' that we might help to transfer the Indonesian experience to the Philippines was the concern that many Mindanao parents were now starting to feel about their own kids. As graduates out of the traditional Madrasah, the young people simply did not have the skills to pick up jobs locally for they fell out of the end of the school system with low levels of literacy and numeracy, poor language skills … just expertise in Arabic language, in quoting the Koran and having a strong traditional knowledge of Islam. The main choice for young boys in particular was to either seek employment in the Middle East or to take on a religious ulama teacher role. Both the Philippines government as well as the parents were consequently concerned that far too often the local Madrasah were fertile recruiting grounds for the extremist Islamic groups such as Abu Sayyaf, the very violent extremist group that rocketed to international attention a few years earlier, as I reported in Chap. 3, when they captured a group of international tourists from a resort on Palawan Island and held them for ransom. (This incident occurred, I should add, just three days after I was on mission in the same area, surprised at the time that the government insisted on providing me with a 24 h close escort of two armed bodyguards.) We had been working in Mindanao in cooperation with the Notre Dame Foundation on our literacy and peace building GENPEACE program for some years now—which I introduced back in Chap. 12. We had mutually built a good environment of trust there. And, the Notre Dame NGO leader of our field work, Myrna Lim, recognized the possibilities that could well follow from extending the Indonesian Madrasah program to the Philippines. She acted as bridge. And I decided to fund a fact-finding tour of key selected people from Mindanao to Indonesia.

As I introduced back in Chap. 12, in June 2004 the delegation arrived, a group of 12 Mindanao Muslim educators and Madrasah heads from ARMM (Autonomous Region of Muslim Mindanao)—where peace between the Islamic rebels and the government had been successfully brokered by previous President Fidel Ramos back in 1996. The group was led by Undersecretary Manaros Boransing responsible in the Philippines for government education policy and strategy in Mindanao. The delegation included regional officials, key school administrators, Myrna—the leader of the Notre Dame Foundation, and the leading Islamic philosopher of Mindanao. Two of the delegation members, as we were informed later, were closely connected with the rebel MILF, endorsed for the mission by MILF and reported back to the rebel leadership later. In other words, the mission was extremely well connected for championing change within the Mindanao context.

UNESCO's engagement in Mindanao through GENPEACE had been an extremely important factor as is UNESCO's 'neutral' position politically. I was told by Undersecretary Boransing shortly after his visit to Jakarta that if the Mindanao Study Mission had been supported under US or Australian bilateral auspices (and these two countries were the main funders of development assistance to education in Mindanao) then the Study Tour would not have happened.

Feedback immediately at the end of the June 2004 Mindanao Study Mission from team members was very positive in terms of the lessons learnt and insights that were opened up by the Indonesian experience. Given that the signs were very positive I decided to 'strike while the iron was hot', and took a follow-up mission to the Philippines just 2 months later. What I found amazed me. Clearly *the time was right*.

There had been considerable progress already. The Mindanao Study Mission team had formed itself into a steering group led by Undersecretary Boransing to progress reform in the Philippines Madrasah system, in particular in mainstreaming the curriculum. A meeting of all key stakeholders (56 participants) had been already planned for 20th to 23rd August (a week after my mission). My mission was very warmly welcomed, and we held long discussions on ways of providing continuing support—particularly in technical support and 'linkage', the curricula as such being firmly the responsibility of the Philippines authorities. Boransing specifically informed me that the idea of mainstreaming the Madrasah had been around for some time, but their way forward had been blocked. The Indonesian experience of UNESCO's CLCC Madrasah schools had quite literally given the team a whole new vision. It was exactly what they were looking for and was not just an idea but an innovation that was already in place and tested. Within two weeks of my visit to Manila the Secretary of the Department of Education signed off on a policy statement of the Government supporting the activity. It was also agreed during a meeting I held with other high level education officials that the Philippines would fully support the prioritization of the Madrasah project within the overall education and peace priorities of the Philippines in negotiation with the UN and with the Multidonor support for Mindanao. Boransing was tasked to develop the official proposal.

Within a year, major changes had been introduced into Madrasah education through the whole ARMM region under Boransing's guidance and with strong local commitment.

I was very sad that at the end of 2005, UN rules being what they are, I had to retire, having reached the statutory age of 62. Sad for many reasons. But, I really hated having to put down the potential impact of expanding this 'Mainstreaming Madrasah' program across the Southeast Asian region. In the context of UNESCO's post-9/11 commitment to dialogue across religions and cultures, the Madrasah support program provided a highly practical initiative to break down the walls between different sections of the community that were riveted into place through the subsequent lives of school graduates by education systems that were isolated from each other—the national mainstream and the religious-based Madrasah. The Mainstreaming Madrasah program perhaps even more importantly, addressed the education shortfalls that were endemic in the Madrasah system itself—characterized as it was by poverty and singular religious focus, together with a low level of educational professionalism of many of the (seriously underpaid) teachers. Our experience in Indonesia and the Philippines showed us that it *is* possible to open up the schooling experience for the Madrasah kids and to *not* threaten the value of the schools for the community in terms of moral and values commitment. As expressed directly to me by the responsible Minister, the Government of Malaysia was interested in extending the program as well, particularly to the northern provinces of the country bordering Thailand. Brunei Darussalam, noted for national commitment to moderate Islam, had already introduced educational programs by which Philippines *ulama* were being trained—in English, and the Government was interested in developing wider cooperation through the region within which Brunei was providing a religious education leadership. I had also found interest in Singapore in being engaged in such a sub-regional peace-oriented initiative. I most sincerely hoped now that a way would be found across the sub-region to foster support for and general mainstreaming of the Madrasah schools, and thus capitalize even further on what we learnt out of handling the crisis that turned Indonesia on its head both politically and economically back in 1998.

As has been the subtext of this whole book though, at heart of the ability to transform was self-empowerment within communities and a strong sensitivity from our side to local culture and its potential power when harnessed. Basically, what we had done really was to stimulate the *idea* and provide the support that allowed the communities to grasp power for themselves *in their terms*.

There was a curious side-play in the Philippines connection though that basically demonstrated to me to never be surprised about anything. In our first meeting held in my Jakarta Offices with the Mindanao delegation in June 2004, their head of delegation, Manaros Boransing, and I, formally introduced ourselves and delegations, then were *both* eyeing each other off, conscious that we had perhaps met somewhere before, but not knowing where. The light suddenly dawned, or glimmered really, for it was glowing out across 36 years of our lives. Way back, like way, way back, he and I had both been students in the very first MBA program in Australia. This was in 1965 at Melbourne University's Graduate School of Business. We had been drinking buddies and had very fond memories of the time, both of us being somewhat curious about what happened in the meantime to the other—as I moved on into a Ph.D. and an academic career and Manaros seemed to disappear somewhere in the more remote reaches of Mindanao. He had in fact been building himself up as an education leader with a firm commitment to his Mindanao roots. Needless to say, our realization of a past life together was a blessing on our ability to now rapidly build trust and develop the cooperation that helped the Mindanao educators so quickly to put the Mainstreaming Madrasah program into place.

Whilst the Mindanao delegation visit and subsequent Islamic education initiative in Mindanao followed from my meeting with Manaros Boransing in June 2004, by the end of the year, as additional stress on our ability to make a difference from within our United Nations role, we were suddenly confronted by the most incredible destructive crisis we could not have even imagined, but which, in our United Nations role, we needed to deal with. This was the December 26th so-called "Aceh Tsunami" that impacted across the whole Asia Pacific region and killed hundreds of thousand people.

18

Tsunami—"The Day the Ocean Moved"

The Monster from The Deep: The Earth Shook

At 7.58 am on the morning of 26th December 2004 the fourth largest earthquake in the last 100 years hit the Indian Ocean floor, its epicenter between the Indonesian island of Simeulue and the west coast of northern Sumatra. The earthquake, with magnitude of an enormous 9.0 on the 'Moment' Scale (or measurement of scale of the original shock)[1] suddenly released centuries of steadily increasing strain on the earth's crust caused by the 60 mm per year movement north by the 'tectonic plates' that carry the continents of India and Australia.

One thousand three hundred km of the India Plate boundary had slipped under the Burma 'microplate' by 15–20 m, causing a rupture in the earth's crust 1,300 km long and 150 km wide, lifting the ocean floor over a 550 km by 150 km surface by 5–6 m, thus releasing energies equivalent to hundreds

---

[1] 1 Originally, the 26 December 2004 earthquake was calculated as of level 9.0 on the so-called 'moment' scale (that is the measurement of size of the original shock), although there remains some debate. Of particular interest is a calculation evaluating very low frequency data from seismograms published in *Nature* in mid-March 2005 by Seth Stein and Emile Okal of Northwestern University, Illinois. Stein and Okal's calculation puts the size of the earthquake at 2.5 *times* that originally thought—magnitude 9.3 on the Moment scale, making it the second largest earthquake *ever* recorded. Official earthquake size still remains at 9.0 by the US Geological Survey. The 'Richter Scale', by the way, is a measure of 'energy released' and requires complex triangulation of measurements from different seismometers so takes time to calculate, is not very good at measuring very large earthquakes because of its mathematical basis, and mainly, is not easily related to physical characteristics of the original earthquake. In spite of it often being quoted in the media the scale is rarely used any more.

of billions of megatons of TNT explosives or a thousand Hiroshima Atomic Bombs.

And the Ocean Moved

Three hundred and thirty thousand cubic kilometers of water moved, releasing a wave pattern in the whole ocean from the floor to the surface that whilst only a metre or so in amplitude in the deep ocean, was 100 km in wavelength and traveling at 700 km an hour.

Fifteen to twenty minutes later the resulting Tsunami hit the coastlines of Indonesia's Simeulue and Nias Islands and Aceh Province. Arriving at the speed of a Jumbo Jet, the energy distributed over the 4 km column of ocean from floor to surface was massively concentrated as the seabed shelved up to land, delivering an initial welling up of water of around 6–8 m, followed by a massive second wave up to 20 m in height and a smaller third wave.

The 'Black Water'

Earthquakes are relatively familiar in this part of Indonesia as the province sits on top of Indonesia's 'Ring of Fire'—one of the most unstable earthquake zones in the world, where the underlying tectonic plates of the planet's crust are crushing into each other with unforgiving resolute force, the stresses of which can only be released by shaking everything above.

The Tsunami however was a totally unexpected horror from the deep ocean that suddenly invaded the land and lives of Aceh.

As one of the rare survivors from the town of Calang on the west coast of Aceh later described it to us, the 20 m wave of dark churning water sped over the land with the menacing curve of a striking cobra, before retreating back into the depths with the land, the trees, the houses …the people … in its clutches. The town of Calang ceased to exist: 90% of its 7,000 inhabitants died—with many of the 10% of survivors having been swept 5 km away from their homes.

The children we spoke with referred to the Tsunami as the 'Black Water'!

These were the children who were left, many severely traumatised by the terror. Nearly 39,000 of their friends or 11% of the entire population of children in Aceh had been killed and 35,000 orphaned as their parents were swept away.

Confronting a totally unexpected crisis of unprecedented proportions, the front-line humanitarian relief Agencies of the United Nations moved in immediately to support the Government's shocked response.

Being There: First Impressions

I flew into Banda Aceh, the capital of Aceh, at 10.30 am a few weeks after the Tsunami had struck.

I had already sent up several of our staff, starting a few days after the disaster, to help re-establish the city's radio communications capability, and on emergency assessment missions.

But as it was the business of other Agencies rather than UNESCO to provide the urgent humanitarian relief that the people so desperately and immediately needed, I had kept our presence on the ground to a minimum. For at that stage, we knew that well over 100,000 people were dead or missing and maybe a half million displaced. Every day the numbers increased as more and more bodies were unearthed from under the mountains of debris. Infrastructure of much of the capital city of Banda Aceh had been destroyed, as had that of all the towns down the western coast. Food was hard to get. We feared a spread of disease. This was a time to focus on finding bodies, bringing in food and medical support, providing emergency shelter, and assisting a heavily traumatized people to cope with simply staying alive.

Things were not easy for the emergency teams who came in with the United Nations and major international relief agencies.

There was no spare accommodation. Hotels simply had ceased to exist. There was little food, disease was hovering in the air, many of the coastal roads were unpassable while transport of any sort was highly problematic until the UN could fly in its own vehicles. There was near chaos amongst the 160 or so voluntary relief organizations which had descended on the place eagerly looking—in a completely uncoordinated way—at how to apply the kind of assistance they had decided back home was bound to be needed, and where to distribute the (often totally inappropriate) aid packages they brought with them—like jumpers knitted by community-minded volunteers in Vienna and intended for Moslem women living in 35 °C tropical heat.

Out in the local community many government officials had been killed and many of those left were paralysed by the trauma, so the heart had been excised from the Acehnese government's ability to respond. The UN even stopped employing local drivers as general practice after too many incidents where the still traumatized driver simply froze with his foot on the pedals and drove straight ahead into whatever object first got in the way. The front-line relief organizations like the World Food Program, WHO, UNICEF—responsible for caring for children-in-trouble, UNHCR—the UN Agency responsible for looking after refugees, and OCHA—the United Nations Office for the Coordination of Humanitarian Affairs, confronted an enormous workload just picking up the pieces and saving the people who had made it past the trauma. Quite frankly, up until now, we would have simply got in the way.

The weather was fine when we flew in and the view was clear. The UN-chartered Garuda Flight circled the city several times for the pilot had decided that we should see the level of physical devastation that the Tsunami had inflicted. The most visible first impression was the dark stain of mud that spread many kilometers out from the shore into the surrounding sea—legacy of the backwash that sucked the life out of the island community as the Tsunami swept back to its home in the open ocean. Then I noticed the ragged edge of the shore where the Tsunami had torn away beaches, headlands, and whole residential suburbs leaving in its wake tiny islands where there previously had been solid land, and further inland a flat almost featureless landscape. This had been a thriving bustling populated cityscape. It was not until later when we had access to before-and-after satellite maps that we could see just how much of the seaside land had simply been carried away, and along with the land, its people.

As we descended closer, features of the city started to emerge—bridges, the backs of which had been broken, a flattened shopping mall, shattered monuments, the scattered bricks of a totally demolished house, twisted rusting wrecks of cars and trucks, rubble everywhere, trees bent and stripped—except curiously enough, many palm trees that had enough flexibility to sway with the force and recover. Strikingly, both the mosque situated right on the edge of the city where the Tsunami struck, and the central city mosque which had been breached by the flood waters 5 km inland, appeared to be quite unharmed. Like the palm trees, their ground floors were largely of columns, so the wave had swept through rather than confront a barrier to be pushed aside. The devastation stretched inland however in contour-determined scallops as far as 8 km from the shoreline. It was quite literally the scene I could only have imagined to follow the explosion of a nuclear bomb.

The plane flew west and landed at the city's Blang Bintang Airport, descending down past misty picturesque mountains and undisturbed tropical forests of what was otherwise a quite beautiful tropical environment. On the ground things were pretty busy. A continuous whap-whap-whap of helicopters flying in and out, the drone of landing cargo aircraft, tents everywhere housing cartons of food and medical supplies, military and international officials bustling as ants in all directions. We were picked up in a somewhat worse-for-wear van driven by a local—fortunately one who had been nowhere near the Tsunami so was not deeply traumatized, accompanied by Roesman, the senior local administrative officer I had sent up to Aceh a week earlier to set things up so I could bring in the assessment team. Roesman took us to our newly leased 'UNESCO House'.

As I said earlier, there was virtually no casual accommodation, so our only option was to find a house to rent on high ground away from the Tsunami affected zone and still intact after the earthquakes. We were following the example of WHO and the World Bank.

Roesman had done well. After considerable trouble he had finally found us a house in a relatively open area normally housing middle-level government officials. Trouble, because houses of any size that remained undamaged by the pre-Tsunami earthquake were rare, their availability to outsiders was at an absolute premium so landlords had suddenly discovered how rich they could become through charging exorbitant rents to visiting aid workers. The UNESCO House was located I might add well above the flood zone of a possible new tsunami—for this fear hovered over us as a constant threat that was made alarmingly present by the standard fare of at least three aftershocks or tremors we experienced every day. Another design criterion we imposed on the choice of house was that we could get out of it quickly to a safe place if a large earthquake struck. So having an open field next to us was a godsend. Indeed in the evening after we came back to the house for the second time after first arriving, I had a large tent erected in the field next door, and we practiced exiting strategies. Our target was to get everyone out from a deep sleep within about 1 min and have somewhere to shelter that was not going to be dropped on by large buildings or telegraph poles. Our people were encouraged to go to bed dressed adequately for instant public display when escaping, i.e.: my 'official' instruction as a UNESCO rule: "always wear pyjamas to bed". We also had had an engineering assessment done on the building by one of the UN experts who checked out whether the house was structurally safe. There were quite a few cracks. But, it seemed the structure was strong enough to withstand another reasonable sized earthquake without immediate collapse. We still said a few prayers.

The house passed the test. Nevertheless, I did find the inside layout somewhat disturbing. It had not quite been completed. In characteristically Indonesian style, the lower floor was connected to an upper half-floor via a sweeping semi-circular staircase in a large central open room. The problem remained however, that the handrails on either side were yet to be installed.

So, I lived in mortal fear of bodies stumbling over the side in the darkened gloom of mid-night earthquake-inspired panic or the whole staircase collapsing onto those sleeping in the open room below. The house was however about the best we could find and it came—admittedly at a significant price—with the owner's old car thrown in and his son as our driver.

When we arrived, we spent just enough time in the house to throw down our luggage, organise who slept where, meet the security guards, and quickly suss out the exit routes—including over the balcony, across the garage roof and down a couple of creepers for those in the furthest upstairs bedroom from the staircase.

Confronting the Task in Front of Us

I had brought the UNESCO team up to Aceh to assess priorities including for rebuilding the human infrastructure of the society so that the people themselves had the strength to do it themselves and knowledge to know what to do and publicly communicate—quite centrally our business. We had a broad brief.

Under our education umbrella we were looking at getting children back into education—although UNICEF was responsible for looking after the kids in the meantime and the massive rebuilding program of schools about to get underway. Our focus was particularly on refugees and children not in school as well as rebuilding the content of schooling. We were also looking at supporting the university and its ability to provide local expertise-based knowledge to support the relief effort rather than have to depend entirely on external consultants. Additionally, many essential labour skills had been lost with the enormous loss of life, yet those left did not have jobs any more as so much of commercial enterprise had been destroyed. There was a pressing need therefore to develop highly targeted training, particularly for people in the resettlement camps. We focused of course on skills in greatest demand in the immediate rebuilding program.

Furthermore, under our science and ecology responsibilities we were assessing what was needed for regenerating the environment. So much land had been swamped by salt, so much of the coastline ecology—both in and out of the water—devastated. In line with our communications mandate, we were already assisting the radio stations that, as I talk about in Chap. 16, we had brought into our own 'Local Radio for Democracy' network a few years before—all of which had been damaged, and two totally destroyed. Again, training was important early. Many journalists had been killed and new skills were needed, so the remaining journalists could guide the process of finding and releasing appropriate information in an emergency situation, for example, notifying people of where to get food and services, helping to find lost members of their families, providing information that people could trust in order to avoid the immensely destructive voice of rumour spreading as a wildfire through a panicked society. We had scientists from UNESCO's International Oceanographic Commission checking out base data on the Tsunami and its impact, such as measured height of the waves, and our own Office staff working out how to develop workable communication and escape plans to cope with a recurrence should it happen. Finally, along with Ministry of Culture officials we were assessing both the tangible and intangible heritage that had been lost. To take one extreme example, the 'frame drum' is a central element in Acehenese traditional music. All but one craftsman who made the drums had been killed.

After we arrived, our first priority for the mission was to obtain field briefings from each of the operative agencies in order for us to assist both to orient and identify where we could make our best contribution plus to obtain a local take on the level of risk we confronted from a recurrence of earthquakes or another tsunami. So, we headed off as quickly as we could to meet them.

We had travelled from the airport to our house by a route that stayed entirely on the south-western side of the city, that is, away from the north-eastern section hit by the Tsunami. Our drive to the UN agencies remained away from the disaster zone as we travelled along a ridge that had escaped the deluge. We did however start to see some of the damage … shopping centers reduced to rubble by the earthquake, collapsed houses, and debris from collapsed buildings. The road itself however was now relatively clear.

We arrived at the UN compound. They had taken over a sporting complex well above the inundation areas of the city, erected twenty or so large tents on the tennis courts where staff could sleep, taken over a half dozen buildings on the site for central administration, a first aid center and a very very basic canteen. Outside the canteen was an open covered area where we could sit while eating the bulk-served meal on offer at that time. At least we had food though. For staff who were on the scene within a few days of the Tsunami the only food they could get was a very basic fried rice once they could find a warung or small café that had been able to open. It took several weeks before small food markets started to appear—again with limited produce mainly transported in from Medan or from further south in Sumatra.

We spent a few hours touring the agencies to find out where things stood. All were desperately busy and reeling from the enormity of their job. As with many emergency situations such as this, the existing UN country team was overwhelmed with handling both the emergency and still maintaining their ongoing business. Consequently, the emergency field offices tended to be populated by many short-term employees brought in for the job. Many were quite young but handling very large budgets. As most were also trying to prove themselves with an eye towards longer term employment, and they had very little knowledge of the local country programs and expectations, we did find real cooperation was difficult. Despite the coordination attempts by OCHA (The United Nations Agency for the Coordination of Humanitarian Affairs), Agencies did therefore tend to work along their own individual lines rather than fully share in a collaborative task—particularly those with the most funding.

I then decided we needed to see what it was we were addressing, so we drove down towards the northwestern side of the city. Around 6 km from the ocean we entered what can only be described as a war zone. Everything, but everything was destroyed. Any vestige of a house that remained was twisted off its foundations or partially in ruins.

We pulled up at the address of one of the radio stations we had been supporting in Aceh, Radio Nikoya. We confronted nothing but piled slabs of cement. I had personally opened this station back in 1999 along with the Danish Ambassador, Michael Sternberg, who had provided the backbone of financial support for our joint venture in building a radio network throughout Indonesia after the fall of President Soeharto's censorship-prone New Order Government. I still had the photograph—bunting across the street welcoming both Michael and I, celebrations with the local crowds, the inaugural broadcast, and .... a suburb of trees, houses, scattered commercial buildings and people—thriving, living and 'normal'. Not anymore. Turning on my heel around 360°, all I could see was a grey debris-strewn flattened landscape. The only people around was a handful of survivors picking through the remains of what once had been their life.

The owner of Radio Nikoya, who came with us to show what was left, told me that his brother, previous operator of the station, had been on the early Sunday morning shift and had been killed there along with two of the station's journalists. Within 3 months, with our assistance, Radio Nikoya was back on air.

We found similar stories of simply 'handling' and breaking through this major crisis with the other UNESCO-network radio stations we visited in both Banda Aceh and Meulaboh, an even more devastated town 150 km south of the capital, Banda Aceh.

The other radio station we visited the next day in Banda Aceh was Radio Prima. Their station and transmission equipment had been totally destroyed.

But here we found the entire staff of journalists camped in tents in the owner's backyard on higher ground, a temporary transmission tower erected next to the house, and the station broadcasting from a kitchen table. In the case of Meulaboh, much of the entire coastal city had been destroyed. Radio Dalka, one of our stations, had been completely gutted, a clear tide mark on the walls at three meters showing how high the wave was when it struck—two kilometers inland, sweeping away or trashing every bit of sound equipment we had provided 6 years earlier. BUT, as signal of the immense drive and courage of the Achenese, the owner then took us up the steps to the attic of his house next door. It survived although water had flooded the entire downstairs area. In the attic in extremely makeshift conditions, Radio Dalka continued to operate with equipment they had either scrounged or had donated as emergency support from other radio stations in our UNESCO network across Indonesia. Radio Dalka was getting on with business in spite of the fact that the owner had lost 44 members of his family although his wife and children had survived. When I walked outside again I spoke with a journalist from the station who had survived. He had lost his wife and two children—just three weeks before. The journalist told me that when the first wave came—around 6 m in height, it swept him and his family away. Through the black water he finally caught sight of a palm tree which he was able to grasp. Holding onto the tree, the journalist only just made it back to the surface through the debris and climbed higher. As the water receded ten minutes later he climbed down from the tree and started to search desperately for his family in the water—now about a metre in depth. Thirty minutes later, and totally unexpectedly however, the second wave came. And this one was enormous—a black wall around 12 m in height. Again, he was swept away and was convinced he would die. Somehow, he managed to swim through the churning walls of debris and back to the surface again. Eventually he found a roof top refuge. He never saw his family again. He was now trying to report the news of other peoples' tragedy but conveyed a very deep sadness behind a brave smile.

Back to Radio Nikoya in Banda Aceh. The owner told me the story of his brother and as I continued to stand in some shock on the collapsed concrete slabs that was all that remained from the station, I had inaugurated just a few years before, I then noticed an old motorbike laying on its side a few meters away. It was covered in mud. On the handlebars was a woman's purse. Still attached. The woman had been carried away by the Tsunami.

We drove further towards the sea. The road towards the ocean was half washed away and littered with the twisted wreckages of cars that had not made it out in front of the wave. We came across the half-demolished walls of a house where someone had written (in English—presumably for the foreign visitors) "26 Dec 2004 Sunday Morning Call" and then around the side, "Knockin on Heaven Doors". The rest of the entire landscape in all directions was flat—the occasional wall or twisted skeleton of a house interrupting the overwhelming perception of total annihilation. Occasional palm trees still swayed in whatever breeze that swept across the land. Amongst the remains of what one could just make out as previous streets and house lots were a few flags—posted there with the owners name, claiming possession against the carpetbaggers coming in from the hills illegally claiming land on the basis that it had belonged to their kin, now deceased, and with the legitimacy of ownership unable to be established given that many property ownership records of the government had been swept out to sea or were seriously damaged. Apart from these momentary glimpses of humanity, what we saw was a landscape of the total bleak grey aftermath of Armageddon.

We saw some people who appeared to be trying to lever a half-destroyed car out of a ditch and stopped our van. A couple of the stronger male members of the team ran across to help. A moment or two later we realized that the supposed owners of the car were in fact looters stripping the car of its tires. We moved on with the feeling we were in a post-Apocalypse Mad Max movie.

Finally, we arrived at 'Ground Zero', the ocean-front village of Ulee Lheue that first received the full-frontal attack of the Tsunami. Virtually the entire community had been obliterated. Just 2% of the children were still alive. We wandered around in a daze. Devastation was so complete. A family came down in a utility truck to what was left of the house next to where we were standing—collecting remnants of a past life from the ruins that remained. They seemed too enthusiastic to have been the original owners. There were tiny poignant remnants of the daily world that had so suddenly been torn apart ... the shattered frame of a family photo, a shard of clothing, a twisted kitchen pot.

We noticed that marketing had already begun. A small 'toko' or tiny shop, had sprung into existence just in front of the ocean-front mosque at Ulee Lheue and was selling cans of soft drink and odd snacks. Further along the road a young man with a small stock of ten or so petrol cans—with petrol siphoned off from who knows where—was selling petrol to any passing motorist who stopped. We bought some petrol as the van was running far too close to empty and we still had to get back. The options were pretty limited.

The village was connected to the rest of Banda Aceh by a road bridge—still, in spite of serious damage, intact. Located on the other side of the bridge, the land side, was the ocean-front mosque I mentioned earlier, still standing and relatively undamaged. On the Ullee Lheue side of the bridge was a tree, one of the very few fully grown trees to survive. We were told by a local who had survived that when the twenty meter wave arrived, *twenty meters!*, 21 people had been saved by that tree. They had been carried into its branches by the force of the first wave, clung on, and waited. The final wave of the Tsunami swept by, and then the people found a way to get down. You could see the height up the tree where the Tsunami had engulfed it—totally stripped of branches from a split trunk. The height of the damage marks was around 20 m.

We talked with a policeman whose police van was parked nearby. As it turned out he was a local. We were standing in the remains of his house. The Tsunami-precipitating earthquake had hit Ulle Lheue at 7.58 am on Sunday 26 December 2004. At level 9.0 on the 'moment' scale, it was a very powerful earthquake so immediately caused considerable damage and scared the hell out of the locals. The policeman told us that his house remained intact however, so he headed uptown to assist where the earthquake had caused the collapse of the central Banda Aceh shopping mall. The Tsunami hit 20 min later, obliterating his home, and carrying off his entire family. He was still uptown so survived, not knowing at first what had happened down on the shore. When he came back to his house nothing was left. We looked at his former house. The tiled bathroom remained partially standing, and that was all … except for a half-broken drinking glass cast into the rubble from its use at the family breakfast that was so rudely interrupted by the arrival of a twenty-meter-high wall of rampaging ocean. When we saw the policeman, he had parked his official police vehicle outside his former house and was watching, monitoring people coming into the neighborhood, perhaps still hoping that something in the will of Allah would change and his family might suddenly reappear.

As we drove uptown again, we passed an open mass grave, a twenty-meter tall oil storage tank swept 500 m away from its companion tanks and into what was left of the local village, a crushed school, pile after pile of debris.

Then we came across a ship—of several thousand tons. It was 5 km inland, and parked in the middle of what had previously been one of the main roads into the central business district, towering over nearby houses that had survived. Already the locals had cleared a way around it for traffic to get by. The ship had been previously moored in the harbor, its enormous generator being used to provide supplementary power to Banda Aceh. The Tsunami had simply picked it up, all crewmembers clinging on, and given them the ride of their lives across the crushed houses of the city. No-one could work out how they were possibly going to move it back, so the ship was likely to stand as a permanent memorial to the sheer power of the Tsunami, but a useful one. Its power generator had not been damaged. Now the auxiliary power source for the city was even more conveniently located than where the ship had been previously, down in the harbor. The house immediately in front of where it had come to rest was relatively undamaged. It was an awesome sight from their front verandah, a ship 30 m high just 10 m away.

In the center of Banda Aceh, not far from the city's main mosque, we came to a people's park—around 3 km from the ocean. It was early Sunday morning when the Tsunami hit. Many people had come out to the park—exercising, jogging, playing with their children, or just sitting having a picnic breakfast. Out of no-where the Tsunami suddenly flooded through …. 3 km inland and 5 m high! No-one could possibly have expected it. Many died. A memorial remains. In the centre of the park is an old DC3 airplane, raised on a pedestal that put it beyond the reach of the ocean surge. This is the Seulaway Plane—donated along with a second aircraft by the people of Aceh to the Indonesian Independence Movement at the end of World War II—one of the many signs of Aceh's continuing commitment to independence and their fight against colonialism of any sort, including the internal neo-colonialism of the Soeharto regime that triggered the founding of the revolutionary Free Aceh Movement or GAM during the 1970s. The Seulaway Plane subsequently pioneered the establishment of the national flag-carrier, Garuda Indonesia. Now, it stood there as the only object not swept away, having presided over the horrific breakfast session of 26th December 2004.

Travelling On

We travelled on this Mission for several days through the Tsunami-affected areas of Aceh—in particular down the western coast to the town of Meulaboh around 150 km south of Banda Aceh. At that stage the roads generally were blocked or torn away by the ocean surge, so in many places access was only possible by ship. For us, we had no choice but to fly, lining up with other UN staff leaving Banda Aceh's military airport by UN charter aircraft. Virtually the whole coast was black—from mud and debris and pools of inky water—deeply salinated up to a few kilometers inland. Very few buildings of any sort remained—except, dramatically, yet another mosque, this time standing totally alone in the coastal town of Calang. The entire town had been annihilated and the people washed away. But not the mosque. We flew over Lhok Nga, just south of Banda Aceh, the place where scientists working with UNESCO had measured the Tsunami surge to have reached its maximum height. At Lhok Nga, the evidence was dramatic, for clearly visible from the relatively low flying aircraft was the skeleton of a totally destroyed large scale cement works, capsized ships in the harbor, palm trees cut off to mere stumps and then draped in necklaces of shattered cement held together by twisted iron reinforcement bars as the wave washed back over the land and retreated into the ocean. The wave, arriving at the harbor at around 20 m in height had washed up the mountain behind the cement works to the height of 34.6 m—or 113 feet for those of us who grew up before decimal measurement arrived.

Officially, access to much of the western coastal area was still under strict military control with travel normally requiring special advance approvals and a military patrol as support. Five kilometers inland were still no-go zones, having previously been basically under the control of the GAM independence movement—although locals told us the rebels only really tended to appear in the villages at night. There was a strict curfew: no-one from the UN teams was allowed to travel after dark, so, given the uncertainty of road conditions, one had to be pretty careful how you planned a trip out to the villages, and delivering humanitarian relief was a nightmare. After landing at Meulaboh however, we did travel out of town as far as we could go, primarily to talk with people at a couple of the displaced people camps. We traveled around 8–9 km inland—well into the so-called no-go zone. However, we confronted no sense of threat. Indeed, although a couple of 'incidents' had occurred with military escorted convoys traveling through the area immediately north of Meulaboh being shot at just on the edge of dusk it was seriously suspected that these incidents were contrived by military sources seeking to discredit GAM. The rebel movement itself guaranteed the safety of all international aid officials and as far as we knew, fully honoured this pledge. GAM leadership was delighted that at last their cause was opened up for the world to see.

I should add, by the way, things were a lot tougher in Meulaboh for the UN staff than in Banda Aceh, as far more of the city's accommodation and infrastructure had been destroyed, and getting goods in was very difficult—with no road access, a damaged harbour and only a small provincial airport to handle air cargo. The 'transit' lounge at the airport, needless to way, was no more than a green military tent; transport was non-existent unless you knew someone who still had a car, and facilities to do anything were either scarce or contrived with considerable ingenuity out of whatever was around. Next to the 'transit' lounge was a small, old, barely functioning motor scooter with rapidly improvised sidecar made from a slab of wood and a bicycle wheel. The vehicle was freshly painted white, and its 'official' status signaled by the letters 'UN' proudly but roughly painted on the side and on the rear. The side-car platform held a computer bag. The motor scooter really was serving as one of the rare UN vehicles that were around in the early days.

Physical Impact of the Tsunami

As I have shown already, the physical impact of the Tsunami was obvious as soon as we arrived.

Infrastructure

The level of damage to Aceh's infrastructure was added up a month after the Tsunami at the end of January 2005 in a World Bank led assessment (in which my own Agency, UNESCO participated) prepared for the donor community within the so-called 'Consultative Group Indonesia' or CGI. The Report found that 1,900 km of local roads and 400 bridges were damaged—with 120 bridges being destroyed through the whole western side of the province, thus cutting the access roads for delivery of humanitarian relief to the isolated villages. Eighty percent of the power lines, and most of the public services were destroyed.

One thousand, five hundred and eight two schools were damaged or destroyed—25% of all the schools across the whole Aceh province.

Meanwhile, the total estimated economic loss for Aceh was 97% of Aceh's GDP—although as the Asian Development Bank reported, the economic impact was surprisingly less severe than in it would have been in other parts of Indonesia or in other countries due to the lack of heavy industry and tourism in the affected areas and little damage to oil and natural gas.

The Environment

Twenty-five thousand hectares of mangroves, 30% of 97,250 ha of previously existing coral reefs, and 20% of 600 ha of seagrass beds were damaged—with an estimated overall economic loss of $(US)675 million. Approximately 300 km of coastal land area has been degraded or lost partly by destruction and removal of land and subsidence (caused by the original earthquake), but mainly from the massive levels of salination that was delivered to the land by the ocean moving ashore.

Coastal reefs—particularly within the first 10 m down from the ocean's surface—were damaged from breakage caused by the force of the waves, debris washed into the ocean from human settlements, and sediment returning to the sea which suffocated the reefs that remained. A team from my own Office led by Jan our marine science specialist along with government scientists who we funded, conducted our own underwater assessment of the waters to the northwest of Banda Aceh. The divers came back with photographs of not only dramatic damage to the reefs themselves but poignant reminders of the associated human tragedy. Resting amongst the remaining coral you could see the shattered remains of household furniture and kitchen utensils, even the odd computer.

Meanwhile, signaled amongst the reefs were contradictory forces of survival. Shortly after the disaster, the diversity of reef fish had markedly decreased, yet fish such as the Powder Blue Surgeon Fish could still be seen around the heavily damaged and silted reef areas. These fish were instrumental in the regeneration of the reefs because their feeding off the damaged reefs keeps the reefs clean long enough for the corals to re-grow. But, given the shortage of food and income for the people, the Powder Blue Surgeon Fish were also targets for fishermen—a terrible tension of immediate survival versus the sustainable ecology needed to support long-term food supplies.

As with the damage to the reefs observed here, there are both primary and secondary consequences of the environmental damage to the land and its flora.

Some areas previously used for aquaculture and rice growing can *never* be recovered due to their salination. Meanwhile, the people could not wait to rebuild their lives. They were coming back and rebuilding almost immediately out of whatever 'found' materials they could scrounge—well before government had a chance to start any form of serious rebuilding program. Additionally, sites for temporary resettlement were being chosen urgently. However, the most basic condition of the viability of human settlement is the groundwater table and its impact on the availability of potable water and capacity to absorb sanitation. This posed a major problem. The Tsunami had wiped out water supply infrastructures in many places. The flooding by seawater and the spreading of pollutants from waste, chemicals, and decomposing bodies during and after the Tsunami had caused deterioration in existing ground water quality. But the basic data was missing so agencies making choices about where to settle the people were operating in the dark. In the short term, immediate assessments of groundwater quality and salination levels were therefore vital.

A number of agencies, in particular, FAO, UNOPS, UNICEF, UNESCO, UNDP and WFP, became involved in establishing these urgent assessments. At the high-tech end we, that is, UNESCO, assisted the Government of Germany to bring in sophisticated helicopter-borne 'spatial electromagnetic surveys' to assess coastal zones flooded by seawater. The electronic beams could penetrate down to 150 m as they mapped the level of saltwater intrusion into the layers of groundwater. At the lower end of the technology spectrum, local scientists started to move in to conduct simple village-to-village assessments of groundwater quality and work directly with communities to help them make the right decisions before their drive to rebuild closed out better location options. The salt pollution in places was horrific: in measurements our own hydrology staff took of some surviving village wells in Banda Aceh that previously provided the peoples' drinking water, the level of salt was so high that the water's conductivity—the indicator we used—was off the scale of our instruments.

Massive infrastructure damage was bad enough. What happened to the people was horrific.

19

"The Human Story of the Tsunami"

Whilst the physical impact of the Tsunami was obvious as soon as we arrived, we could only imagine the terror that the survivors had suffered. However, as we travelled through Aceh and had the chance to talk with survivors, the *human* story of the Tsunami emerged as an increasingly poignant and complex tragedy.

The Deadly Game of Collecting Stranded Fish

The first signs of the approaching Tsunami were seen by the locals as a fascinating curiosity. No-one had any idea of what the signs meant—except, very significantly, people from the island of Simeuleu who had built tsunamis into their folk legends and who escaped by following the guidance of Simeuleu mythology—a story I will return to shortly.

It was early in the morning. Although they had just experienced a very noticeable earthquake, most people believed once the shaking had subsided that the immediate danger had passed. Because it was early on a Sunday morning and a holiday for most people, many families along the coast had wandered down to the beach for a picnic, to exercise, play together, or simply to watch the waves.

Then the waters of the ocean receded—out to up to a kilometer off shore.

Because they did not know what this heralded, many people, particularly children, were enchanted—and ran out onto the sands to collect stranded and jumping fish.

But while they were playing on the suddenly exposed ocean floor, the thin line that had formed across the whole horizon off Banda Aceh grew in height to 6 then 15 m, or 54 feet, and then exploded onto the beach as a 'smelly, oily, black wave' that swept all before it. It was followed 30 min later by an even bigger wave. One survivor interviewed by Mercy Corps Indonesia's Media Officer, Debby Tomasowa, reported that the wave was so high that it left fish on the side of the hill where they sought refuge: the people on the hill survived on those fish for the two days they were stranded.

And it was not only the impact of the wave surges that mattered, but also the wash returning to the ocean—for it was this force that sucked many of the victims out to sea. A Maldives Government Official who I was working with on a science policy project phoned me in late January 2005 and told me that the body of an Indonesian woman had even travelled as far as his own family's island in the Maldives around 2,000 km away from Aceh, and had just been washed up on his beach. And as I observed earlier, the power of this receding current could be seen in high relief at Lhok Nga just south of Banda Aceh where cement and steel remnants of a building were left wrapped around the stumps of remaining partially amputated palm trees.

The Scale of Human Tragedy

The sheer scale of human tragedy was mind-numbing. After the search process was exhausted, BAKORNAS, the Agency for National Coordination, published the final figures: 128,515 people had died in Aceh and been buried and another 93,837 remained missing—presumed dead, with an additional 154 people being killed or missing south of Aceh in North Sumatra. There will be some overlap in these figures for Aceh as many bodies were buried without being able to be identified. What is clear however is that Aceh absorbed the majority of the impact of the Indian Ocean Tsunami—suffering over three-quarters of the quarter million people confirmed to have lost their lives or still to be missing across the whole Indian Ocean region.

Another 513,278 people were displaced in Aceh with 151,600 of their homes being damaged and 127,300 destroyed.

Perhaps most disturbing of all was to see the impact on the children.

Thirty eight thousand, six hundred and eighty three school children were killed, or 11% of all the children in Aceh province. Thirty-five thousand children were orphaned or separated from their families. Along with this, 2,245 of their teachers were killed or went missing and another 3,000 were displaced—thus rendering them unable to teach, and as I mentioned earlier,

1,582 schools were damaged or destroyed. The impact in the most affected areas was of course overwhelming. At the ocean front village of Ulee Lheue in Banda Aceh only 2% of the children could turn up to school again. The rest of their fellow students were dead.

These figures had enormous implications for re-building education, one of UNESCO's mandates—along with UNICEF—which moved quickly in cooperation with the Government to repair damaged schools and get children back. Our own role in UNESCO was mainly with 'out-of-school' children in the IDP camps (or Temporary Living Centres—TLCs as they were locally known).

A disaster of such momentous scale produced deep wounds in the social and institutional fabric, the consequences of which were not always visible at first, like for example, the impact of three times as many women as men being killed—because the women were on the beaches or in their coastal homes while the men were at work on the ocean or out in their fields away from the ocean. And there was a disproportionate number of the people killed who were government officials and professionals—for paradoxically they were more privileged, with houses in pleasant locations near the sea.

However, the story of the Aceh Tsunami was not only one of human disaster. It was also one of the human response and courage of the Acehnese people, a story in which the sheer scale of the disaster shocked both Government and the Acehnese Independence Movement into negotiations that were successful in bringing peace to a province that was previously deeply troubled by civil unrest.

The Shadow of the Wave

What became very apparent on our journey through Aceh was that the danger and the fear had not gone away when the wave swept back into the ocean.

There was a continuous series of earthquakes and aftershocks following the enormous 26th December 2004 quake, indeed 513 in the first 6 months. Even before the day was out on the eve of the disaster, another 13 aftershocks had hit Aceh. As I observed a little earlier, even when we were there on the present Mission a few weeks later, we experienced three or more serious earth tremors every day. And these tremors could not be dismissed as of little importance, for the earth under Aceh and its adjacent Sunda Trench remained very unsettled. Three months after the Tsunami, on 28th March 2005 another major shock occurred, the massive 8.7 magnitude earthquake that struck Nias and Simeulue Islands not far to the west of Northern Aceh.

The people, still picking up their lives from the impact of the earlier earthquake and Tsunami were now visited with even more enormous damage and loss of life as the associated shocks confronted them. On Nias, 623 people were confirmed dead and a further 48,000 people affected. The 26th December 2004 earthquake appeared to have touched off or presaged a cascading impact that progressed southwards down the Mentawai island chain as the earth re-adjusted. The island of Simeulue rose by two meters, Nias tilted—rising one metre at one end and dropping a metre at the other, whilst Siberut, south of Nias, rose one metre, and because of its location down what looked like an evolving chain of connected faults in the earth's crust, Siberut was feared to be the possible site of yet another super earthquake. Indeed, as I mentioned in the last chapter, Siberut *was* hit shortly after the Nias earthquake, in the early evening of Friday 8th April 2005, by another series of large earthquakes, this time with magnitudes of between 6.1 and 6.7. In my Chap. 11 where I was presenting the broader story of our development assistance work in Siberut, I report talking by satellite phone with Koen, project manager in our UNESCO field office there, when the first of the earthquake shocks suddenly started to tear down the office around him. To add a bit more detail and colour to the story, I then stayed connected to Koen while he ran, escaping into the clearing outside, meanwhile hearing with considerable fear the destruction going on around him. Once outside, Kuhn finally returned his attention to the phone and reported what was happening. To my considerable relief Kuhn had escaped without injury. Not quite the more normal conversation one has with a member of staff about project management. Our Office on Siberut and a number of nearby buildings were damaged, but injuries were light as Siberut was a very undeveloped place, so the built environment was largely of traditional houses. Then, on Tuesday 12th April, Mount Talang volcano erupted, 49 km east of Padang on the coast of Sumatra east of Siberut, causing immediate evacuation of 25,000 people on the mainland. A day later, and further south down the progressive chain of disturbances two other volcanoes showed radically increased earthquake activity—Krakatau in the Sunda Strait and Tangkuban Perahu near Bandung on Java. All events were connected. And the cascade of earth movement was very likely continue. Indeed, back in 2005 the US Geological Survey predicted a 1 in 8 chance of a major earthquake in this same region above magnitude 8 in the immediate future. They came close to being absolutely right: on 9th December 2007 a major earthquake of 7.9 magnitude rocked the city of Bengkulu on the West Sumatran coast, south of Padang, but fortunately it was not accompanied by a tsunami. Still, everyone is waiting whilst the earth rumbles beneath them.

The people of north Sumatra and its associated island chain were therefore reminded every day that they should be scared, and they remained very skittish. On 11th March 2005, there was general panic in Padang as city residents reported that a large wave was coming into the city. As a result, a considerable number of the population emptied into the streets in an attempt to flee from the coastal areas. This created massive traffic jams throughout the city which eventually paralysed virtually all movement. As our own UN staff found, even movement by foot to our designated 'evacuation points' was difficult and dangerous with the crowds in a state of panic. We were informed of several people being killed by cars charging frantically and blindly away from the ocean, with drivers paying only marginal attention to the rushing crowds which got in the way. The incident had been generated by someone, already traumatized, noticing that the tide had risen and assuming this was signal of another tsunami, who then yelled it to his neighbours, immediately spreading a massive panic. In fact the tide flux was quite normal, but the impact of the unfounded panic paralyzed the city.

In an environment of fear, rumor can very easily precipitate an irrational terrified response that sets light to an uncontrollable fire of crowd panic. One of the first things that therefore has to be done in handling the aftermath of a disaster such as the Tsunami is to ensure the public can get immediate access to reliable information they can trust and which will extinguish the rumor torch that can so easily be ignited. We found exactly the same thing when we were dealing with the aftermath of the Moslem-Christian conflicts and killings that followed the downfall of President Soeharto in 1998. I talked about this in Chap. 13. Getting radio stations back online, getting radio receivers out quickly into the community, and ensuring the journalists knew how to handle emergency information, were clear immediate priorities for us in Aceh. This was a clear UNESCO mandate.

The Spirit of Survivors

There were some quite extraordinary stories of survival. I spoke with a journalist in Meulaboh, along with Arya, Head of UNESCO's Media Team. The journalist, Lola, dreamed of the Tsunami two days earlier and, when confronted by the earthquake, remembering the dream, she ran … and survived. A particularly strange story, reported in the Jakarta Post, is of Riza, a 26 year old clothes vendor who was living in a rented house near the coast in Banda Aceh. As she and her twin children were carried by the water out of their house—from on top of the cupboard on the second floor where they had sought refuge—Riza claimed, a large snake 'the size of a telephone pole' swept past her. She and the 9-year old twins, who were badly injured, hung onto the reptile as it drifted along on the current until they landed on higher ground where the water was just a meter deep. As Riza says, she 'slapped her face to make sure she wasn't dreaming'. Perhaps apocryphal, perhaps a true story. Myths and spirits and spirit men or dukans are often close to the surface of daily life in Indonesia. President of Indonesia Susilo Bambang Yudhoyono revealed 6 months after the 26th December 2004 Tsunami, as the chain of earthquakes continued to shatter the fabric of northern Sumatra life, that he had been seriously requested to slaughter 1,000 sheep and perform a series of rituals to stop the cascading series of earthquakes. He declined ..... and it should be noted that as an increasing number of natural disasters hit Sumatra and Java over the year or two immediately following the Tsunami, there was an increasing sense amongst survivors of personal moral responsibility, that is, that the society had been breaking the moral principles of Islam and had brought the disaster on themselves in retribution. UNESCO was receiving reports after the earthquake that devastated Yogyakarta in June 2006 that many children whose families had been directly affected by the earthquake were afraid to attend school due to intimidation from other students who blamed them for the disaster. Several reports came in from people we had contracted to assist in the recovery—of ritual collective suicides apparently in response to the victims' feelings of personal moral responsibility and belief in God's retribution. Dreams, spirits, dukans, God's retribution—were all intimately woven into the fabric of meaning that survivors of disaster have stoically worn since the Tsunami.

Recovery

The rapid rebuilding of schools had a very important impact on the wider capacity of the people to recover. People we spoke with observed that the fact that the children were returning to school re-injected the first sense of normality back into their shattered lives.

Not long afterward, that is, by the middle of February 2005, the markets were starting to get back into action and you could see signs of business enterprise re-emerging out of the rubble.

However, even with signs of normality returning, recovery was still a long and troubled process. The Tsunami clawed deeply into every aspect of Acehnese life, claiming not only the survivors' family and children, but also eroding the survivors' moral certainty and ability to respond—even once they have come to terms with the loss and were seeking to move on.

The fact that so many local government officials were killed meant that there were just not many people left in local government who could take action—and many of those who were left remained deeply traumatized.

The same differential impact also affected the expertise base that could be brought in to support recovery, in particular from the main university in Aceh, the University of Syiah Kuala in Banda Aceh.

The University of Syiah Kuala was nominated by the Government of Indonesia to act as the local source of higher level technical expertise to support the recovery and rebuilding process, so the University's knowledge capacity was intended to play a central role in Aceh's regeneration. The core of this capacity however had been quite literally swept out to sea. Fourteen smaller private universities were destroyed entirely.

We went to visit the University of Syiah Kuala and to talk with key senior staff who were left. The University had lost 213 staff through the Tsunami, whilst another 521 lost their homes. The University buildings were completely undamaged as they had survived the earthquake unscathed and were well above the Tsunami wave surge. However, as we sat around the meeting table of the Rector's Office, sipping cups of tea in what appeared to be a quite 'normal' Indonesian university environment, and as the Rector spoke, we increasingly came to the realization that whilst the physical structures remained intact the human capacity of the institution had been seriously hollowed out. What was particularly significant was that the academic leadership of the University was disproportionately torn out of the institution. One hundred and ten or just over 50% of those killed were the most senior faculty, the senior professors, as they, like the government officials, lived in the better suburbs by the ocean—and, as the Tsunami hit early on a Sunday morning, were at home not on campus which, being located back from the ocean on higher ground, was spared.

What happened to Syiah Kuala further demonstrated the second level weakening that followed from the crisis, that is, in the on-ground capacity to plan and implement a government response.

The Problem of Rebuilding

Again though we come back to the complexity of responding to a crisis such as this. At a central level, government was concerned to prevent people moving back to areas that may be affected by a future tsunami of a similar magnitude as that of 26th December 2004. A 500 m Green Zone was originally declared, that is a zone stretching 500 m back from the ocean where no one was allowed to build or develop their communities.

Unfortunately, the local people were not waiting or paying attention. Within months after the Tsunami, they were re-building where their original houses were—near the ocean. Fishermen needed to be near their boats and could not imagine separation by a half kilometer or more from on-going commitment to the practical tasks of protecting, launching, unloading and maintaining them. Inhabitants of fishing communities in particular made it very clear that they simply could not survive if they must live far from the water; and many of the people we spoke with recognized that the chance of a tsunami returning in the near future was quite small, so they were therefore prepared to take the risk. Finally, the 500 m Green Zone concept faded away. When the new supreme authority for rebuilding Aceh, Indonesia's Agency for Rehabilitation and Reconstruction (BRR), came into being at the end of April 2005, the head of this authority, Kuntoro Mangkusubroto, decided that priority had to be given to people getting back to their lives rather than the enormously complex task of moving an entire people away from the ocean and building what were tantamount to city-block sized mountains for their escape—a plan that was seriously put forward by Central Government as a first Action Strategy.

At first there was a general consensus, particularly amongst other Agencies, and even in my own Headquarters, that the science arm of our UNESCO mandate within the United Nations should be held to our side until after the urgent humanitarian relief had been delivered and immediate reconstruction of shelter was well under way. However, it started to become very clear to us at field level after only a few days that scientific assessments were an essential input to the decisions that had to be made very early, even, or perhaps, particularly, during the time when greatest concentration was being paid to providing food and rebuilding houses.

What was urgently needed was science and scientists to work with the communities. I have already talked of how essential groundwater assessments were to choosing where people re-settled. Additionally, scientists were needed to make assessments of the specific local mitigating conditions against the possible impact of another Tsunami, that is, of the specific geomorphology of the ocean floor and land to see which areas were most susceptible to inundation, and to test the ideas that were current that mangroves and other plantations may make a difference in reducing the force of the wave. This is using science to help the people learn, to empower their own decisions.

With little evidence to go on, the Government and many NGOs that bankrolled local communities to do the work adopted the idea that planting mangroves as a set of buffers was the way to go in mitigating the possible consequences of another Tsunami. Quite frequently however, in the rush to implement, little or no expert support was brought in to guide the local communities. As a result, the planting operation all too often was a failure. The seedlings were planted indiscriminately rather than following a strategic mitigation design, and often in the wrong place so even the plantations themselves were unlikely to survive. But the faith in mangroves, even when planted correctly, rested on shaky foundations, and the number of natural mangrove areas remaining on the most vulnerable western coast of Aceh prior to the Tsunami was quite small anyway. The evidence simply was not in. We started to have a good look, and sent off a team to get hold of comparative data for other countries, particularly, Thailand. Still the replanting charged ahead in Indonesia, with the need for scientific evidence swept aside.

Additionally, some early scientific assessments had to be made of the detailed affect of the Tsunami before the signs, for example, of wave height, disappeared. This detailed information was essential in developing field-based plans of settlement areas less likely to be affected by a future Tsunami, and deciding on strategies for mitigating the consequences should another Tsunami arrive on the shores of Aceh.

Responding to a disaster such as the 26th December Tsunami was a complex process—in particular as everything had to be done urgently and there are so many interacting domains. It is also clear that science must work hand in hand with communities from day one to assist both the recapture of peoples' lives as well as the rebuilding of the physical and human infrastructures that sustain their future.

Response by the International Community

Response by the international community was quite extraordinary.

Although the UN identified the need in early January 2005 for less than $(US)1 billion for urgent relief, over $(US)4 billion was immediately committed by governments and private donors. Indeed, by the end of the rebuilding program the world community had pledged $(US)7.2 billion and delivered $(US)6.7 billion.

One hundred and sixty four NGOs came to help in Aceh with a multiplicity of agendas. Many were mainstream and experienced, but also included were some rather unusual groups such as the Prison Fellowship Indonesia, Team Albania, Youth of the Street Australia and the Scientologists.

Outpouring of such generosity brought with it some real challenges.

Management of a complex emergency requires detailed coordination at both federal and local levels. However, communication at all levels—between departments and between Jakarta and Aceh, was problematic at the best of times. Whilst $(US)4 billion may have been 'committed' in the early days, only about 80% of the money found its ways into the UN's hands directly (a lot going into military ships, helicopters and so on, supplied by individual donors). Additionally, donors contributing to the UN's so-called 'Flash Appeal' fund, nominated who they wanted the money to go to rather than contribute to the fund as a whole. This caused us problems. UNICEF, for example, was oversubscribed by 214% whilst at the same time UNDP did not have adequate funding to bring the hospitals back online.

Well experienced NGOs, such as OXFAM, World Vision and Care International moved quickly into effective operation, often acting as implementing 'arms' of UN programs, delivering food and tents and so on. But many others were quite literally falling over each other in an uncoordinated way. One of the problems the UN was finding in the first weeks was the number of volunteers arriving on the doorstep—actually opening the flap of the tent in the World Food Program tent city built on a rapidly annexed tennis court, bringing willing hands but not always relevant expertise, quite literally getting in the way and taking up accommodation and food of those in need, and meanwhile, blaming the UN and larger organised agencies for lack of attention to their generosity of spirit in coming to Aceh in the first place. The volunteers often came with no backup or local knowledge. For example, one group of a half dozen highly specialized neurosurgeons from Egypt arrived offering to operate, but the hospitals that were left were desperately coping with an overburden of seriously injured refugees and anyway had no nursing or support staff even before the Tsunami who could possibly assist in complex neurosurgical procedures.

On the other hand, where well linked into need, volunteers were invaluable. Indeed, volunteers were enormously useful to UNESCO—which, amongst other tasks, took a key role along with the Ministry of National Education and several NGOs in the provision of support for children and young people who are out of school—for example, as orphans, separated, disabled, displaced along with their parents, or who were street-children or out-of-school in the first place.

In addition, in a complex emergency, aid can bring with it entirely unforeseen consequences. Second-hand clothes were often a nuisance rather than a benefit. Perhaps inappropriate for Acehnese climate or customs, the clothes required sorting and were often refused due to Acehnese pride—the people preferring to dig through the rubble for rags, as they were *their* rags. What was needed was cash—for people to buy exactly what they needed and to assist immediate development of local clothes-making enterprise.

Meanwhile, the scientologists and a number of other NGOs offered one-on-one trauma counselling, sometimes, as with the scientologists, by some quite unfamiliar laying-on-of-hands means, but inappropriate to a people who found deep solace in their religion and local community solidarity. Donations from large donors of equipment, such as fishing boats and fishing nets that did not fit local experience or conditions either went unused, or in some cases caused environmental damage from overfishing close to the shore. Other donors were rapidly present rebuilding houses for the people—but in locations that the government had already declared would be forbidden to housing in case of future tsunamis. Generous provision of pharmaceuticals and doctors had the unintended consequence as the World Health Organization, WHO, discovered, of eliminating the income of local pharmacists and doctors, and the creation of a blackmarket of pilfered drugs over the border in Sumatra.

Consequently, in a complex emergency such as we confronted in Aceh, aid does not always translate the generous good intentions of kind hearts who care into precisely what is needed on the ground; and management of the flood of goodwill can be a nightmare. What is essential is connectedness to real knowledge of what is needed at local level and then assistance to facilitate engagement of local communities in their rebuilding of their own lives.

Fortunately, the Indonesian Government acted very sensibly to drive Aceh's recovery and redevelopment towards meeting these needs, and towards eliminating the specter of corruption that hung over the possible input of very large quantities of money into Indonesian affairs. It took 4 months to set into place. However, in April 2005 the President created BRR, the Rehabilitation and Reconstruction Agency for Aceh and Nias, to handle all recovery programs, and handpicked Kuntoro Mangkusubroto as its head. Kuntoro, the former mines and energy minister, company director, academic and civil engineer, dictated his own terms—ministerial ranking, direct access to the President and a salary three times that of other ministers—a condition he insisted on to remove any temptation to dip into the vast money flows that were going to pass through his hands. Kuntoro suffered no nonsense, and with assistance from New Zealand, set up Indonesia's first internal anti-corruption unit, serious anti-corruption and accountability standards and encouraged whistle blowers. All development in the Aceh rebuilding program had to be approved and coordinated through BRR. This could have been a recipe for disaster. Indonesia was ranked 143 on the world's non-corruption index, so cynics were predicting that much of the aid would never reach the people it was intended to help whilst petty bureaucracy would destroy even the best-intentioned aid programs. Instead, however, Kuntoro brought a wind of fresh air into the Indonesian system and managed to maintain both the integrity and efficiency of the Government's operation with extraordinary energy and skill. Some corruption did occur at project level, but BRR's accounts were checked by international auditors and always found to be intact.

Right back at the start however when we first went to see, we found again and again that the Acehnese themselves demonstrated a very strong will to take on the responsibility of looking after their own lives and future rather than continue to depend on outside help beyond the immediate survival period of assistance—a key strength in Acehnese recovery.

The Historical, Religious and Cultural Strength of the Acehnese

Indeed, the Acehnese are a very independent people—strongly guided by a deep commitment to Islam—and have had this character since the ninth century when the first Islamic kingdom of Aceh, Perureulak, was established.

Since these foundations, the Acehnese went out and Islamised the kingdom of Patani in southern Thailand in the 13th Century, but refused to accept colonization from outside themselves, taking on the Portuguese in the 16th Century, the Dutch for much of the first half of the 20th Century, in the course of which they actively became involved in the Indonesian Independence Movement at the end of World War II. Indeed, as I mentioned earlier, as support to the burgeoning independence movement at that time, the Acehnese donated two aircraft, one of which the Seulawah plane, later pioneered the establishment of the national flag-carrier, Garuda Indonesia. It remained undamaged on its pedestal in central Aceh as the Tsunami surged past.

Since Indonesia's independence, relations between the central government and Aceh have been troubled—partly because of dispute over who gained the lion's share of the wealth generated by oil and gas exploration—in particular, during the Soeharto New Order Government period from the late 1960s to the late 1990s. In response to rebellion, Aceh, from quite early in the piece, was awarded 'special territory' status, allowing the province a high degree of autonomy in religious, educational and cultural matters. However, discontent remained primarily because much of Aceh's oil-based wealth was being siphoned off to Jakarta. The rebel movement, GAM, was formed in 1976, and initiated armed attacks on police and military installations.

In response, the Indonesian Government declared the province a Military Operation Zone (DOM) in the early 1990s, then again, over the last couple of years. Many complain of human rights abuses. But the territory has been largely closed to outsiders while the armed conflict continued, so reliable information on how wide-spread abuses were or even whether they had occurred or not was difficult to obtain.

Then the Tsunami hit!

Armed conflict areas are not easy when it comes to delivering emergency relief. For the UN teams it meant dealing with serious security concerns—in particular, as soon as we moved outside the capital, Banda Aceh, where special approvals and military support was required. Humanitarian relief therefore flowed but implementation was still unwieldy.

Meanwhile however, the sheer magnitude of the Tsunami did open up the province to the outside world. The Acehnese independence movement, GAM, welcomed international presence, and whilst quiet for an initial period after the Tsunami, started to re-engage with the military as negotiations in Helsinki between GAM and the Government of Indonesia re-established—perhaps glimpsing a situation of enhanced influence. However, GAM meticulously avoided violence against UN and humanitarian relief workers. In parallel, Indonesia moved strongly to support humanitarian relief to the people of Aceh, a move that was strongly appreciated amongst the people. New opportunities for dialogue had therefore emerged, even though there remained entrenched economic and political interests in maintaining conflict on both sides of the military and GAM confrontation.

Consequently, the backdrop for action by the UN to assist the people of Aceh involved a deep historic and religious legacy and a highly politicized context of armed struggle. For the first time GAM took a step back in negotiations from calling for full independence, so opportunity for a liberating peace became a lot more likely—paradoxically a result of the terrible tragedy of the Tsunami. The product of this new wave of negotiations was finalized in talks during July 2005 in Helsinki and debates in Jakarta. After 30 years of separatist fighting in Aceh the two sides reached a preliminary peace deal in Finland on Sunday 17th July 2005, with a Memorandum of Understanding formally signed 1 month later. The people of Aceh wanted peace, and the Tsunami disaster opened up and brought mutual trust into the relationship between adversaries in what had become a closed and torn society.

The peace has held. The people, including the ex-combatants want it. However, the paradoxical impact of the Tsunami continues. Attention in the post-2004 period was directed to helping the victims of the Tsunami and not enough to the victims of the previous civil conflict. Twenty thousand former combatants from GAM remained largely without jobs or underemployed. Many of the 100,000 victims of the conflict still lived in misery because of the conflicts. Governor of Aceh, Irwandi Yusuf pointed out on Thursday 19th March 2009, over 4 years since the Tsunami swept over Aceh, that there therefore remained a feeling of envy amongst victims of the conflict because of their neglect compared with victims of the Tsunami. Peace remains on a sensitive edge of potential unrest unless the wider unemployment and re-integration of the former fighters is handled well.

Acehnese Cultural Resilience: Staring Down the Face of Disaster

Meanwhile, the strength of independence of the Aceh culture and its religious base was a major positive force for recovery—but also a complicating factor in its management.

We found for example that in the devastated town of Meulaboh there was an enormously strong drive from the people to get back a sense of normality into their lives by their own efforts. Because of the isolation and military containment, Meulaboh was not as easily accessible to humanitarian support as was Banda Aceh. So the people started moving to help themselves. Everywhere you found people seeking to rebuild shelters on their previous land with 'found' wood and just about anything else they could scavenge.

Again we confront the complexity of recovery in the context of total destruction. Not only were the houses destroyed. Also destroyed were the land ownership documents previously held in the local government buildings that were washed away. Without clear proof of ownership and boundaries, and with many vacant blocks remaining from families who were totally wiped out, land could easily be in dispute and legitimate rebuilding prevented.

Basic to any government rebuilding strategy therefore was the reconstruction of the legitimacy of land ownership. The United Nations worked with the National Archives Office to try and restore the water-damaged documents that remained, but this process of restoration reached well into the second half of 2005. Meanwhile, the only way of re-establishing ownership where no documents remained was for the local officials to work with survivors to form agreement on boundaries. But many of the local officials who had some knowledge had been killed. Recapture of who owns what, basic to rebuilding, was therefore an immensely frustrating and time consuming task, particularly for people who are desperate to claim back their lives.

People we talked with virtually all wanted to return and to rebuild—even those who had lost everything and ended up in temporary living centers (TLCs). When we spoke with local officials, or Camats, we found frequently that they were quietly assisting the provision of materials even though officially they were supposed to wait for government approval of a rebuilding masterplan.

And, with the strength of community of Aceh, the entire 'internally displaced people' or IDP situation transformed entirely from what we originally expected. Originally it was envisaged that 24 IDP settlements (TLCs) would be established, each providing housing for between 10,000 and 40,000 people. As it turned out, there would be no more than ten. Instead, people were living with family or their own communities; many were 'boarding' within the houses of people who lived in the zones that escaped the Tsunami. When we talk with them, they virtually all wanted to return, even those with absolutely nothing left.

Furthermore, the strength of the Acehnese religious faith and community solidarity was instrumental in coping psychologically with the trauma. Many were deeply traumatized. The number of survivors in government departments or the university still unable to function was high. However, it was almost unthinkable for Acehnese to question God's mercy or wrath, whatever the degree of their personal loss. Perceptive trauma counselors and psychologists quickly learned that attempts to impose forms of therapy that are not culturally acceptable to the Acehnese have been demonstrably unsuccessful.

Assisting Cultural Strength to Handle the Trauma of the Tsunami

One of UNESCO's programs in Aceh sought to address those still suffering trauma, loss and dislocation of the meaning of their lives through using the local culture to help people find their own voice and find strength in their communal solidarity.

Song is particularly important in Aceh, as is the opportunity for the people to express themselves in ways appropriate to their religion and traditions. Traditional song and dance in Aceh, the Seudati, is a form of Pantun or poem, which often implies the teaching of the Koran, the inherited wisdom of life and nature as well as humor. The Seudati contains a narrative element that reflects a situation, feeling or experience of a current context and is fundamentally about interaction and dialogue—between performers and audience and between performers—providing a powerful dynamic for revealing and dealing with fears within the context of community and sharing. We built our design for action from experience in the more general UNESCO program working with children using music and performance to heal, as I mentioned in Chap. 3.

Implemented initially in a Mohammadiyah orphanage and two TLC settlements—Walubi Barack and Lamjabat region, local traditional artists were trained to emphasise the use of different senses in song and dance—such as listening, feeling and seeing—as post-tsunami psycho-therapeutic tools. The trained local artists then guided the young children to express their past experiences and collective memory through locally relevant narration and dance. Children were taught to make their own simple musical instruments, in particular for percussion, and to develop music performance together to express cooperativeness, solidarity and relationship. The activity—conducted over a six week long period—taught the children to listen, to engage with the leader and to interact with each other as a team—including outsiders—for after three weeks of training we brought the children from the different sites together to learn how to deal with strangers through musical interaction. The initial activity was with 120 children and produced some quite extraordinary results, not only amongst the children—identifiably happier and more confident, but also the performers and the spirit of the whole village community who could now see that their children were again starting to come back from their trauma, as can be seen by checking out the YouTube film "Sacred Bridge Rising Above the Tsunami". One Acehnese parent said, "The children are happier, they eat more, they sleep better and they are more prepared to go to school". The coordinator of the Mohammadiyah orphanage told us "I have never seen the children singing on their own. But since this program took place, the children cheerfully hum and sing the Seudati every day on their own." In each case the settlement communities decided after the UNESCO Program was completed to continue it on their own as a permanent feature of village life.

There was a fascinating side story to this program. President Clinton came to Banda Aceh. He had been appointed Ambassador for the Tsunami by the United Nations so came into town to have a look at how things were going and to assess new needs to take back to the donor community—in particular, business groups who he was particularly targeting. This was Monday 30th May 2005, 5 months after the Tsunami. On the same day we had organized a public performance by the children from the resettlement camps and orphanage who we had been training in music and dance for the last 6 weeks. Knowing Clinton's interest in impromptu saxophone performances—for example, with the King of Thailand—I had approached the former President's Office in New York, with agreement from the other UN agencies, and requested that he attend the performance and play along with the children. Initially, Clinton agreed in principle. Unfortunately, in the last day or so before he arrived, the plan changed. Clinton had had a second (minor) heart attack only a few weeks before and his minders were worried that the performance would not be good for his health, other agencies with much larger programs pumped up the pressure to get Clinton to visit their project sites …. and finally the plan swung around to the former President flying out of Banda Aceh to field sites at the front end of tsunami relief, not leaving adequate time for a quick trip to the kids' performance along the way. Consequently, on his arrival, all of the Agency Heads, including me, had the chance to spend a morning with Clinton, and to meet with him individually, while we talked about progress and needs. We met in a transit room at the airport, all of us impressed by his very relaxed and engaging style and approachability. However, Clinton then was whisked off in a UN helicopter to various project sites, and I made my way out to the IDP camp where the children were about to perform—unfortunately, without Bill Clinton.

Without troubling to tell me at this stage, the local musicians working with the children, aware of my own musical background, had programmed me in to accompany Bill Clinton had he arrived. The music and dance performance of the children started though without Bill Clinton watching on. We were doing this in an open pavilion in the middle of the IDP camp, with around 40 or so others from outside along as spectators and the entire village community hanging over the railings looking on. The children were very excited, their mentors immensely enthusiastic, and the atmosphere built up to a crescendo of appreciation from the audience. At the end, my Sacred Bridge friends insisted we now move on to an improvised session where the harmonica met Acehnese music almost certainly for the first time ever. Four of us stood around in a small circle in the center of the pavilion—the traditional singer, a poet respected locally as a living legend of song, a guitar player, a percussionist, and me. Each of us had a microphone. The children were milling around our legs. The singer started an Acehnese chant and after a bit of testing I found a key I could use to accompany him along with a sense of what might work when performing together—not easy as an Acehnese drone and a blues harmonica are very different genres. And then we started, building up a powerful Acehnese drum rhythm accompanied by the singer's chant …

and the wailing of my harmonica. We were facing each other close up. I saw a look of surprise and then amazement come over the poet-singer's face as he made eye contact with me while we worked out the harmonies. It was only later that I discovered why. I was holding the small blues harmonica in my closed hands along with the microphone to get the best audio sound, and he could not see the instrument. He quite literally thought that I was doing the most incredible sounds just with my voice. Anyway, we worked out a way of putting the music together and created what has to be the first performance of what I would like to call, 'The Acehnese Blues'.

At the end as we started to relax and chat with the people, an elderly man came up to me. He only spoke Acehnese so I could not work out what he was saying at first. After a friend came across to help however, I found out that he was asking if he could have one of my harmonicas. Each of the 'blues harps' is a different key, so to change key one has to change instruments. I could not give him one without destroying, as it were, the whole kit. Anyway, I fortunately had a new spare harmonica back in the room where I was staying. So the next day I returned to the IDP camp and gave the harmonica to the guy. The story then came out. He had actually had a harmonica—maybe even the only one in Aceh, and it was washed away in the Tsunami. He was delighted with the gift, and it helped his own recovery: he had lost his wife and entire family in the tsunami. The harmonica signaled at least a future with his music. As a result, he took up the challenge of looking after the future of the culture program with the kids generally, and helped us expand it across other communities. I never found out if he actually did play harmonica with the children. But I have this fantasy that perhaps the serendipitous meeting at the culture performance on Monday 30th May 2005 may have precipitated a movement towards building a new genre of music, "The Acehnese Blues". Whether this happened or not is not so important and improbable anyway. What did matter was that a harmonica was perhaps a catalyst for his commitment to continue and to champion the future of the children's' culture-based recovery program.

In the context of its mandate as the agency of the United Nations responsible for the world's cultural heritage and empowerment, we in UNESCO had used similar culture-based approaches to deal with social trauma before. We handled the conflicts between children and young people across religious and cultural dividing lines at the time of the 1998 revolution that ousted President Soeharto through putting Islamic and Christian kids together in a project in the National Museum—exploring the variety of Indonesia's cultures and creating activities such as making posters of peace in religiously mixed groups. We used musical expression as a mechanism of bringing together the leaders of street gangs of Jakarta (where somewhere near 100 young people were killed in gang violence each year), also to produce joint posters of peace that became common T-shirts of street gangs across the whole city. Following this, we set up a forum that met every six weeks or so in the UN Building itself. The youth-gang leaders then met regularly to iron out their differences and conflicts—influenced at least a bit by the sense that their negotiations now had a bit of status as United Nations related. I should add though, we had some 'interesting' difficulties when bringing the street gang leaders together initially to share designing the 'Posters of Peace'. I came across two gang leaders arguing, one loudly telling the other, "My (expletive) Poster of Peace is a (expletive) sight better than your (expletive) Poster of Peace"! I paused long enough to point out in Bahasa Indonesian language that this was not quite the point.

Much of the attention in a time of emergency such as we confronted in Aceh becomes focused on the physical needs and infrastructures of the people. But a lesson we learnt very clearly—in particular from our experience working with children—was that it is the human fabric of meaning and existence that provides the community cohesion, will, and drive to act that is basic to the recapture of life for a people so deeply affected and traumatized. And we had to remember that there was quite serious damage to the cultural fabric of the whole community. In surveys we conducted along with the Ministry of Culture and Tourism, we found very considerable loss of peoples' intangible cultural heritage, that is, the social practices, rituals and forms of cultural expression that bind the people together and forge their identity. I mentioned near the start of this chapter that three times the number of women were killed as men—in particular as, being a Sunday morning when the Tsunami hit, they were on the beach watching their children play while their husbands were working elsewhere. This gender imbalance potentially had a powerful impact on the community's intangible cultural heritage. In one town, where only 40 women survived out of 1,000, they were seriously concerned that there were not enough women around to remember and teach the unique ways of preparing food, of dance and expression: one women started what was tantamount to a 'marriage service' to bring women into the community by encouraging the men to marry quickly. She then set up 'cultural training' for the women.

Finally, the strength of Acehnese religion and culture was demonstrated in resistance to what looked like it was shaping up to be a significant security problem for international staff and agencies working within Aceh. Extremists, though small in number in Indonesia, had had a powerful impact on the security and economy of the country—with bombings in Bali, at the Marriott

Hotel and Australian Embassy in Jakarta, a number of attacks on shopping centers, many attacks on churches, a concerted campaign of provocative inter-religious violence in Poso and other parts of Sulawesi, 'cleansing' of night clubs, 'sweeps' of foreigners in the streets, and so on—by extremists relying on a call to Islam as an excuse for terrorist violence. Even the United Nations Building in Jakarta was attacked with a bomb in 2003 as I reported earlier in this book.

A security warning was announced by the Australian Government in January 2005 based on information that extremists were threatening Australian and New Zealand nationals who were operating in Aceh—particularly in connection with resettlement areas. For example, one radical Islamic group, the Islamic Defenders Front, rushed in hundreds of volunteers to "guard", as *Newsweek* reports on 17th January 2005, "Muslim society because there are many infidels here" from the international relief effort, and a number of other radical Islamic groups established presence in Aceh. The test of the influence of these groups came with a well publicized anti-western-culture film and speakers forum at the main mosque in Banda Aceh, the Baiturrahman Mosque, on 24th February 2005. But, as it turned out, most of the only 120 people who attended were non-Acehnese, imported supporters from Java. The Acehnese remained unimpressed and independent and did not participate. The extremist push simply collapsed in a heap of disinterest. As with the experience of many other internationals, I was personally and genuinely thanked on a number of occasions for being there for Aceh. The threat of potential terrorism against international aid for Aceh dissolved .... for no other reason than that the members of the Acehnese Islamic community themselves rejected this kind of fundamentalism as against the values of Islam and the interests of Aceh.

20

"Preparing for Another Tsunami"

As we looked to the future, we were paying particular attention to trying to prevent such a horrendous impact of a possible tsunami of equivalent force if one strikes again.

The possibility of a tsunami cannot be avoided, as they result from geological forces well beyond the power of humanity to control. Consequently, we have to pay attention to getting people out of the way in time and perhaps find ways to diffuse the impact of the wave on the land.

We have some pretty good experience in the Pacific. UNESCO, through its International Oceanographic Commission (IOC) organized the Pacific Early Warning System 40 years ago, based on a regional center in Hawaii, and has continued to coordinate it since through a subsidiary International Coordination Group. Building a warning system for the Indian Ocean was based on this experience and coordinated in a similar way, in this case by the Indian Ocean Tsunami Warning and Mitigation System—ICG/IOTWS, if you would prefer to remember the acronym. Under the leadership of UNESCO the Indian Ocean Warning System came into operation in late June 2006—consisting of 25 seismographic stations relaying information to 26 national information centres, as well as three deep ocean sensors.

Bringing the system into operation was however a political nightmare. There were certainly enough meetings: seven high level political and several technical meetings in the first 6 months—all seeking to promote and coordinate the overall system. A number of countries, notably India, Thailand, Australia, Indonesia and Malaysia (as well as France who wished to establish a 'regional' center in the South West Indian Ocean) were going ahead to build their *own* systems. This was not necessarily a problem as long as they communicate with each other *quickly*, in the first few minutes after an earthquake event, signaling by what can be measured immediately from its size and location that there may be a problem, and then within a very short space of time later, from corroboration with sensors in the ocean, that a tsunami is on its way. In the case of Japan, for the sake of speed, the warning actually short-circuits reliance on accessing *all* measurements, being based primarily on highly sophisticated mathematical models of an enormous range of possible scenarios derived from ocean and coastal measurements and the *exact* location and size of the offending earthquake. Full use of deep ocean and other measurements is used for subsequent ratification rather than the initial warning.

At this stage however, years after the Indian Ocean Tsunami, the solution that has been adopted internationally employs an interim *advisory* system with warnings being broadcast from the long-established Pacific Tsunami Warning Centre in Hawaii and the Japan Meteorological Agency.

A basic problem remains, however. Whilst the technological systems can trigger urgent warnings, the message has to get out to the people along coastlines, generally, in relatively poor communities. People have to have access to immediate reliable information, for example, from radio stations, and *have to believe in the results* of the technical system when the warning system tells them that there will *not* be a tsunami. However, in the case of Aceh—and now, Padang in Sumatra which, being further down the evolving chain of tectonic plate upheavals, is more significantly at risk, there will *never* be much time for a warning as the source of a possible tsunami is so close. If a tsunami is sensed, the people have to know *immediately* as the tsunami could hit within 15 min after the precipitating earthquake. In the case of Aceh, perhaps a way of doing this is to use the mosques that populate every town and village and have a loudspeaker system already set up to call the faithful to prayer. Response in building effective local warning systems still remains incomplete.

Coordination at national levels can be dramatically complicated as well. In Indonesia for example, there were 14 separate agencies involved in one way or another in receiving and broadcasting the warning: they tended to operate as a general rule quite independently of each other. Consequently, following the July 2006 Java earthquake, the Indonesian Government received tsunami warnings from the US and Japanese centers but failed to alert anybody. Even so, 23,000 people did evacuate the coast: it was just that they acted for themselves having experienced the earthquake and remembering well the experience of Aceh. It was not because they were warned by officials.

What really matters is being prepared.

In many cases people simply do not understand what a tsunami is, how it comes about, or what signs to look for, even when they know that if you live close to the ocean an experienced earthquake can be bad news. Advance provision of information at the level people can understand is critical.

But, in a relatively traditional society context, instruction of information is not enough. Given the *geological* time scale of earthquakes that release the pressure of slowly encroaching tectonic plates, there may not be another tsunami for 50 or 60 years—well beyond the generation that experienced the present trauma. Consequently, 'information' provided in the present is likely to be forgotten or disappear into irrelevance as generations pass and life goes on without a tsunami actually occurring. That is, the knowledge will disappear *unless* some mechanism is built into education that assists *generations* to remember.

The story of the North Sumatra Tsunami contained a marvelous example of what works. Traditional people on the island of Simeulue off the Acehnese coast remembered the stories of their 'ancestral experience' about the 'smog', or tsunami of 7.6 magnitude, which hit the island on January 4th 1907. The story of the smog became embedded in continuing rituals and folk lore. As soon as they saw the coastal waters receding in 2004, 97 years later, the indigenous Simeleu people ran away from the coast and up the mountains. They survived—with only eight people dying and one missing out of an island population of 76,000. We understood that the nine people who were killed were mainly visitors—who did not know the legend. And the people had also maintained a traditional system of drumming messages from one village to the next that around the coast carried the warning rapidly through the entire coastal community. The *fact* of a previous tsunami was lost in time, retained only in a timeless folk-lore legend.

Even in the town of Meulaboh, one of the most devastated areas in Aceh, a Simeulue community lived on the point where the wave first hit. Whereas many locals died, all members of the Simeleu community survived as they ran *as soon as they noticed the water receding after the earthquake shook their homes*, that is, being sucked out to feed the wave coming ashore.

UNESCO investigated more about the Simeulue 'smog' legend and how it remained in long-term memory, and we then assisted in the development of tsunami preparedness education for children—involving stories and songs, supported by an initial contest for Acehanese children to make up stories as myths, to embed the idea of tsunamis deeply into cultural expression rather than just school lessons which may be forgotten. The society has to remember and react quickly based on experiences from long ago.

Transnational Versus National Issues: Some Observations

Epicenter of the December 26th 2004 Tsunami was in Indonesian waters to the north-west of Aceh, but rapidly split the earth 1,300 km through international waters towards the coast of Thailand and Myanmar. Although described by *Newsweek* on 10th January 2005 as "relatively speaking … a small blip in the long, violent history of a planet with a molten core, where entire continents have vanished and then reformed", on a *human scale* the consequences of the 'blip' were horrendous. The Tsunami's impact affected the whole of the Indian Ocean region, sweeping across the low-lying Maldive islands with bodies carried from Indonesia before washing up already dead people along the west coast of Africa. This was a truly international disaster.

Relief efforts led by the United Nations and involving many donor countries of the world, hundreds of NGOs and billions of dollars, also were mounted on an international scale. Development of a new regional sensing and warning system for future mitigation of such horrendous human impact was also intrinsically international—with deep-water buoys installed to the west of Indonesia for example, being of little use to warnings in Aceh and North Sumatra due to the close proximity of these provinces to the most vulnerable deep-ocean earthquake sites—and therefore very short potential warning times; but the buoys are of considerable use in providing advance information disseminated further north to Thailand, Myanmar and north-west to the Maldives and India.

Even however, with the clearly present need to move together as an international community to both address the current crisis and prepare for the next, international politics quickly intruded into the debates. Donor countries and NGOs competed with each other to offer the highest profile aid or aid that met *their* interests and capabilities rather than those necessarily of the communities in need. Even, as I noted before, financial donations to the common UN Flash Appeal Fund were usually donations to specific Agencies nominated by the Donor Country rather than to the UN-system as a whole, a factor that strongly eroded the UN's ability to address the whole connected spectrum of requirements that arise in a complex emergency.

Recipient countries were quickly mired in politics in negotiating the development and application of an Indian Ocean wide early warning system— for example, with Thailand, in the context of Prime Ministerial election concerns, pushing hard at Ministerial levels to become the centre of the regional system, India deciding to design their system independently, and a range of donors—Germany, Japan, Australia and China for example—developing separate bilateral aid programs to support separately planned elements of national early warning capabilities and just in the countries of *their* political choice.

The main consequences of these political perturbations of internationalized goodwill were mainly felt in time delays for people in desperate need, and wastage or inefficient targeting of resources. Over time, the effect of these inefficiencies started to shake out, the people affected were indeed starting to get back to a sustainable life—though much more slowly than desirable.

If we were to look to the future and how to improve international cooperation in times of such urgent crises as Indonesia had experienced from 2004, the key would seem to be to strengthen advance international commitments and coordination mechanisms for the planning and response to specific high-risk disasters—a high priority given the incidence already emerging of increased cyclonic and weather disturbance activity associated with Global Warning.

Additionally, however, there were direct interactions between international assistance modalities and interests, and confusion in internal national response. In the case of Indonesia, although development of a Presidential Action Plan for rebuilding was set in motion within two months of the disaster, much of it was subsequently discarded, having been designed under pressure of urgent political priority at the distance of Jakarta and central government agencies rather than from local needs, contingencies, and consultations. It took over four months for the supreme local coordinating agency, the Agency for Rehabilitation and Reconstruction (BRR) to be formed and several months more before it was ready to move into serious action in Aceh. Eighteen months later, and despite firm executive action, there were still significant problems with the level of delivery of BRR's coordinated relief—partly because there were continuous arguments about its authority in relation to all arms of government from local to national. Developing a national Early Warning System involved 14 separate national, provincial, and local government agencies, and although Ministerial authority was confirmed with the State Minister of Research and Technology, lines of authority in implementation remained unclear, whilst response authority remained in the hands of the military and the disaster relief agency BAKORNAS, with unclear boundaries between BAKORNAS and the government's central planning agency BAPPENAS. Inter-agency coordination was a nightmare. And the critical bridge that had to be crossed, but remained incompletely constructed, was across the nexus between technical system advice and local community response. For no matter how effective and timely is the technical system of advice, if the people do not trust the advice, are uncertain about who to pay attention to, or remain unprepared in knowing precisely how to escape, then the early warning quite literally falls on ears that cannot hear. Meanwhile, a complex emergency requiring whole-of-government response is extremely difficult to coordinate in countries that traditionally tend to design Ministries of Government in carefully delineated separate territories with very poor traditions of inter-agency coordination and cooperation, and of community consultation.

Hopefully, *having to respond*, the lessons of disaster may even have a salutary impact on general planning and coordination arrangements of government. But this is a tortuous road to a high mountain yet to be climbed. There are at least signs, however. The Indonesian government responded quickly and in a coordinated way to the 2006 earthquake disasters in the Yogyakarta region. Even so however, as I mentioned earlier, Indonesia received a tsunami warning at the same time but completely failed to respond. At a local level, the place that is arguably in the greatest danger of a further Tsunami is the town of Padang on the western coast of Sumatra. With a population of just under one million people, two-thirds of Padang is below 5 m in elevation above the ocean, and meanwhile the town is directly opposite to where earthquake activity has been building up east of Siberut. If an earthquake of large magnitude occurs in the greatest depths of the 2,000 m Sunda Trench, then Padang is *very* likely to suffer a major tsunami. Here at least the people are preparing. Escape routes have been mapped; tall earthquake proof buildings identified for possible refuge; and sirens—to be triggered by and only by the mayor—have been installed.

What must be finally stressed however is that even though the disaster represented by the Aceh Tsunami is truly international in character, what works in response is intrinsically *local*. Needs must be identified and addressed at this level. Consultations and actions must be conducted at local levels. The *specific* cultural and political context at local levels fundamentally determines how the crisis is likely to be played out and the most effective modalities of response. Aceh is a signal case, for its strong Islamic and community-centered culture was of central importance in housing, rehabilitation and even the understanding by people of what the disaster meant. Aceh was a country at war when the Tsunami hit; it became a country of peace—the magnitude of the shock exploding the barriers to negotiation and international entry that had previously existed.

Some Lessons for the Future

The story I have presented in this and the previous two chapters is about just one disaster. But it sure was a big one and had wide-ranging consequences. Exploring this story therefore allows us to look at disasters more generally, in a broad-spectrum prism as it were, providing a demonstration in high relief of what is likely to be found in all major natural disasters, even though perhaps less dramatically. For what the international and national humanitarian relief agencies needed to deal with was not a relatively simple though perhaps logistically complex provision of survival goods—food, medicine, and shelter. Instead, what the Aceh Tsunami Story demonstrates is that a natural disaster of such magnitude confronts us with a *complex human emergency* created from the tearing apart of the very platform for peoples' existence and creation of the meaning of their world. What is required involves rebuilding the social, cultural, and economic fabric of the society, facilitating the empowerment at levels of will and capacity that allows people to do it for themselves and find their own power over their future, even in times of terrible hardship.

There will be unexpected problems in response. We saw such surprises in Aceh in the impact of the loss of records of land ownership on the timetable to rebuild. We found an unexpected impact on rebuilding in the way that small holes in the economic fabric, such as of the destroyed ice works in Meulaboh, can entirely derail much wider economic initiatives—in this case the re-generation of the fishing industry. There was what I called 'second level weakening', with the relatively higher incidence of deaths of local officials, for this served to cripple the ability at local government level to plan and guide response. And, we saw, perhaps not too unexpectedly, conflict erupting between peoples' need for immediate income from capturing and selling 'Powder Blue Surgeon Fish' and the regeneration of the coral reefs that would sustain the peoples' longer-term supplies of food—because these fish were central in keeping the reefs free of sediment and therefore in a condition where they *could* regenerate.

There were unexpected *benefits*. The sheer magnitude of the Tsunami disaster suddenly overwhelmed the impediments that both the rebel GAM movement and the government had been limited by in negotiating peace. The province *had* to open up for international assistance; the rebel movement *had* to support government and the international community in delivering aid; the government, and most of all the military, acted responsibly to put conflict parameters aside until the job was done and thereby earned the trust of the people. The circle of interests in conflict was broken. And the people were delighted. Peace was an unexpected and critical outcome of the Tsunami Disaster.

From a more negative perspective, we found in the Tsunami Story that with international aid, the good intentions of generous donors do not always translate into effective action as I showed in the last two chapters. To summarize:

> First, always likely to be present in *bilateral* aid, we are very likely to find that the interest of the donor country has some sway over the way that humanitarian relief is offered – including looking for good press for apparently good deeds and being more concerned about bilateral profile than inter-agency coordination and targeting of the overall program.
>
> Second, national interest is still likely to touch funding that flows into multilateral agency coffers such as those of the United Nations. Major country donors gave generously to the UN's 'FLASH Appeal', a mechanism that was created to promote and receive funding for response to the Indian Ocean Tsunami. However, donors were only prepared to donate the funding to Agencies within the UN system which the donor was interested to support. Those Agencies with the most positive profile or those which were most 'fashionable' therefore received disproportionately more money than those which were less known – yet the UN had to deliver a *whole* and *coordinated* response: some areas of urgent need were sidelined whilst others were rolling in money that was sometimes hard to spend in time. Most importantly, there were therefore important holes in the overall fabric of response.
>
> Third, volunteers and civil society NGOs can offer highly committed and competent individuals who are prepared to make enormous personal sacrifices to assist in a major humanitarian crisis. But there can be problems – particularly with the newer and less experienced groups. As in the Aceh crisis, we frequently confronted NGOs that wanted (or, sometimes were only equipped) to do *their* thing rather than fit into the government's plans and priorities. The result was boats that were too powerful and stimulated overfishing of an already depleted ocean, houses built in locations that directly contradicted government planning rules, clothing donations that were totally unsuitable for the tropics or were an antithesis to the Islamic dictates and style of Aceh. Those volunteers without local language or useful skills simply got in the way, took up desperately needed shelter and food, and moreover then virulently blamed the UN for not caring and not using their 'valuable' assistance.
>
> Fourth, the products of aid, even when chosen well, can have a detrimental impact on the economic fabric of the society. We found dramatic examples of this in the way that overwhelming (and quite appropriate) attention to emergency medical support displaced local doctors and their continued employment and income; and free pharmaceuticals flooded local pharmacies out of business.

What matters, and this is one of the most important lessons of the Acehnese Tsunami disaster, is the targeting of humanitarian relief and development assistance to *local needs assessed at local levels,* not determined at a distance in the capital cities of remote donors—and this even included the national government itself.

Finally, to return to the opening note in these three chapters about the Aceh Tsunami, that is, that a natural disaster of such magnitude confronts us with a *complex human emergency* sustained from the tearing apart of the very platform for peoples' existence and creation of the meaning of their world. Attention must be paid to rebuilding the knowledge and cultural fabric of the society *from day 1,* not just 'sometime' later. And this rebuilding task is the particular responsibility of UNESCO.

Consequently, as can be seen in the Aceh Tsunami Story, very early attention had to be paid to science—to address urgent problems of desalination that had to be measured and solved prior to rebuilding; to understanding the role of mangrove plantations in mitigation *prior* to jumping into unschooled planting activity; to measuring *impact* of the Tsunami precisely in order to be sure of where any future event is likely to have greatest impact, and thus to plan zones to be avoided for human habitation, as well as optimal strategies for warning and escape.

Early attention needed to be paid to rebuilding media capacity for the people to have access to *reliable and trusted information,* rather than be commanded—and terrified—by rumor and panic.

Education too was not something to be left until later, or to be forgotten about once the school buildings had been reconstructed. The kids *could not* be left out of school. This was not just because their education was going to be delayed and so their lives would take a step backwards for a while. Returning children to school also had a substantial impact on the whole community for it signaled by a change in the very order of daily routine, that life was returning to some level of normality, a critical factor in helping people adjust and get on with their lives under immensely difficult circumstances. But, as with UNESCO action, it was not just rebuilding schools and getting the children back into them that mattered. Many of the children and youth were displaced or orphaned; many existing employment opportunities were closed down. Attention had to be paid to 'out-of-school' children and youth, and to fostering education and training *in the community* that dealt with their particular needs, with a very close eye on *creating* new employment opportunities and capacities. Additionally, many of the most traumatised children had fallen through the cracks of the system, failing dismally in the national tests that were to determine their whole future. Eighty percent of the children in these most affected areas had failed the national exams. These exams simply were not a priority in a life that had so recently been massively traumatized and destroyed. Rapid intervention in a tiny subsequent August 2005 program (as far as level of funding was concerned, a few thousand dollars amongst millions) made an enormous difference. Alan Bolton, Director of ILO, and myself put together a targeted tutoring program for students from most affected Acehnese regions who had failed the national exams and were about to re-sit for a final attempt. The program cost only around $(US)6,000 or so, emphasized both the substance of the exams as well as techniques in doing exams generally, like reading the questions carefully, working out timing for each answer, and so on. We put together a tutoring team in Aceh. As a result, *95% of the students who had failed then passed*—securing their life chances and confidence in recovering from the incredible trauma they had experienced.

And, usually not glimpsed by humanitarian relief agencies, was the power of culture that was vibrantly demonstrated in the Aceh Tsunami Story. 'Culture' is often viewed as little more than entertainment that people go to theatres and concerts to see, or soft spongy stuff that surrounds everyday life, but is really not so important compared with making a living and getting on with 'important' things. This view is so wrong. A peoples' culture determines the way they *do* things, and *why*. It provides the frameworks of meaning in interactions with others for knowing *how to relate* to them, *who* you are, and *commitment* to particular actions. Take this away and you are left with a totally empty human and societal shell which is simply unsustainable. As well as all this, the Tsunami massively shook the foundations of the meaning of everything for the Acehnese people. Thus, recapturing cultural strength also provided their relief and empowerment to keep going and to rebuild. The most dramatic evidence of this lay in the culture program UNESCO implemented with children, relying on partnerships with traditional cultural performers: the children, and with them, their village communities *came to life!*

So, the people of Aceh were picking up their lives again in cities and towns that quite literally appeared as if hit by an atomic bomb. On Thursday 19 March 2009 the Multi Donor Fund (MDF)—the group of key international donors including the World Bank and the European Commission, declared that reconstruction in areas devastated by the Tsunami was nearly complete—about 93% finished. In April 2010 the government's Rehabilitation and Reconstruction Agency (BRR) withdrew, having finished its work. There is however a downside to completion. Aceh's unemployment level was still very high, around 23% of its 4 million people. Most affected were the 20,000 former combatants from GAM, the Free Aceh Movement, many of whom remain envious of the attention lavished on Tsunami victims. This could become a very sensitive wound unless attended to.

The people of Nias and Simeulue were still recovering from the massive series of earthquakes that followed shortly after the Tsunami, as the earth faults rippled down the Sunda Trench west of Aceh and Sumatra obliterating perhaps 60–80% of their housing and many of their people. The Mentawai population of the island further south, Siberut, and the Sumatrans in the coastal town of Padang .... were waiting .... in fear ... that at any time the earth would move again and the oceans invade. Indeed, since 2005, there have been major ocean-centred earthquakes that could have generated tsunamis in this area. But so far they have been lucky: only ripples.

The Tsunami Disaster, the 'Day the Ocean Moved', reminds us of the incredible power of nature that we so often take for granted, and the complexity of human impact that is a consequence. We can see in the face of the Acehnese also the resilience of human spirit that gives us faith that humanity can live with this power and ultimately survive. And we can see the importance of both UN and international response to the disaster itself and preparedness for physical structures that were destroyed. The key to human resilience lies in the will and knowledge of the people. The path to a secure future is fundamentally about connection with local culture and meaning. With this lesson in mind, it was essential to strengthen UNESCO's focus and action out to where the people and their communities are ... out in the world beyond Paris Headquarters.

21

Bridging the Two UN Cultures—Reform for the Future

An International Agency Ain't All That Simple

Robert England, writing in 2002 as Head of a Field Office in the United Nations Development Program, UNDP, made an observation based on his UN experience that applies with as much strength to UNESCO and all other UN Agencies as it did to UNDP. Taking the root of his idea from the book by organizational guru Warren Bennis, 'Managing People is Like Handling Cats', England observes:

> UN staff behave like cats in dogs' clothing. They appear to be dogs, eager to fit in and easily trained when actually they are cats, independent, individualistic and difficult to unite.

This observation feels so true from inside the organization. But it is not because people attracted to the United Nations are two-faced hypocrites or necessarily all that different from people in other large complex organizations. Rather the observation follows from the *particular structural constraints and dynamics* imposed on doing business as a UN Agency, embedded as it is in a field of political, cultural and economic interests, and with a meaning to its participants that is legacy of a unique organization history. UNESCO, like all complex *human* organizations, does not function in simple straight lines of purpose, authority, and rules. Instead, the organization functions as a complex interaction between people, their interests and personal styles, the formal structures and lines of responsibility and authority within which they are placed and have a specified role, the *in*formal circles of influence and inclusion … and power. And UNESCO's organizational culture provides the meaning of things, woven as it has been over time into a tapestry of formal and informal rules and protocols, expectations and precedents …. 'the way we *do* things around here!' Add to this the external interfaces that set both the priorities and contexts for action—not just at the top but deep into the heart of organizational practice: a high level political environment of Member States to which UNESCO (and particularly its Director-General who is elected by them) is obeisant; multiple local national authorities—including UNESCO National Commissions established by these authorities, NGOs and people from both specialized groups and general communities with which UNESCO cooperates; and other arms of the United Nation System as a whole. Meanwhile UNESCO networks and operations are stretched across the whole world and its staff are drawn from around 150 nationalities.

The result was, as I identified back in Chap. 2, an international organization of two cultures. Culture 1 established the meaning of Headquarters life in its responsiveness primarily within separate disciplinary fiefdoms such as Science, Education, Culture, and Communication, to UNESCO's international political environment and following 'proper procedure' in order to not be exposed to criticism full of 'dogs'—who acted like 'cats' in controlling what field offices could do. Culture 2 on the other hand, established the meaning of life in the field, where staff had to handle very real-world situations across the range of disciplines needed to be effective in making change happen: serving as 'cats' unable to assume a 'dog' façade because of the nature of their work. Action in a field office context required handling crises and suddenly new situations that could not be planned or even expected 2 years in advance when the programs and budgets were approved at the Biennial General Conference of Member States. Add to this, Culture 2 actions could all too frequently lead to our staff handling very real danger while going about their job. I have demonstrated some very dramatic examples of this through this book.

Consequently, when I first joined UNESCO full time back in 1995, its way of doing things appeared fine on paper, but turned out to be much more complex and opaque in practice. Robert England's 'cats' were prowling everywhere, sniffing out political and personal advantage. Meanwhile, every public forum espoused 'dog'-style collaboration. But the organization as a whole was divided, with Headquarters dominating what was planned, agreed, and mandated in field practice—at times with little real knowledge of what was really needed.

At the center of power in Paris what a visitor to UNESCO's Headquarters will find is two building locations. The first is at Place de Fontenoy

21 Bridging the Two UN Cultures—Reform for the Future 349

overlooking L'Ecole Militaire and the Eiffel Tower—built as a showpiece of 1950s architecture, and, in absence of an adequate ongoing maintenance budget, slowly deteriorating since, or at least until 2004 or so when urgent repairs finally commenced. The other section of Headquarters is located a five-minute walk away, combining two buildings, Bonvin and Miollis—again named after their principal street addresses. In both primary locations the buildings descend into the underground—though with central atria and light wells. From both building locations, it is possible to view the Eiffel Tower depending on seniority and vantage point—so there is of course a significant pecking order about how far up the building one's office is located and on which side.

Fontenoy houses the Director-General and his or her Cabinet—on the sixth floor directly overlooking the Eiffel Tower, and additionally all arms of the organisation's Administration. Just one Sector is housed in Fontenoy, Education, largely as this is the largest and most significant of UNESCO's original mandates. The other Sectors, Social Science, Science, Culture and Communications, are housed in Bonvin, while Miollis, joined by a common foyer but separate elevators to Bonvin, largely is occupied by offices of Member State delegations. Oh, and there is a small four-storey Annex to Fontenoy, out in the garden, an adjunct to the main building and housing left-over Administration bits and pieces and the World Heritage Offices. Fontenoy is the center of power and also contains the main conference rooms and exhibition spaces of the organization. Meanwhile, the deepest basements of Fontenoy—far from the coffee machine and views of the outside splendor of Paris—could well be, and were, used as the destination of banishment for those administrative bureaucrats who offend; whilst to be moved from Fontenoy to Bonvin, they said, half (but only half) jokingly, was an act of 'decentralization', separation from the 'center'.

The social architecture of UNESCO Headquarters was therefore very French, that is, centralized, as is French governance and culture, around the center of power—political and administration arms of the organization being close, substantive Sectors being at arms' length and separate from each other. And the field offices? ... Well out at the periphery, absolutely secondary in organization decision-making and interest, but good excuses for interesting mission travel to make sure that Headquarters ideas are being looked after. Indeed, at this stage in organizational evolution, this was 1995, there was a very genuine fear that to be moved to a field posting was the kiss of career death—disappearance away from the centres of attention in Fontenoy, a sentence that might well never allow you to return. This same fear persisted through the whole time I worked in UNESCO. *Both* unions of UNESCO staff (and there are *two* which have found it traditionally impossible to settle differences and amalgamate—but which also primarily represent the interests of Headquarters staff rather than those from the Field) expressed this fear in response to UNESCO's subsequent decentralization policy to 'rotate' staff in and out of the field. A document tabled at the 177th Meeting of the Executive Board in August 2007, using the words of one of the two unions, ISAU, instead of applauding decentralization, warned:

> It is essential to ensure that rotation is not used to inflict punishment or to exile colleagues who are considered undesirable and that the redeployed staff members have the right to return to a post in their professional group after the normal period of assignment.

Needless to say the zone of greatest sanctity was the Director-General's 6th floor arm of Fontenoy—a suite of a couple of dozen offices, entered past a security guard and imperial doors with thick-carpet corridors lined with major art works donated over the years to UNESCO, usually from Member States in recognition of UNESCO's role as the United Nations Agency responsible for the world's culture.

Under the rule of the Director-General in power in 1995, Federico Mayor, the 6th floor inner sanctum largely housed a group of a dozen or so of his personal Advisors, individuals standing outside Secretariat lines of responsibility who usually imported some political support for the DG but whose hiring, advice and authority lay quite outside the formal Secretariat processes. As *personal appointments* by the Director-General the 6th floor Advisors were highly sensitive to his wishes, and all were supported by generous conditions of appointment, complementing an Assistant Director General equivalent status and stipend with a Paris per-diem as if they were on permanent mission from their home countries. Mayor, a charismatic Spaniard, also tended to maintain the odd 6th floor post for senior *female* advisors, perhaps ex-Ministers or diplomats, but now providing particularly close support, especially on long missions.

Meanwhile, the Director-General's Cabinet at that time cringed in total obeisance to the Director-General's wishes. As he travelled on mission, a continuous task for the head of an international organization of around 190 Member States, the DG would frequently wish to leave behind 'gifts' to the countries he visited to shore up his political support—gifts like a small new UNESCO Field Office as promise to a President, or an Education initiative as promise to a key Minister. On his return to Paris it was Cabinet's job to ensure that the money could be found within ongoing Sector programs to feed these initiatives. Every Sector feared the consequences of the Director-General's mission commitments as the budgets, locked theoretically into decisions made up to 2 years earlier at the last General Conference, allowed little flexibility to deal with the unforeseen. The result was an awful lot of juggling with mirrors by those outside the inner sanctum. As one of my fellow field director colleagues commented to me, "I learnt to spend my money quickly before he could nab it."

On the other hand, being *in* Cabinet, meant being intrinsically close to the Director-General thus having direct access to personal interventions and rapid promotions that bore little relationship to the rigid and time-bound promotions procedures available to those outside the inner sanctum.

Indeed therefore, the Director-General *was* very comfortably cocooned away from detailed knowledge of what really was going on, well supported in the grandest of his plans by a sycophantic circle of people who were very unlikely to shake the tree too hard.

Meanwhile, the world out in field offices away from UNESCO's Paris centre, could be enormously challenging, but also rewarding as I have already demonstrated in the case studies of this book—including, for me, in UN staff taken hostage, a national revolution, handling the aftermath of a Tsunami that killed over 200,000 people, major change in educational and media practice, working with people and cultures as different as with the Mentawai people of the Indonesian Island of Siberut versus the modern urban complex of many Asian cities, and with politics that stretched from heavy repression as in North Korea to the democratic practices of New Zealand and Australia.

UNESCO simply *had* to bridge the two internal cultures which otherwise fundamentally eroded its strength and effectiveness in handling this wider world and making a positive difference.

Signs of Change

Organizational transformation to bridge the two cultures had not happened. But a new rhetoric was starting to emerge at the time I joined UNESCO about the need for greater decentralization of authority and practice. The rhetoric was legitimated and promoted by Executive Board decisions that had been brought to the table over the previous couple of years, aimed at strengthening 'Culture-2', the Field Culture, by reaching *out* of Paris with more resources and authority. But rule from the center continued.

The idea of decentralization was not new in UNESCO. The establishment of units away from Headquarters had been an element in UNESCO policy since shortly after the foundation of the organization: UNESCO's

Second General Conference held in Mexico in 1947 resolved to establish as soon as possible regional offices or centers of UNESCO in the major geographic regions of the world. Even my own Jakarta Office had been founded as far back as 1951, though at that time it operated under a somewhat different mandate—as the UNESCO Field Office for Southeast Asian Science Cooperation.

However, large scale decentralization was a relatively recent practice. Thus, during the first 30 years of UNESCO existence, only 18 Field Offices were created, whilst in the 11 years from 1988 to 1999 39 such Offices were established—a clear initiative of Federico Mayor. By the end of 1999 when Koichiro Matsuura came into office there was a total of 70 Field Offices in Member States, plus 4 Liaison Offices, 6 Institutes, and a number of Centers that varied in their status and relationship with UNESCO. The Executive Board however was concerned that no strategy underpinned this development. Many of the offices were established to satisfy political rather than logistic intention so there was very uneven coverage around the world—20 offices serving Latin America and the Caribbean for example versus only 14 for the whole of Asia and the Pacific, many were simply too small to be able to operate effectively, while the link to Headquarters of many offices remained loose, poorly defined, or too complex. As a result, rule from the centre continued and the voice from the field remained weak.

Consequently, as Federico Mayor was exiting the organization in 1999 the General Conference approved 30 C/Resolution 83, calling for a basic policy for the *rational* implementation of decentralization.

Stimulus for us to take action to implement this Resolution was the initiative previously taken by the then Director of the Field Coordination Unit in Headquarters to bring *all* Field Directors for the very first time to the General Conference in 1996 both to support the Member States for which we were responsible and to meet each other and exchange ideas on field strategies. It did not take long in the first of what evolved as a series of meetings for our dissatisfactions to bubble to the surface. These largely concerned lack of responsiveness of Headquarters to field operation needs, particularly staffing and budget and even communications, and absence of our voice in the planning process and funding allocations.

It is invariably dangerous to be most vocal on failure by one's bosses and their 'system', and proved so for me as I was then elected by my fellow Field Directors to take the issues to the Director-General at a special 'expanded' meeting of the Directorate-Générale a few days later. This was a meeting of *all* senior Headquarters staff. As our collective case clearly implied criticism of UNESCO's management I saw the politics of me leading the charge as

21 Bridging the Two UN Cultures—Reform for the Future 353

probably weighted rather heavily against me, so prepared for a potentially contentious time with the Headquarters heavies, in particular the Director-General. However, Mayor, though initially seeming to be a little surprised, actually listened carefully and immediately agreed to take action to seek to redress the problems we had raised, allocating overall responsibility for implementation to the Deputy Director-General (the DDG). An internal group in Headquarters was appointed to come up with recommendations.

Nothing serious eventuated, however. For example, a basic problem we had with staff in Headquarters was that many did not respond to correspondence from the field (and I had started to make a blacklist of people who in my 2 years in the organization had *never* responded to me once). The DDG's group recommended more use of e-mail rather than deal with the underlying problem of the cultural divide between Headquarters and Field priorities. So, we had not reached very far into the organization to start reform happening. But the issues were now on the table, and the discussions continued through 1998 and 1999 between Field Directors, and between some of us and some open minds in senior positions in Headquarters. Mayor was near the end of his tenure as Director-General so, whilst expressing interest, was really not committed to any level of serious organizational reform, instead being more concerned with battling the political flack that was starting to surround him from some of the more vocal Member States.

Finally, Serious Action on a Decentralized Reform Agenda

The doorway to serious change opened in 1999 with the appointment of Japanese former Ambassador to France, Koichiro Matsuura as Director General. Following a high priority of UNESCO for Japan, his Member Country, and wider general support, Matsuura immediately embarked on a path of reform. He appointed a previous ADG or Assistant Director General—for the Communication Sector, to Chair a Task Force exploring organizational change in Headquarters. On the Chef de Cabinet's recommendation Matsuura then appointed me as Chair of his Task Force to Decentralize the organization and Reform HQ-Field relations. This was November 1999. The timetable was horrendous for I had to bring the Principles of Decentralization Reform—with the Director-General's full endorsement—to the Executive Board's next meeting in April 2000, then consult with and gain basic agreement with all Member States across the world's six regions, develop a detailed plan accompanied by preliminary budget options and staffing commitment and bring it back to the subsequent Board Meeting 6 months later in October 2000. In fact the time available between these Board Meetings was substantially shorter than it appeared as I had to wait until May for the Director-General's response to the Board's conclusions before I could act on the April agreements, then finish the whole job by end-August in order for the documents I wrote to be translated, printed and distributed to Member States before a required statutory deadline in advance of the Meeting. The 6 months shrunk to much closer to three.

My Russian Task Force leader—for internal HQ change and I fully agreed and cooperated in our mission. The ADG was a previous media baron from the Soviet Union with bear-like personal style but also a mischievous sense of humor. When I first met him some years earlier, his first observation to me about UNESCO, expressed with a thick Russian accent was,

In Rarshia I thourrght I knew burooooocrrracy. Then I joined UNESCA!

Along with my Russian colleague, and under instruction of the Director-General, I moved into offices of Cabinet in the Director-General's 6th Floor wing of UNESCO's main Headquarters building in Paris, newly vacated by the departing Special Advisors to the previous Spanish Director General, Federico Mayor. Suddenly I found myself—splitting my time throughout 2000–2002 between working on Task Force issues from a base and team in Cabinet while in Paris and on regional field management from Jakarta, whilst also travelling the whole world as Personal Envoy of the Director-General to convince the Member States of our Task Force Plan.

We came up with a series of principles that needed to be applied to make decentralization work effectively. I took these principles to the Executive Board in April 2000 for endorsement, and the 'Action Plan' to the Board in October 2000—with a heap more detail in early 2001.

Our central guiding philosophy was that UNESCO is one organization, with one overall mission, and that the central criterion for its performance is its impact and relevance to its Member States. 'Decentralization' therefore was a tool, not an end, providing a means of ensuring that UNESCO programs, though global in scope, targeted the specific needs and contexts of individual countries—particularly the least developed—to maximize relevance and impact. Bedded into this overall philosophy was a series of strategic principles which were subsequently accepted by the Director-General and Member States. These principles placed a two-tier approach to decentralization at the center of our Action Plan, the two layers of the strategy being 'Cluster Offices' and 'Regional Bureaux'.

On the one hand Cluster Offices serve a manageable number of Member States through multidisciplinary teams, and, apart from difficulties translating 'sub-regional' into regional politics and languages, would otherwise have been called 'sub-regional offices'. This concept provided the core of our proposed strategy, based on our reasoning that given limited resources we could not locate an office in *every* Member State where they were needed, so we would locate a fully equipped multi-disciplinary office *near* each Member State, with groupings of served Member States determined by both local political and logistic factors.

Cluster Offices therefore needed to be located around the world according to rational principles of geographic distribution—negotiated with Member States with a clear eye focused on local political or language sensitivities.

Regional Bureaux on the other hand principally served the Education and Science Sectors—though small Culture and Communications Offices and capacities did exist within some regions. It was the purpose of the Regional Bureaux as 'pools of expertise' to backstop the Cluster Offices, but Cluster Offices had the responsibility to serve as *the delivery platform* for all programming and implementation relations at country-level with Member States, thus avoiding overlap between interventions from different parts of the Secretariat .... a problem that had previously bedeviled Field Offices where we could be suddenly surprised by a Head Office or Regional Office colleague appearing in our country unannounced and speaking with government on behalf of the organization quite independently of us and our on-going consultations and representations. These overlaps of authority continued for a while, but the winds of rationality were blowing particularly through the attention of the Deputy Director-General to whom deviance was reported, so organizational relations and overlaps really did start to come to order quite quickly.

We saw that existing but purely 'National Offices' would be maintained only in exceptional circumstances, and then defined the criteria: participation of the country in so-called 'E-9' initiatives, that is the most populous countries in the world where particular attention had to be paid to literacy and education, or in post-conflict transition countries, and that was about it. The plan called for National Offices to be seen as temporary, destined eventually to be closed after their purpose had been fulfilled .... not always easy as the offices once established could be as difficult to prise out of Member State hands as implanted teeth. UNESCO did however manage to reduce by 13 the 34 National (or Country) Offices between 2000 when the plan was accepted, and 2007.

Furthermore, we sought a *demand-driven* UNESCO, so defined the role of Cluster Offices as one of pro-actively consulting with individual Member States *at the start of the planning process*, thus reversing the valence of the previous planning model, where everything started from the center and was endorsed by regional meetings of Member State National Commissions along the way. We were able to put this fully reversed planning system into place in Asia and the Pacific where several of us were very committed to making it work, but its implementation globally remained rather more problematic and slower to put into place.

Meanwhile, we also took on the lines of authority between Field Offices and Headquarters—now with Program Sectors in Headquarters delegating authority to Field Offices upon approval of their workplans for which the Field Offices were accountable. The new mantra however *was* that Cluster Offices (and National Offices) are responsible and accountable for *all* activities implemented in Member States for which they are responsible. To support the Field Offices we proposed that the previous Bureau that looked after Field Offices, now called the Bureau of Field Coordination (BFC), be strengthened from its previous distinctly peripheral presence in Headquarters to act as the *voice* of the Field within the Headquarters structures and culture. BFC unfortunately did become rather too embedded in Headquarters and into a doctrine of making Field Offices *accountable*—as distinct from supported—and some of the key design features we proposed were never fully implemented, for example, senior professional staff responsible for each region who knew and visited the region frequently and were likely to be destined for one of the next Field Director jobs as they came up. However, BFC did eliminate some of the administrative confusions that previously existed where each Field Office was nominally connected to Headquarters through its 'Parent' Sector, Science, Education and so on—a system that made no sense when the Offices were seen as multidisciplinary platforms for all Sector activity conducted at country level. BFC took over management responsibility for appointment and funding of Field Directors and senior Administrative Staff, leaving Sector relations quite specifically to do only with approval and backstopping of the specific professional activities. Management of local staff (that is, appointed from within the host country of the Field Office) was fully decentralized to the Field Office Director. The system of accountabilities was still a bit messy, but very much more rational than it was before.

Backing this whole system was the assertion for the first time of a serious policy to *rotate* staff from Headquarters to the Field and back on a standard time basis—even making this a general requirement for further

21 Bridging the Two UN Cultures—Reform for the Future 357

promotion—apart from that group of staff who intrinsically could only be allocated to Headquarters—serving personnel, budget, planning, interpretation, and document production functions for example. We developed this policy in consultation with the Task Force involved in reform of Headquarters organization and general personnel policy.

All of this seemed pretty good on paper. The real world is rather more problematic.

Even with what felt like a general emerging consensus amongst the Member States with the draft plan we came up with, my confrontation with the full Executive Board when I presented this plan for the first time was very feisty indeed.

Directly impinging on their interests was the fact that it was fundamental to the planned reform for us to re-arrange the pieces on the chess board of established offices inside Member States. There were far too many tiny offices established (particularly by the previous Director-General, Federico Mayor) on political promise to a President or Government with one professional staff member and an assistant and which were simply uneconomic and ineffective. We identified several tiny offices, for example, where the cost of running the office was up to 10 times that of the budget they administered whilst there were not enough professional staff to cover the range of sector areas for which UNESCO was responsible within the UN system. Representatives of Member States where offices were targeted for closure were generally not pleased. Plus, given that we could not afford offices in all countries, each office that was left had to serve a number of Member States: choosing which ones was a highly political task. We literally re-drew the UNESCO political map of the world and I had to deal with the flack from Member States who did not like the picture from their particular national vantage point.

Consequently, while I was still on my way to the podium for my initial presentation to UNESCO's Executive Board (that sets the Agenda for World Agreement by Member States at the Biennial General Conference) the Ambassador from Uruguay was already on his feet speaking in vociferous and offended Spanish. I had no idea what he was saying so maintained my nonchalant pace to my podium seat, only to be confronted by my assistant with a distinctly worried expression on her face and a pair of translation earphones in hand. "Mr Hill, you've got to listen to this!" she commanded. I had to be on my feet moments later to respond. Fortunately we had worked through the Latin American group of offices very carefully indeed, and had developed a series of compensatory strategies and new initiatives to accommodate countries losing offices. We also had come up with what eventually the Board recognized as a *necessary* plan to deal with the very real problems the organization was confronting in its field operations. It wasn't that hard to explain. So I managed to provide appropriately conciliatory answers to an initially antagonistic Board. And the Decentralisation Reforms proposed were accepted without revision. I left the Board Meeting two hours later after making a series of responses to some pretty hard-hitting questions, feeling like I had lost 10 kg in sweat …. took the elevator back to my office on the 6th Floor and sank back into my office chair with a stiff cup of coffee in hand. The Chef de Cabinet, Francois Rivière, caught me just as I was opening the door, smiling and congratulating, having heard the debate on the in-house speaker system. "We've done it! You totally turned the Board around. This hasn't happened before."

The design of decentralization reform was in place.

I was absolutely committed to the reforms we had initiated, so, as one would expect, maintained a strong interest in what happened after I had completed my Paris-based reform assignment … right up to the time I retired at the end of 2005…. and, of course, beyond, as one does not put down being interested in the results of such interesting personal commitments. But implementation of decentralization reform was handed over to others in Headquarters.

The effect had a little of the character of 'three steps forward, two-and-a-half back', but things did happen although rather more slowly than we might have liked. The Cluster Organisation was set in place, of the 74 offices open in 2000, 24 were progressively closed; three new National Offices were created—primarily to meet the concerted application of education in E-9 countries (those where basic education was most in need of help), but we had still reduced the number of National Offices by 38 percent. The current status of UNESCO's decentralized network included 53 Offices covering 148 Member States comprising 27 Cluster Offices, 10 Regional Bureaux, 21 National Offices (maintained on an exceptional basis). The percentage of Regular Budgetary posts located now (2008–2009) in the Field was 35% compared with 25 percent in 2000; the number of very senior (Diplomatic-1 or D1, and above) posts, in particular in Headquarters, has been radically reduced—from 2000 at end of 1999 to 89 today. From November 2003 it became *mandatory* for all *newly appointed* staff to include rotation into Field postings as part of their career structure, although it proved too hard to apply the rule to all—rotation remains voluntary for all previously appointed staff—and I should point out that it is very much harder to rotate professional staff in UNESCO than it is in our sister agencies such as UNICEF or UNDP which are blessed with much larger staff populations and less specialized requirements. Still, since June 2004, 140 professional staff moved between

21 Bridging the Two UN Cultures—Reform for the Future

duty stations—of which 33% moved from Headquarters to the Field, 22 percent back from the Field to Headquarters (still harder), and 45% transferred between Field Offices. For the Executive Board this level of movement still did not go far enough: at its April 2007 meeting the Board, noting the difficulties bedeviling rotation because of its largely voluntary character and the Headquarters-oriented institutional culture that still persisted, called for the Director-General to give 'due consideration to mandatory rotation of all international professional staff.' Meanwhile, merit-based promotion—an initiative that would introduce considerably more flexibility and motivation into the personnel rotation system—was assuming a little more serious presence in the way staff were managed: what is called the 'reclassification reserve' (traditionally for upgrading people in their current posts if conditions of their appointment changed) had been increased from $(US)1.5 million to $(US)2.0 million for 2008–2009 with the express intention of covering 'merit-based' promotion—a change that was expected to allow 40 such promotions to occur.

Progress in decentralization continued to be monitored. The first Review was conducted in 2004 and concluded that lack of adequate resourcing was slowing things down whilst interactions between the various arms of the Secretariat—including from Headquarters to the Field still needed considerable further improvement. The second Review was held in 2009, this time placing particular emphasis on aligning UNESCO's Field presence and authority with the general reform of the United Nations at country level towards greater coherence and cooperation between UN Agencies. This Review further *strengthened* UNESCO's Field presence, and further bridged the gap that used to be so central in the provision of real support from Headquarters to what we did at Field level in bringing empowerment and change to the real world of developing countries.

Meanwhile, with privilege of my position in helping to create this transformation, I had been left with a very rich understanding of UNESCO as an international organization—textured as an entity within a highly complex political and cultural context—still, at the time I retired, an organization substantially comprising individualistic and Headquarters-philic *cats*, but increasingly having to engage with each other and the outside world in the cooperative stance of Robert England's organizational *dogs*.

22

Final Wrap—The Force of Cultural Empowerment

This book is primarily based on my more than 10 years full time in UN field operations, whilst living in a developing and volatile country and looking after other Member States at field level. I was left deeply affected by what it really meant to inhabit a society that had been torn apart by civil conflict or natural disaster, but which meanwhile was engaging for the first time in explorations of democracy and freedom to feel and express whatever the people truly believed in. Most importantly though, what had indelibly been inscribed on my consciousness was what I had learnt about *the power of culture and local community* within an increasingly globalizing economic and cultural world.

When I arrived in Indonesia in 1995 I was ready to *look*—21 years of previous experience as a Sociology Professor certainly had tuned my awareness of the importance of meaning within the human experience, as had 30 years of previous part-time consultancy with the UN and other international agencies principally across Asia … And I had taken on a job quite deliberately where, amongst other things, I was to be responsible for United Nations action on cultural conservation and empowerment. But what I *saw* was far beyond anything I could have read about or expected—in what I had had the chance to experience everywhere from traditional through to modern societies, within what worked in United Nations practice, and deep into the international institutions themselves.

What I saw was that many people are both economically and spiritually impoverished in a world where their own engagement in collectively creating its social and cultural meaning is denied. More important is the positive side of this same observation. Where people are strengthened at quite local levels—in daily life—to *take charge* of their own culture and community, the empowering consequences are enormous. For the meaning that guides our ability to act and to have a vision of what we *can* achieve is constituted in daily life as we construct how we relate to others and communicate and share, as we go about *doing* things together, and in what we learn about or *change* in taken-for-granted shared assumptions about the 'way we do things around here'. Culture is not the frothy stuff on the top of what really matters in practical living but is the guiding hand on what really *does* matter. Culture is strong, and peoples' ability to make charge of their own world is strong, when they are *actively* involved in *making it* rather than passively *receiving* global messages via the evening TV or fashion billboards, or being lectured by those who wish us to follow *their* path and morality unquestioningly.

The power of culture was revealed at every step along the way of my 10-year experience. Some key examples from the current book:

> The hostage crisis in West Papua that I talk about in Chapters 3 and 4 had been an extraordinary epic, etched with the color of Papuan culture confronting an unknown outside world. Even the negotiations themselves as well as of course the extraordinary courage and caring spirit of the local people for the hostages, revealed at their heart, what humanity is when glimpsed through the lens of human care for shared meaning across difference. We saw how Papuan society was severely impoverished when the central *cultural* commodity, pigs – used in exchange gifts and ceremonies that held the community together, was missing. Sharing in the journey of 'ten thousand years in a lifetime' of the traditional leaders as they confronted contemporary urban life for the first time on their 'Voyage into the Future' as we called it when we brought them out of the Papuan jungles to Jakarta, showed me on the one hand, how people *can* only translate the shock of the new into terms that are largely set by the familiar cultural baggage they are already carrying … but on the other hand, how those with courage to adventure into alien cultural territory and actively *engage* across cultural division, can start to find whole new vistas of meaning and opportunity opening up before them.
>
> When the Indonesian education system was reeling after the twin shocks of economic collapse and political revolution in 1997 and 1998, it was engagement of people and their communities at local level that changed the meaning and therefore culture of schooling, its accessibility and relevance. Schooling came alive as I demonstrate in Chapter 17, because management of the schools was decentralized down to local community levels rather than the parents and children being relatively passive recipients of a rote-based school system designed in detail from Jakarta, and the community accepted the responsibility of directly being engaged for the first time in their own kids' education experience. A fairly straightforward idea, it took a *lot* of work to turn around

22 Final Wrap—The Force of Cultural Empowerment

an education system catering for 29 million elementary school students and 10 million junior secondary school children – intervention right down to local community levels, training of school principals who had never had to seriously manage things before, and in particular, moving the bureaucratic culture of a highly centralized national education system into letting go, and handing over control out to the provinces. But the *idea* was powerful and caught on like wildfire, ultimately becoming national policy, its annual price-tag, once settled into place, of no more than the old centralized system. Meanwhile, the children's learning had improved dramatically – in particular because they were now much more *actively* engaged in learning for themselves, creating their own world of meaning and knowledge, rather than receiving it passively from teachers preaching from the front of the room.

The Mentawai people of Siberut, once they appreciated the value of their own traditional approach to forest management within a modernizing world, and started to connect *in their own terms* into wider society and government that was otherwise riding roughshod over their lives – became empowered, able to develop their own vision and take control over a world that was previously slipping dangerously out of control on both environmental and cultural parameters. Right next door was a criterion case of the alternative: indigenous Mentawai people on the more southern islands of the Mentawai chain, whose island ecology was already destroyed and whose traditional culture had slipped into irrelevance and disuse.

In the GENPEACE project in Mindanao, southern Philippines, that I talk about in Chapter 12, it was the opening up of the voice of the local community – through community radio, and their *active* engagement in education, peace-building and change, that not only helped thousands to become literate and thence be equipped to learn and engage as equals in wider society; it was also this local opportunity to *actively create and express* their own take on the world and its meaning – in a cooperative dialogue mediated by institutionalized 'fair-witnesses', that was instrumental in inter-religious and inter-cultural understanding and peace-building in a province previously torn apart by civil war.

It was the recognition by the local community of Banjarsari, Jakarta, that I presented in Chapter 12, that *they* could choose a whole new local ecologically aware culture for their village, that allowed them to produce not only a healthy 'green' environment for their own lifestyle enjoyment (amongst the slums and expressways of a heavily polluted car-dominated city), but also serious economic enterprise and income.

And finally, as demonstrated in Chapters 18 and 19, it was engagement of the children with their own traditional culture and its expression that *healed* the immense trauma they experienced as their society was decimated by the 20-metre-high waves of the 26th December 2004 Tsunami that rolled over Aceh in North Sumatra.

In this case and every case where people confronted major crises in which we in the United Nations system became engaged, I was continually inspired by the intrinsic strength of humanity that one can rely on to reach positively into the future even when things are *so* bad in the present. And the key to releasing this human potential was to pay attention to people in their daily lives and local communities, where *they* were helped to *redefine* their world of meaning and what was possible—to develop a new more empowered culture for themselves. Indeed, with this perspective in mind, we constantly found extraordinary new *opportunities* for empowering action emerging out of very challenging circumstances. You just had to look through the right lens.

The way the United Nations system operated on the ground therefore needed to cherish this power of the people and help them unlock the potential for themselves. We, in the development assistance business needed to *listen*, to *engage*, *be responsive* with communities and helping them to take over the decision-making for themselves, though perhaps assisting with crossing previously uncrossable bridges to government or wider power interests until the people could stand confidently on the bridges themselves. Certainly, in the interim, we needed to act as 'fair witness' to contestable events … but ultimately, to have *faith* in the intrinsic strength of an empowered local culture and community. All this aligned well with the 'participative' paradigm of development assistance that was emerging during the 1990s. Whereas previously the model had progressed from conducting activities *for* the people to them participating in *our* project, the new approach from the 1990s was one of us learning to participate in *their* project. We did have something to add, introducing new ideas that at the same time were sensitive to the existing culture and which were designed to trigger the realization within the community that they really *can* empower themselves. We needed to introduce knowledge that may be needed and is currently lacking, and to provide resources that allow something to happen. But, what really mattered most was *respect* for the people's own ways of doing thing, constructing meaning and engaging with each other to forge community strength. To take one striking example, we in international agencies and government were surprised after the Aceh Tsunami that many less displaced persons camps had to be constructed than we expected. The Acehnese community had taken the handling of internal refugees on their own shoulders—many had been voluntarily taken in to board with people who previously had been strangers.

Back in the UN organizational house of UNESCO, the developed culture of the internal social and managerial world played a large part in how well the organization was able to respond to world events and the objectives set by Member States … and particularly to the support of local community cultural empowerment. UNESCO's was a cultural world that was intensely influenced by the politics of Member State interests and relations—not just at the top, but deeply into the heart of daily organizational practice. And as I show in Chap. 2, the internal culture of the organization is strongly influenced by the practical and political demands of its immediate environment. Thus, in Headquarters, the culture of business was about responding to the political environment—it was a culture where 'how we do things around here' was most fundamentally about 'administering an illusion of certainty' as this feeds Member State concerns about *their* agreed plans being put into place with implementation responsibly delivered. Headquarters action played a particular role however in establishing through inter-country dialogue universal principles and norms based on shared values, developing the moral compass that would allow the international community to meet the emerging challenges of maintaining 'the common good' across international territory. Political sensitivity and trust by Member States in the responsible handling of budgets and tasks approved at UNESCO's Biennial General Conference that were handed over for Secretariat action were essential to this task. Out in the Field where the organization is dealing with a world of practical problems and which is in constant motion—where plans established two years ago are of little use when you confront the unexpected—a revolution or natural disaster for example, the organizational culture increasingly became one of 'managing change' and balancing accountability against the demands across the world from the organization's Headquarters centre—demands that were mediated via information and accountability systems designed *within* the Headquarters culture, and sometimes not particularly helpful in local management action. Nevertheless, as I did observe in Chap. 12, when I spoke of 'empowerment', the *idea* of locally focused community empowerment was such a powerful idea that increasingly it sold itself—first in activities that we were legitimately able to pursue as a world body with local communities, but also even in the organization itself. As we sought to reform UNESCO towards its greater effectiveness in the 2000s, the primary *intention* of the reform was to bring planning, accountability, and sensitivity of the organization back as close as possible to engagement with the people and *their* interests and meanings at national and at local levels.

What all this reflects is what I have become totally convinced about, the emergence in the agenda of international affairs in the late 20th century and onwards into the present 21st century of a new paradigm of cultural dialogue and empowerment—even, or perhaps particularly, in dealing with the excesses and disempowering impacts of a globalized world. Solutions lie just outside the back door of the globalization experience … in the human integrity and vision of our direct neighbors and ourselves … our community—when we get together. It is here that United Nations action' can best target 'Defense of Our Humanity'—focusing in particular on the force of human empowerment—including across cultures and difference, and particularly in a sharing response to crises—relying on the 'Essence of our Humanity'.

I trust my book will have demonstrated clearly by now that I do not come to this conclusion from just reading the literature, having a strong but personally untested opinion, or even from touring around the world. Instead, my conclusion of the power of our basic humanity, community and meaning, and the way the United Nations needs to operate to make effective change happen, is based on direct experience across a range of national and cultural contexts where I had some responsibility for action to *defend our humanity*.

The evolving story of the book has traced what for me was a very rich set of experiences during the decade in which I had the privilege to join full time in the United Nations quest to make the world a better place. I will never forget signing an international agreement underwater in lipstick with a President, walking behind a sacred ox in a traditional midnight ceremony, sharing a pig feast with the traditional leaders of what is now West Papua, playing blues harmonica along with the traditional musicians of Aceh in our 'healing' of children program. I will never forget the people I worked with either, both inside and outside the United Nations—many of whom were totally inspiring in their commitment, ideas and courage.

But most of all, I will never forget the people we discovered out there in communities, whose worlds I was privileged to enter as a United Nations worker through paying attention to listening and working with the people across many cultures, developing a better understanding of their connection with the wider world …. for it was these and all the other people I had the valued opportunity of meeting at a grass-roots level that taught me to see how the United Nations has greatest power to operate effectively and make a positive difference within the increasingly globalized world of the 21st century.

And I sure had some amazing experiences along the way.

Bibliography

Budjiardo C (2005) West Papua: land of peace or killing field. Paper presented to the 5th international solidarity meeting for West Papua, Manila, Philippines, April

Elmslie J (2001) Irian Jaya under the gun: Indonesian economic development versus West Papuan nationalism. PhD thesis, Department of Government, University of Sydney, p 195

Garrett K (1997) Hostage story, Australian ABC, background briefing, on Sunday 18th May 1997 reported the capture this way. www.converge.org.nz/wpapua/friends.html

Hill S (2014) Merdeka—hostages, freedom and flying pigs in West Papua. Perceptic Press, Sydney

Hill S (2017) Captives for freedom: hostages, negotiations and the future of West Papua. University of Papua New Guinea Press, Port Moresby

Human Rights Watch (2007) Out of sight: endemic abuse and impunity in Papua's central highlands: III. Background.

ICRC Resource Center (1999) ICRC Role during the Irian Jaya hostage crisis (January–May 1996). Posted 27th August. www.icrc.org/eng/resources/documents/misc/57jpz.html

McWilliams E (2005) Response to efforts to deny crimes against humanity in West Papua, East Timor ETAN/US, November. www.etan.org/news/2005/11mcfet.htm

Saltford J (2003) The United Nations and the Indonesian takeover of West Papua, 1962–1989: the anatomy of betrayal. Routledge, London, p 147

Singh J, Loveard K (1996) Now a threat in Irian Jaya—once counted out, a Rebel Group seizes hostages. ASIAWEEK, January 26, p 30

Tapol, Indonesia Human Rights Campaign (1998) TAPOL (Surrey, UK). http://www.tapol.gn.apc.org/reports/r050430.htm

GPSR Compliance

The European Union's (EU) General Product Safety Regulation (GPSR) is a set of rules that requires consumer products to be safe and our obligations to ensure this.

If you have any concerns about our products, you can contact us on

ProductSafety@springernature.com

In case Publisher is established outside the EU, the EU authorized representative is:

Springer Nature Customer Service Center GmbH
Europaplatz 3
69115 Heidelberg, Germany

www.ingramcontent.com/pod-product-compliance
Lightning Source LLC
LaVergne TN
LVHW011000250326
834688LV00003B/45